Housing Transformations

The turn of the century has seen a proliferation of concepts and models in relation to the development of new types of residential environment in the UK. *Housing Transformations* seeks to account for why this has occurred and how it has been made manifest through the shaping of the actual built form. The first part of the book presents a conceptual framework which argues that the built environment derives from a variety of influences: the structural context, the mediating role of institutions and organisations, the actions and proclivities of individuals, and textual representations. The second part includes illustrated case study examples, covering both new build schemes, such as urban villages, gated communities, foyers, continuing care retirement communities and televillages, and refurbishment projects, such as mental hospitals and tower blocks. The result is an original book in which social theory is combined with elements from the built environment disciplines to provide greater insight into how and why we build places and dwell in spaces that are at once contradictory, confining, liberating and illuminating.

Housing Transformations will appeal to academics, students and professionals in the fields of housing, planning, architecture and urban design, as well as to social scientists with an interest in housing.

Housing and society series
Edited by Ray Forrest
School for Policy Studies, University of Bristol.

This series aims to situate housing within its wider social, political and economic context at both national and international level. In doing so it will draw on the full range of social science disciplines and on mainstream debate on the nature of contemporary social change. The books are intended to appeal to an international academic audience as well as to practitioners and policymakers – to be theoretically informed and policy relevant.

Housing and Social Policy
Contemporary themes and critical perspectives
Edited by Peter Somerville with Nigel Sprigings

Housing and Social Change
East–West perspectives
Edited by Ray Forrest and James Lee

Urban Poverty, Housing and Social Change in China
Ya Ping Wang

Gentrification in a Global Context
Edited by Rowland Atkinson and Gary Bridge

Forthcoming:

Sustainable Development
A new perspective for housing analysis
Rebecca Chiu

Housing and Social Transition in Japan
Edited by Yosuke Hirayama and Richard Ronald

Housing Transformations

Shaping the space of twenty-first century living

Bridget Franklin

Routledge
Taylor & Francis Group

LONDON AND NEW YORK

First published 2006
by Routledge
2 Park Square, Milton Park, Abingdon, Oxon OX14 4RN

Simultaneously published in the USA and Canada
by Routledge
711 Third Avenue, New York, NY 10017

Routledge is an imprint of the Taylor & Francis Group, an informa business

© 2006 Bridget Franklin

Typeset in Times and Frutiger by
HWA Text and Data Management, Tunbridge Wells

British Library Cataloguing in Publication Data
A catalogue record for this book is available from the British Library

Library of Congress Cataloging-in-Publication Data
Franklin, Bridget
  Housing transformations : shaping the space of 21st century living /
  Bridget Franklin. –1st ed.
    p.   cm.   – (Housing and society series)
  Includes bibliographical references and index.
  1. Housing – Great Britain.   2. Housing development – Great
  Britain.   3.Housing policy – Great Britain.   I. Title.   II. Series.
HD7333.A3F82 2006
363.50941–dc22   2005032855

ISBN10: 0–415–33618–X (hbk)
ISBN10: 0–415–33619–8 (pbk)
ISBN10: 0–203–42139–6 (ebk)

ISBN13: 978–0–415–33618–5 (hbk)
ISBN13: 978–0–415–33619–2 (pbk)
ISBN13: 978–0–203–42139–0 (ebk)

In memory of Rose, Christine and Jane
friends who cared

Contents

Figures

List of figures

Acknowledgements

A number of people have been of great assistance in the preparation of this book.

First I must thank the many organisations and individuals who gave me access to information or were willing to be interviewed in relation to the case studies. These include: the planning authorities of the City of Birmingham, Brecon Beacons National Park, the City and County of Cardiff, Dartmoor National Park, Harlow District Council, the London Borough of Tower Hamlets, Manchester City Council, Stroud District Council, Teignbridge District Council, and York City Council; the Bournville Village Trust; Birmingham City Council Development and Joint Ventures Department; members of the former BHDC; South West Regional Health Authority; Devington Homes; the Joseph Rowntree Memorial Trust and staff at Hartrigg Oaks; East Thames Housing Group and staff at Harlow Foyer; Urban Splash; Glamorgan Record Office; a representative from Roger Tym and Partners; sales administrators at Adventurers Quay and Acorn Televillage; Nia Blank and a former director of St David, for information in relation to CBDC and Adventurers Quay; David Michael, for access to Stroud Cohousing; and the Stewart Community Woodlanders, for their hospitality.

The material on urban villages in Chapter 6 is drawn in part from an ESRC funded project: *Urban Villages: a Real or Imagined Contribution to Sustainable Development*, Award Number R000223284.

Figure 7.1 is © Crown Copyright. NMR (from Richardson, H. (ed.) (1998) *English Hospitals 1660–1948: a survey of their architecture and design*, p. 163, Figure 163). Figure 5.1 has been reproduced by kind permission of Routledge (from Dovey, K. (1999) *Framing Places: Mediating Power in Built Form*, p. 21, Figure 2.1). Thanks are also due to Tom Garne of Cardiff University for technical assistance with the process of reproduction. All other figures are the author's own, with Figures 6.1, 6.2, 6.3, 6.4, 6.6, 6.7 first appearing in Franklin, B. (2003) 'Success or failure: the redevelopment of Bordesley as an (urban) village', *Urban Design International*, 8, 1/2: 21–35, reproduced with permission of Palgrave Macmillan.

Acknowledgements

This book would never have been started had it not been for the encouragement of Susan Hutson, who persuaded me that I had sufficient material and commitment to bring it to fruition. I must also thank the series editor Ray Forrest for supporting the book, and the staff at Taylor & Francis for their assistance. In addition, I am grateful to David Clapham for valuable comments on a pre-publication draft. Both he and Bob Smith have been a supportive influence during my time at Cardiff University and I owe them much. Finally I extend my gratitude to Jim Kemeny for his interest, encouragement, and wise counsel.

Abbreviations

AARC	Active Adult Retirement Community
ABP	Associated British Ports
ASBO	Anti-Social Behaviour Order
BBNP	Brecon Beacons National Park
BCC	Birmingham City Council
BedZED	Beddington Zero Energy Development
BHDC	Birmingham Heartlands Development Corporation
BHL	Birmingham Heartlands Limited
BME	Black and Minority Ethnic
BRE	Building Research Establishment
BVT	Bournville Village Trust
CABE	Commission for Architecture and the Built Environment
CASPAR	City Centre Apartments for Single People at Affordable Rents
CAT	Centre for Alternative Technology
CBDC	Cardiff Bay Development Corporation
CCRC	Continuing Care Retirement Community
CCTV	Closed Circuit Television
CIH	Chartered Institute of Housing
CMDC	Central Manchester Development Corporation
CML	Council of Mortgage Lenders
CPAG	Child Poverty Action Group
CPRE	Campaign to Protect Rural England
DETR	Department of the Environment, Transport and the Regions
DoE	Department of the Environment
DNPA	Dartmoor National Park Authority
DTLR	Department for Transport, Local Government and the Regions
EMO	Environmental Movement Organisation
ETHG	East Thames Housing Group
FoE	Friends of the Earth

Abbreviations

GEN	Global Ecovillage Network
GMV	Greenwich Millennium Village
HBF	House Builders Federation
IT	Information Technology
JRF	Joseph Rowntree Foundation
JRHT	Joseph Rowntree Housing Trust
LETS	Local Exchange Trading System
MHLG	Ministry of Housing and Local Government
NHBC	National Housebuilding Council
NHF	National Housing Federation
NHFA	National Federation of Housing Associations
NHS	National Health Service
ODPM	Office of the Deputy Prime Minister
PPG	Planning Policy Guidance
PPS	Planning Policy Statement
RIBA	Royal Institute of British Architects
RICS	Royal Institute of Chartered Surveyors
RSL	Registered Social Landlord
RSPB	Royal Society for the Protection of Birds
RTPI	Royal Town Planning Institute
SHG	Social Housing Grant
SPAB	Society for the Protection of Ancient Buildings
STBI	Sustainable Tower Blocks Initiative
SUDS	Sustainable Urban Drainage System
TCA	Telework Association (formerly Telecottage Association)
TCPA	Town and Country Planning Association
UDA	Urban Development Agency
UDC	Urban Development Corporation
UVF	Urban Villages Forum
UVG	Urban Villages Group
UK	United Kingdom
URBED	Urban and Economic Development Group
US	United States (of America)
WAG	Welsh Assembly Government
WCED	World Commission on Environment and Development
WWF	Worldwide Fund for Nature

Introduction

The production of the built form, in whatever time or place, in whatever shape and for whatever purpose, is irrevocably a human and a social act. Hence, whilst a building might be admired for its aesthetic impact, or appreciated for its engineering properties, it cannot be understood without knowledge of the society in which it has been conceived, of the rules and resources of that society, and of the individuals who are the designers and ultimate users. For the built environment does not randomly appear, but is a result of a multitude of influences and a variety of interconnecting factors: spatial contexts; ideological positions; political interventions; economic conditions; societal attitudes; historical traditions; technical knowledge; professional power; and public perceptions. Thus the shaping and the re-shaping of the built environment derives from the intersection of locationally and temporally situated factors: the structural context, the mediating role of institutions and organisations, and the actions and proclivities of individuals. To this end, it is helpful to draw on and integrate ideas from a range of conceptual and theoretical frameworks in order to gain the necessary depth to explain the variety and nature of the built form, and to inspire a greater insight into how and why we build places and dwell in spaces that are at once contradictory, confining, liberating and illuminating.

In thus connecting the social and the spatial, this book contributes to an emerging academic debate from across a range of disciplines including architecture, sociology, geography and urban design (see, for example, Bentley, 1999; Dovey, 1999; King, 1980; R. King, 1996; Lawrence, 1987; Madanipour, 1997, 2003; Markus, 1993; Markus and Cameron, 2002). But, with the exception of Lawrence (1987), these authors cover urban space and the built environment as a whole, and do not make sustained reference to what is perhaps the most essential element of the built environment: the dwelling. Surprisingly, even the newly emerging discipline of housing studies rarely focuses on the built form of housing, concentrating instead on legislative and policy issues to do with the administration, availability, management and financing of housing. It would appear that matters relating to the design and nature of the built form are perceived as more properly the province of the built environment disciplines of architecture, construction, surveying, and even social history.

The fact that housing studies in the UK has been concerned primarily with policy issues has also been cited as the reason why it has been lacking in terms of theoretical and conceptual rigour. Instead it has followed a narrow empiricism which is at the expense of a capacity for reflection, and which tends to reproduce taken for granted assumptions in housing (Jacobs and Manzi, 2000; Kemeny, 1992). This position has derived at least in part from the way in which housing research has developed, reliant almost entirely on funding from central government offices and from housing organisations themselves (see Clapham, 1997). This has cast housing research in the mould of governmental and organisational concerns, dealing with material facts, rules, quantifiable data and normative judgements (P. King, 1996). In this project both the development of theory and the study of the cognitive, creative and humanistic elements of housing have been neglected. This problem has been compounded by the fact that housing studies has struggled to achieve the status of an independent academic discipline, not only because of its largely policy driven concerns, but also because it is a relatively new field of inquiry, with followers drawn from a range of existing disciplines. This has led to the lack of a coherent conceptual or theoretical basis on which housing studies and housing research can build.

To counter this, Kemeny (1992) has suggested that housing should be reconceptualised in terms of the individual disciplines from which housing scholars originate, such as sociology, economics, or political science, and that in this way a more theoretically informed understanding of housing might arise. But it could be argued that as a subject housing is so large in scope and impinges on so many areas of life, that it cannot be conceptualised under the rubric of only one discipline. It may be, as Rapoport and Lawrence have both argued, that what is needed is a more integrated and holistic conceptualisation of housing. Rapoport, from the American school of environment-behaviour research, asserts:

> Housing is a particularly striking example of the need for theory. There is too much information, numerous disconnected pieces of empirical research, which, in effect, become counterproductive ... Even a conceptual framework can help by organizing material, although not as much as theory.
>
> (Rapoport, 2001: 145)

Lawrence has argued more strongly for multi-disciplinarity, stating that it is the lack of an integrating conceptual framework that is impeding the formulation of strategies which will inform more appropriate solutions to the design and management of housing (1987). He highlights the need for a multi-faceted or 'contextual' approach, identifying geographical, cultural, social and individual variables in the use of space, and locating them within a historical perspective (see also Lawrence, 1990, 1994, 1996).

The position adopted in this book, is similar to that proposed by Lawrence. Like Lawrence, who was trained in both architecture and anthropology, I come from a multi-disciplinary background. Trained in social anthropology, sociology and housing studies, I have been employed in both an architecture and a planning school. This has given me a broad base from which to examine housing in all its manifestations and with all its ramifications. Like Kemeny, I believe that one's disciplinary training profoundly affects one's later thinking, even if one moves to new subject matter. However, this thinking may be narrow or broad, depending on the nature of that initial discipline. As a student of social anthropology, I was informed across a range of topics (cultures, social systems, belief systems, myth and ritual, kinship, economic and judicial systems, settlement patterns and house forms) as well as a variety of methodologies and epistemologies (positivism, structuralism, functionalism, participant observation and ethnography). This holistic approach, intrinsic to social anthropology, was assisted by the absorption of a perspective wherein no one version of reality, no one world view, no one way of doing things can be classed as superior to any other – all interpretations and all ways of life are equally valid. The problem here, of course, is that if 'anything goes', it is difficult to create any systematic body of theory as a basis for knowledge, and indeed, since the heady days of structural anthropology in the 1970s, social anthropology has struggled to develop theoretically.

In subsequent study of sociology I was introduced to a more rigorous approach to theory, and have continued to engage with social theory and its application to housing issues. During my academic career I have also been exposed to a number of other disciplines, including environment-behaviour studies, cultural anthropology, urban studies, architecture, urban design and planning, as well of course as housing studies itself – all of which are under-theorised.

What is developed here is not an overarching theory (for, with Rapoport, I do not believe this is possible), but a theoretically informed conceptual framework which is multi-faceted in the way that Lawrence suggests. Whilst such pluralism may disquiet the purist (see also Dovey, 1999), its benefits are intended to create new insights and to extend reflection beyond the boundary of one narrow position. Like Beck (2000) I feel that the issue of theory and perspective is one for pragmatism, and that it is not necessary to adhere rigidly to one particular school of thought, unless of course, one is engaged in a work of theoretical analysis and critique. The book is, essentially, a work of *bricolage*: a term used by the structural anthropologist Lévi-Strauss to describe how ideas and modes of thought are constructed from the assimilation or assemblage of what is to hand (Lévi-Strauss, 1966). And, continuing in anthropological vein, the book does not seek to persuade that what is presented should be interpreted as 'fact': it is but one construction of reality that can co-exist with others, in a world of fluid, open and ever-changing meaning.

As well as developing a more holistic conceptual framework, the book deals with some specific manifestations of the built environment in one particular country and at a particular point in time. In the UK, the turn of the century has seen a proliferation of concepts and models in relation to the development of new types of residential environment. These are on different scales, are often targeted at different kinds of people, and include a fairly extensive and diverse list: the urban village; the millennium community; the sustainable urban neighbourhood; the televillage; the ecovillage; the retirement community; the gated community; the home zone; the loft; the live/work unit; the lifetime home; the smart home; assisted living; extra care housing; very sheltered housing; the foyer; supported accommodation; starter homes; affordable homes; key worker housing; the 'space box'; cohousing; ecohomes; earth sheltered housing; the autonomous house; and the low impact development (and this list is not exhaustive). Although some of these have their origins in former models, either in this country or more usually elsewhere, the way they have been appropriated here in recent years is new. Arguably this has arisen as a response to, and as a reflection of, transformations in social processes and modes of living.

In addition there is another trend, and that is the adaptation into dwellings of pre-existing building types, such as hospitals, warehouses, mills, farm buildings, churches, schools and offices. Here, the impact of social and economic change has brought about obsolescence and redundancy, but what has also been necessary is a transformation of perception in which what was originally constructed (mentally and physically) for one particular purpose can now be reconstructed for another.

This proliferation of concepts and models has become of interest to me, in part as an observer of changing patterns of dwelling, but also in the context of the teaching of housing development. This has raised issues as to the reasons for the appearance of these concepts at this particular time, as well as questions such as who has been promoting them and why, who has been adopting them and why, who is developing them and why. There seems to be no literature that addresses these issues – in part because housing studies itself has not, as has already been noted, overly concerned itself with the nature of the built form.

This book will seek not only to describe these concepts and models, but also to account for their emergence at the present time, at the conjuncture of a particular set of cultural, social, economic and political circumstances. Discussion is confined to the UK, with the focus mainly on England, although some examples from Wales are also used. Cross-cultural comparison might have been a possibility, but the advantage of selecting one (known) country is that it allows greater analytical depth, since cultural and institutional factors are kept constant, and the effect of other influences can be more easily uncovered. The book also does not deal with the individual experience of users, since this is a work investigating the reasons for the production of particular housing types and not an empirical or theoretical inquiry into use.

The book is divided into two main parts with a third concluding section. Part I provides the conceptual and theoretical framework, starting in Chapter 1 with an overview, the production of a model of the influences on built form, and an example of how the framework can be applied in practice. Chapters 2 to 5 elaborate on the elements of the conceptual framework. Chapter 2 discusses the structural conditions of postmodern society in the context of globalisation and risk, and the concomitant loosening of community and family ties and the crisis of identity. Chapter 3 concerns the institutional arrangements which result in certain types of policies, rules and regulations, whilst Chapter 4 deals with issues of agency as expressed in organisational and individual action. Finally, Chapter 5 addresses theories and issues of built form and design as they relate to residential environments.

Part II turns to the variety of emerging concepts and models of housing in the UK, drawing on the content of Part I to elucidate the contextual factors which have led to their emergence. In the space available it is not possible to assess the full panoply of the new concepts and models that have appeared in recent years, and instead a selection is taken which is representative of different scales, of different national and international influences, of new solutions to old issues, and of responses to new challenges. In addition to general discussion, these chapters include a narrative on specific case study examples to illustrate how the defined outcomes of a generic type are mediated by locational, institutional, organisational and individual factors. Again, these have been chosen for their diversity as well as for their geographical spread, although those about which there is already considerable material in the public domain, such as Greenwich Millennium Village, BedZed, and Poundbury, have deliberately been excluded. Specific projects have been identified through a literature and web based search, and then after checking for potential relevance to the study in hand, access has been negotiated. For each project further information has been obtained from relevant organisations and individuals, and every site has been visited and photographed, although in one or two cases it was not possible to access interior spaces.

The first chapter in Part II, Chapter 6, focuses on the recasting of the 'village' as a concept for residential development. The promotion and realisation of this concept would seem to be based on a nostalgic and mythical construction of 'villageness', which is then projected on to a number of different types of contemporary development. These include the millennium village, the urban village, the retirement village, the leisure village, the televillage and the ecovillage. In this chapter it is the urban village and the televillage which form the focus for discussion, with case studies of Bordesley in Birmingham and the Acorn Televillage in Wales.

Chapter 7 turns to significant building types of the past and the reasons why a rediscovered interest in heritage has led to a desire to preserve as monuments some of the more architecturally distinctive examples. This reclassification now applies not only to buildings which might be deemed 'historic', but also, and somewhat controversially, to those modernist forms built as recently as the 1950s. Because of their qualities, monuments cannot be demolished, and hence alternative uses must be found for those which have become obsolescent or unfit. If this involves retrofitting for contemporary living, then in some cases there is a need to overcome the former negative connotations of the building type. This is the case with the two examples which form the subject matter of this chapter: the Victorian lunatic asylum and the discredited tower block, as illustrated in the case studies of the former Exe Vale mental hospital in Devon, and Keeling Tower in London.

For generations, older people and the feckless young have proved something of a problem to the rest of society, and Chapter 8 considers the reasons for this at the present time. It examines two new solutions for these categories of people, both of which have something of the institution about them: the continuing care retirement community and the foyer. Interestingly, both have been imported from other countries, the US and France respectively, and have been adapted to reflect the British context. Foyers are now found quite widely across the UK, and here the case study of a foyer in Harlow, Essex is used. By contrast, continuing care retirement communities have yet to make any significant impact, and the case study of Hartrigg Oaks in York represents the only one in England.

Chapters 9 and 10 present in many ways contrasting responses to a common, even global, human dilemma: how to live more sustainably in an environment under threat. Institutional solutions, which are dominated by the need to ensure continued economic growth, profit and the security of citizens, have turned towards the promotion of city living, and it is this which forms the subject matter of Chapter 9. To make this policy preference more palatable to a population which largely sees inner cities as places to avoid, there has been an emphasis on improved design, on the contribution of new technology, and on measures to achieve exclusivity. These elements are clear in the two case studies presented, Timber Wharf in Manchester, a modernist inspired block of loft apartments, and Adventurers Quay, a gated community in Cardiff. Chapter 10, by contrast, looks at how certain groups and individuals have taken a radical approach to matters of environmental and social sustainability, in which institutional arrangements are rejected in favour of self help and egalitarianism. The chapter looks in detail at cohousing, a concept of collective living derived from Scandinavia and the Netherlands, and low impact developments, a derivative of the concept of the ecovillage. The two case studies here involve a cohousing scheme in Stroud, Gloucestershire, and a permaculture community on the fringes of Dartmoor National Park.

Finally, Part III draws together the threads that have woven within and between the various chapters, and speculates on future trends. Connections are made between the case studies and the way these help to give meaning to the conceptual framework introduced in Chapter 1, whilst it is also shown how the conceptual framework itself creates insight and understanding into the patterns that frame the space of practical action. In conclusion, there is some speculation about future directions in the face of the challenges and problems ahead, and about the nature of the social and spatial transformations which might affect the shaping of our residential built forms.

Part I

Theory, concept and practice

1 Towards a contextual approach

In this chapter an overview is provided of some theories and concepts which are deemed to be relevant in developing a contextual approach to the understanding of residential environments. As mentioned in the introduction, this necessitates drawing on a number of disciplinary strands in order to attain sufficient breadth to address the complexities of the nature of housing. The first section of the chapter briefly examines the way in which commentators on built form, anthropologists, and specialists in environment-behaviour studies have analysed the relationship between culture and dwelling, and refers to the limitations of their approaches. The subsequent three sections concern the constitution of society and take a more sociological perspective. First there is a discussion of the structure/agency debate, including a critique of social constructionism and the contributions of Giddens and Bourdieu. Then attention is paid to the different roles of institutions, organisations and individuals in framing agency, and to the importance of discourse in shaping action and meaning. The chapter then moves on to look at how built form too can have meaning, and how spatial organisation is irrevocably implicated in supporting or constraining social action.

The ideas discussed in these sections form the basis of a conceptual framework which shows the interconnectedness of structural, social, institutional, individual and textual factors in creating and interpreting the built form of housing. This is illustrated in the form of a model and then, by way of practical application, in the worked example of the development of a specific housing scheme, that of Quarry Hill in Leeds in the 1930s. The subsequent chapters in Part I build on the elements of the conceptual framework, starting with considerations of structure, then moving on to discussion of institutions, organisations and individuals, and finally ending with ideas about design and the construction of built form.

Culture and dwelling

The housing of every society in the world has a historic distinctiveness; be it located in the deserts of Northern Africa, in the tropical rainforests of South America, on the steppes of Asia, or in the mediaeval towns of Europe. This distinctiveness is a function of the diversity of cultural context, and it is this which helps to determine how any given society shapes, produces and uses the built forms within which its people dwell. The resultant multiplicity of house styles and modes of dwelling has been given little sustained attention in academic discourse. Architecture, as the discipline which studies the built form, might perhaps have been expected to address this issue, but has shown little consistent interest in the cultural diversity of housing. Exceptions include the cross-cultural work of Oliver (1987, 2003) and the somewhat romanticised accounts of vernacular dwelling from around the world. These have been used to promote the virtues of so-called 'spontaneous' architecture and its perceived ability to achieve more culturally and socially appropriate design than mass produced housing (see, for example, Hamdi, 1991; Rudofsky, 1964; Turner, 1976). In regard to housing specific to British culture, however, the discipline of architecture has been relatively productive, with a number of works which cover vernacular housing, the history of housing types, and particular periods or styles of housing (see, for example, Brunskill, 1981; Colquhoun, 1999; Edwards, 1981; Glendinning and Muthesius, 1994; Gray, 1994; Scoffham, 1984). Together these works illustrate the heritage and tradition of housing in Britain, revealing also the archetypes which are part of the British psyche.

Social and cultural anthropology, as the disciplines which study the cultures of the world, have been remarkably silent in relation to analytical, as opposed to descriptive, accounts of the built environment. The main exception here derives from within the now outmoded field of structural anthropology, popularised in the work of Lévi-Strauss, and based on the structuralist approach popular in the mid-twentieth century. The central idea behind structuralism is that it is possible to identify mental structures and patterns of cognition that can be shown to be common to all cultures. Particularly prevalent is the notion that the human mind classifies through opposition: nature/culture; sacred/profane; purity/danger; insider/outsider; male/female; high born/low born; night/day; left/right (see Douglas, 1970; Lévi-Strauss, 1968). Such oppositions are reflected in thought, myth, ritual and patterns of living, and can also be identified in the ways in which material objects are organised and arranged. Thus, for example, features of the ordering of settlements and dwellings can be shown symbolically to reflect conceptual categories and aspects of social organisation. This results in housing patterns which are in effect 'good to think', since they express a consonance, or homology, between spatial formation and the ordering of social life. Thus the way in which things are arranged in space can assume a metaphorical quality, with particular significance accorded to physical boundaries since they denote the ambiguous and potentially threatening distinction between inside and outside, friend and stranger, culture and nature.

Emerging from the US has been people-environment studies, also known as environment-behaviour studies, which combines aspects of architecture and cultural (but not structural) anthropology. This cross-cultural approach explores the interaction between people and their environments, in terms of identifying the cultural characteristics which influence the shaping of the built environment, and concomitantly, the ways in which the built environment influences people. The most famous exponent of people-environment studies has been Rapoport, whose prodigious output now spans five decades. In his first major work, *House Form and Culture* (1969), Rapoport examines how people organise and use dwelling space, whilst attempting to devise a conceptual framework to analyse the cultural forces that give rise to them. In later work (1977, 1982, 1985) he advances this conceptual framework to develop his theory of systems of settings and systems of activities – a 'non-verbal communication approach', in which housing must be viewed as part of the specific system to which it belongs. This system includes the complete built environment of village and town, monumental buildings, non-domestic spaces, and the links between people and these places. Environments, he states, can be neutral, inhibiting or facilitating for behaviour, with the inhibiting effects becoming acute in times of stress, as, for example, in the case of migrants. Whilst Rapoport has been influential in extending the scope of people-environment studies, he can be criticised both for over-emphasising the determinacy of culture, and for assuming the homogeneity of people within a culture.

The difficulties of providing a conceptual framework sufficient in terms of both rigour and compass may explain why some proponents of people-environment studies have adopted a more focused approach. Thus in a few cases there has been a return to a more structuralist tradition in looking at the significance and symbolic meaning of spaces and places (see, for example, Kent, 1990; Parker-Pearson and Richards, 1994), whilst others have explored place attachment and the meaning and use of home (see, for example, Altman and Werner, 1985; Altman and Low, 1992; Arias, 1993). With their emphasis on identity and the psycho-social, these latter works shift the emphasis from the cultural to the personal, and from society to the individual – in other words to the phenomenological, as encapsulated particularly strongly by Cooper-Marcus (1995). Indeed, whether the emphasis is cultural or phenomenological, people-environment studies can be criticised for the way in which it overlooks the organisations and institutions of society – the political, economic, juridical and administrative framework within which social relations are framed, and the regulations, norms and rules whereby resources are produced and distributed. For an insight into the relationship between these issues and the actions in time and space of individuals, we need to turn to sociology and social theory.

The riddle of society

The question of the relationship between society and the individual strikes at the heart of a fundamental problem in social theory: that of the primacy of the individual or of society; the chicken and egg issue that continues to divide sociologists between those who believe that society is driven by overarching structures external to and independent of individual actions, and those who believe society is constituted by individual action and the meaning given by individuals to those actions. The 'macro' perspective, or macrosociology, is concerned primarily with the large scale institutions and organisation of society, as exemplified historically by the structuralist and functionalist schools of thought represented by Durkheim (1964), Merton (1967) and Parsons (1937). More recently social realism has developed a more sophisticated perspective on this tradition, arguing that social life consists of layers of reality, and that these layers exist objectively at a deeper level from everyday action and experiences (see, for example, Layder, 1997; Sayer, 2000; Scott, 1995). The 'micro' perspective, or microsociology, avers that such reification of social facts is misguided, and that social life consists only of the minutiae of day to day activities, social interaction and personal experiences, as exemplified by the approaches of phenomenology, ethnomethodology and symbolic interactionism (see, for example, Blumer, 1969; Garfinkel, 1967; Schutz, 1972). These two contrasting perspectives can be criticised for failing on the one hand to take individual actors seriously, reducing them to inert bearers and reproducers of systems, and on the other, for failing to take account of the wider social processes which form the context within which action takes place, thus reducing society to the constructs of knowledgeable actors. This dichotomy, or *dualism*, between what can be further defined as 'structure' (objectivist) and 'agency' (subjectivist) approaches, has been somewhat caricatured by Archer (2000) as 'Society's Being' and 'Modernity's Man': the passive dupe and cipher on the one hand, and the active, creative (and rational) thinker on the other.

The central problem of dualism is that each approach represents what many would consider to be a partial and one-sided view of the constitution of society – in one approach individual agency is elided out of existence, and in the other, there is no such thing as society. In recognition of this apparent lacuna, there have been some attempts to make linkages. An early example was the work of Berger and Luckmann (1966), who put forward the theory of social constructionism. For Berger and Luckmann, society has both an objective and a subjective reality, based on interpersonal action and reproduced through knowledge and language. Their contention is that social reality exists in terms of the actions and thoughts, meanings and interpretations of individuals, who thus create the totality of everyday knowledge in a taken for granted environment. This knowledge base equates to the institutions and social rules of society, which are in turn transmitted to the next generation through socialisation. Different forms of knowledge are acquired by different social groups, and are often expressed symbolically through styles of dress, rituals or manners of speaking.

The significance of the contribution of Berger and Luckmann is that it seeks to moderate the extremes of dualism by proposing both that individuals create society, and that society creates individuals. But there remain weaknesses for which social constructionism is criticised, notably that the emphasis is clearly on society as a product of human interaction, with a concomitant neglect of both social and material reality (Gergen, 1994). Furthermore, there is no discussion of conflict and change, of space and place, of the distribution of goods and resources, of power and authority. Despite this, social constructionism has proved influential, and in particular has been central to the development of a more theoretically informed approach in housing studies (see, for example, Clapham, 1997; Franklin, 1998; Franklin and Clapham, 1997; Jacobs and Manzi, 2000; Jacobs *et al.*, 2004).

In the endeavour to develop a more sophisticated and integrated resolution of the structure/agency debate the role of structuration theory has proved influential. The two key thinkers associated with this approach to theorising society are Giddens and Bourdieu, the prolific and scholarly works of whom have been a major force in the social scientific world in both the UK and Europe. One of Giddens' main contributions has been in overcoming the *dualism* of the individual and society and reconceptualising it as the *duality* of agency and structure: 'By the *duality of structure* I mean that social structure is both constituted *by* human agency and yet is at the same time the very *medium* of this constitution' (Giddens, 1993: 128–9, original emphases). Giddens makes a distinction between structure, as the rules and resources of social systems, and the system (or society) itself, which consists of reproduced relations between actors situated in time and space. Structures are both the medium and the outcome of human action. Essentially, social structures do not have independent existence, but are reproduced or transformed by actors who experience the rules and resources as either constraining or enabling. Giddens conceptualises rules as having normative, symbolic and legitimising aspects, whilst resources are either authoritative or allocative (concerned with the control of material products). These rules and resources comprise the structural properties of social systems, which often become embodied in institutions. Among these structural properties, a number of structural principles are also significant and account for changes from feudal and traditional institutions to modern, capitalist institutions.

Structure has an abstract and recursive quality, and is not fixed in either time or space. Human action, on the other hand, is necessarily situated in time and space, and thus action helps to fix structures and social systems, both in the here and now, and through constant reproduction as actions are repeated or re-created anew. For this reason, the settings of action are important to Giddens, providing the contextuality of social life in both time and space. In referring to physical settings, Giddens prefers the term 'locale' (1984: 118) to place, pointing out that a locale can be at any scale, from a room, through a street corner, to a city or the territory of a nation state. Locales are 'regionalised', sub-divided into zones which are of significance for different time-space activities – thus a house can be zoned into spaces used for different activities at different times of day. Regions are generally demarcated by physical or symbolic markers, which help to signal movement between regions and to indicate the need to adopt appropriate types of interaction and behaviour (reminiscent of the 'front' and 'back' regions of Goffman (1971)). Cities, too, are regionalised into areas which can be conceived of as front and back regions, and such zoning is strongly influenced by the operation of housing markets and the consequent social constitution of neighbourhoods.

Giddens' contribution to the theorising of society has been influential, but as with any other theory is not above criticism. In particular, it has operated at the level of 'grand theory' rather than as something which is demonstrably capable of being employed at the empirical level to explain practical action. There is a tendency to see agents as both homogenous and amorphous, without class, gender, age or ethnic group, and with no account of power, authority, or practices of domination. In his early work personality, affect, emotion, and any sense of interdependence or negotiation between actors are ignored, whilst little justice is done to the realities of time and space (see Bryant and Jary, 1991). More recently, however, Giddens has demonstrated a concern for the social predicaments and existential questionings of humanity, particularly in regard to how identity has fared under so-called late modernity, as will be discussed further below and in Chapter 2.

Bourdieu's approach to the structure/agency dichotomy overcomes some of the problems associated with Giddens. Bourdieu's intellectual orientation is towards both philosophy and sociology, but he has been strongly influenced by ethnography and social anthropology and by his fieldwork in Kabylia in Algeria. It was this experience which led him to question both the structuralist ideas of the anthropologist Lévi-Strauss, and the way in which the anthropologist interprets practical action. He believes there is more to action than the account given by the 'native', and hence, like Giddens, takes issue with interpretative and ethnomethodological approaches (Bourdieu, 1977). On the other hand, and again like Giddens, he does not believe that actors are simply passive bearers and reproducers of objective structures. But Bourdieu is less interested in devising a conceptual theory than in attempting to develop a way to analyse practical action at the empirical level, and it is here that his main contribution lies.

Bourdieu's central concept is that of the *habitus* as a mediating factor between structure and social practice. The *habitus* is defined as: 'a system of durable transposable dispositions, structured structures predisposed to function as structuring structures ...' (Bourdieu, 1977: 72). More simply the *habitus*: 'implies a "sense of one's place" but also a "sense of the place of others"' (Bourdieu, 1989: 19). It operates as a strategy generating principle, a disposition to act in a certain way, or a 'feel for the game', which allows individuals to know how they should act in a given circumstance, and in a way that accords with social norms and institutional precepts (thus reproducing them). But the *habitus* is neither rigid nor a predeterminant of destiny, since it permits individual (conscious or unconscious) choice and personal interpretation, albeit within a certain range: '*Habitus* is creative, inventive, but within the limits of its structures, which are the embodied sedimentation of the social structures which produced it' (Bourdieu and Wacquant, 1992: 19). Individuals are socialised from birth into the *habitus* analogous to their position in society, and thus *habitus* is operationalised at both individual and group (or class) level. Classes and groups are characterised by their status as the dominated and the dominating, and each tends to choose goods and services which are homologous with their social group. The dominating classes seek 'distinction' through the determination, by symbolic means, of what constitutes good 'taste' – setting the fashion in house type or clothing, defining which is the 'right' newspaper to read, or determining the 'best' home furnishing style (Bourdieu, 1984). The dominated then seek to emulate the dominating, thus encouraging the latter to move on to new forms of distinction.

The context of action is referred to by Bourdieu as a 'field', with the *habitus* providing a practical sense of how to act within the field. Fields are characterised by the possession of economic, social, cultural and symbolic capital which bestow power and legitimacy – thus the fields of education or the arts possess cultural capital (knowledge, aesthetic taste), the field of banking possesses economic capital, the field of the family possesses social capital, the field of the peerage possesses symbolic capital. But fields can also be the sites of struggle and conflict, with individuals vying with each other for power, through possession or display of forms of capital – the political field is the prime example here (Bourdieu, 1992). His framework helps to account also for examples of 'disharmony', when, for example, a solution imposed on one social group by another, such as the spatial organisation of a housing estate, does not accord with the *habitus* of the dominated group. For space and spatial organisation have social significance in that they govern practices and representations. Thus the estate, the house, even the body, are all forms of physical space and sites which embody or objectify the generative structures of the *habitus*. This is exemplified by Bourdieu through the example of the Kabyle house in which the categories which underpin the social world are shown to be replicated in the layout and assignment of space within the house – thus the child learns by association how the social world is structured and how to act within it (Bourdieu, 1973).

Bourdieu's work has always held a lesser appeal in the English speaking world than that of Giddens', perhaps in part because of its rather obscure style and the opacity of its concepts (see Jenkins, 1992). His insights do, however, have much to recommend them, especially as his approach is more flexible and more grounded in action than Giddens'. However, like Giddens, he remains closer to the objective than the subjective end of the epistemological tradition of sociology. The individual and the group are still largely faceless and undifferentiated, with a somewhat reductive distinction between the dominating and the dominated. There is also a neglect of personality, biography, decision making or negotiation, whilst the capacity and role of institutions and organisations is largely overlooked.

Both Giddens and Bourdieu make mention of place and space, suggesting that structuration can have something to say on these issues, but in essence, there is a failure to elaborate on the variety and reality of place and space, and how place and space in all their manifestations, including built form, both constitute and are constituted by social action. In an attempt to remedy this situation a few authors have subsequently explored the application of structuration in relation to place, environment and housing (see, for example, Donley-Reid, 1990; Dovey, 1999, 2002; Lawrence, 1993; Pred, 1983; and Sarre, 1986). Between them these authors address space in its widest meaning, from ecosystem to geographical area, from localised housing system to actual form. They also demonstrate, with varying degrees of conviction, elaboration and understanding, that structuration theory can provide only a partial elucidation of the connection between the social and the spatial – in terms of how social practices are enacted in space, constrained by space, transformative of space, or deposited in space.

Institutions, organisations and sentient beings

Institutions provide the ongoing framework whereby social, economic, political and juridical systems can be translated into processes activated by human agency. Institutions thus mediate between structure and agency, and are powerfully implicated in the extent to which the structural systems of society are reproduced or alternatively transformed. Institutions therefore have a life beyond the individual or group, have a history and a future, and have powers embedded within them which go beyond the immediacy of human action at any one time and which influence the possible scope for action. Institutions include, for example, the family, the Church, the law, the system of governance, the class system and the monarchy, each of which is characterised by its own rituals, principles and ways of thought and action. Effectively these institutions embody the rules and resources of the social system; they provide continuity and certainty, whilst also helping to shape the boundaries of activity in terms of the normative and the acceptable.

Institutions cannot themselves act: it is individuals who necessarily perform this function. Acting alone or in groups, in loose networks or in tight organisations, it is they who mediate both structure and institutions, with the potential both to perpetuate and to transform the existing order. In Bourdieu's terms, in relation to the *habitus* being a knowledge of how to act in a certain situation, or a feel for the game, then institutions embody the game. Those who play the game are not only those in positions of power who influence policy and decision making, but all those others whose thoughts, speech and action can affect events in ways which are not necessarily predictable, and which may be reinforcing or subversive of the status quo. It is this which prevents institutions from being immutable, making them vulnerable to those maverick individuals who step across accepted boundaries and bring into question the integrity and solidity of the whole institution – as witness the contemporary issues of paedophile and gay priests in the Church, and the transgressions of the Queen's children in marriage.

Within the institutional framework, organisations are important entities, themselves reliant on the actions and interactions of the individuals who compose the membership of the organisation. Organisations include the bureaucracies, professional bodies, private sector companies, pressure groups and so on, in which individuals with a certain common sense of purpose interact. In this regard, the social constructionism of Berger and Luckmann (1966) becomes relevant. According to their perspective, even though the institutional world is internalised as an objective reality, individuals have the capacity to sustain or modify that reality through interpersonal interaction. The significance attached to such interactional encounters has been theoretically explored in analyses based on symbolic interactionism and ethnomethodolgy, relying on intensive observation of people in contextual settings (see Kemeny, 2002). Such contextual settings involve not only the people in attendance and the way they speak and present themselves, but also the context itself: the type of place; the nature of the occasion as formal or informal; the time of day; preceding events; the duration of the encounter; the available props and so on. In regard to the nature of the interaction itself, critical factors are the relative positions of power of those involved, and the role of negotiation in determining outcomes – outcomes which can lead to: 'practical decisions which may have fateful consequences for those affected by them' (Kemeny, 2002: 141).

The importance of such 'negotiated order' is referred to in the work of Strauss *et al.* (1963), who show how outcomes in organisations are dependent on the: 'processes of give-and-take, of diplomacy, of bargaining …' (Strauss *et al.*, 1963: 148). Taking the example of a psychiatric hospital, it is pointed out that staff are all at different stages of their careers, have different ideological positions, different responsibilities, different training, and work in different ways. In discussing diagnosis and treatment they have their own aims and ambitions in mind, as well as the outcome for the patient – an outcome which is demonstrably dependent upon the process of negotiation and the balance of power between the parties. Extrapolating out from psychiatric hospitals Strauss *et al.* suggest that the less clarity there is about organisational aims and the boundaries of individual roles, the more the process will depend on negotiated order. That this is true, has been confirmed by work in other organisations, for example, schools (Hall and Spencer-Hall, 1982), medical hospitals (Mesler, 1989), social services departments (Wilson, 1992) and housing organisations (Franklin, 1998). Hall and Spencer-Hall, and Wilson stress that other factors in addition to negotiation are crucial in determining outcomes. Both point to the significance of individual biography, personality and style of management in shaping organisational culture and objectives, and in creating rituals, rules and procedures which affect the extent to which other personnel may have scope for negotiation.

This perspective reinforces the view that human agency does not consist simply of the passive reproduction of society's objective structures, but instead represents the actions of knowledgeable actors who have the capacity to reflect on what they do, to change the rules of the game, and to act in surprising ways. For this reason we need to know more about what it is that drives human action. An actor is both an individual and a member of one or more classes or groups, and it is through membership of class or group that an individual acquires the resources structurally available to him or her as a frame for action in the world. These resources provide continuity over time, and exist separately from and independently of the individual's own personal attributes, but inevitably impact on biography, experience and life chances. An individual is born into a social stratum, although through choice or circumstance may acquire the attributes of a different one. Similarly, an individual may through accident of birth be ascribed to a particular social group – in regard, for example, to ethnic group, type of disability, gender – but later choose or acquire the attributes of others.

In this context, Archer has provided some helpful ideas from a basis of aspiring to bring humanity back into social realism (Archer, 2000). She believes a sense of self, of self-worth, of individuality, and personal creativity is critical:

> In short, we are who we are because of what we care about ... We give a shape to our lives, which constitutes our internal personal integrity, and this pattern is recognisable by others as our concrete singularity.
>
> (Archer, 2000: 10)

She stresses the importance of recognising that whilst social agency may frame the roles available to us and the ways in which roles are performed, they do not determine how roles are selected or carried out: personal identity, self-consciousness, emotion, biology and experience are all influencing factors. Individuals may have difficulties in deciding on a role that expresses their identity, trying several out, choosing inappropriate or extreme roles, seeking to personify that role, and deciding how much of themselves to invest within it.

In presenting her ideas, Archer is moving towards the subjectivist approach in sociology, and it seems we cannot fully apprehend the nature of 'being in the world' or social action without recourse to phenomenological, interactionist and constructionist accounts. These are more cogent and persuasive in terms of demonstrating how behaviour is produced (as opposed to social structures being reproduced). Of particular significance in this regard is the work of Goffman (1961, 1968, 1971), based on extensive empirical observation. Goffman argues that face to face interaction has its own dynamics, consisting of the nature of the encounter and the personalities brought to it. People engage their own personal identity in an encounter, but this sense of identity is fragile and people may adopt a front to manage the encounter in such a way as to create a favourable impression. Hence people engage in 'impression management' and give 'performances'. Furthermore, identity is many-faceted, with people choosing to reveal different sides of their personalities to different people on different occasions. The result is a distinction between behaviour enacted in public, formal roles, or 'front' regions, and in private, informal roles, or 'back' regions (Goffman, 1971). Goffman and Strauss both demonstrate how in organisations and institutions people manage encounters by drawing on language and shared cultural meaning, negotiating outcomes through verbal and sometimes non-verbal means.

The power of the word

Reference has been made in the above sections, explicitly or implicitly, to language and representation, and the ways in which it can structure versions of reality. In this regard, discourse theory, or discourse analysis, is relevant, since it: 'puts discourse use at the centre of societal processes, assigning it a key role in social relations and in social transformations' (Hastings, 2000: 131). Discourse analysis, which addresses the use and meaning of language both in written text and speech (see Fairclough, 1992), has made a relatively belated entry into the fields of urban studies, planning and housing studies (see, for example, Franklin, 1998; Franklin and Tait, 2002; Gurney, 1999a, 1999b; Hastings, 1999, 2000; Jacobs and Manzi, 1996; Jacobs et al., 2004). As both Berger and Luckmann (1966) have stated, language is the medium through which truth and meaning are socially constructed, and is therefore open to different interpretations. Meaning itself is not fixed, but is fluid, and is created out of the interaction between speaker and listener, writer and reader. Nonetheless, language, as a system of categories and rules, 'fixes a world' (Hodge and Kress, 1993: 5), however temporarily, and is also a tool for socialisation and classification. A child, learning language, learns also how to perceive and interpret the world. In this way, texts: 'perform a range of specific rhetorical, legitimising and synthesising functions' (Jacobs, 1999: 205).

But language has an influence beyond this, in that it can be used as an instrument of ideology and power whereby certain versions of truth and knowledge are promoted as intrinsically more valid than others. Language thus becomes an expression of social structure, with the effect of reproducing or transforming social relations, such that, as Bourdieu asserts, the adoption of new discourses results in a constant repositioning of individuals and groups as they seek to impose their own representations of the world (Bourdieu, 1991). Politicians and the media, for example, continually manipulate meaning in order to cajole or convince the listener or the reader to accept a certain view of how things are (see Manning, 1985), whilst professionals demonstrate their claims to superior knowledge through their use of scientific and esoteric language. This same process is at work in, for example, the production of policy instruments. Whilst policy documents are often considered to be value free, it has been demonstrated that on the contrary, language is used to construct selective versions of the problems in order to render the policy responses not only appropriate but also commonsensical (Hastings, 1999). Such language has a 'normalising' effect, whereby issues, categories of people and events, are judged and treated in a stereotypical way, exerting a 'disciplinary power' on those who might seek to depart from taken for granted interpretations (Foucault, 1977; Gurney, 1999b).

Although there has been some criticism of discourse analysis as being overly involved with the type of intersubjectivity promoted by, for example, Garfinkel (1967) and hence for being relativistic and reductionist (see Burr, 1998), it is clear from the foregoing that this is to oversimplify the potential of discourse analysis. Discourse exists not only in a behavioural context, but also in a social context: it is central to the construction of social reality, but also has a dynamic relationship with practice (Jacobs and Manzi, 1996). Speech and text lay the foundation for action, for social relations, and for policy endorsement, whilst at the same time reflecting the ideological, political and institutional context – the structures of society. In achieving these effects, discourse often resorts to rhetorical or narrative devices, such as 'storylines', irony, wit, euphemism, neologism, hyperbole, simile, metaphor, myth, analogy and metonymy (Fairclough, 1992; Gurney, 1999a; Hajer, 1995). These are powerful tools in cueing an audience to interpret things in particular ways, but they go beyond this in connecting people to a collective consciousness of shared interpretations of such issues as history, tradition and myth, good and evil, exclusion and inclusion, and the power of institutions. It is these issues which are intrinsic to our sense of our place in the social system and in the world.

But this is not to say that new discourses cannot be produced, or that individuals do not have the power to transform, through language, existing beliefs, policies and practices. Thus, for example, in recent years a new discourse of physical disability has been promoted. This has been effected by people who themselves have disabilities, who have countered the accepted 'medical' model of disability with an alternative, 'social' model, effectively challenging and changing not only perceptions of disability, but also professional power and credibility (see, for example, Barnes, 1990; Oliver, 1996). This recasting of disability has also changed a hitherto marginalised group into a powerful force, and it has contested our cultural and mythical legacy of disability as something 'other': sinister, baneful, cursed, and outcast. At a more pragmatic level, it has had a particular impact on perceptions of the built environment, bringing into focus its limitations for those with physical disabilities. This has encouraged planners, designers and policy makers to 're-read' the built environment, and to introduce new practices to ensure greater accessibility.

Form has meaning

To many, the meaning of the built environment is primarily aesthetic: what matters is its visual appearance and the emotional response elicited from those who experience it. But to define the qualities inherent to an aesthetic experience of the built form has exercised theorists and critics since the days of Vitruvius in the first century BC (see Unwin, 1997). Aesthetics denotes beauty and harmony, and these must be derived from form, with form itself made up of all the elements of a building: size, scale, proportion, massing and volume, ornamentation, rhythm, light and shadow, texture, colour. The idea of the perfect interval, of rhythm, of articulation, of harmony, and of emotional response in architecture has also brought comparison with music, notably in Goethe's perception of architecture as frozen music. The succession of styles, schools and movements which has characterised architecture has at least in part been due to the search for the most authentic way to achieve this elusive aesthetic quality.

To concentrate on the built environment as form and aesthetics, however, limits the full extent of its meaning, the fact that it is a spatial manifestation, and that it has a connection to social relations, text and representation. This connection has been captured by Lefebvre, who suggests that space consists of a triad: spatial practices (the way in which space is empirically used in the reproduction of society), representations of space (the objective knowledge about space which can be conceptualised and is particularly the property of those who manipulate space such as architects and planners), and representational space (the space of symbol and imagination which overlays physical space and allows the meaning of space to be continually reconstructed) (Lefebvre, 1991). This triad can also be conceptualised more accessibly as 'practised', 'conceived' and 'lived' (or 'imagined') space (Dovey, 1999: 46), although in practice these categories overlap. Lefebvre argues that a science of space needs to include all the elements of this triad, and that one of the consequences of the capitalist mode of production has been to diminish the level of consistency between the three dimensions of space, in particular causing a potentially harmful dislocation from representational space.

Lefebvre's ideas about the way in which domination and subordination can be expressed through capitalist use of space have been reflected in the work of Foucault (1977), Markus (1993) and Dovey (1999). These authors argue that the built environment is complicit in the capitalist project. Foucault, for example, suggests that architecture reproduces the significant shifts in power relations over the ages, and that the enlightenment that began in the eighteenth century, together with subsequent shifts towards capitalism and industrial technology, have brought about new forms of domination – a 'disciplinary power' which exerts a normalising influence. Architecture is complicit in this since it is not merely a physical element in space, but achieves the allocation and 'canalisation' of people in space, encoding and manipulating social relations (Rabinow, 1984). The disciplinary power of architecture is at its most expressive in the disciplinary institution – not only the prison, but also the asylum, the military camp, and the school. In this connection Foucault draws on Jeremy Bentham's concept of the panopticon, an architectural device whereby surveillance of inmates can be achieved from one central position such as a tower. Unable themselves to observe whether the guard or overseer is present, yet aware that their every movement may be subject to scrutiny, inmates feel they must behave in a conformist way. Hence discipline becomes internalised.

The work of Markus and Dovey shows how the spatial outcomes of both architecture and urban design act as mediators of practices of power, in which the built environment may appear passive and silent but nonetheless is endowed with the capacity to control, intimidate, coerce, manipulate, seduce and authorise. Buildings and the spaces between them frame social action, they facilitate or constrain certain types of activity, and they exclude or include certain categories of people:

> The built environment reflects the identities, differences and struggles of gender, class, race, culture and age. It shows the interests of people in empowerment and freedom, the interests of the state in social order, and the private corporate interests in stimulating consumption.
>
> (Dovey, 1999: 1)

In his work Markus has looked more closely at the design and layout of certain building types of the industrial era, focusing on how the designer, intentionally or unintentionally, reproduces power relations in the design and layout of the built form. The resident or user then has little choice but to reproduce them since the built form facilitates only certain types of practical action. Thus the built environment becomes a classifying device consigning people not only in space but also to their role in society, and thus effectively reproducing social relations and the social structures of society. Thus, for example, the design of the Victorian asylum fixes in form both the asymmetries of power between inmates and supervisors, and the classification of the inmates by gender and type of condition (Markus and Cameron, 2002). Similarly, contemporary building types reflect the power relations of society. Thus the shopping mall represents a temple to the power of global capitalism, a haven of communal consumption, wherein passers by are seduced into consuming not on the basis of need, but in search of a lifestyle or the realisation of their dreams. But those who have no spending power, or who are there for a purpose other than to consume, are subject to a normalising 'gaze' and are excluded or moved on (Dovey, 1999).

In regard to both representations of space and representational space language is important. Indeed the relationship between the built environment and language has been much debated, in terms of both language *about* the built environment, and the language *of* the built environment (see Forty, 2000; Markus and Cameron, 2002, for detailed discussion). In regard to the former, meaning is socially constructed through the discourse of those who perceive and make sense of the built environment. Although the primary impact may be visual, apprehension goes beyond this, for whilst we 'see' a building, we can only give it meaning – 'that is a mosque', 'this is a church' – through verbalisation, and the descriptive and classifying capacity that language gives. Beyond this, language is used to make value judgements about the built environment, whether by lay people, the media or professionals. Each of these will use the type of discourse (unsophisticated, journalistic, technical) that is consonant with their position in society, with the aim of achieving their purpose of commentary, critique, comparison, or instruction and so on. As well as verbal accounts much of this discourse is produced as written texts, such as works of architectural history and appreciation, columns in newspapers, articles in academic and professional journals, textbooks, development briefs, design guides, surveyors' reports, and even marketing materials.

Texts are not only written, they can also be graphic, as for example photographs, plans, drawings and other illustrative devices. One advantage of illustration is that it presents an image which can be absorbed all at once, unlike words which have to be taken in sequentially (Forty, 2000: 39). Hence a different version of reality can be communicated, although just as with words illustrations are not value free and are similarly open to manipulation and interpretation. The production of an illustration requires a particular skill which, like language, has to be learnt. Indeed, the representation of three dimensional reality through two dimensional means is a definitive skill for design professionals, with drawing being the medium through which form and shape is given to ideas and creativity – Lefebvre's representation of space. The possession of this skill, together with the development of an esoteric vocabulary (jargon), is central to the claim to privileged and technical knowledge upon which professional power is based. Its possession is a central part of an elitist mystification process which reduces lay people to onlookers, excluded and frustrated because they cannot decode what amounts to a foreign language.

A model and its practical application

The foregoing has put forward a number of theoretical perspectives and conceptual insights from a variety of disciplinary backgrounds. Some have placed the built environment centrally, others mention the built environment only in passing or not at all. An analysis of social structure or social agency which fails to acknowledge how both are framed by space, misses a central dimension. By the same token, analyses which concentrate only on the built form, its history, design and aesthetics, exclude the richness of the ways in which the built environment provides the context for action. This context is not a mere container, value free, but expresses and encapsulates the norms, ideologies and beliefs of a society, both in production and in use. Furthermore, the ordering and division of space assumes strategic significance in the enactment and expression of social and symbolic relations, emphasising and reinforcing the differences between people. This connects to structuration theory, which can be harnessed to show that the built environment has a place as both the medium and product of social practice. Hence it is a 'structuring structure' for social action, and provides a way of physically demarcating the social spaces inhabited by different groups in society.

Whilst spatial order may be culturally and socially constituted, the influence of organisations and individuals cannot be overlooked. Organisations have cultures, regulations and negotiated orders that shape outcomes. Individuals are unique, bringing to organisations, events and perceptions their own expertise, needs and interpretations, based on experience, biography, personality and identity. Both organisations and individuals have the capacity to reproduce or transform social structures and social relations, and this extends to the way in which they produce, interpret and negotiate the built environment.

Figure 1.1 endeavours to capture some of the richness of meaning described above. It necessarily represents as an ideal type a somewhat complex conceptual framework, but can be simplified by considering the layers of structure, agency and representation, as denoted on the right hand side. Structure includes culture and society, the latter consisting of the social, spatial and conceptual processes which inhere in a particular culture – in the case under consideration in this book, British culture. Agency can be broken down into constituent elements: first the institutions and organisations which mediate structure through tradition, routine and regulatory procedures; second the individuals who are specifically involved in the creation of the built environment, such as planners, designers and developers; and third the people who make sense of and use the built environment. Representation is a term which can then be adopted to refer to the communicative actions of agents which both reproduce (or transform) social structures and express organisational and individual values. These communicative actions consist of spoken, written or depicted texts, and the built form itself. It should be emphasised, however, that although Figure 1.1 may give the appearance of a set of discrete categories these are in fact overlapping and mutually reinforcing in a way which is difficult to represent in two dimensional form.

To illustrate how the conceptual framework can be applied in practice the example is taken of a project of modernist architecture. This is Quarry Hill, an estate of flatted dwellings built by the local authority of Leeds, West Yorkshire in 1934. These flats were an anomaly in the UK housing context, for Quarry Hill represented a modernist inspired construction for public sector dwellers twenty years ahead of its time, the first large scale system-built flatted public housing scheme in the UK, and the only one of this concept or design (see Ravetz, 1974, for a comprehensive account of Quarry Hill; Mitchell, 1990, for an illustrative text; and Franklin, 1996a). It is awareness of the structural context, the workings of human agency, and the ways these are mediated and represented in space that provides the background to the development and form of Quarry Hill.

Modernist architecture was initially culturally specific to continental Europe. Its appearance was in response to the structural conditions of the late nineteenth

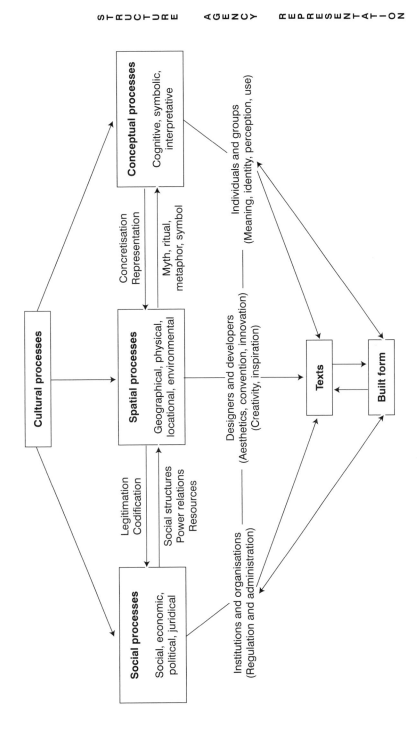

STRUCTURE

AGENCY

REPRESENTATION

Conceptual processes

Cognitive, symbolic, interpretative

Individuals and groups
(Meaning, identity, perception, use)

Concretisation
Representation

Myth, ritual, metaphor, symbol

Cultural processes

Spatial processes

Geographical, physical, locational, environmental

Designers and developers
(Aesthetics, convention, innovation)
(Creativity, inspiration)

Texts

Built form

Legitimation
Codification

Social structures
Power relations
Resources

Social processes

Social, economic, political, juridical

Institutions and organisations
(Regulation and administration)

1.1 A model to illustrate the contextual framework of built form and early twentieth centuries as the old social and spatial order began to collapse, although it took the devastation of the First World War for its design precepts to become crystallised. Thus it became a design statement that represented in built form the desire for a new beginning and a more ordered and cohesive society. In terms of form it was influenced by the geometric shapes of cubist and abstract art, and was expressive of a deliberate break with the more flamboyant historical revival styles. In addition it capitalised on the new materials and technical developments that were being explored in machinery and engineering (see Curtis, 1987).

There was a clear ideological underpinning to modernist architecture: rejection of the past; representation in built form of the imperative of the machine age; cold intellectualism and scientific rationalism; and function as the prime determinant of form. It was this latter that gave rise to the maxim 'form follows function'. It is these attributes which accord with Lefebvre's representations of space (conceived space), whilst in regard to his representational space (imagined space) what is involved is precisely what he feared to be typical of capitalism: an emptying out of meaning; a distancing from the spaces of symbol and imagination; and the negation of the 'poetic space' of Bachelard (1969). At the same time, modernism reflected a crystallisation in space of capitalist responses to the structural situation of employment in the early twentieth century. Throughout Europe there was a need for a supply of cheap but healthy labour to ensure maximum profit for the capitalist economy. Housing to a sufficient standard, located near the place of work, was essential to ensure first that workers would be healthy and would successfully reproduce the next generation, and second to enable them to feel that they were gaining some benefits from their labour. Modernism offered the prospect of a reasonable quality of mass housing in standardised units, thus suiting the ideological needs of capitalism to dominate and control the working populace, whilst at the same time giving an impression of homogeneity and equality – all workers were identical cogs in the wheel of capitalism, and all were to be seen to be treated the same.

Modernist architecture thus represented a transformation of the old rules of design, the concretisation in space of a new conceptual approach, and a meeting of the needs of an industrialised society. But as with any successful movement, the Modern Movement needed influential individuals to drive it forward and promote its principles. In Europe the most influential of these individuals were undoubtedly the famous names of Mies van der Rohe and Walter Gropius, both attached to the Bauhaus school, together with Le Corbusier, famous for his discourse of a *machine à habiter* (machine for living). The teaching, writing and example of these men were central to the paradigm shift that resulted in the widespread adoption of the modernist style, and they and those who followed them shared in the reflected glory of a new field of symbolic and artistic capital. The fact that this was displayed in the very visual evidence of architectural form made their claim to pre-eminence, the 'distinction' of Bourdieu, plain for all to see.

In the traditionally conservative and insular UK modernist architecture was slow to gain appeal. It was only through the agency of architect *émigrés*, escaping from Nazi persecution in the 1930s, that sufficient collective influence was gathered to disseminate the new discourse in relation to design. Up to that time no authority had ventured to follow European solutions to mass housing, even if they were aware of them. In part this was because of the English (but not Scottish) cultural aversion to flatted dwelling, but also because of an ideological commitment to the new, quintessentially English, Garden City movement with its low densities and large areas of green open space. In addition, flats in the imagination of the English working population were associated with the grim 'Buildings', the barrack-like tenements built in the Victorian age by moral housing reformers. However, in many towns and cities, housing problems were severe, with a pressing need to clear vast tracts of overcrowded and run down Victorian terraces – the latter having been the response by profiteers to industrialisation. Given the institutional framework that prevailed (see Chapter 3) subsidies from central government were available to replace slum housing, but local authorities were relatively free to make their own decisions about design provided legislative standards were met.

By the 1930s Leeds was a city with an acute housing problem. Its traditional streets of back-to-back housing were little more than slums, massively overcrowded and in a state of disrepair. A solution was needed, and the one that was eventually proposed derived from the interaction between two committed individuals together with their powers of persuasion and negotiation with the relevant local authority committees.

In the early 1930s the deputy Chairman of the Housing Committee in Leeds was the Reverend Charles Jenkinson, a socialist and committed Christian who had made housing improvement a personal crusade. He was influenced by the currently fashionable tenets of the Garden City movement and the belief that fresh air, light, space and gardens must and could be provided for all classes. The Director of Housing, R.A.H. Livett, was an architect who was intellectually curious about putting into practice some of the stylistic ideas of the Modern Movement in architecture, and keen to adopt new technologies in construction. On a visit to Europe the two men were particularly impressed by the housing in Vienna, notably Karl Marx Hof, built in 1927, with its vast scale, half a mile in length, the range of communal facilities, and even the displays of flowers on the balconies. They began to be convinced that this type of housing could provide the answer to Leeds' problems. In particular it would provide a visual statement of a commitment to the betterment of the social and moral lives of slum dwellers, whilst also creating a 'community' within one functional unit in which all needs could be met.

Their design blueprint for the estate to be known as Quarry Hill was based on Karl Marx Hof, but with the superimposition of a number of features derived from France, such as the construction system of steel and precast concrete panels, and also the lift and waste disposal systems. Internally the flats were to be superior to those they had seen on the continent, to comply with higher English standards and layouts as required by the Tudor Walters Report of 1919. Flats were also provided with open hearths for solid fuel fires, following English domestic custom rather than more innovative European convention. Livett also incorporated external and internal embellishments, such as heraldic Leeds owls as capstones, semicircular and elliptical arches topped with huge flower troughs, and fireplaces with neo-classical detailing (as illustrated in Mitchell, 1990). In not playing according to the rules Livett was allowing personal idiosyncrasy to prevail over rationality, and compromising the principle that the structure should speak for itself and represent nothing other than a pure container of function.

When finished Quarry Hill flats contained over 900 flats in one vast crescent shaped perimeter block enclosing five smaller slab blocks, with a maximum height of eight storeys. But the development was never completed to the original vision. The plan had been to create a Utopian community with all necessary facilities, including a large community hall, twenty shops, a laundry, a swimming pool, a bowling green and tennis courts, gardens, various recreation areas, playgrounds and a kindergarten. In the event it was not so much human agency as institutional and structural constraints which led to the dimming of the vision: at local level the inability of the local authority to meet the soaring costs of construction, and at national level the onset of World War Two. Thus most of the communal facilities remained unbuilt and the landscaping of the open spaces was never completed.

The way Quarry Hill was received and represented varied according to the perspective of those engaged with it – their *habitus* – as well as over time. Initially it had lent Leeds and its housing committee an air of distinction, an example of intellectual and symbolic capital in a most striking form. To some people the estate was an outstanding example of how to achieve good housing for workers, close to their place of work and the facilities of the city. Others saw it as a nasty foreign import smacking of communism and a place where hordes of the poor and disreputable were housed; a place to be avoided. Such opposite perceptions drew the comment that it had a: 'dual reputation as the pinnacle of modern working-class housing and a hopelessly "red" estate' (Ravetz with Turkington, 1995: 48). As for the tenants themselves, initially they were pleased with an environment which seemed a vast improvement on the old back-to-backs, and internally this was certainly the case. But the huge scale, the expanses of open space, the sense of enclosure and separation from the city streets, were all a new and alien experience.

Over time the problems multiplied. The disillusionment of the residents, the lack of maintenance of open space, the concentrations of problem families due to the local authority's policy on allocations, and the inadequate construction which had not taken into account the damp and cold of a Northern city, all took their toll. By 1973, the costs were insupportable, and councillors and officials declared the scheme no longer fit for habitation and ordered its demolition on humanitarian grounds.

Relating the story of Quarry Hill more closely to Figure 1.1, it can be seen that the cultural context is of British insularity, suspicion of new ideas, and preference for domestic scale dwellings modelled on a mythical rural quality. In Europe, by contrast, there was an already established tradition of urbanity, together with a normalised acceptance of the flatted dwelling as an appropriate residential form for all classes. In regard to social processes, in Europe the changing requirements of capitalism required increasing numbers of more amenable workers. The response at the institutional level was to produce new housing, both to ensure a healthy workforce and to seduce the working population into a belief that it was benefiting from the capitalist system. The actual shape this housing took was a consequence of a new movement in architecture, stimulated by the perceived inability of existing design orthodoxies to reflect the changing social order. But this transformation in approach to design may have taken a different course had it not been for the inspiration and leadership of certain key individuals such as Gropius, Mies van der Rohe and Le Corbusier, together with the possibilities afforded by technological advances. Thus the mass housing block of modernist architecture was born, acting at the symbolic level to reinforce the fact that all workers were identical, without either individuality or autonomy. Thus did spatial form reflect and reproduce the social situation of the times, and in particular the way in which the state must be seen to maintain control and order to allow the capitalist project to succeed.

In the UK the catalyst in the advent of modernist architecture was changing social events in Europe, specifically the effects of Nazi ideology and the consequent arrival in this country of some of the most influential exponents of modernist architecture. It was the persuasive discourse of their teaching and writings that stimulated British architects to reproduce their ideas, but institutional interests, particularly national and local governments, were more cautious. This was due to their *habitus* of resistance to change and the fact that their legitimacy derives from reproducing the status quo. But the reality facing local governments was a legacy from the social processes of industrialisation, specifically the deterioration into slums of many of the hastily erected and unregulated rows of terraced housing. In Leeds, a Northern city with an industrial base, the old back-to-backs were overcrowded and in disrepair, and new housing was desperately needed to avoid worker dissatisfaction. The subsequent negotiation of a solution at the institutional level was dominated by two prominent individuals, one motivated by Christian charity and the other by architectural zeal. Without their initiative and collaboration an entirely different solution might have been proposed, and it was the decision to visit the different cultural context of continental Europe that brought to Leeds a built form that they believed would fit contemporary social and institutional needs and, through its aesthetic innovation, bring distinction to the city. However, the purist design principles of modernism were compromised by the need to cater for the specifically English cultural requirement of a living fire, as well as by the desire of the architect to express himself in the detailing – some of which made reference to the local culture.

The resultant high rise, high density built form of Quarry Hill was in complete contrast to the local vernacular of the former back-to-backs, whilst the spatial vocabulary of scale, open space, hierarchy of public and private space, relationship to the street, and lack of connectedness to the city's fabric were all at odds with traditional preconceptions of the ordering of residential space. The *habitus* of the residents did not equip them with the capacity to relate to this language, and furthermore the spatial system imposed had no congruence with their traditions of social life. In effect it was a prime example of Lefebvre's concerns about the disjuncture between spatial practices, representations of space and representational space. It was this lack of consonance, together with the failure to allow for the locational realities of climate and the institutional incapacity adequately to fund the scheme or to manage it once completed, that resulted in Quarry Hill becoming constructed as a place of oppression and a failure. Far from representing distinction it soon became an embarrassment, and eventually the city authorities negotiated its demise.

Through this example it is possible to see the complexity of the inter-connections between aspects of the model presented in Figure 1.1. It is not simply a case of a cascade effect, in which cultural processes lead directly to social, spatial or conceptual processes, with these then being enacted or mediated by the agency of institutions, organisations and individuals, who express themselves in action, discourse and the shaping of built form. This would be a reductive view, and it is important to appreciate that there is a circularity and a linkage between all the elements: individuals are not entirely free thinking and acting agents but operate within the parameters of cultural and social structures and are further constrained by institutional frameworks. However, they do not mindlessly reproduce structures, but have the capacity to alter and transform them. Similarly built form does not appear autonomously through the actions of developers or designers, but is the outcome of a process mediated by cultural, social and institutional preconceptions, and framed by the realities of the spatial constraints and opportunities of specific locations.

It is only through the detail of a case study approach that this type of complexity and the nature of the inter-relationships between elements can be unravelled, and it is for this reason that the case studies in Chapters 6 to 10 form the core of this book. However, in order to fully understand the context within which the case studies are played out, it is necessary to expand on some of the issues which have been alluded to in the current chapter. It is for this reason that the next four chapters examine in more detail those aspects of the social system, of the institutional framework, of the powers of agency, and of the analyses and discourses of built form, which seem to be of most relevance in the context of the shaping of the space of twenty-first century living.

2 Unsettling structures: insecurity and change in a globalised society

Historically the different cultures of the world have existed in a relatively isolated way, albeit with occasional episodes of intermingling due to invasion or waves of immigration. Thus for the most part, the cultural and structural systems of society have evolved only slowly, at a pace which can be accommodated without engendering insecurity. New technologies, new modes of living, new patterns of settlement and house form, have consequently developed incrementally, allowing a gradual adaptation. In the past century and a half, however, this has begun to change, and at an accelerating pace. Increased contact between cultures, industrialisation, two world wars, the spread of global capitalism and the information revolution have triggered unprecedented upheavals across the world in all the established structures of social life: nationhood; monarchy; governance; economy; religion; employment; mobility; relationship between town and country; divisions of wealth and poverty; and connections to community and kin.

This chapter examines the causes and consequences of these changes in the UK in recent times, highlighting globalising tendencies, the spread of inequality, the growth of the consumer society, and the implications for urban space, home and community. What emerges is a picture of instability and insecurity in which authority, community and identity are dissolving, and in which people feel they belong everywhere and nowhere. In this situation of anomie, security and meaning are increasingly being sought through the project of the self and the possession and display of material goods. Amongst these goods can be included the home, although the home is, of course, far more than this. It is the place to be 'at home', the place of security and identity, of comfort and memories, even though for some the home contains a reality far removed from this idealised construction. The same 'feel good' factor that inheres in the word 'home' is also found in the term 'community', but community too can be shown to be a concept that has more meaning in the imagination than in any actual representation on the ground.

The globalising imperative

Britain at the start of the twenty-first century is part of a globalised society in which people, goods, money and information flow from one side of the world to the other and back again with increasing frequency and at increasing speed. Central to these flows are communication links, with the expansion of transportation, telecommunications, and most recently, the world-wide web facilitating the new global network. Capital, too, has become mobile, no longer fixed to locality as in the days of industrialisation. Opportunity is pursued from place to place in search of the lowest costs and the greatest profit, and with little concern for the human or environmental consequences. The countries, firms and individuals who succeed (in terms of increased wealth), are those who are prepared to participate in this new mobility, who are flexible, responsive to market change, looking boldly to the future and not clinging blindly to the past. At the same time, neither countries, firms nor individuals seem to have control over the processes of the new global order, which are random, elusive, evanescent and ultimately baneful.

At the same time as globalisation, and inseparable from it, there has emerged in Western societies another profound shift. This shift has affected all areas of life: the economy; social relations; the political order; the labour market; cognition and world views; the built environment; and patterns of living. Variously referred to as post-industrial, post-Fordist, post-traditional, post-capitalist, postmodern, high, late or second modern, it amounts to the end of the period which began with the Enlightenment, the so called modern period. This was characterised by a belief in progress, in rationality, in objective scientific truths, in mechanisation, the division of labour and a capitalist economy based on waged labour. Central to the modern period in the UK was the industrial revolution and the development of factory and mill based work, with new transport systems and the intensive urbanisation of a society which had hitherto been based on agrarianism. But the period also included the great scientific, literary and institutional advances of the Victorian age, and the subsequent mid-twentieth century ideologies of the nuclear family, the welfare state, full employment, professionalisation, and bureaucratisation. In effect, modern society, or modernity, represented a dislocation from the old traditional society, which was based on feudal relations and the institutions associated with family, religion, morality, hierarchy, locality and community (Giddens, 1990, 1991). All of these began to be undermined under the complexity of the conditions of modernity; a process which has gathered pace under the impact of postmodernity and globalisation.

It has been suggested that the consequences of this postmodern era have resulted in profound effects on both structure and agency, such that we now dwell in a 'risk society' where 'reflexive modernisation' and 'individualisation' prevail (Bauman, 2001a, 2001b; Beck, 1992, 2000; Beck *et al.*, 1994; Lash and Urry, 1994). The adoption of the term risk society has been introduced to designate the nature of society now that the modern industrial period is over. In a risk society the beliefs central to modernity in regard to science, progress, expert knowledge and a hierarchical social order have begun to be questioned and challenged, hence the term 'reflexive' modernisation. Furthermore, there is a new public awareness of the hazards inherent in the pursuit of innovation and aggressive growth; hazards which are often invisible and whose effects are unknowable, and which concern environmental degradation, genetic manipulation, pollution, food contamination, nuclear and biological threats. Since experts – whether scientists or politicians – are no longer trusted, people cannot believe that the systems which exist, or even those that might be developed, can be guaranteed to protect them from harm. In addition the other securities, of family, marriage, community, work, religion, tradition, shared values, continuity, are also foundering, increasing the sense of anxiety and insecurity. Since the established structures and institutions are shaken, people feel cast adrift, no longer sure of who they are, where they are going, and how they fit into the scheme of things. Whilst this disorientation may to some extent give an impression of freedom from the constraints of the old traditional ties, it also has the consequence that people are forced to turn in on themselves and make new decisions. The effect of this is to strengthen the power of agency over structure in a process of 'individualisation'. The central question becomes 'how shall I live?' (Giddens, 1991), with the individual forced to choose what to believe and who to be, to create an identity and construct a biography, to become a 'reflexive' individual:

> The tendency is towards the emergence of individualized forms and conditions of existence, which compel people – for the sake of their own material survival – to make themselves the centre of their own planning and conduct of life. Increasingly, everyone has to choose between different options, including as to which group or subculture one wants to be identified with.
>
> (Beck, 1992: 88)

Ideologies and markets

The effect of globalisation on the UK has been compounded by a historical and geographical insularity which has rendered the British people resistant to external influences. Introspection and retrospection have been key definers of British society, wherein a monarchy and an aristocracy, land and property, tradition and pageant have held sway. But at the turn of the twenty-first century the UK is having to adapt to the new world order, in which it is no longer the leading force it once was in the old imperial and industrial eras. The dominant world power is now the US, and the aggressive 'Disneyfication' and 'Macdonaldisation' of society, the relentless pursuit of growth, the confessional society, the pursuit of pleasure and celebrity status have filtered into the pores of societies across the world. At the same time, the UK has been drawn into greater communion with continental Europe, joining the European Economic Community, now the European Union, in 1973, and subsequently having to accept, if reluctantly, some of the common European policies with their emphasis on social justice and citizenship rights. Perhaps as a result of these influences the UK is becoming less deferential and more meritocratic, society is more open, and apart from a reactionary minority people are by and large more accepting of the values and contributions of other cultures. The UK has also been drawn into global issues, most notably in regard to the 'war on terror' and the environmental debate. The latter has become increasingly pressing since the publication of the Brundtland Report on sustainable development (WCED, 1987) and the convening of the first Earth Summit in Rio in 1992. One result of this is that the term 'sustainable development' has now become part of popular rhetoric, although its meaning remains contested, its principles elusive, and its achievements indeterminate (see Raemakers, 2000).

In terms of national politics the twentieth century experienced relatively frequent shifts in government between Labour and Conservative majorities, and hence between an emphasis on ideologies on the left of the political spectrum and those on the right. During and after the Second World War, however, these differences were overcome in an all-party commitment to the establishment of the welfare state and state intervention in the free working of the market to ensure full employment and a stable economy. This coalition weakened over time, with a marked change in 1979 when the Conservatives came to power under the leadership of Margaret Thatcher. Their ideology was driven by a 'New Right' core which urged that the market should reign supreme, free of state interference, and that hence privatisation and competition should be encouraged. The public sector was pronounced inherently inefficient and unaccountable, whilst the welfare system was deemed to promote a 'nanny' state which encouraged dependency and idleness, sapping the ability of the individual to take personal responsibility.

In pursuing the policy implementation of these ideologies, Mrs Thatcher presided over the dismantling of much of the welfare state, in privatising much of the public sector, and in vastly increasing inequality and poverty – as well as famously declaring that there was no such thing as society. By the time Labour succeeded to power in 1997, the Conservative era had endured for so long that much could never be reversed. In addition the Cold War had ended, the Berlin wall had collapsed, and along with it the belief in the potential of state socialism. Old Labour became 'New Labour', shifting to the political centre and eliding the difference between left and right. New Labour under Tony Blair has continued to perpetuate the ideology of a market led society, albeit with a more inclusive approach which has seen targeted efforts to ameliorate the problems of poverty. However, there is an implicit rejection of any return to true welfare statism or the principles of proportionate redistribution and all that remains is a safety net for the most vulnerable.

In relation to housing, the generally accepted ideological position from the late nineteenth century onwards has been that free market solutions alone are not sufficient. This suggests that housing is perceived as a good which cannot be unproblematically produced and distributed by the market, and that the benefits of housing accrue not only to individuals but to society at large. However, since the 1950s it is owner occupation that has been promoted, popularised by the Conservatives as realising a property owning (or in some cases, owing) democracy (Daunton, 1987; Doling *et al.*, 1988). But reliance on owner occupation is not unproblematic, since the housing market is particularly sensitive to the economy. Thus economic upturns and recessions often have a dramatic impact on the housing market, as proven by the experience of the downturn in the late 1980s and early 1990s. Indeed, the consequences of negative equity and repossession led at the time to a questioning of the idological commitment to owner occupation (see Chapter 3 for further information on housing policy).

The early 2000s saw a new found confidence in housing as a sound investment, especially as mortgages were rendered more affordable by a fall in interest rates, engineered to boost the economy. This resulted in a base rate of 3.5 per cent in mid-2003, the lowest for nearly half a century. Not surprisingly (and especially when allied with the lowest house building programme for over seven decades) this led to high demand and an unprecedented increase in house prices. Furthermore, a falling stock market and concerns about the security of pension funds made property seem a better risk to investors, with a concomitant demand in the second home and buy-to-let market. By 2003 this had led to a severe problem of affordability for those even on average incomes to obtain a foot on the housing ladder in many areas of the country, with the south-east the worst affected (Wilcox, 2003). During 2004, interest rates were gradually increased to try and slow the housing market and rein in excessive consumer spending, but it was only at the end of that year that house prices showed any signs of slowing. At the time of writing it remains to be seen whether there will be a house price crash on the scale of the early 1990s, and while economic rationalists believe that in the context of relatively low unemployment and continuing low interest rates this is perhaps unlikely, the more elusive issue of consumer confidence may well be the key determinant.

The housing market is also directly affected by the labour market. In today's globalised and market led society, the old securities of full (male) employment and a job for life have gone. The manufacturing industry appears to be in terminal decline as either its products are no longer needed or companies have moved production to Asia where labour is plentiful and cheap. Instead the demand is now for a mobile and flexible labour force based on an information and communication society, in which the service sector predominates. But in the new global information revolution at the start of the twenty-first century even here jobs are under threat. For in both the new call centre industry with its relatively unskilled labour force, and in the more highly skilled financial and IT sectors, jobs are gradually being transferred overseas where costs are lower.

The new conformation of the labour market has had implications for the individual, for the community, and for traditional systems of authority. Men fear they cannot support a family, and women have entered the workforce in increasing numbers, challenging the old order of male/female relationships. In the effort to succeed, to progress, and to keep or secure permanent work, both men and women put in ever-longer hours, with the UK now working the longest hours in Europe. Commuting hours have also extended, as investment in transport is neglected, and high house prices force those on even moderate incomes further from their place of work. Many couples now work in different towns or cities, or occasionally even different countries, and run two homes, a 'pad' near a place of work and a family home. Moreover, the fact that the old structures of authority and loyalty in the workplace, in the community and in the home are no longer reproduced in the traditional way has meant that discipline and commitment have become dissolved and diffuse, sometimes absent altogether, sometimes internalised, sometimes displaced and abused (see Bauman, 1998, 2001b; Foucault, 1977). The combined consequences are social and personal distress, relationship difficulties, an increase in divorce, in single parenthood, in undersocialised children, in alienation and in crime: 'A market society takes a terrible toll of the social groupings that represent the building blocks of humanity' (Hutton, 1996: 225).

Polarisation, diversity and demography

Despite continuous economic growth and ever increasing standards of living, Britain remains an unequal society. Indeed inequality in income has increased in the last 25 years, driven by an ideological commitment to the position that the twin incentives of low taxation and low benefits are what make work and individual effort pay. Reward has overwhelmingly gone to those already rich, and by the turn of the twenty-first century the most wealthy 1 per cent in the country owned nearly 25 per cent of the total wealth, whilst some 25 per cent of the population, 12 million households, were living in relative poverty (defined as those with less than 60 per cent of median income) (Howard et al., 2001; Low Pay Unit, 2003). Official unemployment figures (4.7 per cent in the second half of 2004) mask the true situation as only those registered and actively seeking work are counted (Office for National Statistics, 2005). However, statistics on both poverty and unemployment conceal national and regional inequalities, and despite the generalisation that the south of the country is more prosperous than the north, there are pockets of poverty in the south, as well as areas of extreme affluence in the north.

Research has repeatedly shown that those who are poor are disproportionately likely to experience poor mental and physical health, early mortality, low educational achievement, higher incidences of crime, poor housing and political alienation (see, for example, Pantazis and Gordon, 2000; Palmer et al., 2002). The fact that poor people are also excluded from the normal life of society has been recognised in the term 'social exclusion', which was first adopted in the European context:

Social exclusion is a broader concept than poverty, encompassing not only low material means but the inability to participate effectively in economic, social, political or cultural life, and, in some characteristics, alienation and distance from the mainstream society.

(Duffy, 1995, cited in Walker, 1997: 8)

The discourse of social exclusion has been taken up by New Labour who perceive crime, unrest, anti-social behaviour, truancy and joblessness to be the consequences of social exclusion (see Social Exclusion Unit, 1998). Hence their aim is to devise policies to create a more inclusive, cohesive and integrated society. Since excluded people tend to be effectively both segregated and concentrated in the poorer areas of town and cities (see Madanipour, 1998), such policies have been focused on spatially defined areas, notably on so-called 'problem' social housing estates. Whilst area targeting facilitates visibility, it ignores the reality of social exclusion which also affects individuals (including the homeless) in more isolated pockets of deprivation, and is not confined to social housing (see Lee and Murie, 1997). A further consequence of identifying the issue of social exclusion with specific localities and a specific tenure is that these then become constructed as the site of all society's ills, places to be avoided containing an 'underclass' of the dangerous and the disaffected, against whom one must be constantly on one's guard.

The distribution of income and wealth create important and significant divisions in society, and have traditionally, along with accident of birth, been seen as the basis of stratification by class. However, there is increasing recognition of the reality of other divisions and other groupings within society, which has given rise to an emerging discourse of diversity (see Harrison with Davis, 2001). In effect, this is part of the postmodern 'turn', which has marked an end to a dominant metanarrative and an acceptance of the experiential truths of others, from whatever culture or perspective they may speak. Moreover, division into generalised categories of race, gender and disability are now seen as overly homogenised, and it is acknowledged that there are multiple sub-groupings, and numerous ways of constructing identity. Race is not simply a distinction of black versus white, but contains many different ethnicities and personal histories, within which the experience of men and women may vary profoundly. Gender cannot be considered simply as an opposition between male and female, but of different feminisms and masculinities, and a variety of sexualities. Disability too, consists of a multiplicity of conditions and of levels of impairment, both physical and mental, such that one person's individual experience cannot automatically be aggregated with another's. All of these groups, but particularly feminists and disabled people, have begun to take direct action and to organise themselves into social movements. Their aims are to ensure that their voices are heard and that their needs are accommodated, not by being made to 'fit in' or to conform, but by a structural shift in societal attitudes which will lead to more inclusive practices.

This 'politics of difference' has led to a concern for a reduction in discrimination of every sort, framed in discourse and action which is 'politically correct'. In effect, it has:

> ... opened up the way to a 'revisioning' of the political sphere and to the development of new perspectives on the cultural and political processes by which the policy and practice of welfare sustains asymmetrical differences in the organisation of social life.
>
> (O'Brien and Penna, 1998: 185)

Accordingly, and in tune with the recent construction of those who use services as clients, consumers, customers, citizens and users, a more inclusive, less top-down and more participatory approach to service delivery is being recommended. This is requiring a transformation of the monolithic, one size fits all approach of the modern era, in which professionals and policy makers assumed they could impose blanket solutions, to an approach which attempts to be more responsive and individualised.

In addition to the changing perception of the institutionalised groupings noted above, there are fundamental changes to the demographic and social constitution of the UK which are likely to have even more far-reaching effects. The census of 2001 showed that for the first time there were more people aged 60 and over than there are under 16 (Office for National Statistics, 2003a). With a figure of 21 per cent of the total population now 60 or more, and 1.9 per cent 85 or more (both projected to rise) there are serious implications in regard to increasing frailty and disability. Longer life is occurring at the same time as increasing inequalities in old age, with considerable difference in terms of income and health, such that whilst a high proportion of older people are undoubtedly poor and in need of care, a rising proportion are relatively wealthy and independent (see Tinker, 1996). The pattern of retirement has also changed from one of retirement at 60 for women and 65 for men, to one where some take early retirement in their 50s to lead a life of leisure or fulfil their dreams, whilst others work until 70 or more. Within a decade or two, however, this will change again as concerns about pension funds and longevity compel people to endure longer working lives. This 'stretching' of old age means that old age can no longer be considered as a homogenous state; there are multiple experiences of old age and ageing, extending over a period of three and often four decades, and embracing a variety of lifestyles, abilities and dependencies (see also Chapter 8).

There have also been significant changes in family life (see McRae, 1999). Whilst marriage has decreased dramatically in popularity, the numbers of those cohabiting or living with same sex partners has increased. In addition, the incidence of divorce has trebled in a generation, the proportion of children born outside marriage has quadrupled, and lone parents head nearly a quarter of families with dependent children (Scott, 1999). People move in and out of relationships with increasing frequency, and the number of complex families, containing a variety of step relationships, means many households have shifting membership over both time and space. At the same time, many families are smaller, since more women are either opting to have fewer children later or not at all. More starkly, longer life, greater affluence, fewer marriages, more marital breakdown and a greater desire for independence, especially by women, have all led to an increase in single households. These were estimated in the 2001 census as 30 per cent of all households, an increase from 26.3 per cent in 1991 (Office for National Statistics, 2003b). Again, this seems a trend that is likely to continue. The traditional nuclear family, upon which so much institutional decision-making has been based, is now in the minority.

The consumer society

During the 1950s affluence began to increase on both sides of the Atlantic, leaving workers with income to spend on a wider range of goods than those required for survival (see Goldthorpe *et al.*, 1968). At the same time, advances in mechanisation meant goods could be manufactured more cheaply on a production line system, especially when limited to a standard range. This principle had first been grasped by Henry Ford at his car plant in the USA with the production of the Model T Ford, and was soon adopted by others in the manufacture of cheap mass products for consumption by a mass workforce (Miles, 1998). As affluence further advanced, such products began to be required in increasing variety and number for a populace anxious to be seen to have the same possessions as others in their neighbourhood. At the same time, the growth of marketing, the search for greater profits, and the spread of advertising conspired to create in people a desire for more and more goods, a desire which they were seduced into believing would bring them greater happiness and fulfilment. Since greater happiness depended on possessing ever more goods, and ever more goods were always being produced, it was axiomatic that desire would never be satisfied, and more and more goods would be demanded.

By the late twentieth century this vicious (or virtuous) circle had both intensified and diversified. In the postmodern world consumerism has now become a way of life, almost a religion, and it is the relationship to consumption rather than to production that is now the organising principle of society and of the economy (see Miles, 1998; Miller, 1995). Indeed, the economy depends on consumerism, especially at times of sluggish economic growth when citizens are urged to shop and spend almost as a patriotic duty (see Clarke, 2003). The range of fashions and styles, their frequency of change, and the growth of branding and designer labels also encourage greater spending in order to be seen to be a knowledgeable consumer. The situation has become one where the use value of goods has been overtaken by their symbolic or aesthetic value as signs (Lash and Urry, 1994) and what has become important is not what goods *do* but what they *say* about those who display them. By selecting certain types of consumer good, individuals construct their identity, choose who they want to be and with which social group they wish to identify: individuals and social groups who are no longer rooted in familiar neighbourhoods but in fluid movement across time and space. In Bourdieu's terms, these groups are ever searching for new forms of distinction which will give them the necessary symbolic capital to proclaim their difference and superiority over others, whilst lower groups constantly aspire to emulate those above them to show they too have arrived (Bourdieu, 1984).

In effect, the division of society into consumption sectors or lifestyle niches has become more important than the old class divisions, and it is the facility to consume that gives people 'ontological security': the sense that all is well in their lives. This ability to consume has become a marker of well-being, success and status, whilst the possession of goods gives a sense of (false) security in an otherwise insecure world. In such a society those who cannot consume through lack of means are not only excluded but also repressed (Bauman, 1988) especially those who are forced to rely on the shifting sands of state welfare. On the other hand, there has also emerged an anti-consumerism in which the deliberate and freely chosen rejection of consumerism has become a mode of resistance to the imperatives of capitalism and the immorality of big business (see Lodziak, 2002; Miller, 1995). The stand taken by growing numbers in questioning the value and consequences of the relentless commodification of daily life has led to suggestions that we may be entering a post-materialist or post-consumer society. This is likely to be marked by the greater credibility given to the pursuit of more reflexive and alternative lifestyles, as, for example, in the various manifestations of the green movement and the search by individuals for therapeutic healing and spiritual meaning (see Giddens, 1994, and Chapter 10).

As a structural force, consumerism is pervasive and is reproduced in everyday practices. It is also through the act of consumption that people construct an understanding of themselves and their place in the world:

> It is increasingly in the array of commodities as brought to life in the consumption practices of the household that moral, cosmological and ideological objectifications are constructed to create the images by which we understand who we have been, who we are, and who we might or should be in the future.
>
> (Miller, 1995: 35)

In this respect material objects act also as cultural objects, since they help to create order in the world through giving expression to cultural categories such as time, space, nature, class, age and gender (Douglas and Isherwood, 1996). Thus the objects people choose, be it clothing, food, car, leisure pursuit, home or pets, become a communicative or encoding device which both reinforces the system of cultural categories, and also informs observers as to which cultural category a person belongs. Consumer goods can also capture our cultural or individual dreams, such as an idealised golden age, a world of romance, a lost childhood or a vision of wealth (Featherstone, 1991; McCracken, 1990). Thus commodities represent not only material value but are also 'good to think': 'a non-verbal medium for the human creative faculty' (Douglas and Isherwood, 1996: 40).

It is this capacity of goods that has been utilised in market research and in advertising, on the one hand identifying the groups into which people can be classified and the types of objects used to distinguish them, and on the other, connecting with their dreams of what might be or what once was. In this way audiences are targeted with consumer goods whose representation draws on the culturally constituted world, creating a symbolic equivalence between them (McCracken, 1990) whilst also affirming their properties of exclusivity. Visual imagery and carefully chosen words create the desired effect, and are decoded by the potential consumer who feels persuaded that acquisition of the object – be it a bijou residence or farm sourced organic meat – will bring distinction. Such symbols of distinction are all the more potent as they are constructed in stark opposition to the place of residence or consumer products of the poor – the tarnished sink estate and the nutritionally suspect burger and chips.

The framing of urban space

Both urban and rural environments are shaped and re-shaped in response to the human need for advancement, interaction and exchange in the pursuit of social, economic and political ends. These ends and the means by which they are achieved have changed over time, as consequently has the physical environment. Thus new landscapes, both rural and urban, and new modes of life are layered over earlier ones, as people and places adapt to change at an ever-quickening pace. In the UK the most pronounced shift has been from a traditional agrarian society characterised by proximate, face to face encounters, to a modern, urbanised and industrialised society, characterised by ever more socially and physically distant relations. This change has been theorised in various ways, for example as a dichotomy between *Gemeinschaft* and *Gesellschaft*, or between organic and mechanical solidarity, or, in a more fluid determination, as a continuum from a stable, moral, homogeneous folk society to an unstable, immoral, heterogeneous urban society (see Savage and Warde, 1993). But whether dichotomy or continuum, the influence on the urban landscape has been profound.

The significant changes to urban form that occurred in the late nineteenth century and the first half of the twentieth century were due to the demands of capital in the modern period: new factories and other industrial complexes; rows of terraced housing for workers; villas and grander houses for the wealthy; the spread of the suburbs; the expansion of public housing estates; shopping centres; and urban zoning. All of these contributed to a paradigm shift in both the physical and the social construction of urban areas, which were no longer in harmonious symbiosis with the rural hinterland but in a confused and destructive opposition: 'modern urbanism is ordered according to quite different principles from those which set off the pre-modern city from the countryside in prior periods' (Giddens, 1990: 6). The contrast between the 'pastoral' and the 'industrial' lives on in popular imagination, and is reflected also in the way in which the UK is polarised into two contrasting geographies; that of the grimness and poverty of 'up North' and of the gentleness and prosperity of 'down South'.

From the latter part of the twentieth century the demands of capital and the responses to it have changed again, leading to a concomitant effect on urban space (see Harvey, 1997). These postmodern transformations are driven by globalisation, the flight of labour intensive industries to countries with lower costs, and the expansion of cheap communication. The impact on both time and space has been profound, referred to by Giddens as 'time-space distanciation', in which both time and space become stretched and subject to global, rather than local forces. In pre-modern times, the space of social life, Giddens' locale, was localised and immediately present. In modern times this became more diffuse, whilst in contemporary times social space and social relations are ever more likely to be disconnected: 'place becomes increasingly *phantasmagoric*: that is to say, locales are thoroughly penetrated by and shaped in terms of social influences quite distant from them' (Giddens, 1990: 19, original emphasis). This has had the consequence that the ways in which people relate to the local place and community have become 'disembedded', influenced by a range of factors deriving from far distant places, and serving to diminish a sense of local identity.

Urban space has been affected not only by the forces of globalisation, but also by the increasing commodification and consumerisation of society. In addition to the shopping malls that have been constructed as temples to consumerism, the cultural industries so reliant on consumerism such as the media, advertising, music, art, publishing and tourism have appropriated urban space and contributed to its aestheticisation (Featherstone, 1991). This process of aestheticisation has been assisted by the new postmodernist architecture which, in reaction to modernist design, has borrowed (if eclectically) from the richness of classical and traditional urban form and endowed the urban landscape with a superfluity of signs and symbols. This same response to the traditional has led people to appreciate elements of the past as heritage, albeit frequently indulging in a nostalgic haze in regard to the reality of the lives that were lived in the now redundant and neglected buildings and neighbourhoods (Hewison, 1987; Lash and Urry, 1994). This combination of influences has brought about the conversion and rehabilitation of warehouses and mills for both the culture industries and for chic urban housing, whilst at the same time a process of gentrification has seen the wealthy middle classes accruing symbolic and economic capital through the appropriation and renovation of architecturally distinctive but dilapidated properties (see Smith and Williams, 1986a; Zukin, 1989, 1995, and Chapter 9).

Such re-framing of urban space and the 'recommodification of local culture' (Clarke, 2003: 191) has become an integral part of the project of place making and image creation and is constructed as essential in securing advantage in the new entrepreneurial competitiveness between cities for inward investment and economic growth. That fraction of capital that is invested in the development industry has also been able to profit from the resurgent interest in the past as newly profitable opportunities open up on sites that were once passed over as irredeemable (Harvey, 1985, 1989; Jackson and Thrift, 1995). But whilst former docklands, historic housing, and the monuments to Victorian philanthropy and industry experience a renaissance, there are still tracts of urban space which are spurned by capital, by the public sector, and by the public private partnerships which are becoming a feature of the new urban order. These spaces of despair and abandonment remain and even multiply, connected by the threads of misery that constitute the fabric of the displaced, the dispossessed and the disenfranchised.

Under modernity the framing of urban space was mediated by a supposedly rational planning process which saw space as objective and abstract: 'Modern space is objective space as subjectively significant symbols are emptied out' (Lash and Urry, 1994: 55). In postmodernity subjectivity has been restored, and it has been recognised not only that people do not use space in intended or predictable ways, but also that human imagination as well as human action are framed by space (see Jacobs, 2002). This resonates with the representational space of Lefebvre, in which locality, identity and subjectivity are negotiated as groups and individuals interact and compete within the mosaic of boundaries and symbols that constitute urban space:

> Occupation, segregation and exclusion on every level are conceptualized in streets and neighbourhoods, types of buildings, individual buildings and even parts of buildings. They are institutionalized in zoning laws, architecture and conventions of use. Visual artifacts of material culture and political economy thus reinforce – or comment on – social structure. By making social rules legible, they re-present the city.
>
> (Zukin, 1996: 43–4)

In effect, the postmodern city consists of overlapping sites in a fractured and contested world in which the diversity and multiplicity of lifestyles associated with class, power, ideology, gender, sexuality, ethnicity, nationality, income and ability can all find expression and a place to which to belong (Clarke, 2003; Westwood and Williams, 1997). In this kaleidoscopic space new freedoms and acceptance have been offered to some groups formerly excluded from much of public space, such as gay people and women, whilst others, such as prostitutes, the homeless and drug addicts, remain perpetually sequestered and contained in marginal places construed as fearful and dangerous, such as red light districts, skid rows and ghettos (see Shields, 1991). Indeed, constructions of urban space as threatening and disorderly have begun to filter beyond these marginal sites, with the consequence that it is the fear of the unknown and the stranger rather than the celebration of diversity and opportunity that have become the prevailing sentiments in relation to the city (Bannister and Fyfe, 2001). Hardly surprising then, that the public spaces of the city are increasingly being fortified and privatised, allowing people to escape to the illusion of control and the safety of seclusion.

The place of home and community

The project of the privatised home and the retreat to domesticity that began with industrialisation and reached its apotheosis with suburbanisation (see Davidoff and Hall, 1987) has arrived at a new phase. Initially constructed around the Victorian ideology of domestic bliss, the distancing of work from home, and the separation of the (male) public sphere from the (female) private sphere, the meaning and use of the home has in the last two or three decades altered in many significant respects. At the same time, social scientific interest and investigation into the meaning of home has helped to clarify and in part to theorise the diversity of the experience of home, with a burgeoning literature elucidating the role of home in human life and imagination (see, for example, Franklin, 1996b; Gurney, 1990, 1999a, 1999b; P. King, 1996; Madigan and Munro, 1991; Somerville, 1992).

Després (1991: 97–99) captures some of the richness of the meaning of home by distinguishing the following themes:

home as security and control
home as reflection of one's ideas and values
home as acting upon and modifying one's dwelling
home as permanence and continuity
home as relationship with family and friends
home as centre of activities
home as a refuge from the outside world
home as indicator of personal status
home as material structure
home as a place to own

Whilst this provides a helpful framework, it fails to account for the full diversity of the experience and meaning of home as between different individuals and groups in contemporary society, or over the life course. These include: home as a place of cultural identity; home as the place where independence can be maintained; home as an economic asset; home as a location for waged work; home as the site of entry to the virtual world of the web. But there is also a darker side to home which sits in opposition to normative constructions: home as a place of abuse; home as a site of discipline and punishment; home as a place of drudgery; home as a place of imprisonment; home as isolation; home as hospital; home as disabling; home as a financial liability. What is abundantly apparent is that home is not merely a *place*, a container for private human activity, but it is also an *idea*; a set of emotions, a way of being: 'Of all the lexical expressions in the English language "home" is perhaps the most evocative' (Gurney, 1999b: 172). A 'real' home should of course be an owner occupied home, as expressed in the normalising discourse constructed around home ownership in the UK. This discourse, endorsed by the trajectory of housing policy since the 1950s, has reproduced the idea that owner occupation is a natural and ingrained desire and, moreover, that it is the only type of tenure which permits pride of possession, accrual of wealth, freedom and a sense of well-being (see Saunders, 1990; Gurney, 1999b).

If the normative associations of the word 'home' are of well-being, identity and cosy familiarity, so too are those of the word 'community'. However, the parameters of 'community' have been even more resistant to explication than those of 'home', with attempts at definition dating from the early days of sociology and Hillery's identification of 94 different meanings (Hillery, 1955). In the mid-twentieth century intensive 'community studies' led sociologists to the conclusion that traditional communities were characterised by the close knit and face to face relations of people whose roles were prescribed from birth and acted out within a specific and circumscribed locality. In urban settings on the other hand, people's social relations were geographically dispersed and selectively chosen, and usually involved interaction with a variety of different people at different times and in different places – sometimes referred to as communities of interest or communities of association (see Crow and Allan, 1994). However, it also became recognised that the traditional community was not always the harmonious and supportive place of the imagination, and that it could be experienced as restrictive, conflictual and oppressive. In addition, the usefulness of the term 'community' began to be questioned, given that it was increasingly acknowledged that: 'its use was ideological, that is to say, that it reflects widespread cultural assumptions and biases, rather than reality' (Savage and Warde, 1993: 105).

This did not, however, remove its normative associations from popular consciousness, or the belief that in the modern world community had somehow been 'lost' and needed to be regained. In this sense it has also entered policy discourse as the basis for practical action, with the belief that 'community' and 'community spirit' can be created by locality based interventions. Here, community has been linked to the more explicitly physical dimension of 'neighbourhood', and together these concepts have underpinned numerous government endorsed models for development and regeneration (see Biddulph, 2000; Brindley, 2003).

These have encapsulated the notion that if the right conditions can be contrived a 'community' will spontaneously emerge, especially if measures are put in place to achieve a 'mixed' or 'balanced' community.

The search for community has, however, a deeper and more complex meaning under the postmodern conditions of risk, insecurity and individualisation. Society has become more fragmented and fractured, and increased mobility is constantly wrenching people from familiar relationships and known localities. Cast adrift in a sea of uncertainty they seek anxiously, and often vainly, for a safe haven and a lifestyle which will give them an identity and a sense of belonging. In Giddens' terms (adopted from the discourse of the psychologist R.D. Laing), the quest of people as they search for their ideal home or community is for 'ontological security': that sense of all being well with the world which comes from personal groundedness and rootedness, and which is so often bound up with being in a known and nurturing place (Giddens, 1990). However, the significance of 'home' and 'community' lies as much in the image the words convey as in any real place; they are 'good to think' at the symbolic level: 'affectively charged; that is they point to existential meanings as those involved in the temporality of death, love, sexuality, relations with one's children, friendship. The meanings involved here are more important than logical meanings' (Lash, 2000: 53).

In this context the consumerisation of the home has brought an opportunity in the form of the new variety of types and styles of housing. These are now targeted less at the idealised suburban family, but more at individuals pursuing distinctive lifestyles and seeking an individualised environment in which to experience and express their identity (Beck, 1992). At the same time, there is a trend towards the creation of what might be termed communities of sameness; the antithesis of real community. These include the various forms of communal and cooperative living that have emerged, as well as the retreat of like-minded people into walled and gated communities to protect themselves from imagined danger (Bauman, 1998). But it would appear that home and community at either the real or the imagined level are not for all, and that there also exists a new mobile elite which has no desire for rootedness or for existential dreaming. Instead this elite seeks a 'non-neighbourhood' condition (Bauman, 1998: 20), pursuing a transient and globalised lifestyle and indulging in the illusion of freedom. As Bauman indicates, the opportunity to be everywhere and nowhere, to be able to transcend both time and space, to live invisible and unobserved, is perhaps the ultimate security in a world which is replete with the unexpected, the unknown and the unsettling.

3 The institutional framework: powers, policies and procedures

As noted in Chapter 1, institutions provide the ongoing framework for the processes and actions of human life. This framework constitutes the entities and bodies, the rules and resources, the rituals and practices, which are available to embody, initiate and reproduce ways of doing things in human society. Indeed, some of the entities and bodies involved have become specifically referred to as 'institutions', as for example the government, the Church and the monarchy. Similarly, there are professions and even industries that have assumed institutional proportions owing to their long history and their necessity to the functioning of society, and which are characterised by their traditions, their powers, and their resistance to change and to outside interference. These include medicine, the judiciary, the army, certain manufacturing industries, and more recently, the housebuilding industry. In addition there exist certain systems in society which have institutional properties and which have been developed over time as a framework for the ordered working of society, such as the educational system, the legal system and the financial system (see Adams and Watkins, 2002: 5–10, and D'Arcy and Keogh, 2002 for a theoretical discussion of institutions in this context). That part of the framework which assumes particular prominence in relation to the production of housing is that concerned with the political, financial and administrative systems, and their shaping of the planning and the housing systems. But all these systems themselves only come into effect when put into action by human agency; agency which is itself legitimised by the powerful and enduring nature of the entities and systems that are endowed with, or are the outcomes of, that agency. In this chapter it is institutions and systems that are under discussion, whilst matters of agency, and their capacity not only to reproduce but also transform, are considered in Chapter 4.

Given the durability of housing and its centrality to human life, institutions and systems both past and present are of significance, since they have shaped, and continue to shape, present and future provision. However, it is only in relatively recent times that a situation has occurred in which a 'system' for the production of housing can be said to have been developed, since traditionally housing was secured by individual endeavour or private patronage. In the past 100 years, however, first the state and then a nationally organised housebuilding industry have assumed prominence in relation to the transformation of the production and planning of housing. However, the development of housing policy has been fraught with a number of tensions as to the rationale and scope of state intervention in housing. These have centred first around the extent to which state involvement is fiscally and politically beneficial or even desirable at all, and second around whether such involvement should be about quantity or quality, or both. The tensions in regard to the purpose and scope of state intervention in housing have led to frequent, generally reactive changes in policy direction, and have been accompanied by probably the most voluminous amount of legislation, reports and consultation papers of any sphere of government activity. The resulting contradictions and ambivalences have provided opportunity for the private housebuilding sector, with the result that by the start of the twenty-first century it has become a powerful institution.

This chapter concentrates on the way the institutional framework for the provision of housing has developed over the past 100 years. The history of housing policy is traced in brief, from the early days of state intervention, through the period of the world wars and the welfare state, up to the start of the New Labour period. There then follows a discussion of the solutions devised over time to the problems posed by people considered to be marginal or to have 'special needs', such as older people, the mentally ill and homeless people, in relation to whom social policy concerns interface with those relating to the built environment. The chapter then moves on to a consideration of housing issues under New Labour, and how these have become constructed as part of a wider and more inclusive policy discourse. The final section of the chapter examines the scope and operations of the speculative housebuilding industry.

From municipal socialism to the selling of the welfare state

The lack of an adequate institutional framework to deal with the structural events of population growth and industrialisation in the early nineteenth century led directly to the physical shaping of towns and cities as we see them today. This lack also resulted in 'jerry-building', overcrowding, the development of slums, and the growing problems of poverty and poor health (see Burnett, 1986). Recognition of these latter factors in the context of the mid-Victorian social climate with its ideologies of morality and philanthropy, led to a variety of responses. Public health concerns caused central government to produce a series of Acts in the latter half of the nineteenth century which affected the construction of housing. At the same time, local authorities introduced their own by-laws, which were strictly enforced under the increasingly watchful gaze of 'municipal socialism' (Burnett, 1986: 36). Even before this time, philanthropic groups and individuals had begun to appreciate the importance of good quality housing from the point of view not only of health but of social welfare and morality. This led to two particular institutional outcomes. First was the development of model villages by factory and mill employers in order to provide housing and other facilities for their workers, as for example, Bournville by Cadbury, Saltaire by Titus Salt, and Port Sunlight by Leverhulme (see Edwards, 1981). Second were the charitable housing trusts founded by wealthy entrepreneurs, such as the Peabody Trust and the Guinness Trust, whose blocks of tenements were again not affordable to the poorest, and whose buildings and regimen were somewhat harsh (see Malpass, 2000). The aim of the founders of these trusts was to encourage others to follow suit, and for this reason they endeavoured to ensure that a return of 5 per cent on the original investment could be made. Thus it was that this movement became known as 'five per cent philanthropy' (Tarn, 1973).

By the late nineteenth century reaction was setting in against the crowded, dirty and unhygienic conditions of urban areas and the monotony of the rows of terraced housing introduced under the aegis of the by-laws. The middle classes in particular were beginning to indulge in nostalgic longings for an idealised rural past, and those who could afford to were moving to the new villas being built on the outer fringes of towns and cities. But it was also felt that improved environments needed to be created that would enhance the lives of the ordinary masses of working people. One response was the idea of the Garden City. Devised by Ebenezer Howard (see Chapter 4), and drawing on the experience of model villages, this was a concept which was intended to unite the best of the countryside with the best of the town whilst also drawing on the popular Arts and Craft movement in relation to style (Howard, 1960). It was Howard too who first promoted the idea of Green Belts encircling and protecting urban areas, and who promoted the concept of neighbourhood units to foster good relations and a sense of community (Greed, 1993). The Garden City Movement that followed institutionalised his ideas and inspired the design of a series of new planned settlements and suburbs in the early twentieth century, such as Letchworth Garden City, Hampstead Garden Suburb and New Earswick in York. All were characterised by low density housing, vernacular design, cul de sac layouts, parks, boulevards and large gardens.

A far more significant institutional response to the housing of the poor was the provision of housing directly by the state. The Housing of the Working Classes Act of 1890 was a landmark Act in that it recognised that the real issue was not a sanitary one, as addressed by the mid-century Public Health Acts, but one of housing *per se*. This Act gave local authorities the powers to build houses, but as the costs had to be met from local rates few such houses were built in the period before the First World War. During the War the Tudor Walters Committee was established to look at how housing could be more effectively produced, especially in the context of working class agitation and the desire to compensate the populace for the privations of war (Swenarton, 1981). This committee was much influenced by Garden City ideals, and the standards that were recommended were generous, with an eye to space, fresh air and good estate layouts. It was this thinking that lay behind the provisions of the 1919 Housing and Town Planning Act and the introduction for the first time of state subsidised housing, to be built and managed by local authorities.

During the 1930s the emphasis shifted from the supply of so-called 'general needs' housing to slum clearance and redevelopment, whilst standards and quality were reduced. At the same time private housebuilders significantly increased their output of housing for owner occupation, now made a realistic proposition through increased prosperity and the greater availability of mortgages through the expansion of building societies.

After the Second World War, planning and housing became part of the massive reconstruction effort which addressed not only the physical environment, but also the economic and social fabric. In line with the principles of the emerging welfare state, it was felt that it was the public sector which should be the main provider of new housing, and there followed the largest programme of council house building that ever took place in the UK. Once more standards improved, following the recommendations of the Dudley Report of 1944, and indeed, the council housing of this period was the best quality that was ever built (Cole and Furbey, 1994). But by the 1950s, with the Conservatives back in power, the expense of maintaining such a programme led to reductions in both the quantity and quality of council housing. Within a few years new concerns were being raised, first in regard to amount of land being consumed by the new low density estates (both public and private) and second in relation to the continuing shortage of housing. This led to a radical change in the design of council housing in the form of system-built high rise housing, which local authorities were persuaded to build through the extra subsidy it attracted (Dunleavy, 1981, and see Chapter 7). At the same time renewed concerns about standards led to the setting up of the Parker Morris Committee to consider how to achieve higher quality housing more in keeping with people's changing expectations (MHLG, 1961). These recommendations were endorsed by the government and remained mandatory for council housing from 1969 until 1981.

The private sector was also encouraged to play its part in post-war reconstruction, albeit with more control following the provisions of the Town and Country Planning Act of 1947. This Act provided the framework for all future planning legislation, and made it compulsory for local authorities to ensure that all development had planning permission (see Carmona et al., 2003, and Cullingworth and Nadin, 2001, on the history and operation of the planning system). The licensing system which had restricted the building of private houses was removed and the building programme which followed saw towns and cities expand into a suburban sprawl. Indeed the very concept of suburbia became institutionalised: an ideal to be aspired to by the bulk of the population, and typified by low density semi-detached respectability and a nuclear family lifestyle with father at work in a steady job and mother at home caring for the children. In addition, owner occupation was encouraged by the Conservative government of the time as the normative tenure, promoted in a discourse of a property owning democracy and an expedient way for people to accrue wealth (see Daunton, 1987). The Conservatives further supported the private sector through the relaxation of rent controls under the 1957 Rent Act, thus inadvertently ushering in a period of landlord harassment and intimidation that became known as Rachmanism, after the notorious landlord of that name (see Kemp, 1997). This scandal, together with the generally poor condition of private rented housing, continued to give this sector a bad name until relatively recent times.

In terms of development, the period from the 1940s to the 1970s was marked by a 'clean sweep' approach (Ravetz, 1980) in which all that was old should be discarded and replaced with the new: new town centres; new housing; new design; new zoning; New Towns. The latter, a three phase programme of new settlements to relieve pressure on existing cities, were developed and managed not by the local authorities but by a new institutional arrangement established for the purpose: New Town Development Corporations (Morris, 1997). In effect, the New Towns owed a considerable debt to the Garden City idea, and were characterised by the emphasis on self-containedness and neighbourhood units, and by the adoption of the American Radburn approach to the separation of pedestrians and cars (see Morris, 1997). Indeed, this focus on the neighbourhood as the appropriate form on which to base residential areas has endured from the early influence of Howard, through the New Towns to the present day, and has become as much institutionalised in the physical planning context as has its social equivalent of 'community' (see Biddulph, 2000).

By the 1970s there was realisation that the post-war approach to planning was not achieving its objectives. Housing problems were still not being solved, people disliked living in high rise blocks, and the urban environment itself was being devastated. Furthermore, popular discontent at the demolition of old buildings and the destruction of existing communities saw the organisation of ordinary (generally middle class) people into pressure and action groups (see, for example, Dennis, 1970; Simmie, 1974; Wates, 1976). The result was a shift in opinion and the introduction of a number of initiatives. These included measures by the government to conserve historic environments and buildings, to ensure greater public participation in planning, and to replace the policy of slum clearance and new build with programmes of rehabilitation and improvement.

A further consequence of this latter move was an increased role for housing associations. These had spread slowly from an early base in philanthropic and charitable housing societies and operated entirely independently of government. However, by the 1960s the government began to perceive the potential of supporting such an arrangement as a 'third arm' of housing provision. Thus the 1964 Housing Act established the Housing Corporation, a semi-independent body (or Quango) which could receive government loans to finance new housebuilding (see Malpass, 2000). As well as being encouraged to work with local authorities in slum clearance programmes, housing associations began to spring up to address the housing needs of those who found it difficult to get accommodation in any other way, such as older people, the homeless and the many immigrants who were entering Britain at this time (see Malpass, 2000). The 1974 Housing Act further recognised the contribution of housing associations through the introduction of new grants and subsidies, thus enabling them to expand their development programmes. This institutional endorsement paved the way for housing associations, as non-profit making bodies, to become ever more significant players in the housing system as the century progressed.

When the Conservatives came to office in 1979, the problem of the inner cities had come to the fore (see Robson, 1988). In effect, they had been neglected whilst the New Towns, overspill areas and new housing estates expanded, leaving the poorest and most marginalised behind. The unattractiveness of towns and cities was driving a 'counterurbanisation' trend, whereby the middle classes and all those others who could afford to, were fleeing to the suburbs or the rural hinterland (see Champion, 1989). The response of the Conservatives to the problem of urban decline was to seek solutions which would involve the private sector, as indicated in the dominant discourse of 'property-led development'. The aim was to encourage private enterprise through offering grants and other inducements, including the introduction of mechanisms to bypass normal planning controls – notably Enterprise Zones, Simplified Planning Zones and Urban Development Corporations (the latter following the already established model of the New Town Corporations). In addition, there was a presumption towards development, and the expectation that both development and design should be determined by market forces with minimal planning intervention (see Allmendinger and Thomas, 1998, for planning polices under the Conservatives).

Such a strategy undoubtedly benefited the private sector but did not sufficiently address the public interest, since it ignored any environmental and social disbenefits. The property market collapse of the late 1980s provided an opportunity to redress this balance and to usher in new policies which would favour a partnership approach between the private sector, public bodies and the voluntary sector. Such an approach would provide public sector 'pump-priming' to attract private sector investment, and would ensure that social and economic conditions as well as the regeneration of property were addressed (see Bailey, 1995). This led to the introduction of a new (and bewildering) raft of initiatives, including City Challenge, Housing Action Trusts, Single Regeneration Budget, Estate Action, Garden Festivals, Estates Renewal Challenge Fund, City Action Teams, Training and Enterprise Councils. In a further move, a new Quango, English Partnerships, was set up in 1994, taking over the role of the previous Urban Regeneration Agency, and with a particular remit to assemble derelict and vacant land for housing development.

The Conservative era saw significant changes in the balance of the tenures in housing. In 1979 just over half the housing stock was owner occupied, 30 per cent was owned by local authorities, some 10 per cent was in the private rented sector, and less than 2 per cent in housing association control (Balchin and Rhoden, 2002). By 1997, over two-thirds was owner occupied, 17 per cent rented from local authorities and 5 per cent from housing associations, whilst the private rented sector had stayed much the same (Wilcox, 2002). This was the direct result of a policy framework which had advanced owner occupation and private enterprise whilst labelling public intervention as demotivating and counter-productive. The drive to owner occupation was hailed as the 'natural' solution, albeit cast for public consumption not so much as a means to overcome the deficiencies of the public sector but as the only way to satisfy the rightful and deeply held desire of people to feel in control of their own destiny (see Saunders, 1990). Specific measures included continued support for mortgage interest tax relief, and more dramatically, the imposition on local authorities in 1980 of enforceable Right to Buy legislation allowing tenants to buy their council properties at a discount (see Forrest and Murie, 1988). This move, referred to by Forrest and Murie as 'selling the welfare state', has had profound consequences in regard to the dramatic reduction of the council house stock and its transformation into a sector which is both residualised and stigmatised. Once popular as a tenure for a broad swathe of society it has become socially constructed as housing for failures; the poor, the idle, the criminal and the hopeless. Furthermore, the image of social housing estates as run down and crime ridden has contributed to a situation of low demand and even abandonment in many areas of the UK (see Lowe *et al.*, 1998).

Efforts were also made to shore up the flagging private rented sector through rent deregulation, decreased security of tenure and tax incentives, but these in effect had little success (see Kemp, 1997). At the same time, council housing was denied both cash and prestige, whilst local authority powers were further undermined by the wholesale transfers of stock to other landlords, and the promotion of private sector and tenant management schemes (see Balchin and Rhoden, 2002; Cole and Furbey, 1994). The promotion of owner occupation was further assisted by the financial deregulation of building societies, making it easier for them to offer more and higher loans, and at the same time the shortage of alternatives drove even people on relatively low incomes into the sector. As a result, during the early Thatcher years owner occupation enjoyed a period of expansion and house prices rose rapidly, notably in the south-east. To stem the resultant inflationary pressures and to curtail the boom in consumer spending funded from equity withdrawal, the government was forced to increase interest rates significantly. This, together with an increase in unemployment (also a result of government policy), led to a house price slump, negative equity, an increase in the number of repossessions, and the actual or potential threat of homelessness (see Ford *et al.*, 2001). This caused such a lack of confidence in the housing market that in the early 1990s questions began to be raised about its sustainability (see Forrest *et al.*, 1999).

Housing associations were not neglected in this period, and although the government appreciated their potential to provide for those in housing need, they were nonetheless promoted within a discourse that made it clear they were to be seen as more akin to private sector agencies. To reinforce this the 1988 Housing Act significantly reduced their grants and required them to rely on private sector loans for a proportion of their funding. Paradoxically it was also made clear that they were to take over the role of local authorities as the providers of public sector housing, now increasingly referred to as 'social' housing. This Housing Act also had other, unintentional consequences, in that there was a diminution of their rehabilitation work, inherently more costly and more risky, and a shift from traditional procurement, in which tenders are put out to contract, to Design and Build. In the latter the housing association cedes control of the whole design and construction process to the contractor, but in return it is the contractor who has to bear the risk of cost overruns. Subsequently the Housing Act of 1996 cut grant rates further and introduced the term registered social landlord (RSL), signalling an intention that landlords other than housing associations might become eligible for social housing grant (SHG).

In response to the new financial regime and the more commercial and competitive climate, housing associations were forced to become more flexible and diverse. Mergers and takeovers became commonplace, whilst others found it to their benefit to operate in consortia or in partnership with the private sector. But despite these trends the majority still remained close to their community based roots and their tradition of supportive services to disadvantaged and vulnerable groups.

Provision for needy and dependent people

Society has always been faced with the issue of how to provide for those who for one reason or another cannot provide for themselves. Historically, everyone was expected to work or be cared for by their family. If this system failed then recourse was had to the Poor Law, with 'outdoor relief' for those 'paupers' fit enough to work, and 'indoor relief' in a workhouse for those who could not. In the Victorian era, the workhouse system was extended and made more punitive. Outdoor relief was only available for the short term sick, leaving the old, chronically sick, disabled, orphans and unmarried mothers to be confined within the ranks of often newly built, but always large and forbidding workhouses. The only exceptions were the mentally ill who, following legislation in the early part of the nineteenth century, were assigned to equally overpowering and regimental mental institutions (see Chapter 7). People with a mental handicap, classed as idiots, defectives or imbeciles, were also placed initially in mental institutions, until the different nature of their condition became better understood and separate institutions provided. This practice of spatial segregation in places marginal to mainstream provision undoubtedly reinforced the casting of the people thus confined as somehow 'other' and by implication inferior.

By the early twentieth century a more enlightened approach, together with increased provision of alternatives such as hospitals for infectious diseases and children's homes, meant that the main residents of the workhouse became the old. It thus became a place of care rather than a place of work, but its stigma remained. The introduction of the National Assistance Act in 1948 finally saw the end of the workhouse, but even so, its shadow still hung over the older generation. To replace the workhouse local authorities were empowered to provide residential homes for old people, and by the 1960s and 1970s were also required to provide domiciliary services to help to keep older people in the community (Means and Smith, 1998). Also during the 1960s, local authorities and housing associations began to provide sheltered housing for older people, where a degree of independence could be maintained but with the services of a warden. For the very old, the local authority old people's home or the geriatric ward was the next step – and the final indignity. By the 1980s there was also a growing market in private sector residential care, the spiralling costs of which were met by a benefits system which initially imposed no ceiling on fees.

In 1990 the NHS and Community Care Act was introduced, motivated in large part by a desire to cut costs and with an emphasis on care in the community rather than in institutional settings. However, it has meant that more options have become available for older people. The private sector has been quick to spot the gap in the market for the more affluent, and now offers various types of retirement housing, including sheltered housing, in addition to its more established provision of residential care and nursing homes. Given the new limits on state assistance with fees, both the latter options usually mean that an older person is now obliged to sell the family home in order to pay for care. Meanwhile housing associations have taken over from local authorities as the main providers for older people in need, and now offer a greater range of options. These include very sheltered or extra care housing, residential care homes, care services to older people in the community, community alarm services, and the management of some of the care and repair services which local authorities are empowered to provide (see Oldman, 2000, and Chapter 8).

In the past people with physical disabilities in need of long term care were often placed in old people's homes (and occasionally still are). Again, the 1990 NHS and Community Care Act has provided more options, with Social Services being obliged to identify needs and provide a package of care to enable independent living. This has been further facilitated by the introduction of the Part M building regulations which specify improved accessibility within the home and by the Disability Discrimination Act of 1995 which has imposed requirements for accessibility in the public realm at large (Imrie and Hall, 2001). It has been a similar story for those with a mental illness or a learning disability, for whom institutional care was the norm throughout the first half of the twentieth century.

Despite a number of Acts and Circulars from the late 1950s onwards in regard to improved care in the community (see Means and Smith, 1998), it was again not until the implementation of the 1990 NHS and Community Care Act that concerted measures and concomitant funding were introduced to reduce reliance on care in institutions for these groups of people.

In the context of community care housing associations have played an important role. As noted above, they have historically provided for various marginalised groups who were not catered for by local authority housing and received government support for this through additional grants for so-called 'special needs'. They now provide a range of schemes for a wide group of people, including not only the four community care priority groups (the old, the physically disabled, the learning disabled and the mentally ill) but also those with other support needs. These include people with HIV/AIDS, homeless people, drug and alcohol users, ex offenders, single mothers, and refugees and asylum seekers. As the term 'special needs' has fallen into disfavour such housing is increasingly referred to as supported accommodation. Until recently the funding regulations meant that this consisted of semi-institutional group homes, but in 2003 new funding arrangements were introduced under the Supporting People initiative allowing support also to be delivered to independent accommodation (see DETR, 1999). This has facilitated the development of a more personalised form of support known as 'floating support'. Usually provided by a voluntary agency the aim is to provide assistance over a period of six months to two years towards the goal of entirely independent living, after which the support 'floats off' to another person (see Morris, 1995).

One of the most intractable problems facing governments for decades, if not centuries, has been that of homelessness. Historically dealt with under the poor relief system and various laws of vagrancy and settlement, the foundation of the welfare state transferred responsibility to the new local authority welfare departments. In 1966 the release of the film *Cathy Come Home* brought to public attention the punitive approach adopted by many local authorities, and led directly to the foundation of the organisation Shelter to campaign for improved rights for homeless people. There followed a more widespread acceptance that the problem was not one of individual failure, needing welfare support, but one of a lack of appropriate accommodation, needing a housing solution. The 1977 Homeless Persons Act was a recognition of this, transferring responsibility to local authority housing departments and requiring them to find accommodation for homeless people – provided they fell into certain defined categories in terms of the extent of need, vulnerability, and local connection. Those specifically excluded were single homeless people and couples without children. It was this legislation which institutionalised an approach to homelessness which has continued to the present day, with minor adjustments.

During the Conservative era, a progressively more punitive position was adopted, which culminated in homeless people – criticised for 'queue jumping'

– being excluded from priority access to permanent social housing (Balchin and Rhoden, 2002). This exacerbated the already existing situation of recourse to temporary housing in bed and breakfast accommodation, hostels and poor quality private rented housing. But this period also saw an exponential increase in the numbers of homeless people, due not only to the decline in social housing stock, but also to policies which cut the availability of social security benefits, especially for those under 25. Meanwhile, in an effort to eradicate the intrusive and embarrassing phenomenon of 'cardboard cities', the Conservatives introduced the Rough Sleepers Initiative in 1990 to provide more hostel places and encourage people into more settled ways of life.

Under New Labour homelessness has been cast as an issue to be tackled more holistically than in the previously punitive Tory approach. It is recognised that homelessness is not only about access to housing, but about support once housing is found, including advice on jobs and training. In line with its inclusion agenda, the Homelessness Act of 2002 reinstated the right to permanent rather than temporary accommodation for qualifying homeless people, and also extended the definitions of vulnerability to include 16 and 17 year olds, people fleeing domestic violence, and people leaving institutions (Balchin and Rhoden, 2002). Nonetheless, given the continuing shortage of affordable housing, these vulnerable groups of people are still often placed in inferior and temporary accommodation.

The rhetoric of New Labour

Since New Labour came to power in 1997 the rhetoric of home ownership, consumer choice, privatism and performance has continued, but there has also been a widening and deepening of the housing agenda. This is indicated in part by a new commitment to a better balanced housing system in which local authorities, housing associations and the private rented sector all have a part to play. But more significant is a new discourse of housing which reflects Labour's expressed concerns with matters of social cohesion, social justice, social inclusion, decent housing, joined-up thinking, balanced and mixed communities, sustainability and urban renaissance. What has also become clear is that following devolution in 1999 and the establishment of the Scottish Parliament and the National Assembly for Wales, policy in Scotland and Wales is increasingly likely to diverge from that of England. For example, in Scotland, where owner occupation has always been lower than in the rest of the UK, it has been declared that there will only be a single social housing tenure (Balchin and Rhoden, 2002), whilst in Wales, with higher levels of owner occupation and major problems of disrepair and poverty, a new national housing strategy has been produced, together with specific Welsh based initiatives (National Assembly for Wales, 2000).

On first coming to office Labour's main areas of concern in regard to housing and planning policy were to address social exclusion and to consider how to overcome the problems of urban decline and abandonment in a more sustainable way (see Power and Mumford, 1999). In pursuing these aims there has been the introduction of a raft of new mechanisms, such as the Social Exclusion Unit, New Deal for Communities, the Neighbourhood Renewal Fund, Urban Regeneration Companies, Local Strategic Partnerships and the Sustainable Communities Plan (discussed further below) as well as the continuance of programmes such as stock transfer and arms length management companies. Another early move was to try to increase the amount of 'affordable' housing, now institutionalised as relatively low cost housing secured through private developers and the planning system rather than by direct government subsidy to the social housing sector (see Carmona *et al.*, 2003, and Chapter 4). Thus there has been explicit advice to planning and housing authorities on this matter as contained in the Green Paper on Housing (DETR, 2000a) and in government guidance, notably *PPG3: Housing* (DETR, 2000b) and *Circular 6/98* (DETR, 1998a). But these texts make it clear that there is a wider agenda for affordable housing in that it will also assist in the creation of mixed communities and the avoidance of social exclusion:

> Policies for affordable housing must ensure a better mix of housing types and tenures and avoid the residualisation of social housing and its occupants. It is important to provide a mix of housing types if we are to ensure a sustainable future for the large estates built in the past. It is equally important to ensure that diversity exists in all new housing developments. We must seek to develop social housing alongside housing built for homeownership and private renting. Large social housing estates have proved unsustainable.
>
> (DETR, 2000a: 71)

Also linked to the affordable housing issue is that of a lack of housing at prices which can be afforded by so-called key workers in London, the south-east and parts of the south and south-west; key workers being essential public sector workers such as teachers, nurses, firefighters and the police. In response first the Starter Homes Initiative and then the Key Worker Living scheme have been introduced, offering grants and interest free loans to facilitate house purchase and administered by housing associations in the relevant local authority areas (ODPM, 2003a, 2005a). Housing associations have also been encouraged for several years to extend their programmes of low cost home ownership. These include shared ownership, whereby the housing association sells a proportion of the equity to the occupant and charges rent for the rest, and DIYSO or do-it-yourself-shared-ownership, under which a household finds a property on the open market and then enters into a shared ownership arrangement with a housing association.

In regard to the sustainability agenda, Labour's initial focus was on trying to make urban areas more attractive and thus take pressure off the countryside and reduce commuting. Charged with making recommendations as to how this could be achieved a 'Task Force' was established in 1998, chaired by the high profile architect and new government guru on matters urban, Richard Rogers, later Lord Rogers of Riverside. The central recommendations of the resultant report *Towards an Urban Renaissance* (Urban Task Force, 1999) revolved around making towns and cities both more 'liveable' and more sustainable by improving urban design, building to higher densities (involving a tension between 'compact cities' and 'town-cramming') and reclaiming derelict and vacant land for housing. The measures then introduced by the government included increased duties on local authorities to consider design (discussed further in Chapter 5), a presumption towards the re-use of previously developed ('brownfield') sites before greenfield sites can be considered (Carmona *et al.*, 2003; DETR, 1998b, 2000b, 2000c; DTLR, 2001; ODPM, 2002) and targets for at least 60 per cent of new housing to be located on brownfield sites (despite the fact that this is not where many people actually want to live (Popular Housing Forum, 1998)). In pursuing its concerns for better design the government has also established the Commission for Architecture and the Built Environment (CABE) to promote good practice, educate the public and advise government on design issues.

Since then, the emphasis has moved to one of housing supply. Nationally it appears that there is a shortfall in provision, largely due to demographic change and a sharp increase in the number of households. Consequently it has been estimated that 3.8 million extra households will be formed by the year 2021, which, given the continuing north-south divide, are likely to be concentrated in London and the south-east (see Adams and Watkins, 2002; Holmans, 2001). In recent years housebuilding has slumped to its lowest level since the 1920s, with private sector output in Britain in the early 2000s at only around 160,000 units per year, housing association output below 20,000 units (compared with a peak in 1994 of over 42,000 units) and local authorities building virtually no housing at all (Wilcox, 2002). Ever dwindling stocks of social housing mean that this tenure is only available to those in the greatest need, and an increase in homelessness suggests that it is struggling to fulfil even this function. Meanwhile, the surge in house prices between 2000 and 2004 (stimulated by low interest rates as well as lack of supply) has created a serious problem of affordability to first time buyers and people on low incomes. Indeed by the election year of 2005 first time buyers had been priced out of the market in nine out of ten towns in England (Inman, 2005) and housing had become a key electoral issue.

In response to these problems, the government has sought a range of solutions. First was the Sustainable Communities Plan of 2003 which included a number of proposals: increasing housing supply in areas of need; addressing the issue of affordable homes; tackling homelessness; regenerating deprived areas; protecting the countryside; improving design and public space; and, in a somewhat controversial suggestion, tackling the problem of low demand in the north by selective demolition (see ODPM, 2003b). But these points have been overshadowed by the announcement in the Plan of four major growth areas in the south-east. These are to be run by new development agencies on the model of New Town Corporation Development Companies and Urban Development Corporations, and are to support the sustainability agenda by being compact and well-designed, with good infrastructure and facilities, and a high proportion of affordable housing. The first such settlement will consist of a linear city to be known as Thames Gateway and spanning East London and parts of Kent and Essex, with the other three being located in Milton Keynes, Ashford in Kent, and along the M11 corridor between Stansted and Cambridge. At much the same time, a review was commissioned to investigate the problems of housing supply, house price volatility and excessive house price inflation. In the resultant report (Barker, 2004) it was stated that ideally the annual output of new private sector housing should be increased by 120,000, and that an additional 26,000 units of social housing per year were required in order to compensate for the existing backlog and meet anticipated levels of future need. It was also pointed out that the housebuilding industry must take some of the blame for lack of supply by refusing to release sufficient land for building in an effort to keep profits high, and that the planning system too was at fault for its complexity, its slow decision-making processes and its tendency to be unreasonably restrictive.

In regard to planning, the government have sought to address some of the issues through the 2004 Planning and Compulsory Order Act. This has introduced new planning legislation and guidance in order to speed up and rationalise the planning process, and consequently ensure houses can be built more quickly. The government has also endorsed the need for more new homes to be built, again especially in the south-east. Given the 'nimby' resistance of middle England, however, it has been recognised that numbers are unlikely to reach those recommended by Barker. And in the social housing sector, the spending review of 2004 announced a significant increase in funding, although again this will not be sufficient to meet the targets established by Barker. In recognition of the fact that it is not so much the question of supply so much as access to home ownership that exercises the public mind, the government is also anxious to find new ways to extend this opportunity to groups hitherto excluded. Indeed, this ambition has been made even more pressing following the publicity given to a further aspect of the affordability issue:

Ministers have been appalled by the findings of a recent report for the charity Shelter showing a widening wealth gap between home owners and people in rented accommodation. It warned that rising house prices were taking Britain back to the deep social divisions of Victorian society.

(Hetherington, 2005: 1)

Hence in 2005 several new initiatives were declared: a five year plan for £60,000 starter homes to be built on nil cost publicly owned land and using cheap, factory based construction techniques; an increase in the threshold at which stamp duty is paid from £60,000 to £120,000; a scheme to allow first time buyers to buy a 50–75 per cent share in their home with the remainder held by the lender and the government; and a 'social homebuy' scheme to allow housing association tenants to buy a share of their property (see Hetherington, 2005; M. Weaver, 2005). Tackling some of the other issues raised by Barker is likely to prove more problematic. In regard to increased supply, both local people and local authorities are resistant to new housing in their own areas, whilst in regard to influencing the operations of the housebuilding industry, there are difficulties to overcome in the face of their powerful and entrenched position.

The workings of the housebuilding industry

From a historical perspective state intervention in housing and the mass provision of state subsidised housing that took place in the twentieth century was something of an anomaly. Traditionally, housing was provided by private endeavour, whether by owner occupants or by landlords, and was locally produced, constructed of locally available materials, and by builders operating over a small area. However, by the late nineteenth century the demands of urbanisation had brought into being a new class of builder, often referred to as a jerry-builder, who saw the chance for quick profits in supplying the new demand for rented housing for workers and who had no regard for quality or design. As affluence increased and owner occupation became fashionable, there arose a new market in homes for purchase. This in turn stimulated the beginnings of a mass market for housing and the emergence by the 1930s of the speculative housebuilding industry. Most of the inter-war housing was built by small businesses with a handful of employees, but some larger firms also began to appear at this time, including names familiar today such as Wimpey and Laing (Burnett, 1986).

After the Second World War, the growth in the private housebuilding sector was marked, and many firms expanded both in size and in their areas of operation. Taylor Woodrow, for example, which had originated in Blackpool, was by 1954 also operating in the south and the Midlands (Burnett, 1986: 322), whilst Barratt, which started as a family business in Newcastle, also rapidly extended its activities across the country (Ball, 1983). However, the majority of firms remained small, and even by the 1970s and 1980s half of all speculative housebuilding was still being undertaken by firms with fewer than 100 employees (Balchin and Rhoden, 2002). Notwithstanding this factor, a number of the larger firms began to dominate, so that by the end of the twentieth century there were 43 companies building more than 500 units per year and accounting for 71 per cent of housing output (Adams and Watkins, 2002). Amongst them were 14 companies building more than 2000 units per year, a figure qualifying them to be classed as volume housebuilders, the three most productive and profitable being Wimpey, Barratt, and Beazer (Gillen and Golland, 2004). However, keeping abreast of the market leaders and their output is notoriously complex since the industry is in a constant state of flux. Mergers and takeovers are relatively commonplace as companies jostle for an increased market share, and there appears to be an ongoing process of concentration and consolidation (Gillen and Golland, 2004). In addition, some companies have begun to exploit 'niche' markets, as, for example, Crest Nicholson with inner city and brownfield development, McCarthy and Stone with retirement housing, Lovell with partnership housing for the social housing sector, and Urban Splash with innovative and creative urban regeneration schemes (see Chapter 9).

The institutional structure of the housebuilding industry is such that it is underfinanced, has low cost margins, has long time lags between inception and completion, has low productivity and is liable to bankruptcy (Ball, 1983). This means that it is slow to respond to changing demand and is extremely vulnerable both to the cyclical 'boom and bust' nature of the housing market and to fluctuations in costs. (The complexities of the economics of housebuilding and the detailed risk assessments which have to be made at each stage of the development process are beyond the scope of this book, and readers are referred to Ball, 1983; Bramley *et al.*, 1995; Carmona *et al.*, 2003; Guy and Hennebury, 2004; O'Sullivan and Gibb, 2003.) Very often there is a considerable time lag between land purchase and development as most major housebuilders hold land banks, whereby parcels of land both with and without planning permission are bought and held, normally for two or three but sometimes for up to ten years, until the optimum time for development.

On the larger sites which local authorities now prefer to see assembled (Adams and Watkins, 2002), housebuilders may operate in a consortium, sometimes including one or more housing associations. This facilitates a wider and more varied product and brings the benefits of economies of scale, as well as meaning that the more risky aspect of the speculative sector can be underpinned by the assurances of the social housing sector. Since the late 1990s and the restrictions by government on the supply of greenfield land, opportunities have become more constrained. Housebuilders argue that it is this refusal of local authorities to release land that is choking the supply of new housing, and not, as is often argued, any strategy of theirs deliberately to trickle supply in order to maximise profits (Dear, 2003; see also Barker, 2004). There are also problems associated with the policy requirement for development on brownfield land. Whether this involves derelict land or the conversion of existing buildings, different skills are needed than for the development of greenfield land; skills which large parts of the housebuilding industry do not have and do not necessarily want to acquire, especially given the costs of remediation and the assumed lack of appeal to potential customers (Adams and Watkins, 2002). At the same time, the traditional developers of brownfield land, the housing associations, have now been placed in competition with the more favourably financed (if reluctant) private sector – hence pushing up the costs and further reducing the supply of social housing.

An issue of increasing importance is that of planning gain, often referred to as Section 106 agreements after the number of the clause in the relevant legislation (see Carmona et al., 2003). This enables local authorities to secure some public benefit through private sector development and can include contributions to infrastructure, playgrounds, open space, schools, public transport, supermarkets, leisure centres, as well as the provision of affordable housing referred to above. Entering into such agreements is resisted by housebuilders, first because the costs affect their profits and are effectively a tax on development, and second, because where affordable housing is concerned, inclusion is likely to reduce the appeal of their sites to private sector buyers (see also Chapter 4).

In regard to marketing, traditionally the housebuilding industry has been oriented towards three major sectors; starter, middle and executive (Adams and Watkins, 2002). The selection and mix of these will be determined by the state of the market, the potential of the site, local socio-economic factors and the market orientation of the housebuilder. For all sectors, most housebuilders make use of a range of standard types in regard to floor plans and elevations, and these are replicated on their estates up and down the country. However, there is a certain contradiction inherent in this, since the result is a standardised product, and standardisation, or homogeneity, is more typical of the public than the private sector:

> [T]he former is seen to emphasise communal aesthetic and functional values, the latter is predicated upon individualised aspects of design. In a mass market such as speculative housebuilding, the emphasis upon individuality in design is constrained by the economics of the production process, in that individuality in dwelling styles may improve marketability but raises construction costs.
>
> (Hooper and Nicol, 1999: 793)

Hence the necessary appeal to individuality is sought by cosmetic features such as porches, balustrades, fittings and finishes, which have 'kerb appeal' but are cheap and superficial additions to the underlying standard plan.

Both house design and residential layouts have come under increasing attack not only by professionals and government but also by consumers for their standardisation, lack of imagination, and lack of respect for variety and context (Bartlett et al., 2002; Carmona, 1998; DETR/HBF/The Planning Officers Society, 1998; DTLR/CABE, 2001; Popular Housing Forum, 1998). This is not to say, however, that housebuilders are unaware of the impact of image in creating acceptability and interest amongst existing residents and potential customers

(Biddulph, 1995, and Chapter 5). The majority of housebuilders, however, have proved resistant to a more substantive change in their approach to matters of design, given the fact that their standard types appear to give satisfaction and, more importantly, continue to sell (Carmona *et al.*, 2003). In an effort to improve design a number of housing design award schemes have been initiated by government bodies and design institutions, but despite a few innovative and imaginative design responses, there has been little impact on the majority of housebuilders (Biddulph *et al.*, 2004). However, in time and with sufficient urging, the government's increasing emphasis on the design component of planning and development may begin to have an effect (see Chapter 5).

Another area in which the government has endeavoured to seek improvement is that of construction. This is due to the fact that the British housebuilding industry is beset by problems in this regard: it is notoriously slow; resistant to the introduction of new building techniques; over-reliant on on-site labour; and dogged by skills shortages, poor working relations, and a bad safety record (see Ball, 1996, 1999; Barlow, 1999). Other European, North American and Far Eastern countries have for some time made considerable use of alternative building techniques and materials involving off-site construction and with only assembly and finishing being done on site. In order to investigate how the construction industry in this country could be similarly improved the government commissioned Sir John Egan to set up an inquiry. His report, usually referred to as the Egan Report, made a number of recommendations (Construction Task Force, 1998). The main issues involved the reduction of capital costs and construction time, the cutting of the incidence of defects and accidents, making more use of a partnering approach (based on networking and trust instead of traditional procurement with contracts and a hierarchy) and being more innovative in construction methods, notably by making more use of prefabrication and standardisation. Egan's proposal was that the social housing sector (inherently more compliant and accountable) should be the first to adopt his recommendations, with the aim that all new social housing in England should be 100 per cent Egan compliant by 2004. Scotland too, agreed relatively promptly to pursue the adoption of Egan in the RSL sector (Internal Audit Scotland, 2003); however, Wales has taken a more cautious and gradual approach (WAG, 2002, 2005). Currently it remains to be seen whether and how the Egan recommendations will be extended to the private sector, and whether the Housing Forum that was set up in 1999 to disseminate the issues through its 'constructing excellence' programme will succeed in bringing about change (DETR, 2000d). In this as in its other ambitions for the quantity and quality of housing, the government may well find that the institutionalised power and profit driven nature of the housebuilding industry prove to be a source of frustration.

4 Agency and action: negotiation, influence and resistance

The previous chapter looked at the way in which the institutional framework has shaped policies and outcomes in regard to the provision of housing over time. Such policies and outcomes can only be effected through the actions of human agency, and it is this which forms the focus of the current chapter. What is considered here are the actions, proclivities and behaviours of individuals, groups and organisations as they negotiate the construction of the built environment in an increasingly unstable world. Hence the chapter examines the nature of negotiation, action and personal inclination, and how these are played out in the development context, albeit always bearing in mind the constraints and opportunities of structural and institutional limitations. The large number of actors involved includes developers, planners, design professionals and users, each acting within the role accorded to them. In addition there are other groups, bodies and individuals who have an interest in environmental issues, and who seek to influence both policy and built outcomes. These include on the one hand various organisations and institutes which act within the established frameworks of society, and on the other, groups and individuals who gain their influence specifically through their anti-establishment activities. In this regard social movements and anarchists play an important role in society in confronting injustices and dysfunctions and effecting change. They challenge entrenched perceptions and values, resist institutional oppression and problematise the way we live our lives. It is through their actions that we are enabled to confront the possibility of doing things in different ways, of taking alternative positions, of having other lifestyles. Also important are the beliefs, writings and actions of people who have risen to prominence, or even notoriety, because they have challenged normative views about development and design. Such individuals can be shown to have been instrumental or even visionary in terms of their transformative power in reinterpreting and redesigning the built environment.

Thus in the context of planning, development and design there exists a situation in which a number of different and competing groups and individuals have the capacity to influence outcomes. This creates a state of tension in which opinion, conflict, negotiation, agenda setting and personality assume important dimensions. However, it is arguably from the dynamics of such situations that an outcome emerges which is greater than the sum of its parts, and which derives its energy and impact from the stimulus of interaction and struggle:

> ... [a] 'battlefield' problematic, in which actors deploy their resources of economic or political power, valued knowledge or cultural capital, in more or less adroit ways, in attempts to make things happen as they want.
>
> (Bentley, 1999: 42)

Controlling development

The residential development process is inherently a complex one, involving many agencies and individuals who must consult and cooperate in order to achieve a satisfactory end product (see Ball, 2002). These include landowners, developers, land agents, financial institutions, consultants, architects, surveyors, valuers, and central and local government agencies, who together are engaged in brokering land deals, securing financial backing, accessing grants and negotiating the parameters and rationale for development. In the private sector, given the centrality of finance and profit making, it is business astuteness, competitiveness and market awareness that bring success at this stage, often with elements of ruthlessness and underhandedness. It falls to the intervention and mediation of those who represent the public interest to moderate intemperate concern for individual or company gain.

The main (and imperfect) mechanism the state possesses to achieve this is the land-use planning system. As well as legislation, central government produces regular planning policy advice in the form of circulars and planning policy guidance notes (PPGs) (at the time of writing being updated as planning policy statements (PPSs)). Local authorities are expected to take these into account when drawing up development plans and deciding on their rationale for the granting of planning permission for new development, but in practice they assume wide-ranging powers in the interpretation of national guidance. One of the problems for local authorities is that of keeping abreast of the constant shifts in central government policy emphasis and direction, due not only to changes of government but to even more frequent changes of the Secretaries of State with responsibility for planning issues – each of whom desires to leave his or her mark on the policy agenda.

Just as with central government, the political persuasion and leadership of local authorities are constantly changing, and indeed, may be directly opposed to the policy goals of central government. For while it is salaried planning officers with the requisite technical skills and training who advise on the content of plans and the merits of planning applications, it is local councillors, as democratically elected representatives of the people, who make the final decisions in committees established for the purpose. Such discretionary and variable powers result in a situation where different local authorities interpret national policy guidelines in different ways, and pursue different strategies in relation to the plan implementation process (see Carmona et al., 2003, and Healey et al., 1995 for examples).

Since the 1990s, the emphasis has been on a more strongly 'plan-led' system, which is: 'meant to ensure rational and consistent decisions, greater certainty, and public involvement in shaping local policies, allowing the planning process to work faster, and reducing the number of misconceived planning applications and appeals' (Townshend and Madanipour, 2001: 134, and see DoE, 1997a). The fact that the plan now has greater significance in determining whether specific proposals will be accepted or not has been noted not only by developers but also by interest groups and local people, all of whom now take a keener interest in the plan making process and are desirous of making their points of view known (Abram et al., 1996). Particularly controversial is the allocation of land for new housing, something which local planning authorities are required to include in the plan on the basis of projections of housing need. Murdoch and Abram (2002) report on an examination-in-public on this issue, and show clearly how the parameters of what could be discussed were set by the Chairman, who controlled the proceedings under his disciplinary gaze. In the negotiating process those who could put forward technical arguments, or who had financial or political clout, were given legitimacy, whilst others such as parish council representatives and members of the public were not. All had a 'feel for the game', but some did not know the rules, whilst others did not play by them.

When considering development for a particular site, a local planning authority will take into account a number of issues additional to the policy aims of the development plan: the extent of local support or opposition; the likely perspective of the infrastructure agencies; the type of planning gain that might be required; the suitability of the site for a particular purpose; the characteristics of the surrounding area; and the need to conserve any existing features on the site. In addition, both planning officers and councillors will be guided by past experience of what is feasible and acceptable, by their own personal preferences, and by the pressures that are brought to bear on them personally by others (Healey et al., 1995). In considering a specific proposal, a planning officer will apply his or her own knowledge, experience and skills in determining its suitability, but a final decision cannot be made without the agreement of the planning committee. This may necessitate a presentation, effectively in public, since the committee is open to interested parties. Here the planning officer plays a pivotal role, with the outcome dependent on his or her: 'skills at verbal and oral presentation and, yes, advocacy, for he or she is in a sense acting as the applicant's intermediary at the committee meeting, at the same time as being the council's professional adviser' (Parfect and Power, 1997: 55). If permission is granted certain conditions will almost invariably be imposed, and further consent must be sought for any subsequent changes to the initial plans. Disappointed applicants have the right of appeal to the Secretary of State, with the appeal normally heard by an appointed Planning Inspector as representative for the Secretary of State. This brings yet another player into the process, whose knowledge of the local situation is lacking and who will have his or her own priorities, sense (or lack) of vision, and political alignment.

Given its discretionary nature and the legislative requirement for public consultation, negotiation is a key feature in the operation of the planning system. This has become particularly important in relation to planning obligations or planning gain – the system referred to in Chapter 3 whereby some community benefit is to be extracted from private developers. Since the 1980s the expectation by central government and hence imposed on local authorities is that the extent of planning gain should be increased and the process made more transparent: 'creating a system where the suspicion that planning permissions are bought and sold is removed' (Carmona *et al.*, 2003: 143). A wide variety of agencies stand to benefit (or lose) from the planning gain process: local authority departments, such as planning, housing, parks, education, leisure services and economic development; local interests such as parish councils and amenity groups; national bodies such as the Nature Conservancy Councils and English Heritage; and in the development industry itself, developers, consultants, landowners and financial institutions (see Healey *et al.*, 1995: 186). The negotiation and brokering of the competing interests and claims of these groups in what is generally a conflictual situation is a complex skill, requiring experience, interpersonal skills, tact, knowledge, patience and a balanced approach, especially in a situation where no fixed rules apply (see Healey *et al.*, 1995: 187–93 for case study examples). Much depends on the outcome of the negotiation process, for it decides not only immediate issues such as developers' profits, but long term benefits such as the quantity of affordable housing for future generations, the preservation of a listed building, or the availability of open space for public use in perpetuity.

The issue of the provision of affordable housing through planning gain has proved particularly controversial. As referred to in the previous chapter, since the early 1990s central government guidance has made clear that it sees the planning system as an important mechanism for the securing of new units of affordable housing. Indeed, local need for affordable housing can be included as a material consideration in the granting of planning permission (DETR, 1998a), with private developers obliged to enter into Section 106 agreements for the provision of an element of affordable housing on their sites. In some cases this may be waived in favour of a commuted payment to the local authority to provide such housing elsewhere in its area. The system that prevailed until early 2005 was, however, somewhat vague and discretionary, with no fixed rules and therefore often subject to prolonged negotiation. It was suggested that local authorities and developers should be 'reasonably flexible', have 'indicative' targets, and expect only 'suitable' (undefined) housing developments to contain an element of affordable housing (DETR, 1998a, 2000b). The provisions of the 2004 Planning and Compulsory Purchase Act have, however, instituted change, although at the time of writing the details are yet to be finalised. The proposals are that Section 106 agreements should be replaced by 'planning contributions', giving developers the option of making set payments instead of, or occasionally as well as, entering into negotiation with the local authority (ODPM, 2005b).

Such a change may well remove much of the element of uncertainty and delay associated with the often protracted negotiations of the present system, but by the same token it will also act against the interests of the local authority in terms of the loss of flexibility and responsiveness. Developers, however, are more likely to welcome the greater degree of certainty. Although naturally reluctant contributors to planning gain, they have increasingly come to accept that it is the price they have to pay in return for the granting of planning permission. Currently they are put in the position of having to balance the extent to which it is in their interests to draw out negotiations in the hope of winning a compromise against the costs involved in delaying the start of the construction process – for delay spells lost profits. Local authorities for their part, have to ensure that the planning gain requested is not so onerous to developers that they will abandon the site, leaving the local authority with none of the housing units they need to meet demand, either private or affordable. If agreement cannot be reached an appeal may result but there is no guarantee it will go in the developer's favour. The developer's dilemma is clear:

> If the local authority ask for more than we are prepared to offer we have two choices. We just say no and forget the site or we go to appeal. We would go to appeal more often if we didn't have the planning system often stacked against us. So planning gain is often the result of us feeling unsafe with regard to the development plan system in terms of taking sites to appeal. So it's a matter of minimising maximum losses ...
>
> (Developer cited in Healey *et al.*, 1995: 174)

Increasingly development is carried out not by one developer alone but in consortia, where developers can share economies of scale in the provision of infrastructure or requirements under planning gain agreements. There is also a move to development in partnership between the public and private sectors, especially in the context of regeneration. Here a different type of relationship applies than in the traditional situation, in which a range of partners representing both public and commercial interests are engaged on supposedly an equal footing, with a board of directors selected to represent each major interest. In regard to Urban Development Corporations (UDCs), Imrie and Thomas (1993) show how the pre-existing values, alliances and allegiances of board members influence strategy and outcomes. In particular, they identify the impact of the power struggles between local authorities and the UDC itself. Local authorities feel that their statutory powers are being undermined and usurped by the powers bestowed on UDCs by central government, in which private gain is subordinated to public interest. Weaker 'partners' such as interest groups, small firms, minor RSLs and representatives of the public are marginalised, being less likely to possess either the necessary experience and skills of boardroom gamesmanship, or the political and financial weight of those who constitute the elite membership of any board. Only a truly disinterested and proficient Chair would be able to broker the often diametrically opposed interests of all, whilst everyone, including the Chair, has to reconcile the interests they are there to represent with their own personal agendas. The consequences of these power struggles and the partiality of the process then become spelt out in the unequal shaping of the resultant built environment.

Another issue local authorities are increasingly expected to address as part of their development control role is design. In this regard there are often polarised attitudes and approaches, with some believing design is a major concern that warrants tighter control, whilst others feel it should be determined by market forces or is an aesthetic and subjective matter which should be left to the creativity and discernment of the individual designer (see Carmona, 2001). As a result, local authorities have in the past had very diverse approaches. Some, most famously Essex, have produced design guides to which they expect developers to adhere (Essex County Council, 1973; Essex Planning Officers Association, 1997), whilst others have seen it as something for developers themselves to determine (see Punter and Carmona, 1997 for a review). However, since the revision of *PPG1* (DoE, 1997a) and *PPG3* (DETR, 2000b) design has assumed greater prominence, and 'good' design has become a material consideration in determining planning applications and appeals (see also Chapter 5). Consequently, local authorities have been encouraged to produce more prescriptive texts in the form of supplementary design guidance and design briefs, or, for larger development sites, masterplans. Again, local authorities vary considerably in the extent to which they take this duty seriously and in the degree of proficiency they possess to undertake it. Meanwhile, applicants for planning permission are advised to consult and negotiate on design issues both with the local authority planning department and with other interested parties. Design has hence assumed a potential for conflict and a need for negotiation almost as great as that of planning gain, and involving a similarly diverse range of people: architects, urban designers, planners, developers, councillors, community groups, business leaders and the public.

The design professionals

The people who believe they alone are experts in the design process are the design professionals, most notably architects. However, in the policy context of late twentieth-century Britain the emerging profession of urban design also experienced an enhancement in its status, encouraged and promoted by a government which saw the improved design of urban areas as one of the keys to the successful achievement of an urban renaissance (Urban Task Force, 1999). Despite this, urban design continues to be perceived as a specialist branch of planning, without either the long established professional status of architecture or the same superior claim to aesthetic and artistic distinction. For professional architects it is only the design of an individual building which can bring into play that complex blend of creativity, and mastery of functional detail that produces the necessary exemplar of style and individuality:

> Architects find an individualized concept of architecture appealing, since it makes it possible to see themselves as heroic and romantic figures, heirs to a tradition that beckons with promises of fame and a niche in history.
>
> (Papanek, 1995: 135)

The actual process whereby an individual produces a design is inherent to the mystique of the design professional, whether architect or urban designer, involving in part the application of skills and knowledge acquired in up to seven years training, in part a process of analysis and problem-solving, and in part an innate artistic and aesthetic sensibility (see Lloyd-Jones, 2001, in relation to urban design; Lawson, 1997, in relation to architecture). Such training encourages the notion that each design situation is unique and that each design response must be original, but in reality designers are guided and influenced by a number of factors: their previous design experience; their motivation for and interest in the particular project; their familiarity with and preference for a certain style; their classification of a design commission as belonging to a certain pre-existing 'type', such as 'hospital' or 'social housing'; and the reputation, style and management practices of the seniors in the design practice (Bentley, 1999; Lawson, 1997). Increasingly, too, designers work in design teams, in which the process of collaboration, negotiation and compromise inevitably constrains the opportunity for individual freedom of expression and the sense of ownership of the design. Furthermore, designers rarely have free rein, being at the behest of an individual or institutional client who will lay down the parameters of the project in a more or less detailed brief, and who will often have quite different objectives and priorities to the designer. In the case of large scale and prestigious projects, such as significant public buildings and major regeneration schemes, appointment of a design team is often subject to competition. Here designers have to steer a course between the production of a design which is sufficiently avant garde and distinctive to stand out from the rest, but which is not so outrageous or overwhelming that it alienates the judges, who by and large are non-professional and conservative. There is also the tendency to play down the true costs and complexity of the scheme in order to secure the prize (Ball, 2002).

In regard to the design of housing, this became in the latter part of the twentieth century a somewhat insignificant and low status field in a profession which was increasingly defining itself by high profile commissions. This was in contrast to the situation in the 1950s and 1960s when the design of public housing was seen as an area in which an architect could make his (in a masculine occupation) reputation, and most local authorities had their own in-house team of architects. However, since that time public housing has become residualised, local authorities have had to contract out many of their services, and speculative housebuilders have become the major providers. Despite this, some architects have still either retained or developed an interest in housing, and, perhaps because this is in itself a manifestation of a social conscience, have expressed a concern for more user involvement. This interest became associated in the 1970s and 1980s with the rise of community architecture, usually in the context of the redevelopment of inner city slums and social housing estates (Towers, 1995). Generally the architect would initiate and control the process, but would ensure that the tenants and residents had full opportunity to make their views and preferences known, and where technically feasible, incorporated into the design. Pioneering and oft cited examples include Black Road, Macclesfield, under the influence of the architect Rod Hackney; the Byker estate in Newcastle, designed by the Swedish architect Ralph Erskine; and the Lea View estate in London, refurbished by the architectural practice of Hunt Thompson.

Community architecture was somewhat frowned upon by the architectural establishment as detracting from the principles of true professionalism and compromising the quality of design – and perhaps also because it was endorsed by the Prince of Wales, considered by professionals as something of a bumbling amateur (Parfect and Power, 1997). However, the principles of community architecture have experienced a renaissance since the latter years of the twentieth century, given that the questioning of professional powers has rendered the voice and opinion of users more influential. Increasingly, therefore, design professionals are being encouraged to involve lay people in the planning and design of housing. This can be time consuming, especially as lay people need to grasp the essentials of planning and design, and to be made aware why certain solutions are realistic whilst others are not. Often this necessitates intensive days or weekends, sometimes referred to as 'planning for real' or 'design charettes' in which paper cut outs, cardboard models, wooden blocks and occasionally computer aided design may be used to simulate the design scheme (see Wates, 2000). On the whole, however, the designers still have the upper hand due not only to their superior skills and experience, but also to the fact that it is still they who assume the key role in the actual development process.

Professional bodies, pressure groups and social movements

Acting in concert is generally more effective than acting alone when seeking to establish power, ensure commonality of approach, or influence events. This principle has long been appreciated by the professions and aspiring professions, who have founded professional bodies to lend legitimacy to their professional status or aspirations, and to act in their members' interests. Such bodies have a range of objectives: setting standards for training and qualification; ensuring that members act with sufficient ethical and professional rigour; reprimanding those who step out of line; seeking to influence policy; and serving as a conduit to government and other professional bodies in matters concerning legislation, professional boundaries, and terms and conditions. In addition, they exert authority and control over their members in more oblique ways through the content of their training programmes, their professional journals, their practice guidance and their professional meetings, steering members into accepted ways of thought and action and discouraging divergent views or practices.

In relation to land use and the built environment, the main professional bodies are the Royal Institute of British Architects (RIBA), the Royal Town Planning Institute (RTPI) and the Royal Institution of Chartered Surveyors (RICS). The RIBA was founded in 1837 to promote the status of architecture as a profession, and currently sees an important part of its role as challenging government to ensure that good design is valued economically, socially and environmentally (RIBA, 2003). RICS, established in 1869, represents not only surveyors – quantity, general, land, building – but all those who work in property, including valuers, land agents, estate agents, architects, planners and housing managers. The dominant ethos of RICS contrasts with that of the more publicly oriented RTPI, founded in 1913: 'the RTPI being somewhat more sociological, political, interventionist and governmental in outlook; the RICS more conservative, private-sector orientated and commercial in outlook' (Greed, 1993: 45).

Of perhaps lesser status than these professional bodies are various other organisations and institutes with an interest in and commitment to the development and management of the built environment. These include, for example, the Housebuilders Federation (HBF), the Council of Mortgage Lenders (CML), the Town and Country Planning Association (TCPA), the Chartered Institute of Housing (CIH) and the National Housing Federation (NHF). The CML and the HBF are predominantly oriented towards promoting policies which will benefit the private sector, and are accepted as authoritative voices at the institutional level. Both are oriented towards the profit motive, and the HBF in particular, which represents the interests of speculative housebuilders, is seen as somewhat conservative and reactionary. It is generally opposed to the constraints imposed by the planning system, arguing for a presumption in favour of development, the release of more greenfield sites, the relaxation of affordable housing requirements, and the absolute necessity to increase the supply of new housing in order to stem exorbitant house price inflation (Adams and Watkins, 2002). In regard to social housing, the NHF seeks to represent the interests of housing associations in England (and is distinct from the regulatory body of the Housing Corporation), whilst the relatively long established Chartered Institute of Housing (CIH) works across the UK to raise the professional profile of those who work in the fields of the development and management of public sector housing (see Cole and Furbey, 1994). Some measure of its success is that it has secured a position as an influential voice in relation to policy on social housing, including the housing and support of disadvantaged groups and the supply of affordable housing.

In this context mention must also be made of the Joseph Rowntree Foundation (JRF). The history of this body dates from 1904 when Joseph Rowntree (of cocoa factory fame) founded the Joseph Rowntree Village Trust to administer the model village of New Earswick in York, together with two other charitable Trusts. Born into a family of Quakers and philanthropists, Rowntree felt a particular concern to: 'search out the underlying causes of weakness or evil in the community, rather than of remedying their more superficial manifestations' and believed that only thus could human society advance (JRF, 2004: unpaginated). His legacy both intellectually and financially was the Joseph Rowntree Memorial Trust, later renamed the Joseph Rowntree Foundation. As well as its continuing involvement in New Earswick, the JRF pursues research and development in line with the founder's aims and is well respected by academics and policy makers alike. In terms of development the JRF also oversees the Joseph Rowntree Housing Trust which operates as a housing association, and has recently researched and initiated a number of new concepts and innovative schemes. These include Lifetime Homes, Smart Homes, the continuing care retirement community (see Chapter 8), a masterplanned urban extension in York, and the CASPAR projects (city centre apartments for single people at affordable rents) in Birmingham and Leeds (see Chapter 9).

Lay people who are not professionally or organisationally involved in the built environment field are generally powerless unless they combine with others who share their interests and opinions. By taking collective action they are more likely to be able to influence events, to effect change, and to confront those in positions of power. Such collective action can take the form of pressure groups and social movements. Pressure groups often evolve from interest groups or communities of association; groups with a common interest whose primary purpose is not to effect change but to promote knowledge and understanding, exchange information and views, and provide support for the constituencies they represent. As pressure groups they may seek to influence the policy debate and argue for measures which are more informed and less socially and environmentally inequitable, but they continue to act within the established structural and institutional framework. Examples at the national level include the National Trust, Friends of the Earth (FoE), the Campaign to Protect Rural England (CPRE), the Civic Trust, Shelter and Age Concern, while at a more local level are the county Wildlife Trusts, local natural history societies and local civic societies. Due to their knowledge, experience and recognition by the establishment, any or all of these may become engaged in consultation in regard to national and local planning and housing policy, the formulation of development plans, the negotiations around the granting of planning permission, and the location and design of new housing.

Social movements can be distinguished from pressure groups in that they aim to challenge existing structures and institutions and to bring about radical change:

> A social movement is a collective actor constituted by individuals who understand themselves to have common interests and, for at least some significant part of their social existence, a common identity. Social movements are distinguished from other collective actors, such as political parties and pressure groups, in that they have mass mobilization, or the threat of mobilization, as their prime source of social sanction, and hence of power. They are further distinguished from other collectivities, such as voluntary associations or clubs, in being chiefly concerned to defend or change society, or the relative position of the group in society.
>
> (Scott, 1990: 6)

The transformative potential of social movements was first studied in the context of Marxist urban sociology in the 1960s and 1970s, notably by Castells (1977, 1978). Castells argued that 'urban social movements' were the means by which workers endeavoured to improve their conditions in relation to collective consumption – the forms of service provided collectively, normally by the state, such as housing, transport and health services. Hence urban social movements involved confrontation with the state in an effort to win concessions, with notable examples in the UK consisting of the rent riots of 1915 and the squatter movement of the 1960s (see Bailey, 1973; Cole and Furbey, 1994).

Following the fall from favour of Marxist sociology there has been a new orientation to the study of social movements, with a concomitant shift of discourse to 'new social movements' (see Crossley, 2002; Doherty, 2002; Dryzek et al., 2003). In the context of today's dislocated society and the loss of the old institutional certainties, these place the emphasis on the development of new loyalties and identities rather than on the claiming of rights and the winning of concessions from the state. Given the discrediting of party politics they also offer the possibility to take alternative political action organised around issues which have some personal significance; a 'cause' to pursue and with which to identify, and which assists in the project described by Giddens (1994) as 'life politics'. Such causes in recent years have involved people at the international, national and local level, and include feminism, gay rights, disability, peace, the environment, animal rights and anti-globalisation. In the UK there has been less organised activity in regard to the environment than in many other countries (Doherty, 2002), and it was only in the 1990s that a more aggressive and nationally organised environmental movement began to emerge, as expressed particularly in Earth First! and the anti roads campaign (Wall, 1999; see also Chapter 10). Otherwise direct action in relation to planning and housing has been largely restricted to local protests such as community hate campaigns against paedophiles and asylum seekers, and resistance to the destruction of New Age traveller and other 'alternative' settlements.

In a generally conformist and apathetic society the reasons why a certain minority is motivated to become engaged in the radicalising activities of new social movements are not altogether clear (Wall, 1999). Existing networks based on friendship, propinquity or membership of an organisation may play an important role in stimulating the potential for action, but it would appear that there are deeper developmental issues, such as a history of being a rebel at school, a childhood experience which has instilled a strongly held resentment or sentiment, or reaction to the effects of being brought up by repressive and authoritarian parents (Crossley, 2002). Beyond this it would appear that the majority of activists are young, well educated and middle class, with a preponderance of welfare professionals and those on the left of the political spectrum. Action is stimulated by the construction of a specific issue as a challenge or a problem, and the emergence of leadership by an anarchic individual or core group who can inspire others into a sense of urgency and channel their energies into action. Such action ranges from the indirect, such as leaflets, petitions and negative publicity, to the more direct, such as boycotts, demonstrations, establishment of alternative living arrangements, marches, and passive or active resistance. In many instances the protestors also claim to have the moral upper hand, since they act to protect and preserve the interests and freedoms of defenceless people (or animals) against the alienating powers of institutions and the arrogant greed of capitalist accumulation. In extreme cases, individuals may resort to a level of anarchy and violence which is directly opposed to the norms of civilised and ordered society and which risks the loss of public sympathy and hence legitimacy. However, threat and shock form an essential part of the ammunition of those at the extremes, as does the response they provoke, of disproportionate force and repression (Crossley, 2002).

Influential individuals: making an impression

In any society there are individuals who become important and symbolic figures in the public sphere, sometimes indeed because of their anarchic ambitions, but more often because they possess outstanding abilities or have reached some pinnacle of achievement. Such individuals have the capacity to influence events, to change policy directions, to alter the landscape and to transform ways of thinking. In this way they make a uniquely personal contribution which has an enduring resonance across space and time:

> [W]e have cherished and benefited from their contributions; we name buildings and even whole communities after them, we read (and sometimes write) books about them, we construct our courses and our disciplines around their words and their works.
>
> (Gardner, 1997: 2)

In regard to the urban environment, it is architects, planners, designers, politicians, academics, social reformers and philanthropists who have had the most opportunity to exert such transformative power. Given their calling, they already possess status and distinction in the social order through their cultural, artistic, symbolic, political, intellectual, or social capital. The reasons why certain individuals from amongst their number then come to prominence would appear to be due to a range of factors: personal attributes, such as intelligence, imagination, creativity, curiosity, self-belief, religious conviction and even state of health; biographical circumstance, such as cultural and social background, education, parental disposition and assets, interaction with the environment, relationships and friendships; and the life chances and life decisions that stem from fate and opportunity – being 'in the right place at the right time'. These factors then interface with the particular conjuncture of space, time and state of societal progress in which the individual is located, and the institutional framework which provides the context for action.

In the conditions of expanding industrialisation these influential individuals included a number of social reformers, entrepreneurs and philanthropists who despite (or in some cases because of) their own privileged situation, became increasingly concerned about urban squalor and its effects on the labouring classes. The names of such people and their legacy in the built environment live on today, and include the social reformers William Morris and John Ruskin; the moralistic housing manager, Octavia Hill; a number of philanthropic employers who provided model villages for their employees, such as Robert Owen, Titus Salt, the Lever Brothers, Joseph Rowntree and George Cadbury; and those wealthy individuals who endowed housing trusts for benevolent reasons, such as Samuel Peabody, Edward Guinness and Lord Shaftesbury (see Edwards, 1981; Malpass, 2000).

Other key figures in the early industrial age of the eighteenth and nineteenth centuries were concerned not so much with housing *per se*, but with the planning and design of cities. In the UK, the names that have passed into design history and whose urban forms are still seen as the epitome of refined taste are the John Woods (father and son), who were responsible for many of the Georgian squares and crescents of Bath, and John Nash, who designed Regents Park in London. As industrialisation advanced, it became accepted that many of the problems were due to the unplanned and unregulated approach to urban development, and in moving towards the idea of planned environments it also became accepted that these should be both aesthetically pleasing and spatially expansive. Particular influences here derived from continental Europe, notably in the work of Baron Haussman, who redesigned Paris on the basis of the boulevard, and Camille Sitte, who was noted for his ideas on the artistic and the picturesque in the design of urban form (Morris, 1997). Both of these had a significant impact on the early practice of town planning in the UK, ideas which in themselves owe much to the work of two other outstanding pioneers at the start of the twentieth century: Patrick Geddes and Ebenezer Howard.

Geddes was originally intent on becoming a zoologist, but was unable to work with microscopes due to an eye condition. Instead he became involved in the renewal of rundown areas in his native Edinburgh, and became noted for his observation – still followed today – that planning should be a process (Morris, 1997). He argued that this process should be based on a methodology of extensive surveys and their subsequent analysis, and that what was required was a scientific understanding of the inter-relationship between physical, social and economic factors.

Despite Geddes' legacy in terms of the plan making process, his name today is not as well known as that of Howard. Howard left school at 14 to become a clerk and stenographer, but as a young adult emigrated to America where he unsuccessfully participated in the pioneer homesteading experiment (see Fishman, 1982). Returning to London after visiting various towns and cities in America, he became caught up in the intellectual debates about the social problems of the day. It was his conviction that something needed to be done to address these problems that led him to consider planning a model community. In his opinion neither the town nor the country could fulfil all the needs of contemporary human life, and he drew on the American idea of the garden suburb to devise an alternative approach. Famously, he represented his ideas figuratively as the three magnets of town, country, and a hybrid of the two, and called his utopian ideal the Garden City, almost certainly after the alternative name for Chicago in the late nineteenth century (Hall, 1982). Contrary to what is often believed to be the case, Howard had no training in planning or architecture, and relied on others, notably Raymond Unwin and Barry Parker, to implement his vision (see Edwards, 1981).

At much the same time in America, Clarence Perry was developing a concept which also has endured over time. This was the concept of the 'neighbourhood', which he argued should be the basic planning unit in the development of towns and cities (see Biddulph, 2000). This idea was then taken up by Patrick Abercrombie, who was charged with the preparation of the Greater London Plan in 1943. He saw London as: 'a collection of communities fused together with a strong local emotional loyalty' (Morris, 1997: 85), and felt that these must not be disturbed by planning intervention, but rather strengthened. Abercrombie's plan-making skills had a profound impact on subsequent planning practice in terms of spatial forms and processes, but his views on social life were largely neglected. The consequences were the undermining and dislocation of longstanding communities in the drive for the renewal of towns and cities in the 1950s, and it took the ground breaking work of the sociologists Young and Willmott (1962) to demonstrate that the dispersal of existing communities led to the rupturing of traditional social life. There followed a spate of academic work in both the UK and the US which reinforced the significance of 'community', and which included Gans' ethnographic account of the West End of Boston (Gans, 1962). This he described not as a community or a neighbourhood but as an 'urban village', and it was this concept which was reinvented in the UK in the late 1980s and reproduced in planning policy (see Chapter 6). This sociological engagement with ideas of community was reflected also in the work of urban design pioneers who were trying to analyse how a sense of community could be enhanced through 'place making'. Significant names in this regard include Jane Jacobs (1961) and Kevin Lynch (1960) in the US, and Gordon Cullen (1971) in the UK, all of whom were preoccupied in seeking to identify those design features which helped to create distinctive urban spaces memorable and pleasurable. It was their work which was instrumental in initiating new discourses and agendas about urban form, as well as promoting the practice of urban design (see Chapter 5).

In architecture too, certain key figures have been extraordinarily influential, and have produced work which lives on both as built reality and as expressions of belief and ideology. In the public spirited but power obsessed Victorian age it was the design of institutional buildings such as town halls, museums, churches and asylums which endowed architects with pre-eminence. Significant names in this connection include George Gilbert Scott, Charles Barry and Augustus Pugin, who, in adopting the flamboyant Gothic Revival form, were not only displaying their distinction and discernment but also legitimising it as the new and fashionable style. By the turn of the nineteenth century, a new generation of architects had appeared, responding to the challenge of a new century with new styles, and seeking to make an impact through embracing the natural and the domestic in less grandiose types of building. In the UK these included Edwin Lutyens with his revival of the domestic vernacular, and Charles Rennie Mackintosh, famous for his interpretation of the art nouveau style. Also affecting design styles in the UK were voices from abroad, such as Frank Lloyd Wright, who sought to create an uninterrupted flow between nature and dwelling, Antonio Gaudí, with his uniquely expressive and flamboyant designs, and Walter Gropius, the leader of the Modern Movement in architecture (see Curtis, 1987). It was Gropius who founded the famous Bauhaus school of design in Germany, inspiring his colleagues and students to support the new rational, scientific style, in which 'form follows function'. One of these colleagues was Mies van der Rohe, famous for coining the phrase 'less is more' as an aphorism to express how design should be approached. Mies was the last director of the Bauhaus before it closed due to Nazi persecution, and both he and Gropius, together with other architect *émigrés*, fled to England and later to America, practising and promoting their views in both countries.

The architect who played an 'absolutely central and seminal role' in the early twentieth century modernist movement was Le Corbusier (Frampton, 1992: 149). Born in Switzerland in 1887 as Charles Edouard Jeanneret, he took the name Le Corbusier, derived from his maternal grandfather, as a *nom-de-plume* in 1920. Corbusier was sent at the age of 15 to learn watch case engraving and was taught by a former student of fine art who had a particular interest in Ruskin and the Arts and Crafts movement. Observing his pupil's design talents and aptitude his teacher persuaded him to study architecture, and it was this influence which changed the course of Le Corbusier's life (Fishman, 1982). During his subsequent career he studied widely in various European cities, travelled extensively, wrote prodigiously, and designed not only individual buildings and housing blocks, but also whole towns and cities. One of his most enduring concepts is that of the *machine à habiter* (machine for living), expressive of his functional approach to housing, while the apotheosis of his ideas for mass housing was fulfilled in the creation of one of his best known buildings, the *Unité d'Habitation* in Marseilles.

As discussed in Chapter 1, both Gropius and Le Corbusier had an enormous influence on the upcoming generation of British architects, who felt persuaded by them to emulate the modernist style and the use of concrete construction in the planning and design of council housing in the 1950s and 1960s. Prime amongst these architects were the articulate husband and wife team of Peter and Alison Smithson, who, in their translation of Corbusian principles to their deck access housing with its 'streets in the sky', endeavoured to create a more honest and plain style which would replicate traditional working class life. The resulting somewhat severe and inhumane architecture was part of a wider movement known, perhaps unfortunately, as Brutalism, a name in fact derived from the French term *béton brut* or concrete in the raw (see Frampton, 1992).

Following the discrediting of modernism and especially its consequences for urban form, new figures have emerged who have promoted new approaches to design. In reaction to the asceticism of modernism (described by Robert Venturi in parody of Mies as 'less is a bore' (Morris, 1997: 210)) a more eclectic and often nostalgic style has been developed. This style was first named by the American Charles Jencks (1977) who referred to it as 'postmodernism', and the title has endured. However, towards the end of the twentieth century it began to share dominance with the futuristic and High-Tech Modernism associated with certain authoritative and successful individuals (and their iconic buildings), such as Richard Rogers, Norman Foster and Nicholas Grimshaw. Rogers, born in Italy, became probably the most influential architect in the UK in the late twentieth century, and is scathing of styles which denote nostalgia and kitsch and the retrospective and artificial values they represent. His interests extend to environmental issues and the design of cities, and these, together with his celebrated status, have brought him to the attention of New Labour. Described by the Deputy Prime Minister, John Prescott, as 'an evangelist of urban renaissance' (Urban Task Force, 1999: 3), he has been feted as a design guru and given considerable powers to influence policy. He has also received the accolade of a knighthood and has been raised to the peerage as Lord Rogers of Riverside.

Rogers' approach to architecture represents in many ways the antithesis of that of the Prince of Wales, who whatever one may think about the monarchy in general and the Prince in particular, has undeniably become an influential figure in regard both to the built and the natural environment. Given his position not only as heir to the throne but also as a member of the aristocracy and a wealthy landed gentleman, his roots are in the past, whilst his future depends on continuity with long established traditions. It is perhaps not surprising then, that he is driven by respect for old values, for history and for nostalgia, and holds much of modern and even postmodern architecture in contempt.

The Prince's convictions have led him to often outspoken intervention, notably in his criticism of certain landmark buildings in the capital as 'monstrous carbuncles', 'glass stumps', '1930s wirelesses' and 'bores' (Morris, 1997). But as well as expressing withering scorn about these and other built environment issues he has also sought to become constructively involved through the promotion of his beliefs and ideas. This has included visible support for community architecture (Towers, 1995), the devising of his own ten principles of good design (HRH the Prince of Wales, 1989), association with the concept of the urban village (see Chapter 6) and his support for the classical revivalist style.

As a champion of sustainability and human scale design, the Prince is able to apply his symbolic capital to good effect and to use his royal status and connections to seek out those who will support him in order to implement his vision. But equally he can be sought out by others, who perceive his usefulness as a figurehead in supporting their own particular vision. In this regard, he is at times deferred to by political leaders, where his position as being above politics is particularly useful. Thus, for example, he was co-opted in 2003 by John Prescott to lend symbolic weight in persuading the public of the merits of the proposals in the Sustainable Communities Plan. For his part, Prescott, as minister with responsibility for housing and planning at the time of writing, combines his political capital with his bellicose personality to forceful effect. However, in contrast to the Prince, his reign will be short and subject to the vagaries of political infighting and reshuffling. For this reason perhaps, he seems determined to leave a strong and enduring impression on the built environment, not only through the new growth areas in the south-east as laid out in the Sustainable Communities Plan, but also through a variety of other initiatives such as millennium communities, Housing Market Renewal Pathfinders (demolition of unpopular housing in the north) and the £60,000 house. Other ministers and politicians too, have used their role to leave their mark on towns, cities and rural communities: Michael Heseltine, former Secretary of State for the Environment, with his work to redeem the inner cities; Margaret Thatcher, former Prime Minister, with her promotion of the private sector, unfettered development, and the sale of council houses; and the controversial Mayor of London, Ken Livingstone, with his call for higher quotas of affordable housing, his support for a new generation of tower blocks, and the introduction of congestion charging in London.

The individuals mentioned above, and of course many others too numerous to name, have had far-reaching impacts not only on the shape and form of our built environment, but also on the way we live within it and react to it. Whether figures of stature in their own right, or assisted by their establishment and institutional positions, they stand out because they have brought transformative capacity to existing perceptions, understandings, and practices in regard to the built environment. But there are of course many other, lesser and often more prosaic individuals, whose interest is not in achieving fame but in acting according to their convictions, in trying to make a difference or simply in doing their jobs and living their lives. Such individuals too may exert a formative influence on the environment and leave their legacy within the built form, but their names are soon forgotten and they remain anonymous to the wider world. Often acting at the local scale they include the council leaders and local councillors who make planning decisions, the officers who advise them, the myriad architects and urban designers who create designs, the activists and members of pressure groups who resist and rebel, the housing developers and builders, the users and consumers – the actions of each guided by their personality, biography and particular location in time and space. Their footprints may be smaller and less enduring than those whose names survive in collective memory, but nonetheless they inexorably leave an impression for posterity: an impression all the more indelible because it is embedded in the shape of all we see around us.

5 The built form: design and discourse

The planning and production of housing is determined not only by structural events, policy frameworks, and the social and political actions of organisations and individuals, but also by traditions and disciplines in regard specifically to the design of built form. The shape of housing and the nature of residential environments cannot therefore be considered without reference to the precepts of architecture and urban design, and consideration as to how these have informed the production and appreciation of the built environment.

The central preoccupations of architecture and urban design are with the creation of built form and the identification of those styles and arrangements which will achieve the most appropriate and aesthetically pleasing results. Since style and form have varied over time this suggests that built form is not neutral but can be read as an expression of the ideas and fashions of the time. In addition, the built form has an immediate visual and spatial presence which is received in different ways by different people, and which varies according to matters such as interest, experience, perceptiveness, judgement of taste and appreciation of ease in use. For the purist, the professional and those charged with overseeing the production of the built environment, there is a concern to identify the properties of the 'best' or most legitimate form, so that these can then be reproduced in space. Others might be more interested in the relationship between spatial form and social practice, and seek to deduce how the arrangement of space facilitates or constrains certain types of activity, and how this in turn reflects relations of power and control. Meanwhile, for those whose orientation is towards the marketing and profitability of housing, the built form becomes a product whose meaning is subject to manipulation through the subtle presentation of image. This is then 'read' by consumers to see if it accords not only with their traditional perceptions of what a home should be, but also with their values, aspirations and lifestyle preferences. In all of these ways, the built form can be said to have some of the properties of 'text', and like other sorts of text is rich in meaning and has something to communicate. Just as a book, a poem or a work of art it can be read and interpreted in a multiplicity of ways, and in the same way has the capacity to reveal underlying societal norms, aesthetic principles, collective memories, and institutional and individual predilections.

It is these issues with which the present chapter engages. First addressed are matters of aesthetics and style, both of which have been so formative within the discipline of architecture. Attention then moves to the way in which it has been suggested that, within built form, the relationship between elements can be seen as consisting of a sequence of ordered parts and wholes akin to the structure of a language. In this ordering of space, the potential exists for spatial form to reproduce the nature of social relations, particularly in regard to the way in which power and oppression are made manifest. The next section of the chapter examines how and why the newly emerging discipline of urban design has begun to have a major role in informing policy and practice in relation to the urban environment. Finally, there is a discussion of the influences on design of the housing providers, in which it is clear that the authority exerted over the public sector has had quite different outcomes from those to be found in the more independent and market led private sector.

Style, syntax and spatial order

Architects, as the experts in relation to individual buildings, and urban designers, as the experts in relation to urban form, have consistently sought to try and isolate those elements which can be said to create 'good' or 'pure' form. As mentioned in Chapter 1, such ideal form appears to relate primarily to the qualities of beauty, expressiveness and functionality, which themselves are derived from the overall impact of the constituent parts of the individual building or urban ensemble. These parts include size, scale, proportion, composition, ornamentation, rhythm, texture, decoration, colour, and the play of light and shadow. However, for centuries there has been an ongoing debate as to how these elements can most effectively be assembled to make the most sincere or most aesthetic statement, and thus achieve a form which provides a transformative experience of delight, perfection and harmony.

In architecture conflicting and competing discourses as to how such perfection should be attained have led to the 'battle of the styles' and the establishment of successive schools or movements as arbiters of 'good taste'. Some styles, such as neo-classicism or Gothic Revival, have been reactive; a re-interpretation of the imagined idealism of a bygone era in the light of contemporary conditions. Others appear to have been influenced by moral concerns about societal conditions, as for example in the peculiarly British Arts and Crafts movement, which drew its energy from a disquiet about the dehumanising and mechanistic effects of industrialisation. Others again, such as early classicism and modernism, have been the products of an intellectual and abstract aestheticism which has been dominated by rationality, proportion, mathematics and mastery of technique.

Turning to more contemporary times, it would appear that the reductionist and homogenising approach of international modernism (as discussed in Chapter 1) was inappropriate for societies seeking a new identity. In effect: 'it was no longer capable of saying anything of significance about the material or ideological relationships of contemporary society … [it] had effectively been reduced to silence' (Forty, 2000: 77). It was from this feeling of sterility and lack of relevance that what has become known as postmodern architecture was born. Here form has been freed from function, and architects have become more expressive, exuberant and experimental, resulting in an eclectic style that includes nostalgia, ornamentation, historicity, playfulness and kitsch. Buildings designed in this way seem to hold a richer meaning and communicate far more than the spare and sterile functionalism of modernist architecture. Indeed, it has been argued that the aesthetics of architecture have become so overcharged with image and meaning that to the consciousness of the ordinary person they have become an 'anaesthetics' (Leach, 1999). Perhaps as a result of this, the dawn of the twenty-first century has seen a tension develop between the largely retrospective and 'anything goes' narrative of postmodernism, and a disciplined and futuristic paradigm dominated by precision and pure form. This finds expression in the sophistication of High-Tech Modernism, an emerging style which is beginning to add a new dimension to the composition of the city:

> Led by Michael Hopkins, Norman Foster and Richard Rogers, High-Tech Modernism is the developed Modern Movement, evolving from the early struggles of the Modern Movement, allowing architectural pluralism, and diversity of cultures, ideas and philosophies coexisting, if not in discourse, at least in creative harmony.
>
> (Morris, 1997: 216)

With the 'postmodern turn' came not only new design styles but also new intellectual orientations. Thus it began to be accepted that there was no single authoritative voice that could dictate the way in which people should perceive and use the built environment, and that instead there are multiple meanings, each of which is equally legitimate and authentic. The postmodern shift also resulted in an increased interest in the relationship between architecture and social organisation. This was expressed both through a desire to understand the connection between spatial form and social practice, and through an appreciation of design as discourse, in the sense of design as text and semantics (Forty, 2000).

The latter owes much to the science of semiotics developed by de Saussure (1915), whose thesis was that language is a system of signs consisting of a signifier, as for example the word tree, and a signified, the living object with a trunk, branches and leaves. In the same way, semiotics can be applied in the built environment field to show how the physical elements of design make up a system of signs which act as signifiers, and which can be 'read' like other forms of text (see, for example, Biddulph, 1995; Broadbent *et al.*, 1980). Thus a building with a plan in the form of cross, surmounted by a tower, dome or steeple, is 'read' in the Western world as a church, whilst at a deeper level the crucifix form also symbolises the death of Christ on the cross, and hence acts as a mnemonic or metonymic representation of the Christian religion. In this way it can be asserted that just as with language, the signs embedded in the built form possess a culturally specific set of conventions and codes, acting at the unconscious as well as at the conscious level.

Taking the linguistic analogy further has been a new discourse of the syntax of style and form. Such an approach, drawing on the rules of structure and grammar, has been adopted primarily by Alexander *et al.* (1977) and Hillier and Hanson (1984). Alexander *et al.* use the linguistic analogy to devise a 'pattern language' made up of the identifiable elements of the built environment. These elements are in part universal, in part particular to each society, and in part specific to a group of individuals. To create a coherent and consistent overall design it is necessary to select between elements and place them in an ordered sequence, as one would select words to form a structured sentence, and then to combine sequences into a meaningful whole as one would combine sentences into a longer utterance or text. In all a total of 253 patterns are distinguished, extending from the smallest scale of rooms and details of rooms; to the interior layout, external appearance and approaches to buildings; to clusters of buildings and the spaces between them; and finally to the larger scale of neighbourhoods, towns and even regions. Suggestions are made as to how each element can be designed to be more in tune with human needs for delight, interest, activity, privacy, relaxation and so on, and how elements can then be combined to bestow buildings and urban spaces with life and energy. By paying attention to the connectivity of each pattern, each element of design, one is then creating a language, an overall environment, in which the parts create a socially and humanly responsive whole. This in turn is expressive of 'a timeless way of building' which roots us to our human past, and which Alexander believes is particularly necessary in the soulless conditions of contemporary society (Alexander, 1979).

Hillier and Hanson (1984) adopt the syntactical analogy to show how the morphology or 'grammar' of buildings and settlements is implicated in social action, notably in regard to the way that certain types of social encounter are facilitated whilst others are constrained. The 'social logic of space' that they devise relies on the spatial mapping of points and the nature of the linear connections between them, and is analysed through a complex notational system. At its simplest, this involves the identification of architectural genotypes; the spatial structures that determine a certain ordering of social action with a building or an urban form. A linear syntax (an *enfilade*) permits only a linear sequence of progression from one point to the next, with no choice of route from entry to innermost point, and hence facilitates a high degree of control over access and movement. By contrast a 'ringy' syntax is open, allowing a freedom of access and choice of movement which indicates that it is not hierarchically controlled. An intermediate syntax is that of the fan or branch, which controls access to spaces from just one central point, such as when a series of otherwise unconnected rooms open from one central hall or corridor (Figure 5.1). In relation to individual buildings a hierarchical arrangement assigns those of lesser status to certain, generally outer, areas, whilst the person of the highest status occupies the most superior and protected position – an inner sanctum. Similarly, visitors are normally able to penetrate only the more public areas of buildings, usually those nearest the street, whilst staff, managers or other occupants control the innermost parts – as in a typical bank, hospital or domestic home.

This notion of power and control as being inscribed on built form extends beyond abstract considerations of spatial syntax to discussions about the way in which social relations are communicated and reproduced through the disposition of space (see Markus, 1993; Markus and Cameron, 2002; Dovey, 1999). In an unequal society the asymmetries of power are irrevocably reflected in spatial form, and form can be manipulated in a variety of ways: to express symbolic strength; to assign people to different types of space; or to direct and control social practice. Thus palaces, cathedrals, city halls, workers' housing blocks and other types of monumental building symbolise the power of monarchy, church and state

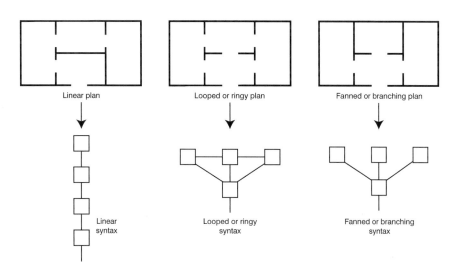

5.1 The three primary genotypes of spatial syntax, reproduced from Dovey (1999), and based on Hillier and Hanson (1984) and Robinson (1994)

as against the domestic scale of the ordinary dwelling. In the same way, there is a hierarchy of space which reflects degree of power, with the most dominant interests securing the most superior locations for themselves and leaving the dominated to occupy the most marginalised places; as for example, when mediaeval peasants were forced to make their dwellings outside the protection of the city walls, or labourers were consigned to the noise, fumes and smoke of the inner cities while the industrial magnates and the middle classes moved out to country residences and suburban villas.

The ordering of social practice through spatial form can be achieved at a variety of different scales and through a number of different devices. Thus, for example, the plans and pattern books of domestic design reflect societal norms about the relative status and place of different family members and of visitors and servants; the spatial ordering of institutions, especially where the panopticon device of the all seeing eye is used, expresses the disciplinarian and classificatory approach taken towards certain categories of powerless people; and the newly privatised spaces of the city, be they gated communities or shopping malls, are indicative of the proclivity of a risk ridden society to exclude and oppress potential malefactors. In effect, in an unequal society there are routines of power and hierarchies of space, in which:

> ... the articulation of space always embeds relationships of power, insofar as it governs interactions between the users of a building, prescribes certain routines for them, and allows them to be subjected to particular forms of surveillance and control. There are, then, no 'innocent', power-free spaces.
>
> (Markus and Cameron, 2002: 68–9)

The emergent field of urban design

In the latter part of the twentieth century a more proactive approach to the design of urban areas came to be seen as important in overcoming the worst effects of the rational school of planning which had dominated the post-war period. Thus the new discipline of urban design has had the opportunity to flourish, distinguished by its concern with the totality of urban space. Essentially, urban design is not confined to the abstract representation of space and form, but with all that which determines, defines and constitutes the urban fabric and public space. This includes an understanding of both historic and contemporary socio-economic determinants, an appreciation of the perception and experience of users, and an awareness of the limitations and opportunities afforded by different types of spatial arrangement (see Morris, 1997; Roberts and Greed, 2001).

A matter which has preoccupied urban designers is why certain types of space and form are pleasurable and successful, and hence 'work', and why others are alienating and unsuccessful, and hence do not 'work'. Here the contributions of urban design pioneers have been influential. In the US Jane Jacobs argued that the post-war planning system based on the separation of human activities into 'zones' was responsible for destroying conviviality and increasing opportunities for crime, and that by restoring the mixed uses of traditional neighbourhoods there would be more interest and activity on the streets (Jacobs, 1961). At much the same time, her compatriot Kevin Lynch (1960) was pointing to the need for memorable and distinctive features to give places identity and aid orientation, such as 'paths', 'nodes', 'landmarks', 'edges' and 'districts'. In the UK, with its longer history of westernised domestic architecture, the debate became oriented around identifying the visual and aesthetic qualities which constituted the concept of 'townscape', particularly as associated with mediaeval towns (see Cullen, 1971).

From these and other influences have developed the theory and practice of urban design, and the more holistic consideration of the creation and use of urban space. An important part of its focus is people: the way people feel about the urban environment; the suitability of spaces for the sorts of activities that occur in them; the ease with which people find their way around; the characteristics of the places in which they linger; the features that they observe and remember; the nature of the places in which they assemble, relax and feel secure, and how these differ from those places they seek to avoid and in which they feel unsafe. This has given rise to a discourse of urban design which is on the one hand descriptive, identifying those features of the urban environment which help people to feel at ease and to orientate themselves (and with a frame of reference drawn from places that are perceived to have grown traditionally and incrementally over time), and on the other hand prescriptive, specifying the essential ingredients of good urban form. In recent years, as urban designers have sought to become professionally established and pursue their claims for distinction and legitimacy, it is this more prescriptive language which has gained in the ascendancy. This incorporates a more assertive and technical vocabulary, and makes specialist use of terms such as legibility, permeability, robustness, identity, sense of place, public realm, organic growth, mixed-use, scale, grain, conviviality, contextuality, vitality, spatial hierarchy (see, for example, Bentley *et al.*, 1985; Gosling and Maitland, 1984; Tugnutt and Robertson, 1987).

Since the 1990s it is the discourse of this newly burgeoning field of urban design (as opposed say to that of the longer established architectural tradition) that has become the dominant one in policy terms in relation not only to urban development but also to housing development. There are several reasons why this might be the case. In terms of both theory and practice it is less overtly subjective, less idiosyncratic, less esoteric, and less aggressive and competitive than the discipline of architecture. Its development of a prescriptive and objective language also seems to have wider applicability, and despite the technical use of terms, the overall impression is of a relatively 'common sense' vocabulary. In addition, the acceptance by government of the need for more effective design in the pursuit of its urban renaissance and sustainability agenda has created a gap in relevant knowledge and experience, and this has provided an opportunity for urban designers and others with urbanist interests to make their voices heard (see, for example, Barton *et al.*, 1995; Frey, 1999; Jenks *et al.*, 1996; Rudlin and Falk, 1999; Tibbalds, 1992). Thus urban designers have ensured that it is their discourse which is relevant and is reproduced, and have thereby secured for themselves a more visible and respected profile as well as a claim to legitimacy, distinction and professional identity.

The policy discourse of design

The policy shift to a discourse of design was first adopted by a Conservative government which had previously been somewhat dogmatic in decreeing that matters of design should be left to the market. However, it was stung into action by the increasingly vituperative attacks on the state of British design from the establishment. These were expressed by the Prince of Wales (as discussed in the previous chapter), the Royal Fine Art Commission, RIBA, the Urban Villages Group (see Chapter 6), and the RTPI, for whom Francis Tibbalds, in a riposte to the Prince, produced his own version of ten design commandments (see Carmona, 2001; Morris, 1997).

Feeling under pressure to act, the Conservatives amended their policy guidance to adjure local authorities to develop design policies which would support 'good design' and reject 'poor design', but at the same time only to control design if the sensitive character of the setting justified it (DoE, 1992). Given this contradictory and confusing advice, in which any definition of good or poor design was further subsumed under the vagaries of aesthetics and subjectivity, it was hardly surprising if local authorities were uncertain how to proceed. As a result they adopted a very variable response, in which only those with an identifiably distinctive built heritage felt compelled to devise prescriptive design policies (see Punter and Carmona, 1997).

The beginning of an effort by government to broaden and deepen the design debate was signalled by the publication in 1994 of *Quality in Town and Country* (DoE, 1994a). The influence of urban design thinking is clear in the emphasis given in the language of this document in regard to quality of design, sustainability, adherence to the precepts of urban design, mixed use, the revival of urban areas, reduced car reliance and citizen involvement. The following year, the commitment to urban design as a mechanism to achieve quality was given further emphasis with the launch of an urban design campaign, which stressed that quality was not so much about the merits or demerits of individual buildings but about the creation of place, identity and civic pride (DoE, 1995, 1996).

It was these sentiments which were adopted also by New Labour, and which lie at the heart of the advice contained within the revised *PPG1*. This has a considerably expanded and more detailed exposition on design specifically constructed around the precepts of urban design (DoE, 1997a; see also Carmona, 2001). In line with its more interventionist ideology, New Labour indicated that it intended to impose greater control over design, to seek to define the parameters of good design, and to suggest how good design could be implemented. There followed a stream of publications from the newly created DETR, one of the first of which was *Places, Streets, Movement* (DETR, 1998c). This set out effectively to critique the prevalent approach to residential development taken by the private sector, and to argue that housing should be conceptualised within the wider discourse of an integrated 'public realm' which gave equal value to people, buildings, open spaces, landscaping, movement and safety.

Of higher profile and broader scope was *Towards an Urban Renaissance*, which as referred to in Chapter 3, was commissioned to assess how urban decline could be reversed and how towns and cities could be made more attractive (Urban Task Force, 1999). Stimulated by the leadership and design idealism of Richard Rogers the document makes clear that there needs to be a transformation of approach, and that this must be design led, or more specifically, urban design led:

> We need a vision that will drive the urban renaissance. We believe that cities should be well designed, be more compact and connected and support a range of diverse uses – allowing people to live, work and enjoy themselves at close quarters – within a sustainable environment which is well integrated with public transport and adaptable to change.
>
> (Urban Task Force, 1999: 8)

The report also has much to say about residential design, urging a national urban design framework, the preparation of masterplans for large scale redevelopment sites, support for the concept of Home Zones (see Biddulph, 2001) and an increase in the number of design led demonstration projects and competitions (see also Carmona, 2001). More substantively there is a plea that new housing should emulate best practice in Europe, with an emphasis on 'long-life', 'loose-fit' and 'low energy'.

The recommendations of the Urban Task Force were central in informing two subsequent policy documents: the Urban White Paper, *Our Towns and Cities: the Future, Delivering an Urban Renaissance* (DETR, 2000c), and the revised version of *PPG3 Housing* (DETR, 2000b). The former continues the imagery of vision, proclaiming 'a new vision of urban living' (DETR, 2000c: 7) in which a greater emphasis on the role of planning and design will result in attractive and well kept towns and cities with an improved quality of life and opportunity for all. *PPG3* is notable for its deletion of all reference to the need to the market being allowed to prevail in matters of design and its urging of local authorities to ensure that applicants for planning permission appreciate the need for 'good' layout and design. In an attempt to stipulate how design quality might be achieved, it is suggested that policies should be adopted which: 'create places and spaces', 'have their own distinctive identity', 'respect and enhance local character', 'promote designs and layouts which are safe' and 'focus on the quality of places and living environments' (DETR 2000b: para 56).

However, there is still a lack of both clarity and definition. Attributes such as 'attractive', 'quality', 'living environments', 'safe' and 'good' design, whilst they convey a positive intention, remain impressionistic, without substance or didactic power. This reflects the fact that aesthetic values, subjective experience and contextual issues are elusive and difficult to capture and express. It is this gap which other, generally more recent texts have been trying to fill with attempts to expand and refine the policy debate and to inform practice (see CABE/DETR, 2000; CABE/ODPM, 2003; DETR, 1998c; DTLR/CABE, 2001; Llewellyn Davies, 2000; ODPM, 2003b, 2005c, 2005d; Urban Village Forum/English Partnerships, undated). These publications endeavour not only to give substance to and 'fix' the elements that can be said to constitute 'good' residential layout and design, but also to specify those aspects of design which will help to achieve New Labour's additional policy aims of sustainability and social inclusion. However, it remains the case that however well informed, well intentioned and well written these texts are, their recommendations are still largely reliant on the cooperation of that notoriously capricious operator; the speculative housebuilder:

> Imagination in good design comes from confidence. Like sports teams, those with most confidence play best. Confidence leads to a virtuous circle that says: I believe in my ability. ... Set backs, criticism and lack of overt management support leads to a vicious circle: I am not confident. ... The housing design process is vulnerable to the vicious circle.
>
> (Planning Officers Society/HBF/DETR, 1998: para 3.17)

The design of public sector housing

Housing provided with public sector subsidy, whether by local authorities or housing associations, has been subject over time to the vagaries of government priorities and the parameters of financial limitations. This has been particularly true of council housing, since not only have local authorities historically been the main providers, but they have also been more closely under government control and scrutiny. A further characteristic of public sector housing is that for most of its history it has been produced specifically for those who cannot access the more socially and economically beneficial private sector, in other words for those with little or no choice.

This situation, of control, powerlessness and marginalisation, has been reflected in the location and design of public sector housing. In regard to location, it has for the most part been the case that such housing has been spatially segregated from private sector housing and assigned either to the less desirable inner areas of towns and cities, or to the windswept perimeter. In regard to design, it is noteworthy that this has often been experimental, as for example with the early twentieth-century tenements, the inner city balcony blocks and grim peripheral estates of the 1930s, the innovation of many of the New Towns, the post-war prefabs, and the modernist tower blocks and deck access housing of the 1960s. All of these styles ran counter to the conservative and traditional image of the British domestic home which continued to prevail in the private sector, and it was only at the time of greatest political support for council housing, after the two world wars, that support was given for the latter to reproduce this ideal. That these were two exceptions in the history of council housing is emphasised by the prominence still accorded to the two relevant texts: the Tudor Walters Report of 1918 and the Dudley Report of 1944 (see Cole and Furbey, 1994). The Tudor Walters Report was the result of a committee of inquiry which included Unwin, of Garden City fame, and the recommendations reflected his influence in regard to low densities, green open space, private gardens, a cul de sac layout, and the emphasis internally on space, light and air. The Dudley Report sought to remedy the shortcomings of the housing that had been built in the late 1920s and 1930s, and recommended improvements to internal standards and development on the principle of the 'neighbourhood'.

A third influential report was the Parker Morris Report of 1961, commissioned in response to falling standards in the 1950s (MHLG, 1961). The title *Homes for Today and Tomorrow* indicates the attempt to take a more far sighted perspective, and the authors might be satisfied that their recommendations are still used as a benchmark today. The report recognises the needs of a changing society, and suggests, for example, more storage space for consumer acquisitions, the replacement of 'through living rooms' with separate rooms where family members can undertake different activities, larger bedrooms for children so that they can be used for playing and homework, more car parking space, and gardens large enough for people to eat outside, play games and relax. It is proposed that overall space standards be considerably increased, but despite observations about the suitability of house types for different types of household, no reservations are expressed about the appropriateness of flats as dwellings for families. Indeed the flats built to Parker Morris standards were initially appreciated since the internal facilities and space standards were far higher than those that the tenants had been accustomed to, and it was only over time that the deficiencies in relation to construction, lack of definition of external areas and social isolation became apparent. The Parker Morris standards were withdrawn in 1981, and one consequence of this has been that since the early 1990s internal standards of all new homes, across all sectors, have fallen. This was brought to public awareness in a report co-authored by Valerie Karn, a respected academic and policy adviser, in which it was stressed that standards in England had become the lowest in Europe (Karn and Sheridan, 1995).

As a consequence of this report, together with the infiltration into housing policy discourse of design vocabulary, there have been new attempts to specify standards for the development of social housing. Unlike England, Wales has possessed from 1994 a pattern book for the internal layout of all new housing association properties, and this was followed a few years later by a set of development quality requirements and a guide to site layout and design (National Assembly for Wales, 1999; Tai Cymru, 1998a; Tai Cymru, 1998b). In England the NHF, the voluntary umbrella organisation for housing associations, produced a more rigorous set of principles in *Standards and Quality in Development* in 1998 (NHF, 1998a), and at much the same time the DETR began to work with the Housing Corporation on devising a more quantifiable approach to the assessment of housing quality. This consists of ten housing quality indicators covering location, the visual impact of the site, routes and movement, and various aspects regarding actual units, such as layout, sound and light levels, accessibility, energy efficiency and performance in use (Housing Corporation/ DETR, 1999). From 2000 all new developments in England which receive SHG have been required to conform to these indicators, with the intention that in due course they should also be adopted by the private sector. In a more recent development, and informed by the sustainability agenda, the government is also supporting an EcoHomes rating system (BRE, 2004). This relates to energy, health, water, pollution, materials, transport, ecology and land use, health and well-being, with assessment of each category expressed on a scale from pass, good, very good, to excellent, and illustrated with a 'star' rating imaginatively represented as an award of between one and four sunflowers. From 2005 all social housing receiving Housing Corporation or Welsh Assembly Government funding must achieve a rating of 'good'.

The issues of quality, standards and sustainability have also meant a greater emphasis on meeting the needs of more vulnerable and disadvantaged groups. In part this has been stimulated by the more general postmodern acknowledgement of diversity and equal rights, but it is also due to campaigns by disability groups, by the feminist movement, and by BME communities, all of whom have pointed to the need for more inclusive design and the unsuitability of the average house for their needs (see Imrie and Hall, 2001; NHF, 1998b; Roberts, 1991). The only impact of this at legislative level has been the imposition on all housing providers of the Part M regulations on accessibility, and it has been left to the social housing sector, with its traditional responsibility for so called 'special needs', to take the lead in articulating and implementing additional design responses. This has resulted in the new concept of Lifetime Homes (see Brewerton and Darton, 1997) and a variety of good practice publications on appropriate design for a range of needs, including disability (e.g. Chapman Handy, 1996), cultural requirements (e.g. NHF, 1998b), old age (e.g. Robson *et al.*, 1997) and even childhood (e.g. Wheway and Millward, 1997).

Another issue which is seen as somehow the province of the social housing sector is that of tackling crime and anti-social behaviour. Here the work of Oscar Newman (1973) on territoriality, surveillance and defensible space has been influential. Based on observation of residents of housing estates in the US, Newman argued that whatever their location in the social hierarchy, people have a sense of territoriality in regard to the space that they occupy, and that people relate to space with a diminishing sense of responsibility in proportion to their sense of ownership of that space. This suggested to him the concept of a hierarchy of space, extending from the most private space of the home, through semi-private space such as the porch, to semi-public space such as the steps up to the porch, and finally to the fully public space of the street. In order to make people feel more secure and to encourage them to look after (or defend) the space immediately outside their home he suggested it needed to be 'defensible', that is, clearly assigned to the individual as private or semi-private space and given an appropriate symbolic boundary. He also urged that in order to prevent concealment, features such as porches, recesses, alleys between houses and thick shrubbery should be avoided, and that passive surveillance should be facilitated by maintaining clear sight lines from the home.

Newman's ideas in regard to the way physical space could be shaped to encourage more socially acceptable behaviour were taken up in this country by Alice Coleman, and are often associated with the approach known as 'environmental determinism'. In somewhat controversial research, Coleman argued that certain design features of estates such as aerial walkways and numbers of entries and staircases, could be correlated with indicators of 'social malaise' such as crime, poverty, litter, graffiti, dog dirt and numbers of children in care (Coleman, 1985). She believed that if the design features were changed then so too would be the indicators, resulting in more socially acceptable and stable environments. Her views were seized on by the Conservative administration of the time which subsequently implemented the Design Improvement Controlled Experiment (DICE) to redesign a number of so-called problem housing estates (often to little effect since tenants were not consulted and the underlying socio-economic factors were not addressed) (see Colquhoun, 2004).

The ideas promoted by Newman and Coleman have led to the standard adoption by social housing providers of certain design features, such as the inclusion of otherwise unusable strips of defensible space at the front of properties, a predilection for easily monitored cul de sacs and 'in curtilage' parking. They have also informed interventions by the Home Office and the police in regard to security against crime. Thus the work of the Home Office on 'safe neighbourhoods' has resulted in recommendations that developments should adhere to certain principles known as 'secured by design', and the incorporation of features such as cul de sacs, enclosure of spaces, CCTV and 'target-hardening' (see Colquhoun, 2004). To oversee this, architectural liaison officers have been appointed to police forces, and new social housing developments are expected to ensure that their layouts and house designs gain a secured by design certificate from the police. However, there is an interesting dilemma here, especially in the context of the discourse of urban design adopted elsewhere in government rhetoric. For much of the thinking of secured by design is anathema to urban designers, who believe in permeability, networks of connections through the urban fabric, the avoidance of enclosure and the encouragement of activity to increase the deterrent effect of more eyes on the street (see Bentley *et al.*, 1985; Hillier, 1988). This has led to an ongoing tension between the alternative merits of the 'grid' and the 'enclave', in which the urbanist perspective appears to be losing out to the more defensive preferences of the majority of residents, social housing providers and the police.

It is often suggested that one of the reasons why social housing estates attract crime is because of their size, their stigmatising and distinctive attributes, and their concentrations of disadvantaged people. As the twenty-first century has arrived, the new discourse of social inclusion, mixed communities and sustainability has begun to see attempts to redress this situation, albeit confined largely to the building of new housing. Thus it is argued that the spatial segregation and design distinctiveness of the past should be avoided, and that social and private housing should be spatially integrated and indistinguishable in regard to design. To some extent this has already begun to happen; for example even by the 1980s local authorities were appreciating the need to build more domestic scale units, and similarly as housing associations have become the main new providers they have continued their traditional policies of building low rise dwellings, albeit often now in larger concentrations. In addition the pressure on private housebuilders to build on brownfield sites means that private sector housing is more likely to be in spatial proximity to social housing. However, real integration would mean the proper interspersing of public and private housing and the end of any design distinction. This is not as yet being achieved, despite the requirement on housebuilders to provide affordable housing in their developments and the new emphasis on public private partnerships. It would appear that the main barrier here is the attitude of the speculative housebuilders, who do not take kindly to interference in their market decisions, and who do not believe that any self-respecting owner occupier would choose to live in proximity to a social housing tenant.

The private sector product

The actions of private housebuilders are dominated not by regulators or by designers but by the pursuit of profit and appeal to the market. Thus historically housebuilders have sought to build what they feel will attract potential purchasers, and have had their own views as to the most suitable style and image to purvey. For the most part this has been informed by the notion that since: 'every Englishman was, or felt he was, a disinherited country gentleman' (Burnett, 1986: 255) then the preferred style would always be a variation of the 'pseudo-rustic'. However, this is not to say that styles in the private sector have not altered at all, nor that they have not been informed to some degree by changing design fashions. But that this has never brought them within the parameters of the prevailing design orthodoxy has been consistently deplored by principled architects and designers, whose animadversions are additionally: 'compounded by an anti-suburban snobbery and lack of understanding of housing as a consumer good that persists to this day' (Carmona, 2001: 20; see also Edwards, 1981).

As discussed in Chapter 3, speculative housebuilding expanded rapidly in the 1930s as for the first time owner occupation came within the reach of ordinary middle class people. The product that was devised was geared specifically to meet their aspirations and deliberately marked a complete transformation in style and location from what had gone before. Banished was consignment to the drab inner city terrace and a life dominated by work, and instead was substituted the idyll of semi-detached suburbia with its emphasis on family and leisure. The low density housing that was built was typically on the theme of the rustic and the traditional, with much use made of features such as gables, overhanging eaves, porches, mock timbering, leaded windows, stained glass, and ornamental brickwork and tiling. Gradually this suburban promise spread along arterial routes and into the countryside, often in large estates that were reminiscent in terms of density, layout, greenery and garden provision of the principles espoused by the Garden City movement and the Tudor Walters Report. However, by this time local authorities had reverted to a predominantly plain and high density terraced form, so the new suburban home remained suitably distinctive for the emerging class of discerning buyers. This sense of distinction was further maintained by a spatial distancing from council housing, a distancing which was felt so essential that when in 1934 a new private sector development was built next to a council housing estate in Oxford, a seven foot wall, famously known as the Cutteslowe Wall, was erected as a symbolic barrier. Significantly, neither in the 1930s nor later, did housebuilders (with rare exceptions) adopt the modernist style promoted by the architectural profession. It was felt that the straight lines, streamlined effects and geometrical shapes would never be appreciated by the mass of owner occupiers in Britain. It was a language with which the majority could not connect in relation to the domestic home.

After the Second World War the expansion of suburbia continued, but housebuilders were initially obliged to provide more 'utilitarian' housing due to post-war austerity. As restrictions were lifted, there was more diversification than had prevailed in the 1930s. This was partly due to the entry to owner occupation of a wider cross-section of the populace, and the concomitant need to reflect a greater variety of purchasing power and taste. Thus between the 1960s and the 1980s more expensive housing exhibited a return to more fanciful and retrospective styles, such as the 'Tudorbethan' and the 'Neo-Georgian', with the occasional interspersion of the 'Colonial' (see Gray, 1994). For the less well off there were more functional and contemporary styles, including what is sometimes referred to as the 'Scandinavian' or 'Anglo-Scandinavian', with large windows, open plan rooms, and the use of timber boarding and tile hanging (Burnett, 1986; Edwards, 1981).

As we have moved into the postmodern age with its emphasis on individuality, identity, image and lifestyle, a more eclectic and diverse mix of house styles has appeared, reflecting also greater affluence and the impact of consumerism. On suburban and greenfield sites these styles tend to be based on a 'Neo-vernacular', with referents to the features of traditional domestic architecture which consumers equate with 'character', such as natural materials, pitched roof construction, small paned windows, decorative string courses, finials, canopied porches, balustrades and panelled doors. On urban and brownfield sites there has been more of an attempt to at least flirt with the more eclectic range of styles of postmodernism, often involving the incorporation of romanticised historic referents such as nautical features on waterfront developments. What is different in both cases, however, is that instead of all houses being identical, as was the case from the 1960s to the 1980s, there is now a variety of finish and ornamentation to give the impression of distinctiveness. Such features are easy to accommodate within the framework of the production and use by housebuilders of their standard types, since many of them involve little more than relatively inexpensive cosmetic detailing. But as with the standard plans of the interiors these still produce a standardised elevational technique, reinforcing what is in effect a language of 'house styles': a Barratt house is recognisably a Barratt house wherever it is located, and it has a different vocabulary from a Wimpey house.

As the twentieth century drew to a close, the new agendas of urban renaissance, sustainability and improved design began to affect even private sector housebuilders. Required to produce more housing on brownfield sites they have been obliged to appreciate the impact on the surrounding urban form, whilst local authorities have imposed ever stricter controls on matters of design. They have also been required to adopt the Part M accessibility regulations, although in other regards their accommodation of the new diversity seems to be limited to the addition of office space in larger houses, and the occasional inclusion of 'live/work' units in city locations. However, as the more advantageous sites have diminished in number, developers have begun to recognise the need to be more proactive in producing innovative and eye-catching design. Hence in a departure from tradition, architects are increasingly being commissioned to design bespoke products and improve on the limitations of in-house expertise and standardised outputs (Biddulph *et al.*, 2004). It is this which has helped to encourage a renewed interest by architects in the design of housing, in which ironically some have been drawn back to the precepts of modernism as a suitable residential style for a certain class of people. Thus have arisen the slick, glitzy and technologically sophisticated tower block apartments of High-Tech Modernism, targeted at those whose lifestyle is go-getting, youthful and affluent.

Unlike the social housing sector, the private sector has to market its product. Here, as Biddulph (1995) points out, speculative housebuilders have become adept at manipulating the visual character, or sign value, of developments in order to appeal to consumers and their aspirations. In the past this has focused on images of traditionalism and domesticity, and whilst this still prevails, there is increasingly an orientation towards the postmodern concerns of individuality, lifestyle, exclusivity and security. This requires attention to instant effect, or 'kerb appeal', through house type mix, spacing of units, layout and landscaping, and elevational treatment, in order to lure prospective customers to the next stage, the viewing of a show home. Here impression management is all, with interiors professionally designed to luxury standards, expensive furniture carefully arranged to maximise the sense of space, and tastefully restrained displays of pictures, coffee-table books and flowers. The marketing process also requires careful consideration of the naming of a development to convey the right image for each market segment (see Collins and Blake, 2004). A variety of themes predominate, such as nostalgia, the natural world, royalty and aristocracy, history and heritage, security and refuge. This accounts for the prevalence of such names as 'Lavender Fields', 'The Village', 'Church Farm', 'Badger's Meade', 'Spinners Meadow', 'Tanners Acre', 'Regents Mews', 'Duchess Court', 'Badminton Park', 'Saxon Mews', 'Brunel Court', 'Austen Grange', 'the Island' and 'Atlantic Haven' (sourced from the publicity material of a cross-section of housebuilders). House types too are subject to marketing scrutiny for presentational impact. Thus, for example, selections of bird or tree names are chosen to conjure up images of rurality, or the names of stately homes, famous race courses and spa towns are used to connote social prestige and grandeur. However, in line with the new sophistication of the urban product, there is also increasing recourse to a more esoteric choice of names, the deciphering of which requires the discernment of cultural and intellectual capital. Thus in inner city Manchester is found the Crosby Homes development 'the Hacienda', located on the site of the famous Hacienda club, and Taylor Woodrow's 'Macintosh Village', so named because it stands where once there was a raincoat factory. In Cardiff, Redrow is promoting two new high rise schemes: 'Celestia', with its subtexts of homes fit for stars, reaching for the stars, and finding the future in the stars; and 'Altolusso', with the latinate overtones of high level dalliance or game playing. Leanings to the highbrow are also conveyed in house type names, as for example, in the choice in the Celestia scheme between the star studded virtues of the 'Maia', the 'Atlas', the 'Capella', the 'Altair', the 'Vega', the 'Electra' and the 'Sirius', or in Wimpey's offering within its classical *optima* 'collection' of the *ultima*, the *libra*, the *lara*, the *maxima* and the *practica*.

Marketing literature too, whether in sales brochures, on websites, or in newspaper advertisements, is manipulated to give developments meanings which will resonate with prospective customers (see Biddulph, 1995; Carmona, 2001).

In suburban or rural areas the imagery almost universally conjures up intimations of history, continuity, rusticity and nostalgia. Appeal is made to people's sense of what the countryside represents: 'the perfect place to put down roots', as an advertisement for a new Redrow home metaphorically proclaims, accompanied by the symbol of a strong tree on a green sward. This language of the rural idyll has a stronger impact if it can be combined with a sense of heritage, tradition, prestige and continuity, as captured in the marketing of a new development by Abbey Manor Homes: 'Enjoy a view at Abbots Meade … splendid traditionally built quality homes set adjacent to Grade I listed former Abbey and Tithe Barn, enjoying a village "street scene" design …'. Much of this is written in Gothic script to reinforce the message of authentic history and venerable erudition.

The image projected for city living is more diverse. The conversion of warehouses and similar buildings into apartments lends itself to evocations of heritage, whilst the concept of 'loft living' has been successfully promoted to create an image of urban lifestyle which appeals to people working in the cultural sector (see URBED *et al.*, 1999; and Chapter 9). But as development activity has had to turn to less attractive locations which do not hold much intrinsic appeal, marketing has had to be ever more carefully constructed. For example Crest, now Crest Nicholson, have 'sold' such a development in Bristol by focusing on both its traditional qualities and its contemporary credentials. Thus its attractions are revealed as those of a place with a historic port, good architecture and proximity to countryside, together with the opportunity for a cosmopolitan lifestyle offering: 'the very best of international cuisine, the lively beat of musical venues and the cultural diversities of stage and screen' (marketing literature, cited in URBED *et al.*, 1999: 10). The imagery adopted by developers also speaks to the individualism and sophistication of those who have demanding but exciting and well rewarded work. Here, by contrast to the recall of tradition and the sense of rootedness in times past, developers are connecting with the reality of the new global, postmodern age, and emphasising individuality, self-obsession, stylish living, discrimination and the ability to relax in a safe and secure environment. Thus for example, a luxury Barratt scheme refers to: 'a home that's the last word in sophisticated style … stunning atrium apartments designed for the discerning and created for those who truly appreciate the finer things in life'. With more dramatic impact, an advertisement by Canary Riverside for a development in London consisting of 322 luxury apartments, 24 hour security, secure car parking, health club, spa, swimming pool, tennis court, landscaped gardens and restaurant, uses metaphor to achieve its desired effect. Accompanied by an aerial view of the site, the text declares: 'the new jet set have landed on their feet', are 'coming in to land' and achieving their destination of the 'arrivals lounge'. The image created is of a safe and contained total living environment, allowing a period of brief relaxation away from vexatious places and noisome people before the transient residents jet off in pursuit of their virtual lifestyles.

The creation of these images, their nuances, their capacity to catch the eye and connect at one and the same time with a fashionable lifestyle, individual aspiration and traditional values, reveals an almost uncanny perspicacity in the marketing fraternity. It also emphasises that the market determinant will never be a willingness to conform to rigorous standards of design or quality for their own sake but only to the extent to which these can be played within the market and turned into presentational impact – and hence into profit. The manipulation of the built form in the achievement of these aims is in effect another manifestation of the way in which built form becomes text; the characteristics of location, style and appearance are utilised to frame and structure marketing discourse, and the discourse then reflects meaning back on the form itself. Beyond this, the discourse has its own story to tell in revealing and reproducing the current preoccupations and structures of society; notably the insecurities and ambivalences faced by individuals, and their desperate desire to find identity, meaning and a place of safety.

Part II

Issues, projects and processes

6 Revisioning the village

> The sounds of England, the tinkle of the hammer on the anvil in the country smithy, the corncrake on a dewy morning, the sound of the scythe against the whetstone, and the sight of the plough team coming over the brow of the hill, the sight that has been seen in England since England was a land … The wild anemones in the woods in April, the last load at night of hay being drawn down a lane … the smell of wood smoke coming up in an autumn evening … These things strike down into the very depths of our nature, and touch chords that go back to the beginning of time and the human race, but they are chords that with every year of our life sound a deeper note in our innermost being.
>
> (Baldwin, 1926, cited in Wright, 1985: 82)

The sentiment portrayed in the passage above resonates with the British psyche as much today as when it was written 80 years ago. The image it conjures up is of a timeless English village set harmoniously within a sunlit pastoral landscape, with a church, a village green, a farm, and a scattering of picturesque cottages. It is of course, an idealised village, but given its significance in providing a symbol both of our history and our sense of identity, its image is deeply embedded in our national consciousness. In essence, it belongs to that category of the imagination that includes the myths of the golden age, the Garden of Eden and the rural idyll.

As well as binding us together in a shared narrative, such myths provide what is perhaps a necessary mental contrast to the hectic and disorienting reality of our urbanised lives. The late twentieth and early twenty-first centuries have brought globalisation, the emergence of new technologies, dramatic social, economic and demographic change, the expansion of the consumer society, and the search for new lifestyles and experiences. The impact of these has been to instil insecurity and the loss of the known and the familiar. It is not surprising then that this is counterbalanced by a search for cultural continuity and rootedness, and a renewed interest in history and heritage. Nostalgia for the past also serves to re-engage us with the primal myths, and this in turn helps to persuade us that a return to a state of innocence, timelessness and communion with nature may yet be within our grasp.

It is in this context that a new discourse of the village has emerged in the UK. This discourse has been appropriated to refer to a variety of somewhat different and often contrasting types of settlement form that have recently emerged within our urbanised society, such as the 'urban village', the 'millennium village', the 'televillage', the 'retirement village', the 'leisure village', the 'ecovillage' and even the 'global village'. Each of these village manifestations has been devised and driven by different interests and with different underlying values, and it is not always clear whether the village rhetoric has been adopted instrumentally or coincidentally. However, the use of the word 'village' would seem in each case to be an attempt to indicate a place which, by contrast to other places, will promise such qualities as identity, intimacy, continuity, cohesion and security. Apart from this commonality, the various 'villages' are inherently very disparate: at the two extremes of scale are the global village, representing the world rendered small, immediately accessible but 'virtual' in the context of instant communication; and the ecovillage, as a group of co-residents living in harmony and symbiosis with the local ecosystem (see Chapter 10). Between them in scale lie the other 'villages', each of which has a different emphasis and purpose.

It is with the village concept that this chapter is concerned. It looks first at the discourses which have constructed rural (village) and urban life as being essentially in opposition, and then at how it was subsequently 'discovered' that certain facets of rural life could nonetheless still be found within the city. It then moves on to consider two of the recent manifestations of the village which seem to have particular pertinence in the context of an urbanised and globalised society; the 'urban village' and the 'televillage'. The way in which specific examples of these have then been implemented on the ground are presented through the case studies of Bordesley in Birmingham, interesting because of its disputed status as an 'urban village', and the Acorn televillage in Crickhowell, Wales, the only representative of its kind in the UK.

The village and the city

The symbolic potency of the village lies not only in the way in which it evokes an imagined rural past, but also in its place within a frame of the imagination in which the countryside is perpetually opposed to the city:

> On the country has gathered the idea of a natural way of life: of peace, innocence and simple virtue. On the city has gathered the idea of an achieved centre: of learning, communication, light. Powerful hostile associations have also developed: on the city as a place of noise, worldliness and ambition; on the country as a place of backwardness, ignorance, limitation.
>
> (Williams, 1975: 9)

Such contrasting views of country and city reflect an opposition between nature and culture, between simplicity and complexity, or between God and humankind, as in the aphorism 'God made the country and man made the town'. And for the most part the image of the country and of village life represents all that is good: the natural, bountiful, unchanging, simple and tranquil. The image of the city, on the other hand, represents all that is bad: the unnatural, alienating, complex, chaotic and dysfunctional. It is the selectivity of this imagery which has proved enduring in the representations of the country and the city, whereas one more tempered with reality would concede that country life has been fraught with episodes of poverty, famine and exploitation, whilst city life can offer opportunity, liberation, excitement and riches. Arguably it is only since the early days of capitalism and industrialisation that the good/evil opposition has become so deeply embedded in consciousness, and it has been suggested that this may well have arisen as a mechanism for coping with adjustment to a progressively urbanising and apparently alienating world (Williams, 1975). Indeed, there is something specifically British about this situation, since on the Continent, which was far less intensively industrialised than Britain, the city remained a centre for urbanity and a focus for cultural life. It is in British literary texts too, that we can see this opposition between town and country reflected and reproduced in the writings of eighteenth and nineteenth century authors. Thus at any time we can visit the romantic poets (such as Wordsworth) to reinforce the view that nature and the natural world are pure, elemental and uplifting, or draw on the chronicles of social commentators (such as Dickens and Engels) to bear witness to the squalor and depravity of the city.

But it is not just in mythical and literary thought that the contrast between city and country has been evoked. It was also reproduced by the early urban sociologists in their search for a science of social systems and social relations. As witnesses of what appeared to be a profound dislocation of social life, they presented rural and urban social life as polarised social realities. Rural social relations were constructed as intimate and personal, binding people together in overlapping and reciprocal roles, whilst urban social relations were constructed as instrumental and isolating, creating distance and alienation in a disintegrating world. The distinction between these two realities was constructed as a discourse of oppositions: the *Gemeinschaft* and *Gesellschaft* of Toennies; the 'organic' and 'mechanical' solidarity of Durkheim, and the 'folk' and 'urban' society of Redfield (see Savage and Warde, 1993). Implicit behind the construction of these essentially artificial 'ideal types' was the perpetuation of the myth that rural, folk and village life was necessarily good, whilst urban, town and city was necessarily bad. Predicated upon this was a second myth, that by their very nature the structures and values attributed to rural life could not exist in an urban setting.

The construction of the structures of rural and urban life as two opposite and absolute kinds was not without challenge. Ethnographic studies of villages and small rural communities showed that they could in fact be riven by rivalries and conflicts (see Savage and Warde, 1993), whilst similar studies in urban areas suggested that there could after all exist there the mutually supportive and enduring social ties formerly associated only with rural life (see, for example, Suttles, 1968; Whyte, 1943; Lewis, 1959). Such an insertion of 'village-like' qualities into the city is more often associated with the American sociologist Gans. In his study of the West End of Boston, he makes a contrast not between the country and the city, but between the 'urban village' and the 'urban jungle'. The former is said to represent a socially functional area in which ethnic migrants have sought to adapt their essentially non-urban (hence rural) culture to the urban setting, whilst the latter refers to malfunctioning areas of transients, psychopaths, criminals and prostitutes, as exemplified in 'Skid Row' districts. In a footnote, Gans states: 'These are purely descriptive terms, and should not be taken too literally. They are not ecological concepts, for neither in economic, demographic, or physical terms do such areas resemble villages or jungles' (Gans, 1962: 4).

This sense of the village within the city is also reflected in British sociology. Young and Willmott, in their study of Bethnal Green, refer to the 100–200 people who make up the population of each street as: 'a sort of "village"' (Young and Willmott, 1962: 109). Pahl expands on Gans' localised application of the term urban village, suggesting that in cities across the world 'urban villages' exist in which the social behaviour of migrants displays elements both of their rural roots and of their urban adaptation (Pahl, 1968: 27). More expansive reference to urban villages occurs in the work of Taylor, who suggests that: 'something called an "urban village" … even if the definition relates possibly more to what is in the mind than to what is on the ground' might bestow the capacity to find in an urban setting both the close networks typical of the village and the wider opportunity provided by the city (Taylor, 1973: 194).

These discoveries of village-like entities in the city are inherently mental and social constructs. The value of such constructs has been in redeeming the negative discourses of urban life, and in giving substance to, or 'fixing', the idea that there can exist within an otherwise oppressive city, areas which offer sanctuary and a sense of belonging. But such a discourse of the village in the city remained for some decades just that, a discourse that existed in the mind and in academic texts, but with no salience for those who designed or planned our cities. Instead it was the discourse of neighbourhood and community that from the 1920s attracted the attention of policy makers and practitioners and informed the urban utopias of, for example, the Garden Cities and the New Towns (Biddulph, 2000). In recent years, however, the village imagery has gained a new legitimacy, and in its guise as the 'urban village' has been appropriated as a new and more befitting model for urban development.

The urban village

The first articulation of the term 'urban village' in the British context is generally credited to the Prince of Wales, first in a speech and then in his book *A Vision for Britain*:

> I am hoping that we can encourage the development of urban villages in order to reintroduce human scale, intimacy and a vibrant street life. These factors can help to restore to people their sense of belonging and pride in their own particular surroundings.
>
> (HRH The Prince of Wales, 1989: 4)

Driven by a conviction that his vision could be translated into reality, the Prince in 1989 assembled a small and elite group of developers, housebuilders, planners, architects and other urban actors. Many of these had already been adversely affected by the structural situation of economic downturn and property recession and were therefore more receptive to alternative development approaches than might otherwise have been the case. A key member of the Urban Villages Group was the European architect, Leon Krier, whose antipathy to the devastation wrought by urban redevelopment was expressed in a commitment to the classical revivalist tradition in planning and design (Thompson-Fawcett, 1998a). This traditionalism naturally commended him to the Prince. Krier was also in touch with developments in the US, where he was an associate of the proponents of the 'New Urbanist' movement. This movement was engaging with the ideas of American urban theorists such as Christopher Alexander, Jane Jacobs and Kevin Lynch in the devising of concepts such as the traditional neighbourhood development (TND) and the transit oriented development (TOD) (see Biddulph, 2000; Calthorpe, 1993; Thompson-Fawcett, 1996).

The members of the UVG visited a number of places in the UK and overseas which were deemed to have 'character' and to 'work', such as the New Town of Edinburgh, Clerkenwell in London, and Montparnasse in Paris. They then sought to distil the principles which underlay the design of such places into a set of criteria which would lead to the development of more humane and sustainable urban environments. These criteria included: an optimum size of 3000–5000 people; a varied townscape; a sense of place; a lively street scene; maximum possible self-sufficiency; reduction in car use; traffic calming; pedestrian friendliness; community involvement and commitment; and a mix of uses, housing tenures, ages and social groups (Aldous, 1992, 1997). However, agreeing a name for the new type of development was somewhat contentious (Thompson-Fawcett, 1998b). Krier strongly urged the adoption of 'urban quarter' in the European tradition, but the others felt this did not have the right resonance for English speakers – it was not consonant with their *habitus*. Thus the term 'urban village' was decided on, although with some apparent hesitation:

> The word 'village' is, to be sure, much abused and over-used. But real villages have many of the essential characteristics we are arguing for; and, in a British context, *urban village* is convenient shorthand for what we are aiming at.
>
> (Aldous, 1997: 29, original emphasis)

There was no indication that any of the members of the UVG had heard of or were influenced by Gans' earlier use of the term urban village.

The first edition of the Urban Villages Report was launched in 1992 amidst much publicity and, by chance, on the very day that the bankruptcy was announced of the prestigious Canary Wharf enterprise in London Docklands. The coincidence of this downfall of capitalist excess and the promise of retrospective traditionalism could not have been more symbolically significant. It also resonated with contemporary institutional and public concern about the state of the urban environment. These factors, combined with the high profile of the group promoting the concept, helped to persuade government actors that the idea of the urban village was worth pursuing. This was illustrated by the emphasis on the urban village as a means to achieve more sustainable development in the revision of *PPG1* and in the document *Planning for Communities of the Future* (DoE, 1997a; DETR, 1998b). English Partnerships, the government's regeneration agency, also promoted urban villages as a model for the regeneration of brownfield sites, setting aside funds to pump prime or 'gap fund' initiatives so that they could be made viable (see Urban Villages Forum/English Partnerships, undated). Thus legitimised and given institutional endorsement the urban village concept was seen by many local authorities and developers as a normalising discourse which, if adopted, might not only secure acceptance for new developments but also attract funding. As a result both local authority led and developer led 'urban villages' began to appear across the UK. These varied considerably in size and type of location, and perhaps most crucially, in adherence to the principles set out by the Urban Villages Forum (UVF), the body which had succeeded the UVG to promote and support the urban village concept and to monitor its implementation (see Biddulph *et al*., 2003; Franklin *et al*., 2002).

In the opinion of the UVF only some 20 of the many manifestations of so-called urban villages are worthy of the name. Perhaps the best known of these is Poundbury in Dorset, built by the Prince on his own land within the Duchy of Cornwall, and masterplanned by Krier (see Thompson-Fawcett, 1996, 1998a). Poundbury exemplifies the initial conception of urban villages as being located on greenfield sites, but in order to accord with the emerging institutional agenda of the re-use of brownfield land the UVF soon altered this position. Hence the majority of the other UVF endorsed developments are regeneration schemes such as the Jewellery Quarter in Birmingham, West Silvertown in London, Little Germany in Bradford, Crown Street in Glasgow and Llandarcy in Wales. However the UVF has not been able to prevent other developers from adopting the urban village appellation, indicating that it has not been able either to control the urban village agenda or to 'fix' the criteria by which an urban village can be identified. For these reasons urban village designation has become little more than a brand; a badge of respectability for any private sector development and hence with little meaning and less credibility.

The legitimacy of the concept has also faltered following its apparent abandonment by New Labour, which has now moved on to millennium villages, sustainable communities and sustainable urban extensions (ODPM, 2002; Prince's Foundation, 2000). The concept of the millennium village, promoted by the Deputy Prime Minister John Prescott, is however, still rooted in the urban village discourse as is clear from its description as a more high profile and sustainable variant of an urban village (DETR, 1998b). To this end millennium villages are to be characterised by a stronger commitment both to the creation of community and, more importantly, to environmental awareness than was the case with urban villages. Thus greater consideration is to be given to such factors as integrated tenures, community facilities, biodiversity, the minimisation of resource consumption, innovative construction methods, energy efficiency and adaptability within the home.

The first millennium village, announced in 1997, was Greenwich Millennium Village (GMV) in London. Despite the dilution of many of the original design, environmental and community targets due to cost implications and lack of commitment (Carmona, 2001; DETR, 2000e), GMV has undoubtedly achieved its intention of being a flagship and even iconic development. This has vindicated the vision of Prescott, for whom GMV was not only to be a symbol of the new century but also a template for future millennium villages. In 1998 the second millennium village was named as Allerton Bywater, a former colliery site near Leeds. Subsequently it was announced that the proposed urban village scheme for the regeneration of Ancoats in East Manchester should be redesignated as a third millennium project, to be called somewhat perversely, New Islington. However, by this time, discourse had moved on again, and this was to be not a millennium village but a 'millennium community'.

This shift in discourse from 'village' to 'community' appears not to have taken place in any overt way, but to have evolved in synchrony with the increased institutional emphasis on a discourse of community – as in mixed communities, balanced communities, New Deal for Communities, and most recently, sustainable communities. This is reflected in the cessation of the link in policy discourse between millennium communities and urban villages, and the substitution of the link between millennium villages (or communities) and sustainable communities (DETR, 2000e; English Partnerships, 2003; Urban Task Force, 1999). Furthermore, the urban village finds no reference in the Urban Task Force Report (perhaps not surprising given the leadership of the anti-traditionalist Richard Rogers), nor has it been included as a development model to be emulated in subsequent planning guidance such as *PPG3* (DETR, 2000b) or the new *PPS1* (ODPM, 2005c). Thus the only agency which now keeps it alive is that of the somewhat elitist anachronism of the Prince's Foundation into which the UVF has now been absorbed, together with the opportunistic appropriation of the term by speculative developers. The latter too, will move on when they perceive that the advantages once afforded by urban village designation have run their course.

An urban village for Bordesley

Bordesley lies one and a half miles to the east of Birmingham city centre and was once a separate settlement. It was incorporated into the City in 1838 and together with its neighbouring districts formed the industrial heartland of Birmingham, enjoying full employment and high output for many generations. However, by the 1970s and 1980s manufacturing was starting to decline. In East Birmingham many industries closed down, unemployment reached 31 per cent, and the whole area became one of the most deprived in England. In Bordesley itself acres of land became derelict. Those who could moved out, whilst those who were left began to experience multifarious social problems. This was exacerbated by the fact that, in contrast to neighbouring areas, the old jerry-built terraces and back to backs had not been cleared and replaced by council housing in the renewal efforts of the 1960s and 1970s. Nor had there been either then or subsequently any significant new housing investment in the older council housing or the private sector. This led Bordesley to be known as 'the land that time forgot' (Allison, 1998: 23).

By the 1980s Birmingham City Council (BCC) was seeking a way to address the problems facing East Birmingham. The then Minister for the Environment, Nicholas Ridley, suggested that it would make a good candidate for a UDC, currently the type of public private partnership favoured by the Conservatives for regeneration (see Chapter 4). However, given the constitution of a UDC as a body which effectively takes control away from local authorities, this was unacceptable to the Labour controlled Birmingham City Council. After much negotiation an alternative solution was found in the form of an Urban Development Agency (UDA), to be set up as a private limited company with representation from the City Council. The UDA was named Birmingham Heartlands Limited (BHL), and was officially launched in 1988.

It soon became apparent that the multifaceted role of planner, property assembler and developer that BHL had attributed to itself was over ambitious. Furthermore, as a UDA it could not receive targeted government funds, and without these the preferred strategy could not be made viable. The new Minister for the Environment, Michael Heseltine, also a supporter of UDCs, recommended that BHL should adopt the UDC model after all. Eventually a compromise was reached, with a 50:50 split between council and government membership, and the appointment of a dedicated team from the BCC planning department. Thus in 1992 Birmingham Heartlands Development Corporation (BHDC) was established, with a life span of five years, later extended to six.

The consultants commissioned by BHL to produce a development strategy for the East Birmingham area were Roger Tym and Partners. In their report (1988) they stressed the need for a privately led initiative to bring in new employment, housing and services. This would need to be stimulated by initial public provision of environmental and infrastructure improvements, and the marketing of the area in such a way that it would seem as attractive a proposition to speculative housebuilders as a greenfield site. It was suggested that design briefs should be prepared to ensure high quality design, and that existing residents should be consulted both about the proposals and their own aspirations. Bordesley was identified as an appropriate area for a new residential community or 'village' (Roger Tym and Partners, 1988: 25), due to its size of 38.4 hectares (95 acres) and its self contained character, bordered by a mainline railway and major distributor roads. Tym recommended that the opportunities provided by the Grand Union Canal and the existing (if derelict) open space should be maximised, whilst a central focus should be provided in the vicinity of the canal with shops, a pub and other community facilities. Suitable sites for housebuilding could be found on vacated land, and the amount could be increased by the relocation of some of the remaining small industries. A diversified mix of tenures of a total of 925 refurbished and new units was considered appropriate, with new houses to be semi-detached or terraced, built in loops and cul de sacs to a density of 13 per acre.

Although it is clear that the Tym strategy did not refer to Bordesley specifically as an 'urban village', nonetheless it was so described in the development framework for Bordesley which was subsequently prepared by the UDA (East Birmingham UDA, 1989). The exact reasons why this occurred and by whom the phrase was first used are unclear. In researching the developments in Bordesley after the event (see Franklin, 2003), it became apparent that different actors put different constructions on the adoption of the urban village rubric. Some were convinced it had been in the Tym report, if not in the published version, then in the previous draft version. The author of the latter was fairly sure it was not, because the concept as promoted by the Prince of Wales had not then arisen (personal communication). Others felt that as a designation it had evolved naturally due to the fact that it had been referred to as a 'village' but was clearly in an urban setting. Others again said it had been introduced due to the connection of BHDC (as an organisation) and the Chair (as an individual) with the Urban Villages Forum, despite the fact that this body was not formed until after the launch of the Urban Villages Report in 1992. This vagueness is reflected in the discourse of the Bordesley Development Framework. For this does not define the nature of the urban village concept, nor detail the design criteria. In relation to housing it states:

> Design of housing should reflect the urban village concept, a variety of building designs and facing materials may be proposed, but linked by a

consistent theme i.e. gate entrances into cul-de-sacs, house styles to vary for each courtyard, treatments of walls, fences, roads, car-parks, walkways, lighting and street furniture.

(East Birmingham UDA, 1989: 15)

The implementation of the £80 million strategy for Bordesley was in the hands of the Bordesley Working Party, and it was this body which had to co-ordinate, negotiate and mediate between the often conflicting interests and activities of a wide variety of agents. These included: a number of BCC departments (planning, economic development, leisure and community services, environmental services, education, housing); various speculative housebuilders; several housing associations; the Bournville Village Trust; British waterways; training and employment agencies; health services; local industries; local community groups; and existing residents, most of whom were council tenants. The latter needed considerable reassurance that the plans for Bordesley would not mean an influx of affluent outsiders and the consequent pricing out of the market of local people.

Three major housebuilders, Bryant, Wimpey and Tarmac, had been involved from the start of the proposals. Rather than following the normal procedure of competitive tender, BCC had offered each a 'footprint' in the area, since without early commitment by the private sector the housing led regeneration scheme would not be viable. Indeed, the centrality of the housebuilders to the success of the strategy gave them considerable powers in the bargaining process. In order to maximise incentives for what would essentially be housing at relatively affordable prices, hence with low profit margins, land was offered at below market value. Further inducements were offered to the housebuilders in the form of central or local government grants for the costs of site decontamination.

The initial three housebuilders were later joined by Woolwich, Bellway and Barratt, but at no stage did they act as a consortium. Instead they were essentially in competition, with a far from unified approach. BCC also involved two housing associations, Focus and Family, as partners for the development of social housing for rent and shared ownership. Again this was done in an informal and unorthodox way, with selection based on the fact that they were well-known, and had current development programmes and assets (personal communication). Two smaller housing associations were offered infill sites at a later date, one of which was used for a hostel for homeless young people and caused some local opposition.

The many, generally small industries in Bordesley were treated in different ways according to their location and nuisance levels. Many were relocated, either to allow the assembly of land with a suitable critical mass for redevelopments, or to remove activities deemed incompatible with residential use. Other sites were offered in the BHDC area of East Birmingham, and in most cases these were accepted without the need for compulsory purchase orders. Others were permitted to remain, hence continuing to provide local employment, and were given grants to improve their premises. One industry, Carrs Paints, created problems for years. This had been in existence on the same site adjacent to the canal for 100 years, and massive relocation costs were demanded in full awareness of the strength of the bargaining position afforded by control over such a prime housebuilding site. After endless negotiation and with the help of a grant from the DoE, a deal was reached and the site released, several years after development elsewhere in Bordesley was well underway.

From the early days of the development of the strategy some discussion had taken place with Bournville Village Trust (BVT). BVT derived from the foundation of Bournville as the model estate for the Quaker owned Cadbury chocolate factory in Birmingham, and was a non-profit making trust with philanthropic aims. It also had a 100 year tradition of development, not only of housing but also of community facilities. The development director of BVT was extremely interested in the urban village idea and BVT eventually agreed to take on the development of the Village Centre, a proposition considered too risky for the private sector. The agreed scheme was for 29 flats, a village hall, a doctor's surgery, a dentist, a chemist's shop, a newsagent and general store, and one further shop unit (Figures 6.1, 6.2). BVT had to compromise on design aspects as Wimpey held the design and build contract, and they further had to compromise in respect of not restricting the general store from selling alcohol – against BVT's founding principles. Another

6.1   Entrance to Bordesley Village Centre. The village hall is on the right, the retained local landmark of the pub on the left, flats and doctor's surgery in the background. Note also the 'Heartlands vernacular' lamp standards and the symbolic 'gateway' entrance.

6.2 The Village Centre, showing shop units, dental surgery in the background, and hard and soft landscaping

6.3 Canal towpath improvements and the Village Bridge. Also illustrated are the rear of the village hall on the left and light industry in the background.

6.4   Bordesley Village gateway sign with private sector housing behind

6.5   'Heartlands vernacular' railings and gateway to the park

advantage deriving from BVT's involvement was their commitment to community involvement and development, hitherto somewhat marginalised in the BHDC approach – despite Tym's recommendations. With limited results BVT sought to involve the public in consultation on the Village Centre, and more specifically in the management of the village hall. There was more success after the appointment of a community development worker to set up and support activities such as a credit union, adult education classes, fun days and festivals, and work with the school. Further stimulation of community involvement derived from the emergence of a key local figure, the much liked and trusted nursery school manager. Her ability to 'speak the language' of both local people and professionals enabled her to act as a successful mediator between them.

By 2000 the regeneration of Bordesley was almost complete, nine years after the first new housing was begun. Fears that the whole housebuilding venture was a gamble proved unfounded as queues built up for the first units of housing, and indeed the entire housing programme sold without difficulty. BCC's aim to retain the existing population and to provide relatively low cost housing for people in Bordesley and adjacent areas was also realised, with 80–90 per cent coming from within two or three miles. In all, 750 new and 350 refurbished houses were provided, with a shift from virtually monotenure council housing to a reasonable mix of tenures. Environmental improvements have also been substantial, involving new landscaping, a new footbridge over the canal (the Village Bridge) and the reinstatement of the canal towpath (Figure 6.3). Throughout, the 'Heartlands vernacular' has been adopted for the design of railings, lighting standards and 'gateway' features, all in a distinctive bright red (Figures 6.1, 6.2, 6.4, 6.5). The school is no longer under threat, there is a new nursery school, old and new places of worship are thriving, and as far as the professionals are concerned there is far greater evidence of a real community than was previously the case. Residents, however, feel there is still considerable community apathy and an ongoing 'us and them' attitude between social housing residents, mainly those in the older council housing, and the new occupants. They are also dissatisfied with the location and limited facilities of the Village Centre, and are sceptical about the future of Bordesley now that the interventions of BHDC are over.

The main ambition for Bordesley was to achieve successful regeneration, and compared to this the application of the urban village concept was secondary. Thus it is not surprising that Bordesley manages to realise few of the accepted urban village criteria. This is particularly the case in regard to the design of the housing. In part this is due to the fact that development was started in the early 1990s when a more *laissez-faire* approach to planning and design still prevailed, and hence little control was exerted by BCC until the time of the two later Barratt developments on the Carrs Paints site. But more important was the housebuilders' position of power, given their centrality to the scheme, and none of them had any interest in the urban village concept or its implications. On the other hand, they did latch on to the emotive connotations of 'villageness' as a marketing device, referring in their promotional literature to 'Bordesley Village'.

The overall impression of Bordesley is of typical suburban development, with low density housing, cul de sac layouts and the standard house types of each developer, all set in enclaves without any sense of relationship either to each other or to the main thoroughfares (Figures 6.6, 6.7). This lack of urbanist design quality is also reflected in the fact that there is little sense of place or of vitality (other than in the school yard), and, despite relative permeability, there is only poor legibility. Although a reasonable mix of tenures has been achieved, new social (Figure 6.8) and private sector housing are generally distinguishable from each other, and there is only a partial attempt to integrate tenures within the same streets. There is some success in terms of mixed uses, but this is mainly in relation to education and leisure with employment limited to the few remaining light industries and few retail opportunities within the Bordesley boundary. It is clear that no attempts have been made to discourage either car ownership or use, and public transport is far from comprehensive in terms of the streets it covers. Certainly if an urban village is to have the vibrancy, architectural distinction, sense of identity or self-containedness of the imaginings of Prince Charles and the UVG, then Bordesley can only be a poor imitation. Indeed, when the UVF was lobbied for the recognition of Bordesley as an urban village, it was dismissed as just another housing estate. Despite this, when judged on its own merits it has won accolades, receiving between 1993 and 1998 a National Housing and Town

6.6   Private sector apartments and houses in typical cul de sac layout

6.7 New housing by two different private sector developers and a housing association (centre left). Note the lack of relationship to each other or the street, also the barrier of the brick wall and its invitation to graffiti artists.

6.8 A street of housing association units with porches, bin stores, and in curtilage parking within defensible space, all typical of the sector

Planning Council award, a prize from Birmingham Civic Society, a commendation by the West Midlands branch of the RTPI and a shortlisted entry for a national award for Partnership in Regeneration.

The televillage

The phenomenon of the televillage has emerged as a response to the structural transformation of the labour market and new developments in technology. The adoption of 'flexible' working practices and the shift from a manufacturing to an information economy has been facilitated by a digital revolution which has allowed much speedier transmission of data across time and space. Meanwhile, the advent of the world-wide web and the ability to create networks of users who can communicate at the click of a mouse, has meant that access to and use of electronic equipment has become at least as important as face to face contact in the newly globalised economy. Furthermore, the development since the late 1980s of portable and affordable personal computers and their marketing as desirable consumer goods has seen a dramatic increase in their purchase for the home (Silverstone and Hirsch, 1992). Once in the home, they are also potentially available for work purposes. This has facilitated the emergence of a new class of homeworking professionals usually described as 'teleworkers' to distinguish them from the traditional 'homeworkers' engaged in low-skilled piecework (see Felstead and Jewson, 2000). Although it is difficult to arrive at an accurate assessment of the numbers involved it would appear that there are increasing numbers of people in the UK who telework for all or part of the week, with estimates of 1.5 million people in 2000 (Dwelly, 2000) and 1.8 million in 2003 (Norwood, 2003).

At the institutional level, public policy interest in teleworking first arose in the US and Scandinavia. The US promoted the advantages of 'telecommuting' in the 1970s as a response to the oil crisis, and it has subsequently been supported by various states as a contribution to the environmental agenda (Gillespie *et al.*, 1995). In Scandinavia, teleworking has evolved from 1980 as a social and economic strategy to assist the populations of dispersed rural communities. Here the emphasis has been on the creation of neighbourhood centres or 'telecottages', which offer access to shared IT resources for both training and employment in a socially supportive environment. The idea of telecottages subsequently spread to the UK, where local authorities and national and regional development agencies have aided the establishment both of these and of similar 'telecentres' in the context of local economic development strategies. As a result there are now over 100 telecottages and telecentres, predominantly in rural areas, and with a particular concentration in Wales (Bibby, 2003). In Powys, for example, an area with the lowest density of population anywhere in England and Wales, there is a network of telecentres across the county which aim to provide the community, businesses and individuals with access to new communication technologies. Some commitment to the principle of teleworking has also been expressed at the level of national government, first through the Employment Act of 2002 which included the right for employees to demand to be allowed to telework under the flexible working provisions, and second through the introduction by Gordon Brown, Chancellor of the Exchequer, of tax allowances for employees working at home (TCA, 2003).

For many people the idea of working from home represents an almost utopian dream. It offers liberation from the daily commute, from the 'panopticon of the workplace' (Felstead and Jewson, 2000: 118) and from office politics. It also presents the alluring possibility of relocating to an idyllic rural situation in which a more acceptable work/life balance seems within reach, whilst the tedium of work will be minimised by its setting in the familiar and relaxing environment of their home. However, such a shift in workplace is not unproblematic. Apart from the potential social isolation, lack of stimulation, and need for the internalisation of discipline, there are also implications for the conceptualisation of the home and the maintenance of boundaries. For by working at home the practices and rituals of 'going to work' and 'coming home' established since the early days of the Industrial Revolution are elided. Furthermore, if work is reinserted into the home it can no longer unequivocally be a place dedicated to privacy, leisure and intimate relations. In many homes there is also the more practical issue of space, not only in terms of the accommodation of the necessary equipment, but also if clients are to be received. These, as outsiders, represent a potentially polluting invasion into the heart of the home. Decisions and compromises must therefore be made as to exactly where work is undertaken: in a spare room; in a corner of an existing room; in a converted garage; or perhaps even in a shed in the garden. In these ways working at home requires a new definition of both 'work' and 'home' in which a transformation of the old boundaries of time and space and the relationship between them must be renegotiated. What emerges is a new routine, with work fitted around domestic chores and able to be carried out early in the morning or late at night, and prepared for by the observance of rituals such as putting on a tie or 'walking to work' by taking a turn round the block or even the garden.

Some sectors of the housebuilding industry have recognised that the emergence of professional homeworking and teleworking has market potential. Thus there is an increasing tendency for new developments to include designated office space within at least some housing units, whilst some developers are experimenting with the more trendy 'live/work' units. Usually in urban areas, these combine living accommodation with dedicated space for a small retail or commercial business. However, the majority of people see teleworking as an ideal opportunity to leave the city behind and to settle in attractive rural locations. The drawback to this is that what at first appeared as a haven of tranquillity can soon be perceived as socially isolating. It is in response to this that the idea of the televillage has arisen. This consists of a 'wired village' (Gillespie *et al.*, 1995: 51); a 'village-like' supportive community in a cluster of dwellings, each of which is provided with office space and fibre optic connections to a local area network (LAN). As a development concept it has not so far attracted much interest, especially by institutional developers, and at the time of writing there are only two known rural televillages in the UK, one in Herefordshire and one in Powys. Both of these were developed by an individual with a personal commitment to teleworking, Ashley Dobbs (see below). There is also a project referred to as an 'urban televillage' in the inner city of Newcastle. Known as Silicon Alley this is part of a larger regeneration initiative and was developed by North East Workspace specifically for the design and multimedia businesses (see Silicon Alley, 2003).

A televillage for Crickhowell

Crickhowell is a long-established and attractive market town situated in the Brecon Beacons National Park in the Welsh county of Powys. The significant domestic architecture of Crickhowell has been recognised by the declaration of part of the town as a conservation area. Within this lies Upper House Farm, built in the mid-seventeenth century as the farmstead for the estate of the local landed gentry, the Rumseys. When the landowners had eventually fallen on hard times, the farm was taken over by the county council as a tenanted smallholding. Given the architectural distinction of the farmhouse it was listed Grade II* in 1963, along with some of the individual outbuildings in the adjacent farm courtyard, listed either Grade II* or Grade II. Despite this the farm was subject to some unsympathetic updating in the 1970s, and in the 1980s became increasingly derelict after the farmer's widow was left in sole charge. The site was then designated for housing in the local plan as part of a more extensive area to include the adjacent former highways depot, also owned by the county council, and eventually developed by Wales and West Housing Association. It was Upper House Farm and the land surrounding it which drew the attention of Ashley Dobbs.

Ashley Dobbs is a man of an entrepreneurial disposition. At the age of 22 he raised capital to develop holiday properties in Britain and in the Mediterranean, running the business from London on a teleworking basis. In 1988 he attended a conference on villages and small towns in Germany, where he heard about Scandinavian experiments with telecottages (Bibby, 2003). This inspired Dobbs to set up the organisation 'Telecottages UK', the activities of which later became subsumed into the Telecottages Association, and of which he is at the time of writing the Chair. He also decided to sell his business and invest some of the proceeds in the development of a small televillage (a 'telehamlet') of eight houses at Perton Farm in Herefordshire, to which he subsequently moved. This was the beginning of the company Acorn Televillages, which was not only intended to be a profit making venture, but was also to incorporate Dobbs' commitment to technology as a means to establish and maintain home office based employment in rural areas (Dobbs, 1993). However, the prime motivation was undoubtedly business discretion and the profit motive, as illustrated by the fact that Dobbs has proved unwilling to pass on any facts which may be used by others to competitive advantage (see Barton, 2000; Upper House Farm, 2002).

In his search for a new and larger site Dobbs became aware in 1993 of Upper House Farm in Crickhowell – not geographically far from his base in Herefordshire and in a county where he knew the telecentre concept was well established. Furthermore, the site had the advantage of being already designated for housing. After establishing that the authorities involved would not be averse to an application for a televillage, Dobbs submitted his plans. These were for a telecottage in the farmhouse; workshops, studios and a youth club in the farm outbuildings; and 32 houses and two flats, all to include home offices. In proposing a diversity of house types, Dobbs argued that he was creating a beneficial 'property ladder', especially when set in the context of the Wales and West housing association scheme for affordable housing on the adjacent site. The application was accompanied by detailed site plans, floor plans and elevations for each house type, and a persuasive 'Concept' statement:

> The recent vast improvements in technology and telecommunications give us a unique opportunity to correct the balance between city and country. In effect, we can work anywhere. This is not a dream ... Yet teleworking as it is known does have a major disadvantage. Humans are very social animals. If you take away their office environment they miss meeting other people, gossiping and exchanging ideas.
>
> (Dobbs, 1993: 1)

The statement goes on to emphasise the aesthetic design, sustainability and craftsmanship that will be incorporated in the design, and the contribution the scheme will make to Crickhowell, especially in regard to the provision of jobs and housing for local people. Opportunistically perhaps, the architects he chose were the in-house team of Powys County Council.

In principle both Powys County Council, as the county authority and current landowners (and in effect, agent), and Brecon Beacons National Park (BBNP), as the local planning authority, supported Dobbs' idea to develop a televillage. It seemed an ideal solution which would address several pressing issues. These included the need for economic regeneration and job creation; the provision of more housing, at least some of which would be relatively affordable; and the solution to the problem of the deterioration of the listed buildings. Powys County Council was therefore minded to sell the site to Dobbs without putting it on the open market. However, the granting of planning permission was far from straightforward, with a number of organisations, interest groups and individuals putting forward conflicting viewpoints and expecting these to be taken into consideration. Powys County Council was already in support of the scheme, but demanded alterations to the initial plans in respect of the upgrading of highways and parking provision. CADW, the quango with responsibility for Welsh historic monuments, had also to be consulted about the plans for the historic buildings, as had the Countryside Council for Wales. This latter body discovered that a number of bat species were roosting on the site and declared that these must not be disturbed. Crickhowell Community Council objected that the plans submitted by Dobbs lacked sufficient detail, whilst the local Civic Society thought that Crickhowell had enough houses without the need to sacrifice a 'green wedge' on the fringes of the town. Furthermore it believed that the County Council had stripped itself of an asset in a private deal without due consultation, and without following the proper procedure of putting the site on the open market. Individual residents of Crickhowell also expressed their concerns in letters to local papers and to BBNP. A few were supportive of the whole concept, particularly the sustainability features, the community benefits and the fact that provision was being made for at least some relatively low cost housing. The majority, however, were in opposition, again raising issues about asset stripping and the loss of open space, whilst those in the immediate vicinity were naturally concerned about the impact on their own properties. There were also complaints that the scheme was for a specialist group of users who by definition would not be locals, together with speculation about the real motives of the developer – as an outsider more under suspicion than if he had been one of their own.

Because of the controversy raised, a public meeting was held, at which Dobbs himself gave a presentation. This did not in itself halt the opposition, and it was the role of BBNP, specifically the planning officer assigned to the case, to mediate between the various bodies. In his report to the planning committee the planning officer's recommendations were positive, and he praised the concept, its contribution to the town, its sustainability features and its design: 'Traditional detailing such as chimneys and cottage style fenestration together with good proportions will result in a pleasing development – which will readily fit in with the town' (BBNP, 1993: 33). His view that planning permission should be granted was an endorsement of the official line of BBNP to adopt the scheme, regardless of opposition. Furthermore, their general satisfaction with the merits of the scheme and its respect for vernacular design (which more than met the sensitive requirements of BBNP's building design guide) was expressed in the way they 'threw the rule book out of the window' in respect of some requirements such as overlooking (personal communication).

A decision was deferred until the requested details were forthcoming, and meanwhile a site visit was held to try and persuade both the BBNP committee members and Crickhowell Community Council of the merits of the scheme. Finally, in March 1994 planning permission was granted. Although not subject to any Section 106 agreements there were 26 conditions. These related to highways, footpaths, drainage, landscaping, materials, use and time restrictions to the youth club and workshops, the granting of listed building consent and the strict phasing of the development. The latter required that the focal building of the Tower and three adjacent plots be completed first, then the listed building complex, and finally the rest of the development. The applicant's attention was also drawn to the presence of bats and the fact that it was an offence to disturb them.

Once building got underway it did not proceed smoothly. Within a few months Dobbs was asking for a change to the planning conditions in respect of phasing as he needed to build and sell some of the larger houses first in order to assist with cash flow. In 1995 the local builders he had chosen, Crickhowell Construction, went into liquidation after completing only two houses. By the end of 1995 the project was running well over budget largely due to infrastructure cost increases, and the delay in the housebuilding programme. The uncertainties this created led to further, somewhat vindicated questioning by local interests who raised issues about the status of the site, the further deterioration of the listed buildings, and the ability of the developer to complete the scheme. Meanwhile, Dobbs was seeking new financial backing for the £7 million scheme which until then had been funded from his own resources. He was somewhat triumphant to secure funding for six months from the ethical bank Triodos, based in Denmark, which assists projects with social and environmental benefit to the community.

Even after the revised scheme got under way in early 1997, now with a new firm of architects (Peter Taylor Associates) and the national company Countryside Properties as the housebuilders, problems continued. Dobbs and BBNP were in continuous negotiation over a variety of issues, including the addition of five further units, landscaping provision, the lack of overall progress, and breaches of conditions in respect of the farm outbuildings. The conversion of the listed farmhouse to a telecottage facility had made no progress due to the renovation costs, the restrictions imposed by fire regulations and the need to retain the integrity of the interior. Dobbs was also asked to remove a prominent weather vane on top of the Tower in the shape of his 'A' logo (Figure 6.9), for which he did not have planning permission, and which in the eyes of the Civic Society was a monstrosity and a blatant advertisement. Dobbs continued to have belief in the scheme, stating with suitable rhetorical imagery in an interview with *The Times*: 'in this case our acorn has fallen on fertile ground' (*The Times*, 1997). Such faith was not, however, well placed. Sales were not proceeding as hoped, and by 1999 although many of the smaller properties had sold, the larger more expensive ones with a £269,000 to £369,000 price tag (even before the price rises of the early 2000s) had not. Furthermore there were complaints from new residents that the fibre optic network had not been connected. The final straw was when Triodos withdrew its support and in October 2000 forced Dobbs into receivership (BBC, 2000). After enquiries from various potential developers, Stapleford Estates eventually took over the Crickhowell scheme to market the remaining houses, finish the landscaping and resolve the problem of the uses of the farmhouse and the remaining outbuildings. At the time of writing BBNP believes the farmhouse will be converted to housing, and the telecottage facility, if pursued, will be placed in one of the outbuildings.

The main access to the finished site is marked by a sign which proclaims 'Acorn televillages: a development of exceptional quality, craftsmanship, energy efficiency and imagination'. Undoubtedly the scheme is visually attractive and has a vernacular feel, although arguably this is more Mediterranean than Welsh. The colour washed houses (all naturalistically named after trees in the way referred to in Chapter 5, such as Hornbeam House, Pear Tree House, Walnut House, Bay Tree House) face on to paved footpaths or courtyards, with winding pedestrian thoroughfares and a central small piazza (Figure 6.9, 6.10, 6.11). Cars are relegated to an access road to the rear of the houses (Figure 6.12) thus giving pedestrians dominance within the scheme and allowing for casual encounters and sociability. The former farm outbuildings have been improved in readiness for conversion to workspace, with adjacent parking space and pedestrian access through to the rest of the scheme (Figure 6.13).

A commitment to sustainability is evident throughout the development. As the illustrations show, much use is made externally of natural or reclaimed materials including stone, cobbles, slate, oak cladding and wattle fencing, and the majority of wood is Welsh sourced and, where possible, fashioned by local craftsmen. Front

6.9 A courtyard within the Acorn Televillage scheme. Terraced units are located on each side, with The Tower enclosing the space at the head, still displaying its gold 'A' logo.

6.10 A pedestrian way leading past the Tower and flanked by wattle fencing and a natural stone wall

6.11 The central piazza framed by some of the larger housing units

6.12 The rear access road and the garages of the larger houses. Smaller units are provided only with parking bays.

6.13 The former farmyard showing the outbuildings, hard and soft landscaping, and pedestrian access through to the housing units. The archway symbolically defines the transition from semi-public to semi-private space and discourages outsiders from entering.

131

doors are sheltered within solid oak porches, and internal doors are of oak with dowels, hand forged hinges and oak latches. Floors are also of wood, using poplar or alder and including end grain pieces that are normally discarded, whilst kitchen cupboards are of ash or oak. Windows are oak framed with double glazed heat reflective panes. Internal paints are mostly organic whilst external paints are made of natural minerals (raising an environmental dilemma as they had to be imported from Germany). Most houses are designed for maximum flexibility with few or no load bearing internal walls, and a gallery loft in the master bedroom can be used for a multitude of purposes. High insulation standards mean that 20 per cent less energy than normal is required, and energy saving combination condensing gas boilers have been fitted, together with efficient wood burning stoves to be supplied by renewable coppiced wood. Rainwater is collected, and bathwater can be recycled for garden use.

There has been some acclaim for the design achievements of the Acorn Televillage, and in 1999 the scheme was awarded the RTPI prize for innovation and sustainability. Its attractiveness as a development has also secured a varied clientele, including in 2002 a pharmaceutical company, a blacksmith, a music and dance school, an alternative medicine centre, an eco-tourism charity, an environmental scientist, a computer programmer, a music producer, an artist and a translator (Upper House Farm, 2002). However, in other respects the scheme has not lived up to expectation. Purchasers have almost all come from outside the area, whilst the high price that accompanies the high specification has priced the larger homes out of the local market. Although some units are used for home based working, many others are occupied by those who commute beyond Crickhowell, whilst others have been bought for holiday or second homes. At the time of writing the telecottage is still awaiting completion. The youth club has not transpired and the workshops have had mixed success. In terms of the planning objectives the scheme has failed in its principal objectives of bringing economic regeneration, providing homes for local people and securing the future of all the listed buildings. To Acorn Televillages as a company and Ashley Dobbs as an individual the ambitious aims brought the prospect of financial ruin. Perhaps in the belief that these problems were caused by the small scale of the project and that the British people are not yet ready to embrace the concept, Acorn Televillages is now developing a much larger televillage of 3,000 units in Nevada, Missouri.

Conclusion

This chapter has looked at the various ways in which the village has been represented over time and then at two contemporary manifestations of the village concept which have recently been promoted. Referring back to the contextual framework proposed in Figure 1.1 in Chapter 1, it can be seen that the cultural context is one in which the word 'village' has assumed considerable resonance in the English language, with connotations of identity, tradition, continuity and harmony with one's fellow beings and the natural world. However, these associations emerged only with the changing social processes of modernism discussed in Chapter 2. Prior to that villages, like the rest of the countryside, were constructed as backward and untamed, and it was only under the dehumanising and alienating conditions of industrialisation that the countryside became reconstructed as a romantic and nostalgic haven; a necessary contrast to the squalor of the city. But under the new social processes of postmodernism and globalisation there has been a further change, with the impact of 'time-space distanciation' rendering local places such as villages 'phantasmagoric' and no longer able to maintain their traditional qualities and isolated status (Giddens, 1990). Arguably however, this has only increased the mythical potency of the idealised village, since it allows the village to assume the symbolic resonance of those other non-existent utopian idylls such as arcadia and the promised land.

As noted in Chapter 1, discourse is central to the way in which the world is socially constructed, and it is through the texts of literary figures and sociologists that the notion of an opposition between the country and the city has been reproduced. But sociologists have also 'discovered' that it is possible for village-like enclaves to be found within otherwise alienating urban environments, and in turn this has offered a way forward in tackling the potentially depersonalising and dysfunctional effects of city living. Thus over time city planners have been encouraged to believe in the artificial creation of urban neighbourhoods and communities, and the more recent resurfacing of the village discourse is yet another manifestation of this belief. That this has occurred at this particular conjuncture in time is indicative of the resonance of all that village-ness conveys in the context of today's thoroughly urbanised, dislocated and risk saturated postmodern world.

The contemporary salience of the village epithet is emphasised by the way it has been appropriated by different agents for a number of different and contrasting development models, ranging from the millennium village to the televillage, the retirement village to the ecovillage. In each instance the adoption of the village rubric would appear to be an attempt to promote and popularise the relevant concept in the knowledge that the imagery of the word village is 'good to think'. In the case of the urban village, the agency involved was an elite and privileged group led by the figurehead of the Prince. Indeed, it was the symbolic capital inherent in the position of the Prince which helped to endorse the concept and legitimise it as one rooted in retrospective traditionalism. In turn this also meant that the concept was of appeal to the Conservative administration of the time – it resonated with their *habitus*. However, the lack of rigour in regard to its interpretation either at the institutional level through the policy agenda or by the Urban Villages Group has rendered it deficient in terms of authoritative power. This has left it open to manipulation by both local authorities and developers, whose motivations have been variously directed towards appeasing the public, securing financial support and exploiting opportunities. It is through these processes that the urban village appellation has become adopted for its symbolic value as a sign (see Chapter 5), thereby further undermining any intrinsic credibility it may once have possessed.

The agency which led to the televillage was, by contrast to the urban village, not institutional leadership but individual conviction. This conviction was grounded in a desire to transform established practices in regard to the routines and places of work, and based on models of 'telecommuting' derived from the different cultural contexts of the US and more especially Scandinavia. However, as a concept the televillage has not achieved either institutional endorsement or popular appeal, due to a combination of the lack of the necessary capital (symbolic and financial) by the person who has introduced it, and the apparent unreadiness of people to embrace a concept which, at least as yet, is not in tune with their *habitus*. Perhaps this is also due to the inherent (and ironic) contradiction in the concept of the televillage, for the possibility of returning to a rural past and pursuing a lifestyle supposedly more in tune with the natural rhythms of time and place, is made feasible only through the very processes of globalisation which, as noted above, have rendered the village a phantasmagoric place in a virtual world.

As indicated in Chapter 1 it is only through analysis of specific examples that we can fully comprehend the complexity of the processes whereby generalised concept becomes specific built outcome. In this regard the spatial attributes of the locale and the thoughts and actions of local agency become significant. In the case of Bordesley there had been decades of industrialisation followed by further decades of disinvestment, and the result was a disconnected and desolate patchwork of housing, industrial premises, pubs, churches, shops, neglected open space, and economic and social deprivation. Given the institutionally endorsed discourse of regeneration through public private partnership (discussed in Chapter 3) it was unsurprising that local actors would perceive this as the best way to transform Bordesley's deterioration from abandoned 'back region' into showcase 'front region'. Here the significance of the powers of negotiation discussed in Chapter 1 can be seen, for the imposition of a centrally determined model was resisted and a locally acceptable compromise secured. Negotiation was also required to assuage the fears of existing residents, and in this regard a crucial mediating role was played by the local nursery manager, trusted by both the regeneration actors and local people.

Reversing the decline of Bordesley was always the central aim of the regeneration effort, and it would appear that urban village designation crept in almost accidentally and without ever being fully elaborated in the discourse of the various texts pertinent to the scheme. Consequently, attention to the design aspects supposedly so intrinsic to the urban village concept was lacking, with no prescriptive design guidelines, little explicit design control by the city council, and minimal input by architectural or urban design professionals. Only those at the apex of the hierarchy, 'networking' in the somewhat exclusive circle of the UVF, were really interested in any claims to distinction or symbolic capital that the urban village appellation might bestow. The realities of the situation on the ground meant that the emphasis was on encouraging any development at all, and this resulted in BHDC pursuing somewhat irregular means to attract developers and then exerting minimal control. Thus Bordesley has been redeveloped in a piecemeal way according to the market decisions of individual (and competing) housebuilders. This has created a built form that reproduces the standard types of any speculative suburban development (as discussed in Chapter 5), and lacking in cohesion, legibility, spatial hierarchy or sense of connection between the different elements of the new environment. Given this essentially anti-urbanist design it is hardly surprising that Bordesley failed to gain distinction under the judgmental gaze of the urban village purists of the UVF. On the other hand, it more than satisfied those whose main concern was to see a rejuvenated housing market, an improved landscape, and the lifting of the blight that had affected the area for so long.

The spatial situation of Crickhowell televillage was quite different from Bordesley, having the advantages of location in an attractive market town and the cachet (although associated difficulties) of some listed buildings. Instead of the complex framework of the numerous and often competing agencies that characterised the multi-objective and large scale regeneration of Bordesley, here there was just one pioneering individual with a single aim. His prior experience with telecottages and property development equipped him to realise this aim, but it seems that ambition and a sequence of practical problems compromised its actual achievement. His initial efforts to win over those to whom the televillage was unfamiliar relied on the powers of discourse through the submission of persuasive written and spoken texts. The local planning authority then took the lead in offering support, making the site available to him (again through irregular means) and exercising a mediating role between the conflicting representations of the various interested parties. The developer was also able to use his powers of persuasion to convince the Triodos bank of the merits of his scheme, although eventually it was through their agency that his financial collapse occurred and he was replaced by a more institutionally approved developer.

Apart from minor details, the overall design concept of Acorn Televillage was universally applauded, since it resonated not only with the *habitus* of the main actors concerned but also with the existing architecture, scale and setting of the small market town. The end result has been a compact, varied, well-proportioned, pedestrian friendly and subtly colourful scheme, with focal points, a landmark building, a clear hierarchy of space, a human scale, and a sense of durability and rusticity deriving from the use of natural materials. In a reversal of the situation in Bordesley therefore, it is not the design outcomes that have been criticised, but the economic and social aims of the scheme. These have not fulfilled the initial vision of homes for local people or of a community of home workers contributing to the local economy.

It is clear from the cases of Bordesley and Crickhowell that the ability to reproduce in built form the vision of the imagination becomes compromised and diluted by the conflicting perspectives of the multiple actors involved and by the realities of conditions on the ground. Even so, some small part of that vision lives on simply by the coining of the emotive appellation 'village'. In Bordesley, even the developers have appreciated this, and although they have shown no interest in the idea of an urban village *per se*, they have grasped the marketing advantages of referring to Bordesley as 'Bordesley Village'. And in Crickhowell, despite the fact that an authentic televillage (if such exists) has not been achieved, the development is still known as 'Acorn Televillage'. In effect, it would seem that the power residing in the generic word 'village' transcends the specificities of any particular residential environment, since it acts as a metaphor and symbol of what once was and might yet be regained. It is on this chimera that the village analogy relies for its strength. Its weakness, and its ultimate downfall as a development concept, is that it is predicated on myth. And myth, as we think we know, has no basis in reality.

7 Monuments made good

There are some building types that are prominent in both our physical and our mental landscapes. Their prominence derives from their size and scale, which, in turn, are born of their function and purpose. And their function and purpose, and the relative way these are inscribed on to the built form, are framed by the cultural and social systems of which they are part. Thus the built form acts as a code for cultural and social systems, endowing each building type not only with a particular internal and external form, but also with meanings and associations, all of which become reproduced over time. Churches, castles, lighthouses, stone circles, town halls, mills, stately homes, hospitals, garrisons and windmills, to name but a few, are each characterised by a generic form which makes them instantly recognisable to those informed about British culture and society. But beyond form they also have meaning, and this becomes etched in memory and imagination such that form and meaning are inextricably entwined. Thus a church represents Christianity, reverence and peace; a castle a history of war and siege and the need for fortification; a lighthouse a beacon to guide the shipping of an island nation through stormy waters; a stone circle the mysteries and mysticism of an ancient past; a mill the advances and exploitations of an industrialised age … and so on.

For the most part, these building types have continued to resonate over time in a positive way, reflecting back to us images not only of a visually impressive physical form but also of a symbolically charged narrative of achievement, moral superiority and pride. They thus become 'good to think'. Any negative connotations, such as episodes of repression, pain, indignity and loss, are elided in the nostalgic haze through which we prefer to see our history sanitised. For these reasons, many of these types have achieved the status of monuments, preserved and protected as cultural icons for future generations to learn from and enjoy. And even when their original use has been superseded by cultural, economic and social change, as when falling congregations render churches redundant or the decline of manufacturing causes obsolescence for the mills, it is only with reluctance that they are demolished. Instead they are where feasible converted to new uses which, whilst requiring some internal modifications, leave unaltered the external elevations and hence the value of the built form as sign. But there are a few building types where this has been less easy to achieve, and where associations of stigma and repugnance have proved more enduring than those of esteem and celebration. This has made it more difficult to bestow on them the same adulation and protection as those types socially constructed in a more favourable light. Consequently, their acceptance and their potential for adaptation should they become superfluous or unsuitable in terms of their original use has been made more problematic. Such types include the nineteenth-century workhouse and mental hospital, and the mid-twentieth-century residential tower block. It is the rise, fall and transformation of these latter two which form the main subject of this chapter, with specific reference to the histories of Exe Vale mental hospital in Devon, notable for its unique radial form, and the tower block of Keeling House in London, the first council tower block to receive listed status.

The badlands of modernity

Under the structural conditions of modernism the spatial arrangement of social divisions and cultural classifications that had been inherent to human organisation since primitive times assumed new forms (Shields, 1991). Population explosion and mobility, greater apparent extremes of wealth and poverty, increased social stratification, the growing role of the state, improved access to education and knowledge, new approaches to the causation and treatment of health and sickness, and expanding opportunities for employment outside the home, all led to a society that was more complex, more fractured, more compartmentalised and more paternalistic than hitherto. These changes, together with advances in technology, led to the burgeoning of new building types in which the new diversity of activities and social categories could be accommodated and classified. In this the state took a leading role, and thus from the mid-nineteenth century there emerged new built forms such as town halls, railway stations, museums, libraries, municipal baths, hospitals and schools (see Markus, 1993). Their significance in social and cultural terms was further signalled by the fact that eminent architects were invited to compete in their design, the winners thereby gaining merit and distinction. The resultant imposing and resplendent styles reflect both the social and symbolic importance of the buildings, and the mastery of the architect over the eclectic design fashions of the time.

As well as being paternalistic, this was a society that functioned on the principles of individual and collective discipline, and where the sanctions of punishment and exclusion kept people within the boundaries of accepted, productive behaviour (see Foucault, 1977). One mechanism to achieve such discipline and control was by spatial containment and ordering, with the ranking of the individual *vis-à-vis* the rest denoted by their relative place or position:

Discipline proceeds by the organisation of individuals in space, and it therefore requires a specific enclosure of space. In the hospital, the school, or the military field, we find reliance on an orderly grid. Once established, this grid permits the sure distribution of the individuals to be disciplined and supervised; this procedure facilitates the reduction of dangerous multitudes or wandering vagabonds to fixed and docile individuals.

(Dreyfus and Rabinow, 1982: 154–5, cited in Shields, 1991: 39)

Such dangerous multitudes and wandering vagabonds were a threat to the capitalist enterprise of the maximisation of profit, which depended on the requisitioning of each and every unit of labour. Those unwilling or unable to labour were, through government edict, to be confined in specific places or spaces sequestered from the everyday locales of activity. Such places and spaces included the prison, the lunatic asylum and the workhouse. These were often built on an intimidating and monumental scale, the very fact that they loomed large in the landscape serving as a visible sign or warning to others. Within these 'badlands of modernity' (Hetherington, 1997) regimes were harsh, surveillance was total, and a rigid system of classification and hierarchy was imposed.

In the twentieth century a new style of monumental building began to appear, emerging first on the Continent. Throughout Europe the horrors of the First World War and fears of worker revolution had resulted in a desire by governments to compensate and placate the labouring poor, whilst at the same time keeping them under control. As discussed in Chapter 1, the promise of better quality state subsidised housing to replace the overcrowded and unfit tenements was seen as one way to do this, and the building type that was chosen was the slab housing block. Mass construction was made possible by the technological advances in materials and engineering, whilst the symbolic and aesthetic importance of the blocks, both institutionally and architecturally, was signalled by the engagement of eminent modernist architects. Consequently, such blocks began to be erected in their thousands across Europe, dominating the urban landscape, and effectively acting as homogenising containers for the anonymous units of labour necessary to serve the needs of capital. In Britain this example from the Continent was at first slow to gain ground, but from the late 1950s local authorities built increasing numbers of similar mass housing units (see also Chapter 3). These included not only the slab blocks or *Zeilenbau* so popular in the rest of Europe, but also the British transformation of this style into the building type of the residential tower block. Within these tower blocks the working classes were under control, segregated from the wider society and stacked up in a seemingly endless repetition of blank and faceless units.

The modern period thus saw the creation of certain specific, identifiable and often monumental building types which have remained indelibly associated with people constructed as in need of containment and control. The stigma and disdain with which such marginal and powerless people have been regarded has inevitably been projected on to the respective building types. Thus these too have been perceived as alien and other: 'placed on the periphery of cultural systems of space in which places are ranked relative to each other. They all carry the image, and stigma, of their marginality ...' (Shields, 1991: 3). It is these hostile associations as sequestered and shameful places that have problematised the possibility of rehabilitation and preservation after they have outlived their period of usefulness. This has posed a difficulty for a society which is keen to preserve the past as a heritage of which to be proud, and from which a new and lucrative 'heritage industry' has been spawned (see Hewison, 1987).

Preservation of the past

In the context of the insecurities of the present and the uncertainties of the future, the past seems to represent a state of order, rootedness, and familiar tradition. For this reason, symbols of the past, whether real or imagined, become eloquent; expressive of a sense of collective continuity and shared identity, and hence deemed worthy of preservation. This desire to admire and preserve the past first emerged in the era of the romantic poets, but it took the activities of an intellectual elite to bring about institutional change. In this regard those famous social and moral reformers of the late nineteenth century, William Morris, John Ruskin, and Octavia Hill (also famous for her methods of housing management) had enormous influence. It was they who were directly responsible for the foundation of two national conservation organisations still in existence today: the Society for the Preservation of Ancient Buildings (SPAB) and the National Trust for Places of Historic Interest or Natural Beauty, now the National Trust (see Pickard, 1996).

During the course of the twentieth century concerned professionals and committed individuals established various other organisations to champion either specific architectural periods or heritage in general, as for example, the Georgian Society, the Civic Trust, the Thirties Society (now the Twentieth Century Society) and SAVE Britain's Heritage. Meanwhile, interest in built heritage was also being disseminated to the wider public through works of architectural appreciation in relation to historic buildings. These included the series of Shell county architectural guides written by the well known poet John Betjeman in the 1930s (see Ross, 1996), and the prodigious works of the émigré Nikolaus Pevsner. The latter, published between 1951 and 1974 in 46 volumes, consist of detailed surveys of all the significant buildings of England: 'filled with wonderful scholarship and a liberal dose of heavy prejudice ... they made the nation's heritage accessible to all. Pevsner's lucid prose and down-to-earth style did much to educate a public that was beginning to awake to the concept of heritage' (Ross, 1996: 27).

In the context of this increased awareness of the value of the built heritage, together with pressure from organisations and individuals, the government was stimulated to pass cumulatively more effective legislation. Measures were first introduced in the Town and Country Planning Acts of 1944 and 1947 for the listing of buildings of architectural and historic interest, and during the 1960s and 1970s these powers were strengthened and the concept of conservation areas introduced (see DoE, 1994b). Until 1987, only buildings dating from before 1940 could be listed, but in that year a Statutory Instrument was passed to permit the listing of buildings over 30 years old, and even of those over ten years old if under threat. This has resulted in a number of modernist buildings being selected for listing due to their perceived architectural merit, despite the fact that to many their style is seen as sterile and inhumane (Cherry, 2001). Thus even some tower blocks have been listed as excellent examples of their type, especially those designed by eminent architects: 'A comparison can be made with workhouses or prisons, which lack popular appeal, but where we have established the principle of listing for historic and planning interest as well as for aesthetic appeal' (Croft and Harwood, 1999: 165).

Due to the obsolescence of their original use many listed buildings have fallen into disrepair and decay, with many now included on the Buildings at Risk Register established by English Heritage. If such buildings are to be preserved then alternative uses must be found. This is often far from straightforward as the form and scale are often such that they cannot readily be converted and, moreover, original features must be preserved and authentic materials carefully sourced. The consequence is that costs are often prohibitive whilst available grants are pitiful given the scale of the problem. Nonetheless, facilitated by a combination of the burgeoning heritage interest, government persuasion and a shortage of sites, even risk averse private sector developers have been prepared to experiment with rehabilitation and adaptive re-use (see DoE, 1987). Initially this was in the context of the property led regeneration initiatives of the late 1980s, when the first few pioneers of mill and warehouse conversions encouraged other developers to follow suit. Subsequently both the private and the public sector have tackled a diversity of other redundant building types, including hospitals, market halls, churches, offices and schools (see DETR, 2000f). Driven by the intensity of the housing and land shortage, many of these are now being transformed into residential space, ranging from basic affordable homes to luxury executive units. In recent years, even formerly stigmatised building types such as the workhouse and the mental hospital have been included, rendered a more realistic proposition as the more distanced postmodern gaze has romanticised the memory of their former use. But interestingly, there has also been a reprieve, even a renaissance, for that other stigmatised type of the modern age, the tower block. For after several decades of being denounced, reviled and even blasted into oblivion, it is now being reconstructed both physically and socially as potentially desirable living space.

The story of the mental hospital

In the early nineteenth century the impact of industrialisation signalled massive structural shifts in regard to the political and social economy, with institutional reform in many areas of public life. More enlightened, although still partial, understandings about mental illness led to changes in the haphazard and punitive ways that had prevailed hitherto in the treatment of the mentally ill (see Scull, 1982; Skultans, 1979). Particularly influential in regard to the transformation of treatment methods was William Tuke, a Quaker, who in 1796 founded the Retreat in York. His view was that a comfortable and aesthetic environment should be provided in order to instil feelings of appreciation and tranquillity, and that inmates should be managed by a system of surveillance and moral judgement (Edginton, 1997). Despite initial resistance from the 'mad-doctors' of the time, it was this 'moral treatment' which slowly began to prevail.

This shift in attitude was also reflected in a series of parliamentary enquiries to discuss provision for the mentally ill. These resulted in the passing of two key Acts, the County Asylums Act of 1808 and the Lunacy Act of 1845, with the latter imposing the building of an asylum in each county as a statutory duty. Suitable locations for these new asylums were deemed to be elevated and secluded, removed from the overstimulating influences of urban life and untainted by 'miasma', the putrescent vapour emanating from low-lying swampy ground and believed to cause debilitation and fever. Within the asylum inmates were to be classified according to type of illness and likelihood of curability, with those of different categories consigned to different parts of the asylum.

Asylums effectively constituted a new building type and the first were somewhat experimental, drawing on the familiar types of the prison and the workhouse. Many therefore adopted the same 'panopticon' design, a form conceptualised by the philosopher Jeremy Bentham in regard to the supervision of prisoners and workers from one central point (Foucault, 1977; Markus, 1993). However, as time went on the numbers of people classified as 'mad' increased and asylums became ever larger and more numerous. This led not only to a need to rethink asylum design on a grander scale, but also a new opportunity for the architects of the time to enhance their reputations through innovative and creative design. For this reason many eminent Victorian architects such as William Stark, Edward Godwin and George Gilbert Scott became involved in the design of asylums, whilst the merits of the different design styles and their contribution to effective treatment were regularly debated in both construction and medical journals of the time, such as *The Builder* and the *Asylum Journal* (Franklin, 2002a).

For several decades there was considerable experimentation to achieve the best plan form (see Richardson, 1998; Taylor, 1991). Internally the requirement was a layout which would provide separate wards for men and women and for different classes of illness, with each ward ideally facing south for maximum sunlight and opening on to an enclosed exercise yard. An administrative area needed to be located in a central position giving sight lines into the wards, with a dining room and kitchens readily accessible. But there was far more to the average asylum than this, and effectively each became a self-contained 'village' with a laundry, a bakery, a brewery, a gasworks, a water tower, workshops, a farm, a church, a mortuary, a graveyard, even a ballroom for regular entertainment. Often the grounds of the asylum were vast, with landscaped gardens, playing fields, parkland and an approach through lodge gates up a sweeping drive to an imposing façade. Given the constraints of internal layout it was only on this façade and the other elevations that the creativity of the architect could be freely expressed. It is this which accounts for the diversity of architectural styles in asylums, the different materials and detailing, and the variations of Palladian, Gothic or Italianate design.

As the nineteenth century progressed into the twentieth asylums became ever larger, many containing up to 2,000 inmates. To the rest of the population asylums became places of revulsion, stigma and scorn, with the threat of being sent to the 'loony bin' or the 'funny farm' acting as a powerful deterrent. This threat was all the more potent given the massive and intimidating scale of the asylums and their physical and social segregation from the rest of society. The reality of what went on inside the asylums was largely left to the imagination, but gradually tales emerged of neglect, cruelty and generally inhumane and inappropriate treatment.

By the mid-twentieth century concerns about the effect of such treatment had been endorsed by the findings of academic research (Barton, 1959; Goffman, 1968) and this, together with medical advances in regard to more effective diagnosis and suppression of symptoms, led to a reappraisal of the desirability of incarcerating people in such large, monolithic institutions. To this effect a series of government reports and Acts from the 1950s sought to create more enlightened conditions within asylums, and, more significantly, to gradually end reliance on them altogether through alternative care in the community. Thus by the 1980s and 1990s many asylums had been made redundant, their scale too large, their associations too oppressive to be easily employed for other purposes. This situation was captured in the words of the politician Enoch Powell in 1962: 'There they stand, isolated, majestic, imperious, brooded over by a gigantic water tower and chimney combined, rising unmistakable and daunting out of the countryside – the asylums which our forefathers built with such solidity' (Park and Radford, 1997: 71). Their disposal was in the hands of the health authorities who owned them and who, in their determination to maximise the value of the site, often demolished the actual buildings in order to offer more marketable vacant land. However, as more asylums were lost, attention was drawn to the destruction of a valuable architectural asset, resulting in the listing of the better examples.

The consequent decline into disrepair and vandalism aroused the indignation and even outrage of many, with increasingly vociferous voices demanding viable alternative uses for these impressive buildings (see, for example, *Architects' Journal*, 1991; Burrell, 1985; Spring, 1987). Particularly active has been the organisation SAVE Britain's Heritage which has surveyed threatened asylums, monitored progress and lobbied for appropriate re-use (SAVE, 1995). Some asylums have also been the subject of campaigns by local pressure groups set up either to prevent demolition or to resist inappropriate development, and in recent years a national website has been established as a forum for discussion and exchange on asylum issues (www.worldofasylums.com).

In the context of this reassessment of asylums the government began to produce guidance to encourage the disposal of sites and local authorities were instructed that suitable alternative uses would be institutional or commercial (Audit Commission, 1988; DoE, 1991; NHS/English Heritage, 1995). However, as the housing recession of the late 1980s and early 1990s faded into memory, developers began to see the potential of residential rehabilitation, especially in the context of the successful conversion of other historic building types and the emphasis on brownfield development.

Given the dominant beliefs at the time of their original construction, many asylums are in fact on prime sites, located on high ground in rural settings yet not far from centres of population. They also have the advantages of being predominantly oriented to the south, set in attractive grounds, and distinguished by often exceptional architecture. Both institutional and occasionally individual developers have begun to capitalise on this, despite the difficulties of working with heritage buildings and the complexities of subdividing institutional space into units of a more domestic scale. The outcome has been often unique, varied and interesting dwellings which give their residents a sense of history and distinction, and which have rewarded the developer's risk by proving popular and saleable (Franklin, 2002a, 2002b). What is notable however, is that in the marketing literature allusion is rarely made to their former use.

Exe Vale mental hospital

Exe Vale Mental Hospital was built as the Devon County Pauper Lunatic Asylum between 1842 and 1845, and hence was one of the earlier asylums. It was located on rising land on the edge of the village of Exminster, five miles from Exeter, with far reaching views towards the estuary. The competition held for the design was won by a local architect, Charles Fowler, noted for his work on bridges, churches and markets, including Covent Garden. As befitted a designer of markets, his approach was pragmatic and functional, and he was also motivated by a desire to improve on existing asylum design. The significance at the time of both the commission and the nature of the debate on asylum design is illustrated by the text of an address by Fowler to the Institute of Architects (later RIBA):

> The first idea that naturally presents itself is to place the seat of government and administration in the centre, and to bring each separate portion or department,

into as easy a communication with it as compatible with the requisite distinctness or classification. Hence have arisen the various radiating plans, in most of which directness of supervision, and facility of inspection, have been obtained by the sacrifice, more or less, of separateness, light and ventilation … The desideratum, therefore, is to obtain the advantages without the sacrifices alluded to, so as to possess concentration without confusion or obscurity. This has been attempted in the instance now adduced (the Devon Asylum) by the introduction of a large semicircle, embracing within it all the administrative departments, and connected externally with the several radiating buildings, for the separate classes of inmates. The chord of the semicircle being 264 feet in length, the subdivisions of this range of buildings have each so small a degree, either of curvature or obliquity, as not to detract from the convenience, or interfere with the construction; on the contrary, the outward bend of the front walls of the day rooms gives them the advantage of a more open and cheerful aspect.

(The Builder, 1846: 349)

Fowler's plan, based on six radial wings and a central administration block (Figure 7.1), achieved a minimal circulation area but with maximum supervision on the panopticon principle, allowing long sight lines into wards and exercise areas. The separate ward wings allowed classification by severity of condition and gender: the three northern wings for females, the three southern for males. Good ventilation was part of the Victorian obsession with health and fresh air, and at Exe Vale this was achieved by an elaborate system of cross ventilation, including the ingenious use of self operated shutters at floor level in cells on the outer walls, and portholes of iron meshwork above the doors on the internal walls. Additional cross draught was

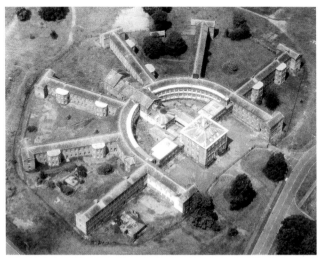

7.1   Aerial view of Exe Vale mental hospital as designed by Charles Fowler

7.2 Centre House under reconstruction

provided by the innovative shuttered opening dials in the segmented arching of the iron framed gallery windows. Given the contemporary belief in the importance of a pleasant and calming setting in promoting cure, Fowler also specified landscaping for the 80 acre site as well as designing a ceremonial entrance gateway flanked by decorative lodges. The tree lined avenue that led onwards effectively framed the pleasing and symmetrical Queen Anne façade of the administrative block, Centre House, whilst obscuring the grim and utilitarian ward wings beyond (Figure 7.2).

Exe Vale was one of the earlier mental hospitals to be run down, with closure completed in 1987. To pre-empt initial proposals by the health authority to demolish all the asylum buildings except Centre House these were listed Grade II* in 1985, together with the lodges, lodge gates and chapel, which were listed Grade II. The merits of the hospital were also recorded by Pevsner in his Buildings of England series (Cherry and Pevsner, 1989). Defeated by this consensus over the building's worth, the health authority decided the best financial reward would derive from parcelling up the land and disposing of it in separate lots for residential development. The planning authority, as guardian of the best interest of the listed buildings, was not in favour of this piecemeal approach and took it to appeal. However, the appeal was lost and development proceeded. Less controversial was the sale of the freestanding chapel for conversion to a pre-preparatory school and of the nurses' accommodation block, a separate twentieth-century addition, for office use by the Environment Agency.

The asylum buildings were sold for the sum of £1 to a developer who planned to convert them into offices, the type of development favoured by the health authority and English Heritage as most likely to secure the future of the building. At that point, however, the office market collapsed and the developer reneged on the agreement. The buildings were in a parlous state of repair, vandalism and theft had taken their toll, children were using the site as an adventure playground, and vagrants, including former inmates, were finding shelter there. English Heritage was forced to step in to make the building weatherproof and also placed it on the Buildings at Risk register. Eventually the planning authority drew up a 'rescue package', which resulted in a change of use from office to residential, and the preparation of a planning brief setting out the parameters of an acceptable development (Teignbridge District Council, 1999).

The only interested purchaser was Devington Homes, a local company with prior experience of conversions, and a subsidiary of Frogmore Developments. They bought the site for £250,000, and in the middle of 2000 began the conversion process. Considerable interaction with the planning authority then ensued, involving submission of successive planning applications and negotiation on matters relating to the listed status and Section 106 agreements (see Chapter 4). The latter included provision of a bus shelter and a cycleway, traffic calming, an educational contribution and the incorporation of an interpretation centre on the history and background of the asylum. There was no requirement for social housing as it was accepted this would compromise the viability of a project that needed £1 million of repair work before conversion could even begin. Additional conditions applied to the external areas, such as extensive landscaping, a management plan, restoration of some parkland and retention of scrubland and other habitat for the resident wildlife. This included rare cirl buntings and wasp spiders, identified following inspection by the RSPB and countryside rangers.

Respect for the original design and the need to preserve what remained of the setting were paramount considerations:

> Key design objectives must be to preserve its simple geometric plan form, the unity of design and its elevation integrity. The building demands an open setting, a respectful foil in which it can live and breathe.
>
> (Teignbridge District Council, 1999: unpaginated)

Consequently no new build was to be permitted and the original elevation had to be retained as it was, or, where necessary, restored with sympathetic materials. The integrity of the overall design concept had also to be respected, and hence parking and small garden areas were to be contained within the old exercise yards, but without unsightly drying areas or any fencing. Private garden space was to be demarcated only by hedging, to a maximum of one metre in height (Figure 7.3). In regard to the internal features there was more scope for negotiation. The local conservation officer was keen to preserve as many original features as possible, including the cast iron and tile ceiling construction, the barrel vaulting at cross passages, the cell doors with peepholes and portholes, the shuttered ventilation panels, the curved and in places chamfered window reveals and the integrity of the double height ballroom as one coherent open space. The developer for his part, wanted to rip out as much as possible and start anew. In some instances compromise was based on the requirements of contemporary building regulations; in others preservation was achieved, as for example in using the old ventilation panels as heating vents. But for the most part the conservation officer had to accept defeat, given the over-riding objective of achieving a financially viable solution.

The development proved instantly popular, and many units were sold off plan even before a show home was opened. At the time of writing the work remains to be completed, but eventually there will be 119 town houses and apartments, each unique, and with prices ranging from £150,000 to £400,000. The town houses have been created through vertical subdivision of the wards, and the apartments are located in the hammerhead cross wings of the wards (formerly service space), on the perimeter of the old semi-circular service corridor, and in Centre House (Figures 7.3, 7.4, 7.5). This new disposition of dwelling units in effect alters the former horizontal cell arrangement into a vertical redistribution, with minimisation of the old corridors and passages and the effective removal of the panopticon effect and the possibilities of a supervisory gaze. After a variety of suggestions for the ballroom it too has been turned into apartments on the ground floor, with expensive duplexes above. A gym and sauna are planned in the basement of Centre House,

7.3　One of the radial wings restored as town houses. Note the parking arrangements and the narrow garden strips with gated access and low hedging.

7.4 Two of the radial wings before restoration. The external space between the wings was originally an exercise or 'airing' yard, and the projecting bays provided internal socialisation space within the linear ward. In the middle distance is the rear aspect of the semi-circular corridor, with the clock tower of Centre House visible beyond. The roof of the former chapel, later the ballroom, can also be discerned at the extreme left.

7.5 Almost the same view after restoration. This illustration also shows the hammerhead cross wing.

7.6   One of the two gated entrances

and there are hopes that the planning authority will eventually permit a tennis court. The perimeter is surrounded by railings with the two access gates controlled by an electronic entry system; effectively gating off the new development from its intrinsically non-threatening surroundings (Figure 7.6).

The development is being marketed as Devington Park, and the naming of the different parts of the site appears to have been carefully considered. Each wing has become a 'Walk' with a local association, as in Powderham Walk, Dunster Walk, Dartington Walk, Buckland Walk. Centre House has become 'Mansion House', the ballroom 'The Orangery', the corridor 'The Cloisters' and the central courtyard 'The Italianate Gardens'. Further 'impression management' (Dovey, 1999: 114) is apparent in the tastefully illustrated marketing brochure, which makes no reference to the former, stigmatising use. The front cover depicts the naturalistic and distinctive symbol of the rare cirl bunting, and within much is made of the: 'exclusive opportunity to live within an important and elegant landmark Grade II* listed building set within 11 acres of private grounds' as well as the wider amenities of the area. In describing the facilities the emphasis is on the high specification and the attractions of landscaping – somewhat exaggerated in the eyes of anyone familiar with the site:

> The classical elegance of the mansion house and the symmetry of the terraced walks, which radiate off the central crescent cloister, are framed by soft hedges and shrubs bringing year round variety and colour to the front vista

… . Within the cloister walk a formal garden based on a period Italianate style with shaded terraces and water features will form a peaceful oasis at the heart of the community … Features include a small lake with an island and ornate Victorian style timber pavilion … . In the secluded northern corner of the Park an area will be created for the rare and protected Cirl Bunting, a native bird of South Devonshire whose numbers have dwindled in recent years.

(Devington Homes, undated: unpaginated)

After a problematic period of over 12 years of neglect, the transformation of the Fowler asylum from institution to self-contained and relatively luxurious housing units has proceeded in a way which has for the most part respected the original design. However, the site when taken as a whole has been badly compromised due to the early policy of the health authority in allowing various sections to be randomly sold and developed in isolation. The result is that the nineteenth-century asylum buildings themselves are surrounded on all sides by an inappropriate network of roads providing access to a series of small housing estates, unrelated in terms of design and materials either to each other or to the asylum and in typical cul de sac layouts totally at odds with the geometrical and symmetrical asylum plan. Even the health authority has belatedly acknowledged the mistakes that were made (personal communication). It is the result of these mistakes which will continue to offend the eye and detract from the setting of a listed building which, perhaps ironically, is itself a monument to another health care mistake, that of the mass institutionalisation of the mentally ill.

The story of the tower block

In Britain, somewhat insulated from developments on the Continent and culturally resistant to flatted dwelling, there was little initial enthusiasm to emulate the new modernist mass housing design styles. However as discussed in Chapter 1, a new generation of British architects could not remain altogether immune from the burgeoning ideas on modern architecture emanating from Europe, especially following the arrival in London of *émigrés* escaping persecution, such as Walter Gropius (founder of the Bauhaus school), Mies van der Rohe and Berthold Lubetkin (see Curtis, 1987). Debate about housing design in particular was further stimulated by the work of Le Corbusier, with his notions of a *machine à habiter* and the *unité d'habitation* (see Chapter 4). This aesthetic and intellectual transformation was taking shape at the same time as institutional concerns about the apparently conflicting needs to overcome post-war housing shortages and minimise the effects of suburban sprawl. The result was a new commitment to the idea of building upwards rather than outwards, as endorsed by the Housing Act of 1956 which provided local authorities with increased subsidies proportionate to overall storey height (see Cole and Furbey, 1994). This was given further impetus by the pressure put on central government by construction companies in the mid-1960s in view of their falling profits, and the consequent encouragement of local authorities to adopt systems built construction methods (Dunleavy, 1981). It was through a combination of these influences that by 1975, 440,000 high rise flats of five storeys or more had been built in the UK, the majority of which were in inner urban areas (Dunleavy, 1981). However, the numbers constructed varied between local authorities and were dependent on the degree of acceptance and resistance to the concept by officers, councillors, property developers and residents (Glendinning and Muthesius, 1994).

The prominence given at institutional level to provision by the public rather than the private sector also offered an opportunity to the architectural profession. Indeed it was architects who were at the forefront of proposals for high rise building at both the Ministry of Housing and Local Government (MHLG), and the London County Council. Initially they reproduced the massive and monotonous slab blocks or *Zeilenbau* advocated by Gropius, but gradually a quest for a more aesthetic interpretation arose. This led to an increasing emphasis on tower or 'point' blocks, which were heralded in the architectural journals as a new kind of specifically British residential space, and enthusiastically promoted for their capacity to provide focal points, imposing scale, dramatic interest and sculptural quality (Glendinning and Muthesius, 1994).

During the 1960s tower blocks were enthusiastically embraced by those local authorities who appreciated their advantages and perceived the building of ever taller blocks as a matter of civic pride. But despite this endorsement it was only a few years before disillusionment began to spread; a consequence of a number of countervailing tendencies. On the design side was the fact that architects were losing interest in the repetitiveness of public sector housing design and instead were looking to the new and distinctive opportunities afforded by the expansion of retail and commercial space. Here those of a modernist persuasion could experiment with the new and exciting materials of plastic, steel and curtain wall glazing. In addition there was emerging a new design philosophy in reaction to the monotonous and alienating spaces of modernist design, which was promoting a return to the merits of 'townscape' and the vernacular tradition. On the institutional side, in 1967 central government withdrew the extra subsidy for high flats, believing that the housing problem was more or less solved. Consequently local authorities had less incentive to build high blocks, and in any case, they were already facing a reduction in their role in new housebuilding as private developers increased their output. And from the point of view of residents, a series of studies demonstrated that they did not necessarily see high flats in the same way as those designers or authorities who had been so enamoured of them:

> They dislike concrete surfaces, greyness, dark colours, car parks (…), and an institutional appearance, which leads to frequent comparison of high rise schemes with prisons, barracks, or even concentration camps.
>
> (Dunleavy, 1981: 95)

Such a comparison was given added resonance by evidence of social isolation, anxiety and mental illness, and in particular of the problems being faced by families with children (see Jephcott, 1971; Stewart, 1970). The final, and most dramatic, death knell was sounded in 1968 when one side of Ronan Point, a 21 storey block in East London, collapsed after a gas explosion, killing several people.

By the 1970s, the era of the tower block seemed to be over, and they remained reviled throughout the 1980s and into the 1990s, a: 'risky, expensive and wasteful experiment' (Ravetz, 2001: 105). They even attracted the condemnation of that mild Conservative Prime Minister, John Major: 'There they stand, grey, sullen, concrete wastelands, set apart from the rest of the community, robbing people of ambition and self respect' (Meikle, 1995, cited in Towers, 2000: 44). Even so, they still provided homes for a million or more people, and they could not simply be erased from the landscape. Consequently solutions to what was now perceived as 'a problem' had to be found, with some authorities favouring selective demolition, often as a form of public spectacle; others selling or transferring stock to housing associations, universities, private sector landlords, housing action trusts or tenant management organisations; and yet others seeking funds for refurbishment (Towers, 2000). Design and construction improvements have included such remedies as the proper assignment of confused external and internal space to defined uses, providing a better sense of connection to the surrounding area, the overcladding of the original structure to improve weatherproofing and energy efficiency, and the toning down of the impression of solidity and mass by the introduction of coloured panels. In addition the introduction of concierge schemes has helped to rehumanise and supervise amorphous space (see Franklin, 1996c), and security has been further improved by the more mechanistic use of CCTV and other electronic systems. The results suggest that in conjunction with more sensitive allocations policies tower blocks can provide both acceptable and appropriate accommodation – for example for single people, couples without children, or even as sheltered housing. This potential has been reinforced by the recent establishment of the Sustainable Tower Blocks Initiative (STBI), an informal grouping of voluntary organisations whose aim is to work with residents, practitioners and policy makers to discover and implement ways to make tower blocks more sustainable places to live (see STBI, 2004).

There has also been a reappraisal of the architectural form of the tower block. This was first signalled in 1993, when pressure from the architectural profession led to the listing of the threatened tower block Keeling House in London, the first of several examples of post-war council housing to be listed (see O'Rourke, 2001). However, listed status does not necessarily ease the problems for local authorities, who then no longer have the option of demolition and who are usually given no recourse to additional public funding. However, if listing is accompanied by the cachet of design by a signature architect and a desirable location, then a new market may be opened up and a private developer attracted to undertake refurbishment. The evidence is that this is beginning to occur. The rapidly rising house prices of the early 2000s led to a situation in which increasing numbers of young professional people decided to purchase former Right to Buy apartments in newly improved and secure high rise blocks, especially in London. Thus endorsed by a pioneering few, former council blocks have become subject to a gentrification movement in which high rise living: 'formerly rejected as an industrial relic' (Weaver, 1999:16; see also Jacobs and Manzi, 1998) can become both acceptable and fashionable. This perception is supported by estate agents who report that first time buyers, young couples and even 'empty nesters' are willing to consider living in tower blocks (Garrett, 2002). Such an inclination chimes well with government concerns to achieve high density inner city living, with for example, Ken Livingstone, Mayor of London, being particularly keen on increasing the numbers of tall buildings.

This policy shift – or reversion – has been reflected amongst the design professionals. In 2001/2 the RIBA exhibition 'Coming Home' included futuristic tower blocks as one solution for delivering the requisite supply of new housing in the next two decades. Thus encouraged, a number of architects have begun to work with private developers and sometimes housing associations in the refurbishment of older tower blocks and in the design of new ones. Moreover, High Tech Modernists, including famous names such as Richard Rogers and Nicholas Grimshaw, have begun to compete to design the tallest and most dramatic forms. Usually including both residential and other uses, those currently under way include Ian Simpson's 38 storey Holloway Circus in Birmingham and 47 storey Beetham Tower in Manchester; the 30–50 storey 'Skyhouse' prototype of Marks Barfield, planned to house keyworkers, professionals and executives across the country; the 40 storey Eco-Tower in London for a mixed community; and the mixed use London Bridge Tower, nicknamed 'the shard of glass' and, at 306 metres and 66 storeys high, the tallest habitable building in Europe to date. With their striking and innovative design, these new towers are being advanced as models of quintessentially elegant, distinctive and sustainable living for twenty-first-century urban pioneers. However as such, they are a rather different proposition to the more prosaic refurbishment of existing 1950s and 1960s tower blocks.

Keeling House

Keeling House was designed in 1955 by Denys, later Sir Denys, Lasdun for the London Metropolitan Borough of Bethnal Green. Lasdun was born in England in 1914 of Russian Jewish extraction, his father being employed in the construction industry and his mother engaged as a musician. Lasdun himself studied music before he turned to architecture, and in later life suggested that the sense of rhythm, ratio and proportion in his architecture derived from this early musical background (Curtis, 1994). As an architect of his time, he was inevitably influenced by the modern movement, reading Le Corbusier's *Vers Une Architecture* in the 1930s,

7.7 Keeling House. This view illustrates three of the four wings of the 'butterfly' formation.

embracing the potential of concrete, and reflecting on the idea that architecture should not only be functional and mechanical but also capable of expressing social values. In 1938 he joined Lubetkin's influential Tecton architectural group in London until this was dissolved, whereupon he established his own practice.

After the Second World War Bethnal Green had a serious problem of bomb damaged and uncleared slum housing, and in common with many other councils, looked towards the emerging trend of mass housing blocks as a solution to its rehousing crisis. Having already successfully commissioned Lasdun for a scheme in Usk Street, the council decided to appoint him also for the larger scale redevelopment of the Claredale Street area. Lasdun's proposal was to tackle the project in two stages, starting with the building of a tower block. This was seen as the most effective means of rehousing the maximum number of tenants from the slum dwellings, leaving these then to be cleared, and in their place two low rise blocks constructed. The tower block, named Keeling House, was 16 storeys high and consisted of four angled wings in a 'butterfly' formation (Figure 7.7). The principle behind this arrangement was to provide protection from the wind and to permit penetration of the sun into all main living rooms at some point of the day. Between the wings was a central tower which contained the stairs, lift shaft, refuse chutes and other services. Each of the residential wings consisted of 14 double storey two-bed maisonettes with two single storey bed-sits inserted at fifth floor level. A high degree of privacy for occupants was attained by ensuring that access balconies served no more than two units and did not pass in front of living rooms or bedrooms, and by providing each unit with a private balcony to the front elevation. Entrance doors between each pair of vertical towers led directly to the central core of the circulation tower, and at each level a partially covered bridge and platform provided access to the dwelling units. These spaces were designed both to provide drying and storage space, and to afford views through the structural supports to the surrounding neighbourhood. Construction (in the hands of the construction company Wates) included both precast and in-situ elements, with the use of concrete, Portland stone facing slabs and black brickwork.

Although unique in its execution, Lasdun's solution owed much to the design orthodoxies which were part of his formative experience. In form and materials referents were apparent to the 'Tecton vocabulary', notably Lubetkin's 1935 design for High Point One (Curtis, 1994: 49). But Lasdun was also familiar with emerging insights into the desirability of respecting physical and social context. Thus he attempted to incorporate the ideas of the American urban designer Lynch in regard to 'urban grain' and 'cluster', and those of the British New Brutalist architects, the Smithsons, on the need to reflect the natural and cohesive social unit of the working class street (see Chapter 5). It was these ideas which lay behind Lasdun's rationale for designing Keeling House as what he called a 'cluster block', a solution which he himself seems to have seen as a pragmatic solution to a functional problem:

> The Cluster Block has been evolved as a solution for large residential units which, because of its small ground area, materially assists in the problem of decanting. They [sic] have been designed for the irregular and restricted sites commonly available for high density urban redevelopment. The basic idea of the Cluster Block is three-fold:-
>
> > Firstly, to reduce the apparent mass and repetitive content of the building by creating within it recognisable visual groups.
> > Secondly, to allow the environment to penetrate the body of the building and be experienced from within.
> > Thirdly, to separate the core with its services and communal amenities from the dwelling areas which remain private and quiet.
> >
> > (Drake and Lasdun, 1956: 125)

Lasdun's solution was greeted by the architectural world as both creative and ingenious, and the acclaim it was given at the time has continued into the present day (see, for example, Architectural Review, 1960; O'Rourke, 2001). Particularly admired have been the aesthetic impact, the sympathetic contribution to the urban landscape, the treatment of public and private space, and the vertical interpretation of the horizontal street, all of which have been interpreted as an unusually elegant sympathetic model for urban reconstruction:

> Seen from a distance the cluster's separate wings stand out from a vertical recess of shadow and repeat the scale and rhythms of the surrounding nineteenth-century facades in their balconies and sills. The instinct to sculpt has been strong and the forms shift into new relationships as one moves by ... the cluster has something of the presence and solidity, in a transient industrial environment, of an East End parish church steeple standing above the rooftops ... the transition from public to private has been handled gradually from the streets outside, to the space enveloped by the wings, to the bridges and alleys adjacent to the kitchens, into the private, double-storey 'maisonettes-in-the-air' themselves ... the alleys may be used to keep bicycles, to hang washing or to chat, so that the previous backyard world of Bethnal Green is to some extent re-created in the air.

> (Curtis, 1994: 49–50)

Although initially popular with residents, defects became apparent in Keeling House as early as 1976. Despite major repair work in the mid-1980s, the block remained so unsafe that by 1992 all the residents were decanted. The London Borough of Tower Hamlets (into which Bethnal Green had been absorbed in the 1965 local government reorganisation) was unable to meet the repairs bill, and it seemed likely that Keeling House would be demolished. Perceiving a threat to a landmark building, the Chair of RIBA's London region working party on post-war historic buildings wrote to the Department of National Heritage (forerunner of English Heritage) and requested that Keeling House be considered for listing as: 'a principal work of this leading architect and crucial to the development of his design philosophy and an understanding of Sir Denys' contribution to urban renewal and housing' (Building Design, 1992: 4). The ensuing consultation led to a conflict of opinion between those who admired the building and wished to see it retained (including Lasdun himself), and those who deplored it as an eyesore and as being totally out of character with the surrounding area, by this time a mix of traditional brick housing and low rise 1960s blocks.

Keeling House was listed Grade II* in November 1993 – to the delight of Lasdun but to the surprise and dismay of local residents, who had nicknamed it 'Keeling Over' (Baillieu, 1993). The listed status only added to Tower Hamlets' problems as the option of demolition was now effectively removed. Feasibility studies estimated the costs of a modified upgrade at £4 million and of a full refurbishment at £8 million, far beyond the capacity of the council. An alternative might be for a housing association to take it on, and for a time the Peabody Trust pursued the idea of using Keeling House for key worker housing. The benefit of this would be that higher rents could be charged than would be the case with typical housing association tenants, and this would help to defray costs (Baillieu, 1995). However, even then it could only be made viable on the basis of Tower Hamlets being willing to sell it for the nominal sum of £1, and the successful outcome of a bid to the National Heritage Lottery Fund for £11 million. The bid failed and Peabody was forced to withdraw.

By 1998 there was still no solution for Keeling House. It was now on the English Heritage buildings at risk register, and was costing Tower Hamlets thousands of pounds a year to keep secure. However with an improving property market new opportunities were beginning to open up, and private sector developers were beginning to express an interest in properties they would once never have considered. Thus Tower Hamlets revised its opinion that in an area of deprivation Keeling House must be used for affordable housing and decided to ask interested development teams to submit competitive bids. In May 1999 the site was sold to Associated Design and Management Services for the sum of £1,130,000. This team consisted of the developers Lincoln Holdings, a company with a history of converting both old and unusual properties for residential uses, and the modernist inclined architects Munkenbeck and Marshall, who had experience of projects which required them to: 'make a silk purse out of a sow's ear' (Sudjic, 2004). These architects had considerable respect for Lasdun, and despite the fact that he had been involved in a failed rival bid, they involved him in their plans until his death in 2001.

The redevelopment process required ongoing negotiation with the various bodies involved, specifically Tower Hamlets, English Heritage and the Twentieth Century Society. The problem they faced was the need to preserve the essential character of the listed building whilst also bringing it up to acceptable standards for twenty-first-century owner occupiers. This resulted in a number of fractious meetings and exchanges over how these objectives might best be reconciled. The issues included: securing an accurate photographic record of the interior; the restoration of one maisonette to its exact historic state; disputes over the acceptability of reversing the relative position of kitchens and living rooms and dispensing with the dividing wall; the retention of the bed platform or storage space above the stairs; the refurbishment rather than the removal of some of the internal fixtures and fittings such as the quarry tiled kitchen floors and metal framed doorways and windows; the height and visibility of new rooftop rooms; the external landscaping; and the choice of internal and external colours to replicate as closely as possible the originals.

Particularly contentious were three new additions the developers wished to make: a steel perimeter fence; an entrance foyer; and a new penthouse in the void created by the removal of the large water tank on the rooftop. Both the Twentieth Century Society and the conservation committee of Tower Hamlets felt the suggested plans for the fence and the foyer were inappropriate. The proposed 2.4 metre steel fence, referred to by the architects as a 'sculptural enclosure', was seen as obtrusive, impenetrable and cage-like, and counter to the original permeability of the building at street level. Also rejected were the first designs for the foyer, since the projecting canopy was considered too prominent and self-conscious, and detracted from the lines of the main structure. English Heritage, by contrast, endorsed both the fence and the foyer, arguing that in present day circumstances residents would appreciate the level of security they represented. The compromise eventually reached in regard to the fence was that it should be reduced in height and given a less solid appearance, with more openings inserted to the surrounding streets. Similarly, the scale of the foyer was reduced so as to ensure that the line of the canopy was contained within the wings of the adjacent two towers.

The issue of the penthouse was less easily resolved. Although supported by Lasdun and English Heritage, Tower Hamlets felt the proposed two storey apartment was not sufficiently in keeping with the design of the original cluster concept of Keeling House, and refused planning permission. There followed a period of appeal, modification, further appeals and further modifications, and at the time of writing the matter is still ongoing, by now several years after the original application in 1999.

The new flats in Keeling House were ready for occupancy in late 2000. The dwellings have been sold on long leases, with one bed apartments priced at £135,000, duplexes (the former maisonettes) at £195,000 and triplex penthouses (the former top storey maisonettes with added rooftop rooms and access to a roof terrace) at £310,000. Despite the hyped marketing, sales did not proceed particularly quickly. Since this equated into low take up of units, initial residents began to be concerned that there was an underlying intention to let some units as social housing, especially given the high number of council and housing association properties in the area. However, eventually all the flats were either sold to owner occupiers or to landlords for the private rental market.

Externally Keeling House dominates the surrounding streets as it has done since first built, and its refurbished profile is little different from before (Figure 7.8). At ground level, however, the new grey steel perimeter fence with its locked gates provides an effective barrier (Figure 7.9). In addition it also signifies the redesignation of space; what was formerly open to the public is now closed, and what was once the living space of social housing tenants is now privately owned. This is further emphasised by the symbolically striking and illuminated glass-fronted entrance foyer with its aluminium canopy (Figure 7.10). This is approached almost processually from the street by way of an electronic pedestrian entrance gate, a short path, and a paved bridge over a pool where fountains play spasmodically. Within, a new concierge presides, ensuring that all is in order and

7.8   Keeling House in the context of what remains of the adjacent Victorian
housing

that the activity of strangers and the access of visitors are closely monitored. This
presence of the concierge is part of the change of use and rehumanising of ground
floor space, with the concierge's office and two new ground floor flats occupying
the voids left by the removal of the old service plants. External space too has been
redeployed, with 34 marked car parking spaces and the softening of the new and
refurbished hard landscaping with a limited amount of planting.

Lasdun's contribution has not been forgotten, and on the entrance path is a plaque
commemorating his life and his role as the original architect. His involvement
with Keeling House had endured for over 40 years and his support was continuous
despite his regret that it would no longer be used by the social tenants for whom
it had been designed (Building Design, 1999). It was fitting therefore that he lived
just long enough to see the rehabilitation and transformation of Keeling House
completed: '[D]esigned with a working-class community of the 1950s in mind
[it] has been reborn, after years of dereliction, as an oasis of chic living' (Powell,
2001: 25). In recognition of this achievement it received in 2002 an architectural
award from RIBA and a commendation from the Civic Trust.

7.9 The steel boundary fence and pedestrian access gate. This image also clearly shows the rhythm of horizontals and verticals and of black and white surfaces.

Conclusion

The focus in this chapter on buildings of the past and the way in which they have been preserved illustrates a cultural proclivity for the preservation of artefacts as emblems of a shared history and national identity. The fact that such artefacts are often sanitised, romanticised and viewed through a nostalgic haze serves only to reinforce the propensity to construct a heritage which is essentially illusory, since all unfavourable elements have been erased. Buildings are an important part of this heritage, and whilst it may be their material presence which assumes dominance, they also have sedimented within them the ordering of social and economic life. Different periods have brought different orderings, and under the social processes of the modern, rational and scientific age it was the desire for mastery through classification and control that came to prominence. Assisted by new techniques of engineering and technology, this proclivity for classification and control was reflected in the construction of a range of new building types, some of which were specifically designed to contain those whose position in society was seen as antithetical to the aims of the capitalist project: the criminal;

7.10 The canopy and reflective glass of the foyer and the approach over water. The stepped base of the fountain can also be seen, and the plaque commemorating Lasdun is just visible in the foreground.

the indigent poor; and the lunatic. Hence arose the building types of the prison, the workhouse and the asylum; 'structuring structures', in which marginalisation, domination and oppression were represented both in the monumental form, and in the layout and sequencing of space within (see Chapter 5). Of these building types, it was the spatially segregated asylum that aroused the most fear and revulsion. Its associations were with madness, perhaps the most bizarre, frightening and least understood manifestation of cultural and social 'otherness'.

The improving economic and social conditions of the mid-twentieth century, together with better understanding of mental illness, meant that the role of the asylums was diminished. But there now emerged a new building type, less overtly punitive but still on a monumental scale and similarly symbolising the modernising zeal and oppressive power of the state (see Jacobs and Manzi, 1998). This was the utilitarian mass housing block, initially resisted in the UK but soon to become an increasingly visible residential form in its manifestation of the tower block. This new type of housing, with its identical cells in faceless blocks, symbolised the anonymity, homogeneity, commonality and powerlessness of working people. As time went on however, such housing was found to be not only structurally flawed but also socially oppressive, and increasingly associated with an 'underclass' of the unemployed, the feckless, the criminal and the destitute. Thus it began to attract something of the same stigma and shame associated with the earlier building types of the asylum and the workhouse, and became similarly a place to be shunned and reviled.

At the institutional level it was local authorities who were charged with enacting central government expectations in regard both to the provision of the nineteenth-century asylum and the twentieth-century tower block. However, willingness to respond varied considerably and depended on the outcome of negotiation between officials, councillors and other interests, as well as the perceived local degree of need and the availability of sites. But once action had been decided on, most authorities were anxious to gain distinction through the production of the most imposing design, and hence sought to appoint the best architects. For their part individual architects were keen to grasp the opportunity to earn symbolic capital and enhance their reputations through commissions for buildings on such a monumental scale. In addition, architects and the architectural profession as a whole played a significant role in reproducing trends in the construction of both asylums and tower blocks, as reflected in the texts of Fowler and Lasdun cited in this chapter and in the dominant role of architects at the MHLG.

Since the latter part of the twentieth century there has been a change in social processes whereby the more reflective conditions of postmodernity have begun to challenge old 'truths'. A greater acceptance of diversity has led to a questioning of the entrenched and illiberal attitudes that were responsible for the assignment of marginal people to marginal places, and there has also been, in this time of dislocation and commodification, an intensification of the desire to identify, preserve and consume heritage. It is through these processes that there has gradually been a shift from the reactive views of those who have constructed asylums and the tower blocks as entirely negative and oppressive (as in the discourses of Enoch Powell and John Major) to a more enlightened approach which has concentrated less on the former degrading use and more on the present monumental form. This has been encouraged by the discourse of individuals such as Pevsner and other architectural devotees, and by the campaigns of pressure groups. It is they who have helped to transform attitudes to both the asylum and the tower block, creating a situation in which both of these can be appreciated for their architectural distinction. However, it has only been with more favourable economic conditions and a booming housing market that institutional interest has also been stirred, with the private sector now willing to step in and take on the risks of redevelopment and a new generation of architects experimenting with twenty-first-century modifications of the high rise form.

The case study examples of Exe Vale and Keeling House show how the original designs were individual interpretations of newly emerging building types: Fowler at Exe Vale adapting the theme of the panopticon, and Lasdun at Keeling House combining the vocabulary of the Tecton practice with Lynch's urban design concepts and the Smithsons' notion of high rise working class life. In their designs they had to allow for the arrangement of large numbers of people in space whilst allowing also for access, circulation, socialisation and services. In Exe Vale this was achieved on a horizontal axis with long wards fanning out from a semi-circular panoptical corridor. Keeling House was organised on a vertical axis, but access was freely available at ground level from all sides and with no supervisory gaze deemed necessary. Once within, tenants were allocated to identical individual flats (or cells) in the same way as at Exe Vale, with access from a series of semi-private spaces on a vertical rather than a horizontal alignment.

In adapting these built forms the challenge for the developers has been to alter the existing organisation of space to render it suitable for twenty-first-century residential use by a more privileged class of occupant. But they have not been free agents and the final form has been shaped by the outcome of negotiation between the often conflicting priorities of the planning authorities, conservation interests and the developers themselves. At Exe Vale the axis has been altered from horizontal to vertical with the formation of town houses or flats accessed from their own private external doors, and the panopticon effect of the corridor has been eliminated. The symbolic gardens serve to reinforce a sense of control by residents over their own space (by contrast to the former users), whilst the perimeter railings and gates symbolise the privacy and social exclusivity of the development: ironically this is now a place from which the criminal, the poor and most certainly the mad must be debarred. Exclusivity is signalled too by the ceremonial approach reminiscent of a stately home: through grand entrance gates and up a long tree lined avenue with a vista to the aesthetic frontage of the former Centre House. This impression management is further emphasised by the extravagant discourse of the marketing texts and the stylish names chosen for the various parts of the development.

At Keeling House the existing form has offered less flexibility than Exe Vale due to its verticality, but change has been achieved by transforming the internal layout of each flat (now redesignated an apartment). Here the re-arrangement and opening up of rooms is expressive of the liberation of the new residents from the old imposed ordering of space. But the greatest change is at ground level. Here the former permeability to the street and its surroundings has been eliminated by the erection of a barrier fence far more conspicuous and intrusive than the one at Exe Vale, with the symbolic effect of emphasising the social and spatial distance between the new private residents and their public sector neighbours. The installation of CCTV and a concierge reinforce the imposition of surveillance and control; a new form of panoptical gaze and a neat reversal of what has occurred at Exe Vale. This is balanced by the illusion of import and grandiosity created by the addition of the glitzy foyer and the approach over water, smaller in scale but not dissimilar in symbolic value to the ceremonial approach to Exe Vale. In both cases it is this re-framing of spatial form which has been instrumental in transforming the old and the disdained into the new and the desirable.

8 Settings of structured dependency

In all societies the trajectory of the life course is marked by the life stages of childhood, adulthood and old age. Although having a physiological basis, the different expectations and responsibilities inherent to each stage are culturally and socially constructed, and the social significance of transition from one stage to another is often marked ritually as a *rite de passage*. This can involve, for example, an elaborate initiation ceremony, accession to wealth, the bestowal of symbolic gifts or tokens, entry to a special type of dwelling, or admittance to the ranks of those with special knowledge or wisdom. In traditional societies, the most complex, dangerous, painful and emotionally charged rituals tend to be associated with the transition from childhood to adulthood, whilst the transition to old age is a more gradual process accompanied by a change in status to an elder. Elders are often revered as a fount of wisdom, for they are perceived to be the custodians of judicial and ritual power and as such must be respected.

In Western societies there has emerged a dichotomy between the traditional and the contemporary ordering of the life stages of childhood, adulthood and old age. Historically, both childhood and old age were risky and of short duration. Children were treated as miniature adults and entered the labour market from an early age, unless they were from wealthy parentage. Old people worked until they were incapacitated or died, since the concept of retirement was unknown. Only gradually and in the latter stages of industrialisation did childhood and old age begin to exist as life stages somehow apart from and contrasted to adulthood, and given special treatment through income assistance and liberation from the labour market. Thus by the early years of the twentieth century both childhood and old age were becoming constructed as arenas of dependency and vulnerability, a situation further underpinned by the activities of the welfare state from mid-century.

One result of this has been that the narrow categories of 'childhood' and 'old age' are no longer deemed adequate to span the many years they now represent. Thus the extension of dependency for the young has led to the emergence of the new stages of adolescence and youth, whilst the extension of the post-retirement years has led to concepts such as the 'third' and the 'fourth' age (see Laslett,

1989), 'active' and 'frail' old age, or even the 'young old' and the 'old old'. The invention of these new life stages has concomitantly involved new transitions: of the young from dependency through semi-dependency to independence; and of the old from independence to semi-dependency to dependency.

One of the consequences of this stretching of the ages of dependency is an increase in those who, quite legitimately, do not work. But in our society it is engagement in the labour market which brings status and reward. Those outside it are on the margins, and pose a potential threat. If their numbers grow too large they are likely to be constructed as a 'burden' on society, inviting a 'moral panic' as to their legitimacy and the requirement of society to care for and contain them. As with any threat, society has adopted strategies to limit the risks not only to itself but also to the categories of people concerned. These strategies include protection, regulation, surveillance and control, all of which may involve an element of spatial containment. In some cases this has resulted in the provision of places specifically devised for the problematic young or old, where risk can be managed and dependency given structure. These settings are in effect spaces of transition, entered into at the boundaries between dependence and independence.

It is with such settings that the current chapter is concerned, with the initial sections looking first at the general issues in regard to older people and then at the concept of the continuing care retirement community (CCRC). Later sections address the problems facing younger people in the contemporary world and the recently imported 'solution' of the foyer. The case study examples consist of Hartrigg Oaks in York, the only CCRC of its kind in England, and Occasio House, a foyer located in Harlow, Essex.

Accommodating age

During the latter decades of the twentieth century there emerged concerns that the increasing numbers of older people and their greater life expectancy, together with the prospect of a pensions 'time bomb', might pose significant problems for the rest of society (see Bernard and Phillips, 2000). Increasingly these problems have been constructed as a burden, with old age cast as a state of inevitable and expensive welfare dependency:

> The social reality of later life (...) is largely determined by compulsory retirement, the old age pension (social security), and state maintained systems of long-term care. Deprived of the opportunity to exercise a more socially productive identity, older people are consigned to the position of a pensioner who is forever at the mercy of state welfare policy.
>
> (Gilleard and Higgs, 2002: 370)

This situation has been referred to as one of 'structured dependency' (Townsend, 1981) in which older people undergo a process of 'disengagement' from socio-economic activity and are then expected to withdraw into a twilight existence. Dismissed by society as of no interest or account, they are relegated to the margins or the back rooms of society: 'made to share a space on society's fringe' (Hockey and James, 1993: 5). In this space, their lack of status is further reinforced by comparison to the helpless life stage of infancy; a 'second childhood', in which dignity and autonomy are denied.

This perception of old age is however undergoing a gradual transformation. The notion of passive submission to structural forces is being challenged both by older people themselves and by academics and other commentators. Increasingly the situation is recognised as one of active agency in which people no longer feel precipitated into a stereotypically dependent old age at a set age, but themselves create their own more flexible boundaries according to individual capacity and proclivity. Hence at the start of the twenty-first century old age has become a more ambivalent social and personal construct, and the reality is that the years of later life normatively associated with 'old age' are multifaceted, that they can span a period of 40 years or more, and that they involve a multitude of lifestyles within an increasingly polarised socio-economic set of circumstances.

Despite this transformation, the legacy of the 'structured dependency' construction of old age is perpetuated through many of the arrangements for the support and care of older people. These have relied on the cumulative provision of segregated and communal settings, such as the post-war local authority old people's home (replacing the workhouse), the sheltered housing of the 1960s, and the burgeoning of private sector residential care in the 1980s (see Means and Smith, 1998). Inevitably, the effect of this expansion of specialist provision has been to normalise institutional and segregated settings as a 'solution' for the housing and support needs of older people. Furthermore the system that was established has created a continuum, or conveyor belt, of care, along which people are shunted until they reach the final destination of the nursing home or the geriatric ward (Heywood et al., 2002; Higgins, 1989a).

Within this continuum the site that has received most criticism is 'the home' (itself a charged description, see Higgins, 1989b). This has been portrayed as a 'last refuge' (Townsend, 1962), a 'last resort' (Oldman and Quilgars, 1999) and a 'warehousing' solution for the 'storage' of redundant people (Higgins, 1989b). Moreover, as an example of a 'total' institution, dependency in such a setting is reinforced, the older person disempowered and 'infantilised' by an institutionalised routine that promotes degrading and demeaning practices such as the wearing of communal clothes, punishment for minor misdemeanours and the distribution of 'pocket money' (see Goffman, 1968; Hockey and James, 1993; Higgins, 1989a). Such treatment is symptomatic of the domination that society has chosen to vest in professionals over those who are in any way disabled, and is characterised by an inability to see beyond the impaired and enfeebled body and its functional limitations. Furthermore, in sustaining the idea that in such circumstances a person is best served in an institution, there is little heed to the potential impact of dislocation from the family home, with its locus as a repository of memory, a source of identity and a place where independence can be maintained (see Gurney and Means, 1993; Higgins 1989b).

In addition to such critiques of institutionalisation there have been government concerns about the spiralling costs of institutional care. The consequence has been a new emphasis on independent living, as endorsed in the rhetoric of the 1990 NHS and Community Care Act (see Chapter 3). Thus the 'mantra' of independent living has been constructed as the ideal, with the implication that this is the only way to achieve well-being and empowerment, and in effect: 'liberating older people from the structured dependency forced upon them in the past' (Heywood *et al.*, 2002: 35). But the danger is of independent living being constructed as the only way in which 'success' can be achieved and the reality is, as so often, more ambivalent. For to some, independent living is experienced as isolating and imprisoning, whilst supported collective living can bring not only security and social activity, but also a sense of identity and place attachment (see Clapham, 2005; Franklin, 1996b).

It is debates such as these which have been favourable to the emergence of new concepts and models, with even the government calling for more flexible forms of housing and support (see DETR, 2001). Some of these have introduced more choice and flexibility in supported living options, such as the arrival into the sheltered housing market of the private sector, keen to cash in on an increasingly asset rich older population. A second innovation has been the introduction by the voluntary sector of 'very sheltered housing', also known as 'extra care' or 'category 2.5' housing. This offers higher levels of support than traditional sheltered housing but without the more institutionalising elements of residential care – thus 'blurring the boundaries' between the two (Oldman, 2000). In addition, new design guides have emerged which aim to humanise institutional environments through, for example, the provision of more domestic scale spaces, respect for privacy, opportunities for personalisation, seating which overlooks scenes of activity and attention to outdoor spaces (see, for example, Robson *et al.*, 1997).

Other concepts have focused on independent living, moving beyond the provision of adaptations or personal support to more fundamental modifications of the home environment. Significant in this regard are Lifetime Homes and Smart Homes. The idea of Lifetime Homes, initially devised by the Helen Hamlyn Foundation (Kelly, 2001), was enthusiastically taken up by the JRF (see Chapter 4) as relevant not only to old age but to any stage or condition of the life course. Amongst the 16 criteria to be included are space for a through floor lift, strengthened ceiling joists to accommodate tracking for hoists, a downstairs cloakroom with sufficient space to accommodate a shower at a later date, and a drive wide enough to allow manoeuvrability of a wheelchair and assistant (Brewerton and Darton, 1997).

The Smart Homes concept is associated with the work of the Science and Technology Policy Research Unit at the University of Sussex, and has also been supported by the JRF. The concept involves the harnessing of new technology to assist people with impairments in the negotiation of the everyday activities of life in the home (see Gann *et al.*, 1999). Hand held devices can perform a range of functions, such as opening and closing doors and windows, and switching on central heating and cookers, whilst remote sensors can detect gas leaks, raise the alert to scalding water, and monitor state of health. However, arguably there are issues here about the substitution of technology for people, the ethical implications of the 'tracking' of an older person, and the imposition of complex, fiddly and sometimes poorly understood technology. Indeed the effect can be such that the home itself may begin to take on the qualities of an institution.

In addition to the above, there are new models for older people which have been introduced to the UK from overseas, and which are notable for the greater degree of agency they can, in theory, confer on older people as they make their later life transitions. One of these is cohousing, which is not confined solely to older people and is further considered in Chapter 10. Another is the larger scale and more diverse concept of the retirement community, which has been in existence in some other countries, notably the US and Australia for some time. Originally conceived for active older people, it has been recognised that provision also needs to be made for the more dependent stages. It is to meet this need that the continuing care retirement community (CCRC) has been devised.

From the retirement community to the CCRC

Retirement communities in the US first appeared after the Second World War, some being based on particular interest groups such as church membership or professional affiliation, and others on a more market oriented notion of the pursuit of leisure. The trailblazer for the latter was Sun City, developed in the Arizona desert in 1960, and the success of this project led to the consolidation of a niche market across the US for affluent retired people in search of leisure. By the start of the twenty-first century there were numerous such developments, varying in size from a few hundred to over 25,000 units (Suchman, 2001). Referred to as Active Adult Retirement Communities (AARCs), the emphasis is on lifestyle:

> Talk to developers of active adult retirement communities (AARCs) and they will tell you that what they are selling is not housing but lifestyle ... What creates lifestyle is more than simply a clubhouse, a swimming pool, and a calendar of social events. For example, lifestyle also embraces the residents' image of the community and of themselves within it ... Often they want a resort environment where their life will resemble a perpetual vacation, providing comfort, quality, independence, companionship, choice, security and freedom from responsibility.
>
> (Suchman, 2001: 58)

What AARCs do not offer is a home for life; for in a setting in which the ethos is one of health, leisure and activity, the visibility of decrepitude and dependency would be anathema. Hence the target age group of AARCs is 55–74, the years when an active lifestyle is a normative expectation. The age of 75 marks a new transition, one to frailty and infirmity, and these deficiencies, together with the costly and non-profitable nursing care which accompanies them, have no place in the AARC.

It was to include this more frail section of the population that continuing care retirement communities were devised. First introduced in the US in the 1950s, they were also a feature of post-war Germany, and in both countries have been adopted with increasing enthusiasm as an alternative model to institutional and expensive residential care (Hearnden, 1983; Martin, 1990; Rugg, 2000). The principle behind them is to offer independent self-contained accommodation to which support can be delivered on a flexible basis, and, on the same site, a nursing home to which people can move temporarily or permanently for more intensive care. Residents generally enter at a later age than to AARCs, but the same emphasis pertains of a challenging and active lifestyle – at least initially. The difference is that the CCRC offers the reassurance and security of knowing that there will be no compulsion to move away at the transition to full dependency.

A unique aspect of most CCRCs is the funding mechanism. For instead of purchasing a home and then paying charges as and when support and care are needed, residents pay an entry fee together with a monthly or annual service fee. This covers the provision of accommodation, be it in an independent unit or the nursing home, as well as all the care and support that might be needed for the rest of life. For residents it operates as an insurance scheme; the risk being that they are paying up front for costly care that they might never need. The risks for the provider are more complex. Initially it is necessary to calculate a viable balance between the number of independent units and the number of nursing home places. Then for each individual who enters the CCRC, the organisation will for a time operate in surplus, but as health deteriorates this will slip into deficit; a deficit that increases the worse incapacity becomes and the longer it endures. In addition to setting the fees at an appropriate level there is therefore a need to ensure the right balance between fit, self-caring people and those reliant on support. This involves 'vetting' those who wish to enter, not only for their long term financial circumstances, but also in regard to health status and likely prognosis. The dangers of these risks are illustrated by the failure in the US of many private sector schemes (Nyman, 1999), and for this reason the majority of CCRCs have been established by non-profit making organisations.

In the UK, retirement communities have only begun to appear in the last decade or two. Here, speculative housebuilders have begun to appreciate the potential of cashing in on an affluent 'baby boomer' generation, desirous of escape from the risks and turmoils of everyday life to a secure and tranquil environment. Thus they are moving on from the occasional block of retirement apartments to the development of larger scale retirement communities, often emotively referred to as 'villages' (see Chapter 6). However, what these private sector led retirement communities generally do not offer, is support and care.

It has been the voluntary sector, sometimes in partnership with local authorities, which has extended the notion of retirement communities from the affluent to those in housing need. The first such scheme was Bradeley Village completed in 1995 by Staffordshire Housing Association, but without any provision for meeting the care needs of residents as they aged. With more vision and foresight, the ExtraCare Charitable Trust has recognised the reality that 'residential care as a model has had its day' and has sought to devise a new model of housing with support (Payne, 2000: 8). It is also concerned to challenge the stereotypical view of old age as a time of dependency and passivity:

> At the heart of this challenge is the principle of independence. By encouraging older people to take charge of their own lives, to stay active both physically and mentally, we give them the opportunity to embrace life, rather than wait for it to slip away.
>
> (ExtraCare Charitable Trust, 2003: 1)

The first two schemes, Berryhill in Staffordshire and Ryedale in Cheshire, offer not only a range of amenities, such as fitness centres, pubs, craft rooms, internet facilities, shops and libraries, but also the chance to participate in extreme sports such as abseiling, hang-gliding and canoeing. Those who need care can be supported in their own homes by ExtraCare's own staff, but not to the extent of specialist nursing and continuing care. This means that once again, the most frail have to move elsewhere.

CCRCs, with their lifetime guarantee, have attracted little attention amongst providers in the UK, even though there is a precedent in the few that were established by charities in the late nineteenth century (Hearnden, 1983). This is no doubt related to the fact that, unlike the situation in America and Germany, this country developed a system of 'cradle to grave' welfare provision. However the phasing out of this welfare settlement has seen suggestions that CCRCs could be an appropriate alternative to meet the needs of older people in twenty-first-century Britain (see Hearnden, 1983; Martin, 1990). Many housing and care organisations have expressed reservations, due in part to fear of a step into the unknown, but also in regard to the nature of the risks involved, the high costs which restrict such schemes to the more wealthy, and the segregationary principles which seem to contradict the care in the community ideology (Rugg, 2000). To date the only exceptions appear to be Inchmarlo House, opened in Scotland in 1987 by a private development company (see Inchmarlo House, 2004) and Hartrigg Oaks, discussed in the case study below.

Hartrigg Oaks

The attention of the JRF was first drawn to the idea of continuing care communities by Dame Eileen Younghusband, a prominent and much travelled figure in the world of social work. Further interest was aroused in 1982 by an academic paper presented at the Policy Studies Institute which stated:

> The first retirement community in this country should be worthy; it should be designed as a demonstration and give the idea a fair test.
>
> (Robin Huws Jones, cited in Dennis, 1989: 8)

Subsequently the Centre for Policy on Ageing was commissioned by the JRF to investigate whether CCRCs could be a viable option in Britain. The ensuing report (Hearnden, 1983) inspired some of the trustees of the Joseph Rowntree Housing Trust (JRHT), the housing association arm of the JRF, to visit CCRC schemes in the US, many of which were run by Quakers. At the same time, the JRF began a consultation process with relevant organisations, and also engaged the Research Institute for Consumer Affairs to assess the extent of interest in a CCRC amongst older people themselves (Rugg, 2000).

Encouraged by the findings JRHT decided to develop their own CCRC. A potential site was identified on land they owned at New Earswick, the garden village three miles from the centre of York (see Chapter 3). The advantage of this site, apart from its nil cost in development terms, was that it would allow the integration of the CCRC into the existing community of New Earswick. A major drawback, however, was that it was designated as part of the Green Belt, even though the local council of Ryedale had included it as 'whiteland' in the local plan for possible development after the mid-1990s.

The architect appointed was John McNeil of McNeil and Beechey, a local firm chosen for their expertise in the design of supported housing and health care facilities. The planning application for the scheme, initially named Beechland, was accompanied by a copy of the Hearnden report and statements from various members of JRHT. These stressed the unique potential of the proposed CCRC as a vital scheme which would be of national significance. Also emphasised were the Joseph Rowntree credentials, the suitability of the organisation to undertake the work, and the fact that in accordance with JRF principles the development and ongoing activity of the community would be monitored and evaluated to inform future decision-making and promote change.

There was considerable opposition by local people and others to the scheme, with concern expressed about increased traffic, loss of amenity space, expansion of an already elderly local population and the unaffordability of the project to most New Earswick residents. In the eyes of the planning authority, the main issues were the Green Belt location and the fact that sufficient residential land had already been designated in the York area. It was on these grounds that planning permission was refused. In their appeal JRHT argued that the unique nature of the scheme justified special treatment – an assertion that led planning officers to remark that JRHT was unjustifiably trading on its reputation to secure an exemption from planning policy. Given the novel issues that had been raised, the Secretary of State decided to determine the appeal himself. In his opinion the merits of the proposal were insufficient to outweigh the greenbelt argument, especially as JRHT owned land on the opposite side of the road which could equally well be developed. In a second appeal JRHT made the most of the ambivalent development status of the land and the fact that they had addressed the affordability issue by creating ten bursaries for local residents. However, the Secretary of State again disallowed the development.

In 1994 JRHT presented a new and successful application for the site on the opposite side of the road. The conditions imposed included: the implementation of acceptable landscaping; restriction of occupancy to people over 50; a prohibition on garages, sheds, greenhouses, or extensions; and satisfactory site access and diversion of a footpath. Finally able to proceed, a contractor for the design and build construction was selected, over whom JRHT retained an unusual degree of control: 'We were vetted like we have never been vetted before' (Marketing Manager, Kier North East, cited in Smit, 1997: 22). Also at this stage several changes were made to the initial plans, in part inspired by a second visit to the US. These included the provision of higher space standards and flexible roof space, the location of communal and nursing facilities more centrally, and the creation of a north–south axis to give a stronger pedestrian and visual link through to New Earswick. It was also decided to include a crèche to serve the people of New Earswick who had no existing such facility. This would help to integrate the scheme into the surrounding area as well as helping to offset any sense of isolation from other age groups (Sturge, 2000).

Throughout the planning stages JRHT had been taking actuarial advice in regard to fees and the maintenance of balance between those with low and high dependency needs. JRHT had two concerns in this regard, one was to be financially transparent to achieve the aims of viability and replicability, and the other was to be able to offer flexibility of packages to residents so that those with varying financial circumstances could benefit. The fee system that was set up consisted of two components: a residence fee reflecting the market value of each bungalow; and a community fee to cover care and services, each with three payment options (see Rugg, 2000; Sturge, 2000 for details). The residence fee is normally refundable on death or on leaving but is not increased in line with either inflation or increases in property prices; an issue which may have to be revisited in the light of recent house price increases (see Croucher et al., 2003). As part of a non-profit making organisation JRHT itself accrues no monetary gain; on the other hand, the substantial reserves of the JRF ensure that the scheme is fully underwritten.

In regard to balance, JRHT had to change the initial 'first come first served' waiting list policy, since this would inevitably soon have skewed the age distribution to the older and more frail. Hence applicants in their 60s, especially couples (who to some extent care for each other) are currently given preference. There are also rigorous financial and health checks which ensure that the initial and ongoing fees can be met, and that on first admission a resident is unlikely to need care. Conditions leading to exclusion include, for example, rheumatoid or osteoarthritis, Parkinson's disease and history of heart disease or stroke. On admission the rights and responsibilities of both residents and JRHT are clearly explained, and each party signs a lease agreement for the property and a care agreement for care delivery. A care package of up to 21 hours can be delivered to each dwelling, and this can include elements from a pop-in or home help service, personal care, or emotional support. If more than 21 hours is needed then a respite or permanent transfer to the care home facility has to be arranged. Lifelong care is guaranteed, and in the rare event of a place not being available in the care home JRHT would fund residential care elsewhere.

The original name of Beechlands was changed during the development stage to the more resonant name of Hartrigg Oaks, with its associations of rootedness, strength, longevity and connection to the earth. However, the intention to describe the scheme on the entrance sign as 'Hartrigg Oaks Continuing Care Retirement Community' was soon rejected by residents in favour of a counter-ageist one which declares instead 'Hartrigg Oaks and Little Acorns Day Nursery' (Figure 8.1). In the naming of the routes within the scheme (e.g. Jedwell, Beeforth,

8.1 The entrance sign to Hartrigg Oaks, with hart and oak leaf logo

Toremil, Lasenby), a sense of history and local continuity has been drawn on, for these are derived from the strip landowners of the ancient Forest of Galtres. Similar close attention has been given to the message conveyed in the marketing materials, whether through advertising, through the promotional video or in the pack sent to potential applicants. The setting in the historic Garden Village of New Earswick and the variety of facilities and landscaped gardens are both stressed, whilst other attributes mentioned include: the 'unique approach to retirement living'; the 'quality accommodation'; the 'stimulating environment'; the 'full and active life in a vibrant and friendly community'; the 'financial security'; and the 'peace of mind'; all endorsed by positive quotations from existing residents, and, in the case of the video, by a few choice words from the Director, Richard Best. However, the initial proud claim to being the first CCRC in the UK had to be modified by the addition of the words 'on the insurance principle' after the existence of Inchmarlo House was recognised. That the scheme is meeting a need is reflected in the interest both from local people and from Quakers across the country. Indeed, the marketing that was required was, and continues to be, minimal, and advertising in local papers and the Quaker journal *The Friend* has been sufficient to ensure a waiting list for some years to come.

The £18 million scheme was opened in 1999 by the Trust's Chairman, Sir Peter Barclay. The 152 bungalows, some in terraces but the majority semi-detached, consist of two types, the one bed Rigg and the two bed Hart. All are built to lifetime homes standards (apart from the parking arrangements), and include

8.2 A close of bungalows. Note the picket fence, the 'caboose', parking bays, dropped tactile kerbs, and symbolic change of road surface to denote entrance to semi-public space.

8.3   A cluster of bungalows within surrounding landscaped open space

features such as low sills, lever taps, double glazing, a call alarm system, and low level baths and toilets. Each bungalow also has a (very) small picket fenced garden, an attached brick shed (known as a 'caboose'), and a designated car space in a parking bay rather than in curtilage (Figure 8.2). Materials are traditional brick with some concrete rendered detailing, wooden doors and window frames, and red concrete roof tiles. Only the care centre has the clay pantiles common to the rest of New Earswick. Security is provided by a discreet CCTV system.

The layout is such as to maximise the amount of landscaped open space, with most of the bungalows clustered symmetrically in closes on the outside of a looped distributor road (Figure 8.3). Lying more loosely within the circle of this road and closer to the care centre are some of the one bed bungalows, initially planned for those who had higher care needs. These, perhaps unfortunately, convey something of the impression of a local authority old person's scheme. A noticeboard near the entrance shows a plan of the site, but wayfinding and legibility are somewhat indeterminate, especially given the lack of distinctiveness between closes and their confusingly enigmatic names. The purpose of the north–south axis as a link through to New Earswick is not strongly defined on the ground, and most visitors to the site would miss the much lauded life size bronze sculpture of a hart which stands on this path (see Darton, 1999), and which, together with an oak leaf, forms the logo of Hartrigg Oaks (Figures 8.1, 8.4). However, the design is highly permeable to pedestrians, with a network of wide, flat footpaths, dropped tactile kerbs at crossing points, and a change of surface to signal the entrance to each close (Figure 8.2).

8.4 The statue of the hart and the porticoed entrance to The Oaks

The main focal point is 'The Oaks' which houses the care centre, administrative offices and communal facilities (Figures 8.4, 8.5). The porticoed entrance leads past the CCTV and alarms control centre to a large stone flagged reception area, intended to represent a street or courtyard (Figure 8.6). Full noticeboards display a range of information and advice, although the notices for resident activities are in a separate niche from those maintained by staff. The care centre is accessed through automatic doors adjacent to the reception desk, which is staffed by a white-coated, hence somewhat clinical looking, receptionist. The doors lead into a short corridor where a visitors' book invites the signing of names, then further automatic doors lead through to the care home itself. Here attempts have been made to avoid an institutional atmosphere by, for example, installing a dado rather than a grab rail, referring to the individual en suite rooms as 'bed-sitting rooms', fitting solid 'front doors' with door bells, supplying each room with a balcony, and enabling the residents to bring their own items of furniture if they wish. Nothing can however conceal the large array of wheelchairs, the rather cramped feel of the internal corridors with no natural lighting, and the presence of uniformed care assistants. Activity is monitored from a nurses' station, and in close vicinity to this are the rooms for people affected by dementia. Initially the complex needs of such people could not be met on site, but now there is a specialist dementia nurse and a dedicated suite of rooms.

The communal facilities are accessed from the reception area, and include a small IT and interview room, a hairdresser's, a small shop, a much used arts

8.5 The Oaks, housing the communal facilities, care centre, and administrative offices. The pedestrian path provides the north–south axis linking The Oaks to New Earswick. Note also the amount of open space, the generous number of lighting standards, and the slightly jarring asymmetry of the building ensemble.

8.6 The entrance foyer with its stone flagged floor and 'stage set' of carefully arranged seating area with coffee table, magazines, and flowers. This impression management is perhaps somewhat undermined by the wheelchair in the background, a symbolic reminder of the function of Hartrigg Oaks. Behind it can be seen the small shop.

and crafts room (most of the artwork displayed throughout The Oaks is the work of residents), a health and fitness centre complete with spa pool, and a coffee shop, restaurant and lounge. In the roof space above are a library and a music room where a wide array of meetings and activities take place. Externally, as well as the large amount of semi-public landscaped open space, there are eight well used allotments, located near the entrance. Residents are actively involved in the management of all of the facilities, both as volunteers, and as representatives on the Residents' Committee, from whose 12 members three also sit on the Hartrigg Oaks Management Committee. Apart from the crèche, attached to The Oaks but with its own entrance, the facilities are open only to residents, their visitors and staff. Residents have differing views on this; many would like to see the facilities shared with local people, but others wish to maintain exclusivity – even to the point of some having requested a 'gated' community. Indeed even within the community, there are issues of the included and the excluded, since the few bursary residents, the visibly infirm, people with dementia and even non-Quakers, are constructed by many as not quite 'one of us'.

Containing youth

By contrast to old age, youth occupies a relatively short span of the life course. Generally constructed as the period between the years of approximately 16 and 25, it is an interstitial stage between the dependence of childhood and the independence of adulthood: 'Youth is principally about "becoming". Becoming an adult, a citizen, autonomous, mature, responsible, self-governing' (Kelly, 2003: 171). In the past this process of becoming involved a relatively ordered and predictable transition from childhood to adulthood, involving first a move from school to work, and second the establishment of an independent household. However, the taken for granted nature of such routinised transitions has been profoundly disrupted by the socio-economic changes of the last two or three decades. These have resulted in transitions which are more protracted, fractured and individualised, so that arguably the process of becoming is now more uncertain, more diverse and more burdensome than ever before (see also Furlong and Cartmel, 1997; Jones, 1995, 2002; Rugg, 1999).

A particular problem for many young people has been the newly globalised and flexible labour market. This has seen the disappearance of many traditional school leaving jobs and apprenticeship schemes upon which school leavers, especially boys, used to rely. Instead the emphasis is on staying on at school where individual performance is all important, and then embarking on more training, either through a plethora of government schemes or through further or higher education. Those who do not follow one of these paths, and especially those who leave school without qualifications, are at real risk of long term unemployment – or, if they are girls, of single motherhood (see Bynner et al., 2002). The result is a situation of anxiety and perplexity, in which false starts and even resignation to no start at all are commonplace. For those who persist there is all too often a period of several years duration before any stability is acquired; a period characterised by an episodic cycle of study, short term working, unemployment and retraining.

The hazards of this episodic cycle have been compounded by the actions of government in relation to the social security system. Under the benefit cutting regime of the Conservatives, 16 and 17 year olds were deprived of state benefits, whilst the benefits for those aged 18–25 were set at a lower level than the adult rate. This inclination to construct young people as occupying an inferior status to full adults has been reproduced in the legislation under New Labour for the minimum wage, with lower rates for those aged between 18 and 22, and 16 and 17 year olds initially excluded altogether. Furthermore housing benefit restrictions have disproportionately affected young people, and there is now only in exceptional circumstances any funding to assist with a deposit, rent in advance or furnishing.

The combined result of these structural and institutional changes has been to render the transition to independence more prolonged, a period of 'social semi-dependency' (Furlong and Cartmel, 1997: 41) in which young people are in a state of flux. This situation has also affected the ability to leave home, which has become an arena of difficulty and risk. In the mainstream housing market opportunities are restricted: the supply of social housing is in decline; owner occupied housing is increasingly unaffordable; and the private rented sector, the traditional recourse for those who cannot access social housing or owner occupation, is not only in limited supply, but is expensive and often in poor condition. Consequently a transitional 'youth' housing market has arisen, in which those most in need occupy the worst and most precarious housing and are often at risk of homelessness (Ford et al., 2002).

At whatever age, it is the state of homelessness which has come to be seen as the epitome of social exclusion – especially if it involves the sight of young people in their teens begging in the street. Homelessness legislation, however, retains the Victorian ideology of the deserving and the undeserving poor, and single people are only deemed to be deserving if they fall into certain administratively defined categories (see Chapter 3). Amongst single people it is those who are young who are most likely to be homeless, but assessing the actual numbers involved is fraught with difficulty, with estimates ranging from a few thousand to over 200,000 (see Hutson and Liddiard, 1994; Quilgars and Anderson, 1997).

Research, particularly that of an ethnographic nature, has established that the young people most at risk of homelessness are those who are the most disadvantaged or vulnerable (see Fitzpatrick and Clapham, 1999; Hall, 2003; Hutson and Liddiard, 1994; Jones, 1995). Often what ensues is a cycle of moving from rough sleeping to hostel dwelling to a bed-sit and back to rough sleeping, sometimes by way of a stretch in an offenders' institution or a brief return to the parental home. But contrary to some stereotypes of young people's preferred lifestyles, such a 'chaotic' pathway is not actively chosen (Ford *et al.*, 2002; Kelly, 2003). Instead it almost always derives from a miscellany of adverse circumstances beyond any young person's control, and sometimes even their comprehension. Finding a way out is fraught with anxiety and complexity, especially as homelessness is generally accompanied by the inability to find or keep a job.

In the light of the moral panic about homeless young people, government has felt obliged to take remedial action. The reaction of the Conservatives was to cast young people as authors of their own misfortune and to try and make families responsible for discipline and support. In the 1990s New Labour, more accepting of structural causes and consequences, sought more coordinated and holistic responses through the New Deal for young people and the joined-up working of the Social Exclusion Unit (see Folkard, 1998). In addition the legislative instruments of the Children's Act 1989 and the Homelessness Act 2002 have extended the duty to assist those deemed to be the most vulnerable or at risk. But these amendments still affect only a minority of young people who face homelessness, many of whom in any case are unwilling to subject themselves to the disciplinary paternalism of statutory services.

In this regard the role of pressure groups and voluntary organisations has proved vital in providing advice, support, and temporary or permanent accommodation. Indeed, it is increasingly recognised that it is only through the provision of support that the transition to independent living and stability can be achieved (see Franklin, 1999). Such support has in the past often been *ad hoc* and haphazard, but in recent years new solutions have emerged which render more structured support, and in some cases more institutionalised support. Such solutions include, for example, supported accommodation in shared housing or clusters of individual flats; supported lodgings, in which ordinary households act as hosts and befrienders to a young person; and floating support schemes, providing individually tailored support in self-contained accommodation for a time-limited period (see Folkard, 1998, and Chapter 3). Another such setting, enthusiastically embraced by both statutory and voluntary services, is the foyer.

The foyer

The word 'foyer' derives from the French system of *Foyers de Jeunes Travailleurs*, a hostel system which had its origins in the nineteenth century but which came to prominence as a solution to the chronic lack of accommodation for young workers following the Second World War (see Anderson and Quilgars, 1995). By the 1990s there was a network of 500 or so foyers in France with places for some 50,000 young people, each offering a range of accommodation and facilities according to the needs of the local community.

The umbrella organisation for the French foyers, the *Union des Foyers de Jeunes Travailleurs*, actively sought links with other countries, and in 1990 attracted the attention of Sheila McKechnie. Then director of Shelter, McKechnie was increasingly concerned about the negative impacts of policy changes on young people. After a fact-finding visit to France she became convinced that a foyer system in Britain would offer an innovative and integrated solution, although she recognised that: 'Transferring models between one culture and another is fraught with difficulties' (McKechnie, 1991: 52). Despite the mixed response from housing organisations, there was sufficient support to render the idea of introducing foyers to this country viable. The Conservative government was persuaded to endorse a pilot scheme in their election manifesto of 1992, and it was this which led to the establishment of the first five foyers in this country (see Quilgars and Anderson, 1997).

An evaluatory study commissioned by the JRF argued that the foyer system was effective in assisting young people in their transitions to independence and in supporting them into training and employment (Anderson and Quilgars, 1995). The New Labour government was minded to support these findings, especially given the work culture ethos, and made it a policy ambition to develop at least one in every town. The result of this institutional endorsement of foyers was that by 2004 there were nearly 200 foyers in existence, assisting over 10,000 residents a year (Foyer Federation, 2004).

The aims of the foyer movement were first set out in 1993 by the umbrella organisation Foyer Federation for Youth, which pointed to the: 'integrated approach to meeting the needs of young people during the transition from dependence to independence by linking affordable accommodation to training and employment' (Tomlin and Sewell, 1993: 5). The essential elements were seen as providing good quality accommodation for 16–25 year olds in a well-designed non-institutional setting, together with support in training and job finding, access to leisure and recreational facilities, and a safe, stable and secure environment. However, this somewhat mechanistic description obscures the underlying philosophy of the foyer system with its emphasis on community, holism and a person centred approach. Indeed it is this which distinguishes a foyer from an ordinary hostel:

> Foyers provide accommodation with opportunity for young people, and a community in which they can grow and thrive. By integrating training and job search, personal support and motivation with a place to live, they provide a bridge to independence, and a chance for young people to realise their full potential.
>
> (Foyer Federation, 2004)

The idea of community extends also to the members of the foyer, with an emphasis on a balanced community of young people of different ages, sexes, needs and abilities, and in which peer support is seen as a key element. Access is normally by referral from another agency, and on entry a young person is assessed in regard to their qualifications, interests and aspirations. From this an agreed action plan is formulated covering personal support, life skills training (including cooking, budgeting, cleaning), vocational training, assistance with job search and leisure activities. The aim is to facilitate the transition to full adult independence within a period of 18 months to two years, with the young person established in a job and in their own accommodation. Breaches by the young person of the action plan, or of the rules and regulations of the foyer (for example in regard to non-payment of rent or possession of drugs, offensive weapons or alcohol) may result in sanctions and withdrawal of privileges – or, as a last resort, eviction.

There is no one universal model of a foyer, since the intention is that they should be flexible and responsive to local needs. Hence they vary in regard to type, size and range of facilities. The numbers of residents range from under 30 to over 200, with living accommodation in self-contained flatlets, in single rooms with shared kitchen and bathroom, or on a more traditional hostel basis with communal living and eating facilities. In design terms the recommendation is for welcoming and well laid out reception areas, together with clear circulation routes and information boards (Tomlin and Sewell, 1993). The provision of communal living space and dining areas is more problematic since on the one hand they may encourage socialisation, but on the other may be avoided in favour of smaller and more informal spaces, such as residents' own rooms. Hence the latter should be designed with sufficient space to facilitate at least some social interaction, as well as allowing scope for personalisation. The more formal facilities, generally also open to members of the local community, may include any or all of a learning resource centre, an IT centre, a crèche, a restaurant, an advice centre, a drop in centre and a health care centre. In many foyers residents are encouraged to pursue 'inspirational activities' such as music, sport, photography and volunteering in the community (McKenzie, 2003: 16).

Given the multi-purpose function of foyers in terms of accommodation, training and support they rely on an inter-agency approach. Usually initiated and developed by housing associations as either new build or conversions, partners may include local authorities, central and local government training and employment agencies, voluntary sector organisations and private businesses. For the same reason, there is a multiplicity (and complexity) of potential sources of funding. Such sources include: government departments; the Housing Corporation; county and district councils; the development agencies; European funds; regeneration funds; national and local charities; the lottery charities board; the Supporting People programme; and private sector loans. Creating a funding package for a new foyer is thus time consuming and unpredictable, especially as continuity of revenue funding is threatened by the fact that many grants are offered only for a finite period of time (McKenzie, 2003).

Despite the hailing of foyers in many quarters as the answer to the no-home, no-job, no-home syndrome, they have not received universal acclaim. There are, for example, concerns about unrealistic expectations of foyers and their reliance on a flawed interpretation of a linear transition from dependency to independence (Jones, 1995). Furthermore 'success' is based on a bureaucratic and cost driven measure of output in terms of those who actually find jobs (see Nother, 1995). Other reservations revolve around the desirability of housing being conditional on employment search or training, which has been likened to a return to the environment of the workhouse (Nother, 1995). Such a Victorian analogy is given added weight by the perception that foyers offer places only to the 'deserving', given the exclusion of those deemed undesirable, such as people with disruptive behaviour or high support needs, or those assessed as being lacking in commitment (see Anderson and Quilgars, 1995; Shelter, 1992). There is also a risk of institutionalisation, especially in the larger foyers; a risk exacerbated by the imposition of often 'draconian rules and regulations' (Quilgars and Pleace, 1999: 118) and the high degree of supervision which fosters dependency rather than self-reliance. This perception of control is supported by ethnographic research which suggests that many encounters between staff and residents are conflictual, with a 'zero tolerance' of rule infringements and the construction of certain non-conforming residents as disruptive and dangerous 'outsiders' (Allen, 2003).

Occasio House

Harlow in Essex was one of the first generation of post-war New Towns (see Chapter 3). By the mid-1990s it was decided that part of the town centre was in need of regeneration, and at much the same time it was acknowledged that there was a lack of housing and information services for young people. In the light of this Harlow District Council formulated a Single Regeneration Budget bid based on a strategy of 'regeneration through youth'. The development of a young persons' information centre and a foyer within the town centre regeneration area were seen as the lynchpin of the strategy.

In 1997, an architect/developer competition was initiated for the construction of a foyer of 76 fully supported units and 40 slightly larger 'move-on' flats. The competition was won by the architects Wilkinson Eyre and East Thames Housing Group (ETHG), a housing association based in London but active also in Essex. ETHG seemed a good proposition as it already had relevant experience of running a foyer in Stratford, London. The design proposed for the new foyer in Harlow was innovative, consisting of two curved aluminium clad blocks, and despite concerns by local people about the location of potentially disruptive young people in the town centre, planning permission was granted in 1998.

The first construction company appointed by ETHG priced the scheme at £5.6 million, considerably above the budget of £4.85 million. Even with cost saving measures the price could not be reduced without compromising quality of materials or viability of scheme size (Building, 2001). Meanwhile ETHG and the council had also to assemble a package for the capital costs. This was eventually put together from a number of sources: the successful Single Regeneration Budget bid; the

Partnership Investment Programme administered by English Partnerships; Essex County Council; the Harlow 2020 Partnership; the Housing Corporation; and the National Lottery Charities Board. Some of this funding was time limited, and the ability of ETHG to start work by the deadline of 10 February 2000 was threatened by the apparently insoluble issue of the costs. However, four months before the deadline a seminar was held at ETHG on the CASPAR scheme, a concept initiated by JRHT with completed schemes in Leeds and Birmingham (JRF, 2005). The architects for the Leeds site were Levitt Bernstein, whose innovative construction used factory assembled and relatively low cost semi-volumetric timber framed modular units. By coincidence the design was uncannily similar to the Harlow foyer design, with the same curvilinear form.

On the basis of this ETHG decided to secure the services of Levitt Bernstein, who were thus put in the unusual position of having to develop another architect's original design concept. They confirmed that the Harlow foyer could use the same construction methods as CASPAR, and that this would bring the total costs within budget. It was this cost element which won over the council, otherwise reluctant to embrace new construction methods and materials. The construction firm of Llewellyn and Sons was then appointed, largely on the basis of their attitude to partnering, and in line with the commitment to partnering by ETHG even before the Egan report of 1998. The foyer was completed in 2001, and opened by the Olympic gold medallist Tessa Sanderson with the name Occasio House, *occasio* being Latin for 'opportunity'. The success of the partnership process secured the accolade of the 2001/2 Room National Partnership Award, whilst the perceived merits of the design were recognised by the 2002 Evening Standard New Homes Award for the best new housing association development.

The foyer is located in Playhouse Square on the site of a former technical college, and although its large mass provides a sense of closure, the scale of the building, the curvilinear form and the grey aluminium cladding are somewhat at odds with the context. This represents a confusion of styles and materials and consists of the Playhouse itself, a 1950s church (due to be listed), a covered shopping area, a multi-storey car park, some amorphous green space, a taxi rank and a busy thoroughfare which runs past the foyer buildings. The battleship grey of the foyer (which some members of the council tried unsuccessfully to have modified) is relieved only by the contrasting blue surround of the main entrance, the blue doors of the move-on block and the large yellow and blue OH logo (Figure 8.7).

Entrance to the main foyer block is from the pavement through large glass automatic doors (Figure 8.8). Inside, the walls of the reception area are covered with notices, and there is a sense of activity as young people and staff come and go. The young persons' information centre, managed by the council, is accessed from one side of this reception area, whilst on the other is a doorway to the various administrative and interviewing offices. To the rear of the reception area is the reception desk (Figure 8.9), staffed 24 hours a day and with a closely monitored

8.7 Occasio House. The main block is to the left and the move-on block to the right. Note the OH logo and the perimeter railings.

8.8 The entrance to Occasio House, open to the street

8.9 The reception area. Access to the accommodation is through the door beside the reception desk, supervised by the reception staff. The flip chart board displays the day's activities: shiatsu massage, study skills, and diversity awareness training.

control panel for the numerous CCTV cameras inside and outside the building. At the reception desk is a visitors' book and the controls for the electronic door which leads to the central well of the building. Here, stairs and a lift provide access to the accommodation. Each young person is provided with a small sparsely furnished flatlet consisting of a bedsit with large double glazed windows, and an internal shower room and small kitchen. Each flatlet has its own 'front door' to which post is delivered, and personalising effects such as posters and rugs are encouraged.

There are no common rooms within the foyer, as previous experience suggested these were either under-used or vulnerable to being trashed unless supervised. However there is communal external space in the form of the garden shared by both foyer blocks (Figure 8.10). This was redeveloped in 2002 with the assistance of charitable funding, and with resident involvement in regard both to design ideas and to the actual labour (see Ambrosi, 2004). The finished product includes planting, lawned areas, mosaic paths, totem poles and a small 'amphitheatre' for outdoor meetings.

The young people who come to the foyer are effectively homeless, and have experienced problems such as family breakdown, difficulties after leaving care or inability to maintain a tenancy. Referrals come from a variety of agencies, including the young persons' information centre, the council housing or social services departments, local housing associations, the government Connexions scheme and

8.10 The garden of Occasio House, clearly defined for residents only

the probation service. Admission is dependent not only on being in housing need, but also on having training or job search needs and having a local connection. Even so, gaining a place is not automatic as all young people have to be assessed to ascertain if they will benefit from the foyer programme. In this only about 50 per cent are successful. Once in the foyer, each resident works with a key worker on a mutually agreed and structured action plan covering two main areas: education, training and work; and tenancy maintenance and life skills. Skills and confidence can be further developed through optional participation in activities such as football, art classes (residents' art is displayed in the staff offices), voluntary service, and, more adventurously, visits to Romania to contribute to a programme for orphaned and sick children. It is also recognised that the young people should as far as is feasible be respected as adults and that proscriptive rules should be kept to a minimum. Thus, for example, alcohol is allowed in residents' own rooms. On the other hand there are strict rules relating to visitors, with only three per week permitted. These must be signed in and out, and the frequent infringements are punished by visitor bans. The most serious problems arise in relation to anti-social behaviour and here the recent extension to RSLs of the ability to apply for anti-social behaviour orders (ASBO) has been of notable assistance. A system has been introduced which starts with behaviour diaries and behaviour contracts, and moves on to a court application for an ASBO with its ultimate sanction of eviction.

When sufficient progress has been made in meeting goals, the resident can advance to the less controlled setting of the move-on block. Unlike the main foyer block with its secure entrance and railed perimeter, this balcony access block is open to the street and visitors can come and go at any time. Residents have a small unfurnished flat with an entrance hall, a living room plus kitchen, a bedroom, a shower room and a small balcony. It is from here that the young person will move to full independence, albeit with the offer of floating support if needed.

As with any foyer, Occasio House subscribes to the principles both of a balanced community within and good relations with the community without. At most times a reasonable balance between the sexes is achieved, and of ages between the two limits of 16 and 24. Degrees of vulnerability vary significantly, and for those with the highest support needs, including those with physical disabilities, there are designated rooms on the ground floor where staff supervision is more readily available. The large size of the foyer provides scope for friendships to develop, but on the other hand it is this large size which also brings problems, both in terms of managing the numbers of young people and in regard to external perceptions. For the large numbers, especially when combined with the central and prominent location of the foyer, tend to result in foyer residents being blamed for any trouble in the town. Indeed, the general perception by the public is of the foyer as a place for criminals, drug pushers, down and outs and asylum seekers. For these reasons constant efforts are made by staff to engage the community through, for example, forging links with local businesses, opening sessions to local people, offering space to community groups and inviting individual complainants to see the foyer facilities for themselves. Overall, there is considerable pride both by Harlow Council and Network East, the subsidiary of ETHG responsible for foyers in its area of operation, in the achievements of the foyer. This is made explicit in the newsletters of these bodies which praise the facilities of the foyer and the benefits to the individuals who have passed through, as described in the pen portraits of various appreciative young people (Essex County Council, 2004; Network East Foyers, 2003).

Conclusion

Conceptualisations of old age and youth vary between cultures, as do the associated rituals of transition and the ways in which the frailties of the old and the energies of the young are accommodated. In twenty-first-century Western societies both age and youth have become more protracted life stages, and this is in large part due to the social processes of the modern period. Driven by the demands of industrialisation and the work ethic of capitalism, this period marginalised those who were not a productive part of the labour market. In regard to old age this has led to a situation in which older people are no longer appreciated for their wisdom and experience, but instead seen as past their usefulness and more or less invisible, both metaphorically and literally. This has been reflected in the shift of the locale of care from the family and the domestic setting, to the state and the segregated and institutionalised settings it has provided. Such 'residential contrivances' (Kellaher, 2001: 226) have reproduced structured dependency both spatially and socially through depersonalising environments and routines, and the systematisation of Foucauldian surveillance and control.

The spiralling costs of this institutionalised system, together with the projected increase in numbers of old people, has resulted in a moral panic expressed in a discourse of older people as burdensome. However, this has occurred at the same time as the new postmodern emphasis on individualisation, lifestyle and choice, and this has had an impact both on older people's perceptions of themselves and on views about institutional settings. Thus older people are becoming more active agents, resisting the stereotypes of old age and constructing it as a lifestyle project in which dependency is postponed and individuality asserted. Meanwhile, academics, policy makers and public and private agencies have begun to question dependent models of care and to introduce more affirmative types of housing and support.

With regard to young people, the waning of industrialisation has threatened the established transitions to adulthood. Denied the familiar and traditional trajectories of the past, the disengaged and semi-dependent young pose the threat of inhabiting a 'wild zone' of deviance and defiance (Kelly, 2003). Hence the institutionalised agency of the state has intervened to impose surveillance and control, and to minimise the sense of risk and mistrust inspired by youth. The most problematic, and often the most visible young are those who are homeless on the streets. Constructed as 'failures' and a 'burden', they are given assistance only on the basis that they fall into the 'deserving' categories of 'priority need' and can demonstrate that they will be compliant (Hutson, 1999).

In seeking solutions to the perceived problems posed by age and youth, recourse has been had to models from different cultural contexts. Thus the CCRC derives from the US and Germany, and the foyer from France. The specific ways in which these have been interpreted in the UK has been through the effects of agency. The CCRC was first promoted within the field of social work, and then elaborated by a socially concerned and respected trust with a desire to lead by example. The foyer was championed by a high profile individual in the field of homelessness, and then adopted at institutional level by a government seeking solutions not only to homelessness, but also joblessness. However, the CCRC and the foyer are in effect directed at people with quite different resources: the CCRC is for the more affluent, with an initially self-selected community of like-minded people who in facing the rigours of old age are also looking for autonomy, companionship, peace of mind and tailored care. By contrast, the foyer is for those lacking in resources, and is not a matter of choice but of a lack of alternatives and of coercion by institutional agents. Despite these differences the CCRC and the foyer both share certain expectations of conformity, not only in regard to the rules of the organisation but also in relation to a 'shared narrative' (see Biggs et al., 2000).

In the CCRC this is constructed around a fit, energetic, and even daring lifestyle, with those who descend into infirmity and dependency being seen as 'failures' and consequently marginalised both socially and spatially. In the foyer the narrative is about acceptable behaviour (albeit with allowances for the exuberances of youth), socially useful activity and the attainment of the goal of independence. Those who conform reap the reward of social and spatial liberation, whilst those who transgress experience exclusion, oppression, disempowerment and ultimately abandonment and despair (see Allen, 2003).

Turning to the specific case study examples, it is clear how the eventual shape of the built form results from a process shaped by the vision and resources of the initiators, and the outcome of mediation and negotiation between actors. In the case of the retirement community of Hartrigg Oaks, JRHT had the relevant experience, financial reserves and land, but was initially thwarted by opposition from local people, the planning authority and eventually the Secretary of State. Even so it pursued its objectives with a persistence underpinned by a conviction of its national and local distinction and seemingly bemused that others did not necessarily feel that this should over-ride other considerations. Occasio House was driven by the belief of the local council that the newly introduced foyer system represented the best solution to problematic youth, but this had to be achieved within the constraints of a finite budget, and again, in the face of local opposition. The search for partners for the project brought an established RSL which had already experimented with the foyer idea in another location, and by coincidence, an innovative architectural practice which had also worked with JRHT.

Not surprisingly perhaps, the contrasting locations of the two schemes reproduce the stereotypes of appropriate spatial settings for youth and age: centres of activity and quiet spaces of retreat. This is reflected too in the final scheme designs; the futuristic, bold and vibrant Occasio House with its multi-storeyed profile; and the traditional, sedate and leafy Hartrigg Oaks with its stereotypical older person bungalows. But there are other factors too which have influenced the built form: the realities of the site and its context; the priorities of the initiating agencies; the perceived needs of the specific client groups; the attitudes of the planning authority; and the creativity of the architects. At Hartrigg Oaks the aim has been to respect the materials, organic form and low density character of New Earswick, and to cater for older and impaired people. The result is a scheme with a suburban feel, and whilst it is indeed low density, the layout is symmetrical and repetitive rather than organic, with the access road unaesthetically off centre. The bungalows (each with their tiny plot of defensible space) are arranged in a 'ringy' structure on the outer side of a somewhat disorientating distributor road and distanced from the central communal and care facilities. Throughout the scheme the facilities and accessibility standards bear witness to consideration of older people's needs, but even so it is clear from the spaciousness, the landscaping and the finishes that this is a setting of distinction, for an elite of the affluent.

At Occasio House the central site has dictated an urbanist design, but the effect is of an individualistic design statement rather than of respect for context. Layout, materials and finishes reflect the need to contain disorderly youth, and convey a sense of basic functionality to be managed at the lowest cost. The trappings of surveillance are more prominent than the discreet provision at Hartrigg Oaks, with locked doors, bundles of keys, security patrols and highly visible CCTV cameras. Interestingly, however, the spatial syntax of the approach to the core within which those most at risk are to be contained is the same in both settings: an *enfilade* consisting of a progression from outer semi-public space, through the scrutiny of a reception desk and guarded doors, to a transitional corridor or lobby space (the semi-private status of which is reinforced by the signing of visitors' names), and finally through the divide of further doors or a flight of stairs to the private setting of fullest dependency. Those with the greatest supervisory needs (dementia at Hartrigg Oaks, vulnerability or disability at Occasio House) are placed in the position nearest to the gaze of duty staff, under continuous surveillance. However, in both places attempts have been made to try to soften the most anonymising effects of institutionalisation through such measures as 'front doors' and opportunities for personalisation within each person's own space – the potential to create at least some representation of home.

The control symbolised in the text of the built environment is reflected also in the application of regulatory systems. Initial selection is based on assessment and the passing of tests. At Hartrigg Oaks the exigencies of the insurance system and the necessity of balance mean that it is effectively not those most in need who are admitted (contrary to normal housing association policy) but those *least* in need, who will make fewest claims on costly care resources. At Occasio House need in itself is only a first step in the crossing of additional hurdles which include local connection, commitment and ability to benefit from the programme. Once within, written plans are drawn up to assist in progression through the system, in the one case to frail dependency, and in the other to active independence, accompanied by allocation to the next stage of accommodation. In effect, and despite a rhetoric of independence and autonomy, residents are never free agents but must subject themselves to the professional domination so characteristic of settings of structured dependency. This is particularly true of the more repressive regime of the foyer, for this seems to encapsulate many of the features once so criticised in institutions for dependent people and which are now generally regarded as antithetical to their interests. For these reasons, and despite the rhetoric, the principles behind both the CCRC and the foyer cannot be said to be entirely new, for segregation from society and an imposed ethos of structure, routine and sense of purpose effectively reproduce a system first established in the days of the workhouse and the asylum.

9 Constructing city lifestyles

The cities of classical and pre-modern Europe developed as centres of civilisation and urbanity; sites for the generation of cultural, social, intellectual and political capital (see Madanipour, 2003). As edifices of human achievement they offered both real and symbolic distinction from the perceived chaos of untamed nature that held sway beyond the city walls, whilst the citizens enjoyed a way of life deemed far superior to that of the rustic, unenlightened and ever-toiling peasantry. As mentioned in Chapter 6, in much of Western Europe this characterisation of the city continued into modern times, but this was not the case in Britain. Here the concentrated industrialisation that distinguished the nineteenth century gave rise to a vision of the city as a smoke-filled, tumultuous and festering place, teeming with an underworld of criminals and vagabonds: a vision reproduced in the imaginings of literary figures such as Charles Dickens and Elizabeth Gaskell.

As the twentieth century progressed and a more interventionist state emerged, the response to the chaos of the city was to try to impose order through regulation and control. Amongst other measures such order involved the zoning of functions, in which particular uses were assigned to particular areas. This artificial and imposed order ran counter to the grain of the versatility and diversity of city spaces, leading inevitably to the proliferation of monofunctional and non-adaptive areas, and an increasingly segregated and alienating city. Even so, the city managed to maintain an allure, offering to certain sections of the population a variety of aesthetic and cultural opportunities – amongst them the legacy of the Victorian municipalisation of city life with its libraries, art galleries, theatres, museums and parks for cultural delectation; the department stores with their hitherto unimagined experience for the purchase of goods; and the *frisson* of being a stranger in a city of other strangers.

Post-industrialisation and postmodernism have signalled a new period in the city narrative. With a shrinking manufacturing base, cities have had to embrace the new knowledge and service economies; to seize the opportunities afforded by the so-called cultural industries of the media, the arts and tourism; and to find new uses for the vast acres of now abandoned industrial land. At the same time, institutional awareness of the problems caused by the old zoning laws, together with environmental pressures and demographic change, have led to a new emphasis on a more effective mix of uses within city spaces and the encouragement of the private sector to reinvest in the city. In stimulating this the projection of a positive image of the city has become all important to city entrepreneurs, as has the ability to offer a wider range of experience for an increasingly discerning and fragmented population, for whom lifestyle and consumption, security and freedom are central concerns.

This chapter examines these trends and changes, showing how a more ambivalent culture of cities has begun to emerge, and how governments and city authorities have reacted to the need to present a new image both of cities and of city living. In this context the production of new forms of residential environments is of interest, especially in regard to the way in which they reflect that dilemma of postmodern society, how to balance the desire for freedom with the need for security. It is for this reason that the two manifestations of city living which are discussed in this chapter are lofts and gated communities, both of which are relatively recent phenomena. The examples considered in more detail are Timber Wharf in Manchester and Adventurers Quay in Cardiff, both located in areas of industrial decline which have faced the need for regeneration.

The city of image, opportunity and fear

Over the modern period cities were generally seen in terms of the functional and material spaces of policy makers, planners and developers, and it is only through the lens of postmodern awareness that they have also been regarded as the fractured spaces of multiple lifestyles, imaginations and representations. In this regard recent texts have engaged with the way in which sign, image, spectacle, gaze and entertainment shape our newly aestheticised relations to the spaces of the city, as well as pointing to the impact of individualisation in reconstructing the city as a site in which identity and meaning can be found (see Clarke, 2003; Featherstone, 1991; Zukin, 1995, 1998). This transformation in perception has accompanied the shift from the city as a landscape of production, based on an industrial and material economy of output and growth, to a landscape of consumption, based on post-industrialisation and the 'culture' of cities (Zukin, 1995). A particular aspect of this culture of cities is the way in which individual cities have sought to achieve popularity and success through mechanisms such as the manipulation of image and the promotion of identity. Thus in the selling of the city attempts are made to overlay the negative perceptions of urban life which prevailed during the industrial period with a new image constructed around the real or imagined qualities of specific places (see Boddy and Parkinson, 2004). It is this approach which has given rise, for example, to the identification by city entrepreneurs of iconic 'Quarters', such as the Jewellery Quarter in Birmingham, the Lace Market in Nottingham, the Brewery Quarter in Cardiff and Little Germany in Bradford. In the same way the symbolic potential of architecture and urban design has been utilised to appeal to particular lifestyle niches. Thus the bold statements of innovative, high-tech and futuristic design seem to promise progress, excitement and freedom, whilst on the other hand more retrospective and eclectic styles convey an impression of tradition, security and rootedness: 'selectively harvesting the local and the past and reassembling the desired elements in an orchestrated pastiche' (Jacobs, 1998: 255).

The contemporary city also has a role to play in offering new and different opportunities. For the 'mobile élite' (Bauman, 1998: 20) or 'flexecutives' (Blakely and Snyder, 1998: 66) it is a backcloth for a hectic, global lifestyle, in which certain spaces of the city are exploited to indulge an 'aestheticized, ludic existence' in the manner reminiscent of Benjamin's *flâneur* (Clarke, 2003: 87). Secure in their affluence, they display their distinctiveness through such markers as their designer goods, their patronage of exclusive restaurants and health clubs, and their occupancy of modish penthouse suites: the symbols of distinction which all can read, and to which many can only aspire. For others, the city represents opportunity in a different way. Here it is the very diversity of the city, its ability to offer freedom and anonymity in a setting of strangers that proves attractive. Many of the individuals who thus choose the city are seeking to escape the oppressions and repressions that coexisted with the modernist processes of conventional suburban living: domesticity; the nuclear family; traditional employment patterns; stability; and normative masculinities and femininities (Fincher and Jacobs, 1998). Thus for gay people, single women, the mentally ill, artists and writers, the city has become a place of self-expression where alternative lifestyles and a variety of subjectivities and desires can be realised. It is through these processes that vibrant gay 'villages' have emerged in numerous cities, including San Francisco, London and Manchester (see Bell and Valentine, 1995).

However, such freedoms, although sought and sometimes found, remain in many respects illusory. For the fear and mistrust which became the dominant emotions of the city in the modern period have if anything intensified, and despite the renewed attractions of city living, the ability to engage with the city and with the stranger in the emancipatory and democratic way evoked by Sennett is still a distant dream (see Jacobs, 2002). In a risk society, fear of the other has become all pervasive, and the stranger continues to be a dangerous figure to be spurned, regulated and contained. Such containment is often symbolised through the disposition of space: 'Nearly all cities use spatial strategies to separate, segregate and isolate the Other, inscribing the legible processes of modernism in urban form' (Zukin, 1996: 49). Under postmodernism these processes have become yet more prevalent, with an increasing tendency for the enclosure and surveillance of both public and private space. This is exemplified by covered and patrolled shopping malls, residential enclaves, gated communities and the use of security guards and CCTV cameras. Such a 'fortress city' approach not only represents the antithesis of diversity, vitality and community, but also reproduces fear.

The redevelopment of the city

At the institutional level it has been a preoccupation with economic growth and competitiveness that has led to attempts to try and reverse the harmful effects of the rise and fall of industrialisation. During the early 1980s the focus was on housing led revitalisation; however, following the property collapse of the late 1980s and early 1990s institutional investors and development professionals reverted to their traditional *habitus* of a risk averse approach. In recognition of this, both central and local government sought to intensify the inducements of their pump priming measures, such as the lifting of planning controls, the distribution of grants, the assembly of land and further support for the public private partnership vehicles of the Urban Development Corporations and City Challenge.

Nonetheless it was this early housing activity which succeeded in attracting a small *avant garde* of new city dwellers, and which also saw for the first time in the post-industrial era an increase in the resident population of some city cores, notably in Manchester, Leeds and Birmingham. However, this was in the same context as a saga of continuing out-migration, further neighbourhood collapse and increasing social and spatial polarisation (see Robson *et al.*, 2000). It was to redress this balance that the New Labour government felt that a more co-ordinated and holistic approach was needed in which more concerted efforts must be made to persuade a wider range of people of the benefits of city living:

> Policies to attract people back to cities [...] have the potential to kill three birds with one stone. They could reduce the loss of the countryside and promote more sustainable patterns of development, while at the same time addressing the root cause of urban decline by making the inner city into somewhere which people no longer wish to escape. This of course needs to be handled with care, to prevent gentrification and the displacement of deprivation to other parts of the city.
>
> (URBED, 1998: 15)

An Urban Task Force was commissioned by Labour to investigate how people's attitudes to urban life were shaped, and in the light of this, how city living could best be promoted. The two resultant reports (Urban Task Force, 1999; URBED *et al.*, 1999) acknowledged that: 'anti-urban sentiments in the British public are deep-rooted and remain as strong as ever' (URBED *et al.*, 1999: 4), and argued that to overcome such sentiments it would be necessary to reprise the continental model of urbanity from which England had misguidedly departed in the industrial era. It was suggested that there were emergent niche markets of people seeking new and distinctive experiences, consisting mainly of single people, couples without children and more active and affluent early retirees. These groups might constitute a source of 'city persuadables' but they would need to be seduced by a new commitment to attractive and 'liveable' design, as well as perceptive and sophisticated marketing.

It was also necessary to persuade housebuilders that profits could be made through developing in the city. Particularly important in this context was a new breed of independent developer, led as much by personal experience and inspiration as by the lure of historic properties to convert or cheap industrial land. Such developers included, for example, Harry Handelsman, whose company Manhattan Lofts is credited with introducing the concept of loft living to London; Tom Bloxham, founder of Urban Splash, who expanded the concept into the north-west; and Roger Madelin of the Argent Group, who took the risk of investing in Brindley Place in Birmingham in the early 1990s (Compton, 2004). These individuals and their companies are distinguished from institutional developers by their 'maverick' attitude and their alertness to the potential of small, depressed areas which institutional investors do not even 'see' (Guy and Henneberry, 2004). This visionary approach has given them not only the intrepidity to develop 'where institutions fear to tread' (Guy and Henneberry, 2004: 227), but also an awareness that good design and the impact of development on local populations are as important as profit margins.

More recently the government's prescription that at least 60 per cent of new housing development should be on brownfield land, together with the policy commitment to urban renaissance and the promotion of the sustainable and compact city, has helped to convince all housebuilders that city development needs to be a key part of their portfolio. In addition, the effect of the property boom of the early 2000s and the unprecedented expansion of the buy-to-let market has also boosted city demand, with the result that at the time of writing there is keen competition for city centre sites with or without government incentives, and extending to areas that would once have been overlooked or rejected outright. Increased demand has also brought increasing profits, and many housebuilders have set up subsidiary companies specifically to focus on city centre construction, as, for example, Redrow's 'In the City' and David Wilson's 'City Homes' (see Blake and Golland, 2004).

From gentrification to loft living

It has been suggested that the government's commitment to the idea of an urban renaissance is essentially a manifestation of 'state-led gentrification' (Ley, 2003), in which the people to be encouraged back to central city living are the middle classes with their beneficial social and economic capital. As a concept, the term gentrification was first coined in the 1960s to describe a movement in which 'urban pioneers' or 'gentry' set about restoring cheap, run down but aesthetically pleasing Victorian and Edwardian homes (Glass, 1964). The people attracted to this movement represented a new middle class constituted by the processes of economic and social restructuring, such as artists, new public and private sector professionals and individuals in search of alternative lifestyles (Ley, 1996).

Seeking to differentiate themselves from other social groupings, they developed lifestyles based on particular modes of consumption, and in which the cultivation of an aesthetic taste, the search for authenticity and the display of cultural capital were important markers of distinction. Disdaining suburbia as *passé*, repressive and synthetic, they sought authenticity within the city in places resonant of history, culture or distinctive architecture.

Once such areas showed signs of improvement through individual effort, they inevitably began to attract the attention of institutional developers, now ready to re-invest in previously abandoned urban space (see Harvey, 1985). For the most part such developers were interested not in residential development alone but in the maximisation of profits through large scale upmarket operations in attractive locations:

> In reality, residential gentrification is integrally linked to the redevelopment of urban waterfronts for recreational and other functions, the decline of remaining inner-city manufacturing facilities, the rise of hotel and convention complexes and central-city office developments, as well as the emergence of modern 'trendy' retail and restaurant districts.
>
> (Smith and Williams, 1986b: 3)

Initially this activity was confined to London, as was the earlier gentrification led from below. But gradually regional cities such as Glasgow, Liverpool, Manchester and Leeds also began to experience gentrification, but in a way which responded to the locationally specific impact of changing socio-economic processes:

> The development of gentrification in a regional city is less reliant on the outcome of a set of historical-geographical conditions, based upon a set of interrelationships between property developers, financiers and a particular fraction of the middle class. Rather, place-specific cultural producers and other place engineers, become important intermediaries in marketing and selling this culturally symbolic residential form.
>
> (Dutton, 2003: 2561)

A specific instance of this 'culturally symbolic residential form' has been the loft, a type of residential space favoured by a particular fraction of the new middle classes. As a residential concept, it originated in the US, where it first became a popular urban form in the SoHo district of New York. Here artists were attracted both by the low rents of the vacant industrial buildings and by the perceived authenticity and aesthetic quality of the distinctive cast iron construction (see Zukin, 1989). As more artists moved in, art galleries began to open, followed by cafés, restaurants and bars. By the mid-1970s rents were rising, and professional developers, encouraged by the city governors, realised that there was development potential. Their activities meant that by the 1980s most of the artists had moved out, displaced by the institutionalisation of loft living and by the commodification of the space they had 'discovered' for the benefit of those pursuing a lifestyle of 'bourgeois chic' (Zukin, 1989: 2). It was through this process that: 'loft living [which] started as a trend, turned into a "movement", and finally transformed the market' (Zukin, 1989: 12).

The concept of loft living has subsequently spread to other areas of North America and to Western Europe. Often, but not inevitably, it has been associated with an influx of artists. Such artists act as catalysts in 'softening up' areas into which more risk averse capital can then move, safe in the knowledge that a new market can be established (Atkinson, 2003: 2348). This market derives from the distinctiveness given to the location by the initial artistic *avant garde* and the way this then attracts intellectuals, media workers and other professionals, who feel their social capital will benefit through the cachet of proximity to the aesthetic and cultural capabilities of the artist (Ley, 2003: 2540).

In the UK it was in London that lofts first appeared, but this was not so much the result of the actions of artists as part of a developer led and planned intervention in the abandoned but newly revalorised warehouses of the Docklands area (Zukin, 1989). The luxury loft apartments, conservation landscapes, waterfront locations and mixed use amenities were designed to attract the highly paid employees of the new locally based service and financial industries (often referred to as 'yuppies').

The success of lofts in London, albeit only as a small segment of a larger apartment market, has led to experimentation in provincial cities such as Birmingham, Manchester and Leeds. However, it has not so far been the domain of speculative housebuilders but instead of smaller specialist companies, such as Manhattan Lofts and City Lofts of London and Urban Splash of Manchester. Initially these companies acquire obsolescent warehouses and other industrial structures whose large spans lend themselves to loft construction on the upper floors, and retail and commercial uses on the lower floors. Then as a market develops for this type of space and suitable existing buildings become in short supply, recourse is had to a programme of new build. In the absence of the cachet afforded by a historic building the tendency is to search for culturally resonant sites such as heritage or waterfront locations, whilst the built form itself seeks to reproduce the scale, mass, and interior of the former lofts.

Loft living comes to Manchester

The revival of the city centre

Manchester is known as the world's first industrial city, brought to prominence through its role in the manufacture and trade of cotton goods. By the mid-nineteenth century Manchester was also a flourishing commercial and financial centre with numerous offices, shops, factories and warehouses in the city centre. However, a century later the general decline that was affecting so many other industrial cities was under way, leaving behind: 'a ravaged post-industrial environment' (Williams, 2003: 55). By the 1980s it was recognised that the problems of this environment, together with Manchester's continuing economic and social deterioration, needed urgent resolution. Despite the instinctive opposition of the 'far left' local administration to Thatcherite policies (see Williams, 2003), it began to be accepted that if Manchester was to regenerate its inner core and compete as an entrepreneurial city then it would have to be open to both private sector investment and to central government initiatives. It was this shift in thinking which eventually resulted in the establishment in 1988 of the Central Manchester Development Corporation (CMDC) (see Deas *et al.*, 1999).

The area of operation of CMDC extended over a narrow swathe of land immediately south of the city centre, from Castlefield in the west, along the so-called Whitworth corridor, to Piccadilly in the east. Some of the advantages CMDC aimed to capitalise on were the significant numbers of listed warehouses and other historic structures in the area, as well as the potentially attractive waterfronts of several canals. In this regard Castlefield was particularly well endowed, its distinctive townscape characterised by numerous trading wharves and warehouses, and a variety of brick and cast iron bridges and viaducts. Indeed, the potential of Castlefield as a tourist attraction had already been recognised by the city council, which had designated it in 1979 as a conservation area and in 1983 as an Urban Heritage park.

By the time CMDC was wound down in 1996 there had been a transformation, not only in Castlefield but across the whole area of operation. A particular success had been the stimulation of interest in city centre living, with significant numbers of affluent young professionals being enticed to relocate to gentrified industrial buildings. It was this success, achieved despite the unfavourable state of the property market at the time, which the city council hoped to emulate as part of its new proactive approach of 'making it happen' (Deas *et al.*, 1999). Indeed in this regard the momentum generated by CMDC continued, and by 2004 the city centre population had expanded to over 6,000 (from less than a thousand in 1990), with an expectation that this would increase to 10,000 or more (Manchester City Council, 2004).

Such progress was in part due to the intensifying efforts of the city leaders to market the city as an ideal place in which to live, work and invest; an ambition assisted by high profile events such as the bid for the 1996 Olympic Games and the successful hosting of the Commonwealth Games in 2002. In addition Manchester had already attracted international interest in the late 1980s and early 1990s as the centre of the UK pop music scene. This had generated a night club culture, attracted a host of new artists and their followers, given the city a trendy image and drawn in a large gay community (see Mellor, 1997). This community had converged in an area beside the city centre canal which became known as the 'Gay Village'. This, like Castlefield and later the 'Northern Quarter', became 'branded' as a cultural quarter by the city council, and used to enhance the image of Manchester as an exciting and vibrant place.

Much of the development that took place in these cultural quarters was initially not the work of institutional developers but of independent individuals, as for example Carol Ainscow, whose company Artisan has been responsible for much of the refurbishment in the Gay Village (see Manchester Online, 2002). Considerably more prominent has been the company Urban Splash led by Tom Bloxham, which has been active in Castlefield and the Northern Quarter. Bloxham first came to Manchester from London in the early 1980s as a student, and in order to supplement his grant began selling records and posters on market stalls. As this was a success he sought for a shop unit, sub-letting the space additional to his needs. It was the realisation that the rent from sub-letting was more profitable than his own sales that led him to consider property as a speculative activity. At the same time he was mixing with others on the popular culture scene, many of whom were finding it difficult to find appropriate and affordable spaces in which to live and work or from which to market their wares.

Bloxham's first ventures into property were conversions of under-utilised buildings not only in Manchester but also in Liverpool. Here he met the architect Jonathan Falkingham, and in 1993 they jointly founded the company Urban Splash to extend their activities from retail and commercial space to residential conversions. It was at this stage that Bloxham decided to introduce the concept of loft living to the north-west. He felt that many people were looking for something different, and that the redundant commercial buildings in Manchester would provide appropriate space for lofts as well as offering opportunities for mixed use development. To be successful it was felt these must be of high quality and good design: 'Our mission is to create great buildings and neighbourhoods in which to live, work and play. By taking existing buildings or creating new ones, we aim to promote the value of modern design and practice sustainable development' (Urban Splash, 2002). The aim was to be innovative and imaginative, to enhance people's lifestyles and to create unique urban living space: 'Beauty with personality. Style with substance. Form with function' (Urban Splash, 2004).

The first loft apartments in Manchester were at Sally's Yard in central Manchester and Smithfield Buildings in the Northern Quarter. Urban Splash then began to look for a new area in which to develop in a more concentrated way, and which had not been 'discovered' by other developers. The site they found was the run down Britannia Basin; an area of wharves, warehouses and struggling small businesses beside the Bridgewater Canal on the western edge of Castlefield. This had been largely ignored by the now defunct CMDC, and was designated by the council for industrial use. Urban Splash produced a masterplan for the area, illustrating how a mix of conversions and new build, together with attention to the public realm, could create both a thriving residential community totalling some 1,000 people and an architecturally distinctive area. The council was persuaded not only to accept the proposals, but to adopt the principles as supplementary planning guidance.

The first project, the only one to be assisted by public sector subsidy from English Partnerships, involved the conversion of the Victorian Britannia Mills into lofts. This was followed by the renovation and partial rebuild of the art deco Smurfit Mill, renamed the Box Works, and a range of new build schemes, including Timber Wharf, Burton Place and the modular Moho, all on the loft principle.

Timber Wharf

In 1998 Urban Splash embarked on its first new build residential project on derelict land close to Britannia Mills, with a frontage to the Bridgewater Canal and immediately adjacent to the Box Works site. The design was the subject of a competition supported by RIBA and English Partnerships, with the requirements of the brief specifying a number of principles: an innovative and visually interesting contemporary design at low cost; new construction techniques; scope for mass production on other sites; flexibility of layout; energy efficiency; and environmentally sound materials. From the 162 international entries six were shortlisted for interview by the competition panel, chaired by Lord Rogers. The winner was Glenn Howells Architects of Birmingham, a firm priding itself on: 'projects that have a clear legible and efficient design whilst at the same time are exciting and enjoyable' (Glenn Howells Architects, 2004). Their design was for an eight storey continuous strip along the canal front using mainly pre-cast concrete construction, together with glass, timber and stone.

A planning application was put forward in 1999 for 136 apartments, together with underground car parking and the closure to through traffic of the facing street, Worsley Street. Given the fact that this was a conservation area and in the vicinity of several listed buildings, the consultees included English Heritage, the Ancient Monuments Society, SPAB, the Victorian and Georgian Societies, and Manchester's Conservation Area and Historic Buildings Panel, as well as other relevant bodies such as the Coal Authority, the Environment Agency, the Manchester Ship Canal Company, and the Environmental Health, and Traffic and Transport Departments. Most of these were supportive of the plan, given its regeneration aims. The Conservation Area and Historic Buildings Panel, however, had some concerns about the design: 'It was felt that this approach did not relate well to Manchester and was more akin to 1960s new towns. This element gives a "hutch-like" appearance, lacking in human scale and roofscape devoid of interest' (Development Control and Traffic Regulation Committee, 1999: para 23). This view was not supported by the planning department whose members felt that the design offered an acceptable contrast to the existing buildings and that: 'the form of the building with its structure expressed elevationally could be seen to make a visual reference to other, highly engineered structures (such as the railway viaducts) within the Conservation Area' (Development Control and Traffic Regulation Committee, 1999: para 29).

Planning permission and conservation area consent were granted in September 1999. The main conditions related to a reduction in car-parking due to the proximity of public transport and the city centre; improved access for disabled people; submission of further details about the layout, landscaping, boundary treatments and lighting of the external areas; improved permeability to the canal; provision of a new fully accessible pedestrian route from Worsley Street to the canal; and the submission to the city council of samples of the intended materials for approval. There was no requirement for affordable units given the significance attached to the regeneration contribution, and the general unsuitability of the site with no local primary school. Later in 1999 a variation was allowed to increase the number of apartments by the addition of an extra storey, whilst a subsequent variation for shops, businesses and live/work units on the ground floor became the subject of a new planning application. This readily gained consent as it was consistent with the city's policies of mixed uses, more active street frontages and the encouragement of working from home.

Construction commenced in 2000, based on a formal partnering agreement between Histon Concrete Structures and Urban Splash, and the latter's favoured in-house construction management approach. Completed in 2002 the scheme consists of 181 apartments including 17 penthouses and 17 ground floor duplex live/work spaces. In fact these are used solely as work space, housing the head offices of Urban Splash, an art gallery, a film production company, an internet based wedding list service, and a delicatessen, bar and small gym combined. There are nine plan forms of apartment, varying from one to three bed units, and with larger duplex and dual or triple aspect penthouses on the top two floors. Individual units are accessed by long, wide internal corridors, painted white and with drop ceilings. The stark impression is softened by the glow emanating from the low set blue spotlights beside each front door, and blue is also the colour of the full length carpet, bordered by a strip of concrete and a margin of slate chippings. The horizontality of this arrangement is offset by the regular verticals of concrete pillars, and the overall effect is of a long perspective which is both expansive and calming (Figure 9.1). Inside the units the feeling of expansiveness continues, with an open plan layout, double height rooms with mezzanine floors, and floor to ceiling windows opening to a timber and glass balcony. It is this design, together with the plain 'fair-faced' or white painted finish of the concrete walls and ceilings, which give the apartments the characteristics of lofts. In addition the dominance of glass floods the interiors with light whilst also giving the external appearance of the building an 'unexpected degree of transparency' and a 'simple layered rhythm' (Evans, 2003: 26) (Figure 9.2). Light is also a predominant feature of the eight storey, full width lacquered concrete and glass atrium set slightly off centre,

9.1 One of the internal corridors in Timber Wharf. This illustrates the long horizontal perspective, the concrete walls punctuated by vertical pillars, the dropped ceiling with concealed lighting, and the floor level spotlights. It is also possible to discern the strip of transitional space claimed by the positioning of door mats within the recessed doorways.

9.2 The main elevation of Timber Wharf. This shows the predominance of glass, including the glass-fronted balconies and the full height glass atrium, positioned slightly off centre. The three life-size sculpted cows stand in the shared and terraced lawn.

and comprising the circulation core between the main front and rear entrances together with the stairs and lifts. This space is given additional drama by the series of paintings by the controversial Turner prize winning artist Damien Hirst entitled *In a Spin: the Action of the World on Things*; 14 separate etchings with titles relating to popular songs and rhymes.

Timber Wharf has a frontage parallel to Worsley Street, and when the Moho scheme opposite is complete there will also be a new public square. The ground floor mixed use units are open to the street, albeit separated by a semi-public boundary of decking, whilst the main door giving access to the residential units is operated electronically with an audio-visual link to each apartment. To the rear of the building is a large triangle of landscaped and terraced open communal space, shared by residents of both Timber Wharf and the Box Works. Here as well as soft landscaping there are concrete chess tables with seating, a concrete table tennis table, and a *boules* pitch, together with a sculpture of an allium by the well known artist, Ruth Moilliet, and three life-size sculpted cows, contributions to the 2004 Manchester Cow Parade Trail (Figure 9.2). This garden area is overlooked on two sides but is well used in summer, serving its intended purpose of community interaction. It is separated from the canal towpath by a high mesh fence which contains three locked gates along its length giving access to the network of canal routes beyond (Figure 9.3, 9.4). This containment of the site has been insisted on by

9.3 The side elevation of Timber Wharf showing its position in relation to the canal and the elevated railway line. The mesh fencing protects the parking space of another Urban Splash development.

9.4 The protective fencing and one of the access gates from the canal towpath into the communal external space of Timber Wharf. Note also the sign advertising the Urban Splash website, designed to be visible from passing trains.

Urban Splash, despite the council's view that there should be greater permeability through the development to the canal as well as a stronger visual relationship. The resistance of Urban Splash to this idea is based on the opinion that the canal towpath is already accessible from several points in the vicinity, and that the absence of a physical boundary would compromise the residents' personal security.

Timber Wharf was popular from the start with 75 per cent of units sold off plan, and this being a city centre site, the majority of occupants are professional single people or couples without children. Most sales also occurred at the height of the buy-to-let market and this has resulted in a 50:50 ratio of owner occupied and privately rented properties, with the latter consisting of both individual and institutional investors. Sales take place from an eye-catching aluminium tube the 'Loft Shop', used for all the Castlefield properties, and prominently located beside the inner relief road (and bearing more than a passing resemblance to the exhibition tube of the Cardiff Bay Visitor Centre). Inside is an interactive model of the whole Castlefield site, and floor to ceiling photographs of the individual schemes. This flamboyant approach to marketing is reflected in the various marketing brochures, DVDs and CDs used by Urban Splash. The promotional CD for Timber Wharf contains information about both Urban Splash ('Our buildings work for the people inside them as well as for the city beyond') and the scheme itself. Timber Wharf is described as: 'the very height of city centre luxury', and, to the accompaniment of trendy music and moving images, it is emphasised that Timber Wharf is: 'a vivid expression of city living as it should be' and 'part of the evolving community of Britannia Basin'. Its connection to the city is also stressed: 'situated in Castlefield at the gateway to Manchester city centre […] a location second to none with the ambiance [*sic*] of the canal but the proximity to the major shops, bars, restaurants and theatres'. It is suggested that the presence of the two railway lines across the canal and the Mancunian Way emphasise the strong sense of arrival into Manchester, a city offering 'a truly contemporary lifestyle' and now 'firmly on the map – a place to live, work and play'.

Timber Wharf has secured a total of five design awards and was featured in RIBA's recent *Coming Homes* exhibition. In this it has continued Urban Splash's tradition of winning awards not only for architectural quality but for regeneration, business and marketing, with over 100 such awards to date. Tom Bloxham, himself recipient of an MBE in 1998, is now head of a multi-million pound enterprise which is beginning to expand its operations beyond the north-west. Further establishment endorsement has come from the upholding of Urban Splash by the Urban Task Force as a model of urban regeneration, and by its selection by English Partnerships as lead developer in the New Islington Millennium Community in East Manchester (see Chapter 6). However, it is Timber Wharf which has given Bloxham the biggest sense of achievement to date: 'It's modern, it's new, it's different, it's got a great sense of simplicity … it just feels really calm and beautiful' (Pride of Manchester, 2003). For one who has cited Le Corbusier's *Unité d'Habitation* as one of his favourite buildings (Mulhearn, 2000: 26) his enthusiasm for Timber Wharf is perhaps not surprising.

Gated communities

Gated communities are defined by Blakely and Snyder, the leading American researchers in the field, as: 'residential areas with restricted access such that normally public spaces have been privatized. Access is controlled by physical barriers: walled or fenced perimeters and gated or guarded entrances' (Blakely and Snyder, 1998: 62). Walls and gates are not, of course, an entirely new means of controlling and enclosing space, as evidenced by the protective fortifications of the towns and cities of Roman and mediaeval times. However, walls and gates have today re-emerged in a transformed guise: 'the walls, the physical walls of division, are inside the city rather than around it' (Marcuse, 1997: 106). In the residential context this 'forting up' (Blakely and Snyder, 1997) has been most closely associated with the US, but it is increasingly apparent that the gated community is emerging as a worldwide phenomenon (see Low, 2003).

In the US, a few gated communities emerged as early as the late nineteenth century, but only increased in numbers with the advent of exclusive retirement communities in the 1970s. Gradually they spread to other types of affluent residential development, and then filtered down from the elite to those on middle incomes. In part this expansion is explained by the decline of the suburbs, once the epitome of the American dream but increasingly threatened, like the inner cities, with crime and degradation:

> Gated communities seek to counter these trends by maintaining the ambiance of exclusivity and safety the suburbs once promised. They exist not just to wall out crime or traffic or strangers, but to lock in economic position.
>
> (Blakely and Snyder, 1998: 63)

Thus gated communities, whether located in the city or the suburbs, seem to offer both safety and the maintenance of an exclusive and homogenous way of life. So popular has this fortress living become that by the early 2000s it was estimated that somewhere between nine and 16 million Americans resided in gated communities (Low, 2003).

Evidence suggests that for residents the sense of safety goes beyond physical protection and containment to a deeper psychological level, in which the gates and walls have the power symbolically to: 'order personal and social experience' (Low, 2003: 10). Furthermore through their promise of the construction of an ideal (albeit illusory) community they present a way in which to suppress and deny the: 'inherent anxieties and conflicting social values of modern urban and suburban life' (Low, 2003: 11). This multi-layered power and meaning of gated communities has been recognised by developers, who in their marketing strategies have learnt that housing in a postmodern world has to be commodified as lifestyle and as sentiment:

> Selling houses is showbiz. You go after the emotions. We don't go out and show a gate in the ad. But we try and do it subtly. In our ad, we don't even show houses. We show a yacht. We show an emotion.
>
> (Developer, cited in Blakely and Snyder, 1998: 64)

In the UK, gated communities have so far had a lesser impact. One of the first to come to public notice was the Barratt estate in Dulwich, London, where in the late 1980s the former Conservative Prime Minister Margaret Thatcher bought an exclusive town house for her retirement. Other select gated communities of the period were built in rural locations where they attracted celebrities and footballers, keen both to display their status and to be protected from unwelcome media attention. But as in the US, gated communities have begun to appeal to the ordinary middle classes as well as to the affluent elite, with the result that more and more developers are adopting this form as the urban type of choice (Atkinson *et al.*, 2004; Webster, 2001). But it is also interesting to note that many developers are building gated communities not so much because of their security aspects but because they have become a fashionable concept:

> Gated communities are very important in the overall development market. In all developments there is a preference to gate, even if it is just car parking spaces. If possible, we do try and get planning approval for gated living.
>
> (Developer cited by Atkinson *et al.*, 2004: 24)

In regard to the obtaining of such planning approval the policy context is unclear, not to say contradictory. Currently there is no official planning policy for gated communities at a national level, and, indeed such a policy would run counter to the government's policy commitment to 'good' urban design and mixed and integrated communities. Essentially gated communities are anti-urbanist, due to their lack of permeability, their enclosure and their privatisation of previously public space (designated by Webster (2001) as 'club' space). It has been left to local planning authorities to resolve these contradictions and to decide whether to establish their own policy on what to most is a new, but increasingly pertinent issue. It would appear that at the time of writing few if any authorities have such a policy, and that the approach adopted in the granting or refusal of planning permission is *ad hoc*; based on personal discretion, reaction to the extent of local opposition or the need to encourage development at any price (see Atkinson *et al.*, 2004; Gooblar, 2002; Manzi and Smith-Bowers, 2005).

Although a few commentators, notably Davis (1990) are emphatically opposed to the fortified aspect of gated communities, others appreciate that they have both benefits and drawbacks (see Blakely and Snyder, 1997, 1998; Manzi and Smith-Bowers, 2005; Marcuse, 1997; Webster, 2001). On the positive side, it is suggested that the apparent security offered by the gates has given some middle income and professional people the confidence to live in the inner city. Without this shift the ability to regenerate marginal brownfield land would be compromised, as would the creation of a more balanced inner urban population. At the same time it is argued that gated communities do nothing to achieve *integrated* populations and merely reproduce segregation in a new guise:

> It is pertinent to ask … whether social fragmentation is exacerbated or inhibited by middle-income professionals moving back into the city to live in gated apartment blocks … Which is worse – the traditional segregation of the twentieth century where house prices and distance separates the richer from the poorer, or the new segregation in which rich and poor live in physical proximity separated by smart-card-operated gates and entry phones?
>
> (Webster, 2001: 155)

As well as reinforcing social and spatial inequality there is a concern that gated communities represent an impoverishment of democratic life. For the implication is that residents of gated communities have chosen to disengage from social interchange and from the processes of ordinary civic life – especially in the US where a new form of privatised governance is emerging (Webster, 2001). Even within the gates there is no real 'community' since residents tend to constitute a largely homogenous group of people of similar socio-economic status, many of whom are there for only a short duration, and moreover, have little inclination for interaction. Furthermore, they contribute little or nothing to the immediate locality that exists outside the gates, commuting to distant places of work, patronising exclusive services and facilities, and in general avoiding the 'messy intimacy' of the outside world (Bauman, 1998: 54).

A gated community for Cardiff

Reconstructing Cardiff Bay

Cardiff in South Wales was a small, undistinguished coastal town until the early nineteenth century when a local landowner, the Marquis of Bute, began to build a series of docks for the export of iron and coal from the Welsh Valleys. In recognition of the growing prominence and prosperity this brought to Cardiff it was granted city status in 1905, although it was not until 1955 that it was made the capital of Wales. After a decline in population in the 1970s, Cardiff began in the 1990s to increase in size again. It also began to gain in national and international importance following the formation of the National Assembly for Wales in 1999, and initiatives such as the building of the new Millennium Stadium, the hosting of the European summit and the bid to be European Capital of Culture (see Thomas, 2003). By the early 2000s Cardiff was being described by its promoters as: 'Europe's most dynamic capital city' (Cardiff County Council, 2004), with an expanding business sector, a population of over 300,000, and an extensive new housebuilding programme. Some of this housing was to be located in new or converted blocks in the city centre, but the majority was destined for the former docks area.

The need for a strategy for the decaying docks had been noted by the County Council of South Glamorgan in the late 1970s, but Cardiff City Council, then responsible for planning matters, had concentrated instead on city centre redevelopment. The whole district, known as Butetown (colloquially as Tiger Bay), was by then in serious decline, and its population of 5,800 was marginalised and relatively deprived. Being a mile from the city centre and located beyond the symbolic boundary of the main line railway, the district was all but invisible to the majority of policy makers, developers and the population at large – especially given the reputation of Tiger Bay as a lawless and dangerous place. In casting about for a solution, the county council recognised that access to public money could be gained if the area were to be included in the government's Urban Development Corporation initiative. After considerable negotiation the Cardiff Bay Development Corporation (CBDC) was established in 1987 to regenerate the whole of the extensive waterfront and its immediate hinterland, but with the concession that the planning powers of the local authorities should be retained (Thomas and Imrie, 1999).

In formulating a vision for the area CBDC took much of its inspiration from the successful regeneration of Baltimore in the US, but with an ambition which extended far beyond physical regeneration alone. Thus its prime objective was: 'to establish Cardiff internationally as a superlative maritime city, which will stand comparison with any similar city in the world, enhancing the image and economic well being of Cardiff and of Wales as a whole' (CBDC, 1988: 4). The strategy that was prepared included new business, retail and leisure facilities; 6,000 new dwellings of which a quarter were to be social housing; the re-unification of the city centre with its waterfront; and a barrage across the mouth of the Bay to maintain a constant water level. The Bay was also to be the location of two new high profile institutional buildings: the National Assembly and the Millennium Centre for culture and the arts. High among CBDC priorities were the preservation of the historic environment and a concern for design quality – despite the emphasis at the time on market forces (CBDC, 2000). CBDC itself retained design control powers, and established a design and architectural review panel (with Richard Rogers and Tony Aldous amongst its members) to prepare guidelines on urban form. As well as prescribing, for example, high densities and a maximum building height of eight storeys, there was also a public realm strategy aimed at giving identity to the Bay through common themes. These included standard widths for walkways; the use of selected ranges of street furniture, planting, paving and other materials; and a commitment to public art.

The whole of the CBDC area was divided into a number of discrete development zones, the most important of which was the Inner Harbour. This was to be redeveloped as the main focus for attracting in both visitors and commercial interests, and included the land around the main waterfront together with Roath Basin, connected to the Inner Harbour by a lock. The planning brief for this zone envisioned it as: 'a centre of cultural, commercial and festival retail activity' with 'a quality environment in which to work, relax, live and play' (Benjamin Thompson and Associates, undated: 1.1.0). Roath Basin was suggested as a prime location for one of the first phases of development since its several feeder canals and locks would allow developments to have an 'intimate focus' and 'to front and have an address to the water' (Benjamin Thompson Associates, undated: 3.1.1). The proposal was that the first housing in the Inner Harbour area should be located here, offering a range of different styles and sizes of unit, and in the hope that it would attract retirees, second home owners and employees in the burgeoning commercial sectors of Cardiff and the M4 corridor beyond.

These strategies were being proposed at the time the housing market began to collapse, and for this reason housing was not initially given high priority by CBDC. However, as the housing market picked up housebuilders themselves began to demand the release of land, and at the same time the then Secretary of

State for Wales, John Redwood, instructed CBDC to achieve more housing starts. The initial phases of housebuilding that then ensued were something of a test case for assessing demand for housing in the Bay, an area suffering from a: 'perception held by most outsiders [...] of an unappealing area with intransigent social problems' (CBDC, 2000: 82). However, the gamble paid off: sales proceeded apace, further national housebuilders were attracted to the Bay, and by the time CBDC was wound up in 2000 the resident population of the Bay had increased by 250 per cent, with nearly 5,000 units built or planned:

> Demand for these [early] developments was instrumental in proving there was a serious market in Cardiff Bay for such properties. The Bay, instead of being seen as a suburban satellite, could be regarded as a high density city location, a convenient and desirable place to live for young working people, small households and empty nesters.
>
> (CBDC, 2000: 87)

Adventurers Quay

The land around Roath Basin was owned by Associated British Ports (ABP) who from the first had shared the vision of CBDC and were one of the partners in the venture. Rather than selling land to CBDC, ABP set up its own development arm, Grosvenor Waterside, and in 1994 it brought forward a planning application for the wedge shaped site of Tyneside Yard at the head of Roath Basin – one of the areas identified by Benjamin Thompson Associates for early development. The proposal was for land reclamation works, highway improvements, foot-ways and landscaping in order to prepare the site for housing development. Planning permission was granted in January 1995, with conditions relating to decontamination and soil quality, the preservation of the dock edges and any maritime artefacts, and adoption of CBDC guidelines in regard to landscaping, surfaces, and the inclusion of public art.

The further development of the site was subject to a limited architect/developer competition (see Architecture Today, 1997). This was won by the housebuilders St David and the architects Richard Reid Associates of Kent, the latter describing themselves as urban design consultants to the former CBDC and as having a commitment to 'place making' (Richard Reid Associates, 2004). At the time St David was a subsidiary of the Berkeley Group which in the early 1990s had made the decision to concentrate on urban regeneration and brownfield schemes (Berkeley Group, 1999). Although there is no direct evidence, it is likely that as one of the largest housebuilding companies the Berkeley Group would have been invited to the 1993 launch of the Cardiff Bay project by CBDC at the Mermaid Theatre in London (a location reflecting the sinuous mermaid logo of CBDC). The specific aim of this event was to draw the attention of nationally based investors and property developers to the possibilities of Cardiff Bay. However, there were few contenders for the risky project of the Tyneside Yard site: this would be the first housing project in the Bay; the demand was unknown; the market was only just beginning to recover; and the site was surrounded by dereliction, with an operating port the nearest neighbour. St David was aware that what was required to meet CBDC's ambitions was something bold, significant and different, but at the same time there was the constraint of an unpredictable demand and hence of an uncertain profit margin. This meant that the budget had to be kept low; as did the eventual house prices if interest were to be attracted.

Richard Reid Associates were responsible for the overall design concept, and the detailed plans were prepared by local architects Osborne V. Webb and Partners, in consultation with the housebuilders, the CBDC design panel and the planning authority. The construction firm used was Birse Construction Ltd, and although a standard procurement contract was adopted, considerable reliance was placed on a Charter agreed and signed by St David and Birse at a team building seminar. The design was based on a high density urban form of 225 apartments, town houses and penthouse suites to be built in two phases, each arranged around a landscaped courtyard and presenting a tight building line to the three waterfronts of Roath Basin, a former dry dock and a canal link. Storey heights, roof lines, and materials were varied to introduce interest, and the elevation overlooking Roath Basin, visible from across the Bay, was purposefully designed as a landmark feature (Figure 9.5). Parking was provided in the courtyards and in an undercroft to the first phase. In

9.5   The waterfront elevation of Adventurers Quay

addition it was decided by St David at an early stage, albeit with some reluctance, that the development should be secured by walls, railings and a gated entry.

At the time (1996) the notion of a 'gated community' was not in popular parlance, and nor were the debates about their perceived merits or drawbacks. To St David the issue was one of trying to make this new, isolated development in 'frontiersland' (personal communication) attractive to customers, and to give them a feeling of identity and security in the context of surroundings dominated by derelict industrial land and traffic to the functioning port beyond. Whilst CBDC did not have any objections to the gated nature of the development, the officers of the planning department were more hesitant. This was a new concept and their instinct was that this was a type of development they did not want to encourage. However, they could see the reasoning behind the desire to create a secure environment and were prepared to consider the scheme on its merits. To this end they visited a gated scheme by Berkeley in Brindley Place, Birmingham, another waterside regeneration site, and concluded that although on the whole this particular scheme was impressive, the fact that it precluded access to the external perimeter of the site was detrimental to the public interest. After much debate, the planning committee finally agreed to the St David proposal for gating, but with the caveat that there must be full pedestrian access around the site. They also decided this should not be a precedent for the future shape of development in Cardiff (personal communication).

Planning permission was granted in February 1997 and was subject to a variety of conditions. These included the provision of public open space outside the development, measures to ensure protection from contamination and flood, and the submission of more precise details in relation to site enclosure, materials, finishes, landscaping and parking. There was no requirement for an element of social housing since it had been decided in consultation with the housing department that the isolation, the lack of public transport and other facilities, and the proximity to a working dock made the location unsuitable. In 1997 and 1998 further planning approvals were granted to increase the number of townhouses and reduce the number of apartments in the light of marketing experience.

St David named the development Adventurers Quay. The marketing brochure, with its glossy cover of a silver yacht above stylised blue waves, refers to Cardiff Bay's slogan: 'Europe's most exciting waterfront' and promises: 'a new style of living in Cardiff Bay ... where a glorious past interacts with a positive and vibrant future' (St David, undated). Cardiff is extolled as a city replete with tradition, new opportunities and unsurpassed facilities, whilst the Bay itself is lauded as a new focal point to: 'take Cardiff into the 21st century'. Adventurers Quay is described as a 'concept' rather than a housing development, and the various house types, with names such as The Mansions, The Astorias, The Madisons, The Bloomingdales, The Chrysler, offer: a 'unique sense of style', as well as exceptional exterior and interior specifications. However, Adventurers Quay is not described as a gated community even though a list of special features notes the: 'video entry system controlling gates and apartment entrances' and the 'secure private parking'. Indeed the gated aspect of the development is not given particular prominence at all, a fact which is attributable to the ambivalence of St David in preferring not to convey the impression of a 'fortress' and instead to let customers determine their own responses to the gates (personal communication).

The completed scheme is approached from a cul de sac spur from the road to the port of Cardiff, and is no longer so isolated as it was initially, with a new office block across the road to the north and new high rise housing currently being constructed across the narrow dock to the west. However, the road and the waterways surrounding the scheme maintain an impression of separation, an impression further intensified by the high walls which front the road and the existence of the electronic gates, supervised from the adjacent caretaker's office (Figure 9.6). Access is also possible by foot from the Inner Harbour. This involves an almost processual route along the length of Roath Basin, across a canal bridge, then over the narrow dock by a decorative structure reminiscent of a drawbridge (Figures 9.7, 9.8). The perimeter walkways requested by the planning department are little used by either the public or residents, not least because the terraces of the apartments and townhouses which front it are barricaded by railings and afford no egress for those who might wish to take advantage of the waterfront (Figure 9.9). Within, the units overlook a smaller and a larger courtyard, where the sense of containment creates a feeling of seclusion despite the circular access route for

9.6 The gated entrance to Adventurers Quay. Note the decorative A and Q on the gate pillars.

9.7 The canal bridge on the pedestrian route to Adventurers Quay. The A frame support neatly frames the landmark elevation.

9.8 The 'drawbridge' approach over the former dock. This image also illustrates the varied design treatment of the roofscape and elevations and the decorative lighting standards.

9.9 One of the waterfront walkways, with no direct access from the external private space of the housing units. The grilles conceal the undercroft parking, and the seating, bins, bollards, railings, and down pipes conform to CBDC design guidelines.

vehicles and the ubiquitous parking (Figures 9.10 and 9.11). The central raised landscaped area might appear conducive for relaxation, but the fact that it is overlooked on all sides by a myriad of windows means that it is constantly in the public gaze (Figure 9.12).

Adventurers Quay undoubtedly achieved what CBDC had hoped in being a striking flagship development and on this account has achieved acclaim. It was highly commended for its contribution to the quality of the townscape in the Lord Mayor's 2000 Civic Awards, and has also been praised for its distinctive contribution to housing in the Bay, notably in regard to the way the homes: 'embrace their waterfront environment and provide a luxury lifestyle' (At Home in the Bay, 1998: 4). Neither has it had any difficulty in attracting potential purchasers, be they owner occupiers, investors anticipating future price rises as the Bay develops, landlords in the buy-to-let market or people planning to move there at a later date. The majority of occupants are professional single people or couples, and there are few families with children. Resale values have increased markedly, but despite the proliferation of gated communities nationally and the appearance in Cardiff Bay of a second such development, Century Wharf (at the time of inception in a different planning authority), for the most part local estate agents have continued the indirect allusion to security rather than stressing the presence of gates.

9.10 The larger of the two internal courtyards with surface parking

9.11 The smaller shared courtyard. Note here the pseudo-Georgian design style which even includes the emphasis given to the centre units, with larger window openings and parapet

9.12 The central raised landscaping designed for sitting and relaxation but in full view from the surrounding windows

Conclusion

The cultural image of the city has in recent years begun to change, with a new (or reprised) sense of urbanity and opportunity overlaying the more negative perceptions of the city as a place of dirt and disorder. It is the social processes of post-industrialisation which have played a large part in this, and the concomitant shift from a landscape of production to a landscape of consumption has brought display and spectacle to the newly valorised spaces of the city. This is evidenced in the language of heritage and popular art, and in the way the new continental style bars and cafés now animate the edge of city streets and squares. These commodified spaces also meet the demand from certain fractions of the middle classes who (as discussed in Chapter 1) are seeking to find identity and meaning through different forms of lifestyle. Consuming the city in a way more typical of continental Europe than the UK helps to provide that sense of difference, and it is but one further step for this to extend beyond work and leisure interludes to 24-hour possession of the city through city centre living.

This change in perception of the city has been reflected at the institutional level. Central government, city authorities and property developers have all begun to devise new policies and strategies to achieve an urban renaissance, and city centre housing has become an essential element in this. But they have also been obliged to consider the impact of a number of other issues: the implications of demographic change; changing lifestyle and housing aspirations; the realities of the poor image of the decaying inner city; the often impoverished state of the local economy; and the potential that can be harnessed from the positive aspects of geographical location and heritage sites. The most difficult spatial locations to tackle have been those most adversely affected by the processes of economic restructuring, and the cities discussed in this chapter have provided examples of this. Manchester developed as a major manufacturing city, and has experienced first inner city depopulation and then the closure or relocation of many of its city centre industries and warehouses due to the impact of the new global economy. In Cardiff, the spatial implications have been somewhat different. Here, in a newer city, the only significant industrial activity was not in the city centre but in the outlying docks which served the coal industry of the hinterland. By the 1980s this industry was in decline and the docks had become an abandoned and marginalised place, defamed in popular imagination and conveniently beyond the gaze of policy makers.

In a postmodern era of city boosterism and competitiveness city actors in Manchester took some time to make the necessary transformation from mid-century urban managerialism to late century city entrepreneurialism. In this they were also hampered by the *habitus* of opposition to central government. But having managed to make the necessary shifts, they learnt to exploit both government resources and the advantages of the city: as a regional centre; a site of industrial heritage; a tourist destination; a centre of culture, sport, and popular music; and a possessor of iconic quarters. City centre living was encouraged through the institutionally endorsed model of a UDC, but this covered only a small area of the central city. Elsewhere it was the actions of individual developers on the fringes of the cultural industry which brought about revival, most notably Tom Bloxham and his company Urban Splash. Bloxham's personal experience, vision and entrepreneurial flair led him to spot a gap in the northern market for a type of urban living space being newly promoted in the UK: the loft. The success of his early experimentation resulted in a search for new areas in which to develop more ambitious schemes, and this brought him to Castlefield, an abandoned site but rich in heritage potential.

In Cardiff the preferred institutional model of a UDC was again employed as a regeneration mechanism, but here concessions were successfully negotiated in regard to the retention of more local control. By contrast to Manchester the initial driving force was tourism and commerce rather than housing, and it was only through the intervention of a Secretary of State and pressure from institutional housebuilders that the release of housing land was achieved. Even then, in a stagnant housing market it needed some courage for the first housebuilder to undertake the initial risky flagship development. Success encouraged new institutional developers, with the result that far from being an invisible site beyond the pale, Cardiff Bay has become a newly revalorised location, its array of upmarket apartments hailed as exemplars of dynamic city centre living.

In both Cardiff Bay and Castlefield, the type of residential form adopted has been derived from a different cultural context, that of the US. Lofts: 'a historically contingent, culturally specific response to disinvestment in the city's core' (Zukin, 1989: 193) initially represented a new form of gentrified living. Then they were appropriated by developers who learnt to remodel signs of artistic and alternative lifestyles into symbols of distinction for an affluent elite wishing to engage in the apparent freedoms, cultural opportunities and diversity of the city. The lifestyles thus constructed are lived within a new configuration of domestic space suggestive of the ambivalences of the contemporary age:

> This suggests that loft living is appealing, in part, because it is paradoxical. The incongruity of living in a factory does not cease to surprise us. From the outside, of course, a loft building looks like a factory, but inside, we find a home. Although homes are considered private space, the openness of a loft makes it public space ... Its success in the urban housing market demonstrates that at this time paradox sells.
>
> (Zukin, 1989: 60)

Gated communities, by contrast, are for a different type of elite, those who are rendered fearful by an internally divided and anxiety ridden world and seek protection from its apparent threat. The walls and gates maintain an impression of security and certainty, excluding people 'not like us', the outsider, the 'Other' and the malefactor. Here too is paradox that sells, for in suggesting to the imagination that there is indeed something beyond which must be feared they intensify the very fear they seek to overcome.

On the former industrial site of Castlefield, the new build Timber Wharf has recreated the loft in an indisputably modernist design. It contrasts in style and materials with the existing Victorian townscape, and yet in mass and form it reflects its neighbours, both old and new. It also engages with these neighbours, looking outwards and inviting interaction through its urbanist approach to design and permeability. However, this urbanity alters in the face of the potential threat of the untamed canal, retained at a distance by an uncompromising barrier. Once within, the spatial form of the full height atrium has in effect a panoptical function (see Ellin, 1997) and the fact that one might be under observation from any point above or below deters inappropriate activity. From the controlling space of this atrium lead the identical corridors and individual flats, a branching spatial syntax effectively denoting the equal status of the residents. Externally lies the semi-private space of the communal garden where opportunities for interaction are encouraged by facilities for the playing of games – although true relaxation might be deterred by the sense of surveillance from the vast array of windows. The iconic cows and the allium sculpture, together with the Damien Hirst pictures, serve not only to add interest and distinction, but also connect the development to the cultural interests of the founder. This is further reinforced in the manipulation of image, sign and symbol in the marketing material. Here several messages are simultaneously conveyed: that Manchester is exciting and 'arriving'; that Urban Splash as a company is culturally distinctive, innovative and dynamic; that the iconic quarter of Castlefield has the makings of a vibrant community; and that loft living provides a prestigious and modern space in which to create a new type of urban lifestyle.

In Cardiff Bay the isolation of the site and its vicinity to vacant and undeveloped space led to the somewhat hesitant suggestion for a gated community, but this still had to be negotiated with a reluctant planning authority. The consequence is that even though the design of the units has the urbanist ambitions sought by CBDC, the effect of the gates is to create an anti-urbanist development, segregated from its surrounding context and looking not outwards but inwards. Access is monitored not only by the electronic gates, but also by surveillance from the adjacent caretaker, and even within the inner courtyards there is a constant feeling of an all pervasive gaze. It is interesting then, that little explicit reference is made to gates and security in marketing the scheme. Instead image and impression are all, as reinforced by the emotive brochure cover of a yacht riding free on the crest of a wave. The suggestion is of buying into a romanticised seafaring past of adventure and discovery, but with any element of danger and risk removed and an exciting and exclusive lifestyle assured.

In many ways the design inspirations for Timber Wharf and Adventurers Quay are drawn from two contrasting cultural and spatial ideals, informed on the one hand by engagement with diversity, creativity and modernist design, and on the other by withdrawal, reaction and postmodern eclecticism. However, both have made compromises which suggest an underlying unease and lack of conviction: at Adventurers Quay the commitment to gates has been half-hearted and seen as a necessary and pragmatic component within a scheme that would otherwise like to profess to be urbanist; at Timber Wharf the intention to link the geometric built form into the grid of its surroundings has been compromised by the secure and impermeable boundary to the untamed line of the canal. These similarities within differences can be seen as a product of the emergence of these two types at the same time in history, characterised by the postmodern shift to commodified lifestyles, the tensions between the desire for freedom and security, the institutional promotion of city centre living and urbanist built forms, and the climate of fear and uncertainty.

10 Alternative modes of dwelling

Preliterate and traditional societies possessed (and where they continue to exist, still possess) an organic world view in which the 'other' world, the natural world and the human world were intimately connected. Gods, spirits, plants, animals and people were seen as essential and equivalent elements in a harmonious whole, with any failure to acknowledge and respect the balanced interdependence of parts likely to lead to chaos and disaster. Thus gods were honoured and propitiated, the land was blessed and appreciated for its bounty, rain was greeted with ceremonial thanksgiving, and the sacrifice of animals for food was endowed with ritual significance. And above all, people accepted as preordained reality the need to live with each other and the land in a symbiotic relationship of trust, esteem, restraint and humility: a relationship of which they were daily reminded through myth, symbol, and the disposition and design of their artefacts.

In Western societies this world view of the earth as a living organism which must be revered and respected continued even into Renaissance times (Merchant, 1992). However, as the Enlightenment dawned and the new sciences developed, it was replaced by a perspective which constructed nature as beyond and outside human life, and something which could, and even should, be mastered in the pursuit of progress, power and wealth. This mechanistic and exploitative approach to the natural world heralded the start of a period of control and domination which brought about the machine age, the industrial and the technological revolutions, capitalism and consumerism. And as time went on the ideological imperative of western societies became more and more explicitly articulated as one of economic growth: this and this alone would secure individual, societal and global well-being.

However, it was also being recognised by the latter part of the twentieth century that the pursuit of economic growth was resulting in certain negative externalities, notably in relation to the unsustainable exploitation of the products of the natural world and in the undesirable effects on the environment of the processes of manufacturing, of the use of chemicals, and of the production and combustion of energy. It was as a consequence of this that new concepts and discourses began to emerge, constructed first around 'environment' in the 1960s, and then in the late 1980s and 1990s around 'sustainability' (Dryzek, 1997). Whilst in themselves these discourses often overlapped and merged, elements of them were appropriated in different ways by groups with differing agendas. Thus institutional interests, forced to accept that (some) environmental problems were real and must be addressed, argued that these could be solved, and were not irreconcilable with continued economic growth. On the other hand, anti-establishment groups and individuals, deeply concerned about the potentially irreversible damage being done to the planet, urged the need for ideological, economic and social change before it became too late.

This chapter considers some of the events which have shaped the recognition and articulation of the environmental problem, focusing in particular on the various manifestations of the environmental movement. It then moves on to look at how ideas which are representative of the environmental movement, such as balance with the natural world, the use of natural and healthy products, energy efficiency, spiritual awareness, personal fulfilment and harmony with one's fellow human beings, have been translated into the production and design of dwellings. More detailed consideration is given to two emergent concepts in this context: the relatively new phenomenon in the UK of cohousing, a form of collective housing imported from Scandinavia; and the ecovillage movement, which advocates and supports a more natural and holistic way of life. Two British case studies illustrate the application of these concepts: a cohousing scheme in Gloucestershire, and a low impact settlement on the edge of Dartmoor in Devon.

The environmental imperative

In the early days of the industrial revolution anxiety about the potential devastation of nature and the dehumanising effects of machines was articulated by an intellectual minority with an often romantic approach to nature and the simple life (see Doherty, 2002; Dryzek, 1997). The musings, treatises and actions of such respected figures as Wordsworth, William Morris, John Ruskin and Octavia Hill gave rise to a more general appreciation of landscape, along with a growing awareness of the need – even the moral duty – to conserve and preserve the countryside and the wildlife within it. It was as a result of such conservation discourse that institutionally endorsed organisations such as the RSPB, the National Trust, the Royal Society for Nature Conservation and the CPRE were founded in the late nineteenth and early twentieth centuries (see Dryzek *et al.*, 2003, and Chapter 4).

During the years of depression and world war, conservation was not a matter at the forefront of most people's minds. However, by the 1960s and 1970s the publication of several influential texts drew attention to the threats posed by unbridled capitalism, notably pollution, population expansion, industrial activity and materialistic lifestyles. These texts included Rachel Carson's *Silent Spring* (1962) and Schumacher's *Small is Beautiful* (1973) and the reports *The Limits to Growth* (Meadows *et al.*, 1972) and *Blueprint for Survival* (Goldsmith *et al.*, 1972). Particularly influential in terms of its wide reach was Lovelock's *Gaia: A New Look at Life on Earth* (1979), in which was expounded the theory of Gaia (named after the earth goddess Gaia) as the living, self-regulating earth. As a respected scientist Lovelock appealed to the establishment, where he gained the ear of Margaret Thatcher, whilst his philosophical and spiritual outlook also attracted followers of the 'green' movement for whom he became something of a guru. It was largely from the challenge presented by the combined impact of these publications that the environmental movement, in all its various manifestations, was born.

This environmental movement has been articulated over time through a variety of different discourses or storylines (Hajer, 1995). These have been appropriated by particular interest groups to shape opinion, urge caution, arouse fear and stimulate action. However, in a world where scientific 'facts' are open to interpretation and disputation, there are competing versions of the extent to which problems can actually be said to exist and what type of action is needed – or even if any action is justified at all.

At the institutional level, the approach adopted has become associated with the emergent paradigm of 'ecological modernisation':

> This policy discourse ... recognizes the ecological crisis as evidence of a fundamental omission in the workings of the institutions of modern society ... [I]t suggests that environmental problems can be solved in accordance with the workings of the main institutions of society.
>
> (Hajer, 1995: 3).

According to this interpretation the solutions that are required are technocratic, regulatory and economically rational, and will be achieved through a combination of government intervention and market efficiencies. It was this thinking which led in the 1970s to the introduction of Departments of the Environment in many countries, including the UK, and which underpinned the 'sustainable development' rhetoric of the Brundtland Report of 1987.

By contrast to this institutional discourse is that articulated by members of the environmental social movement. This movement began in the 1970s, and increasingly became referred to as the 'green' movement (see Doherty, 2002; Dryzek, 1997, and Chapter 4). As time has passed this green movement has evolved into two distinct arms; one seeking to work with and within the existing political and social structures, and the other believing that the only way forward is to reject existing structures and establish alternative systems. The former includes groups such as FoE, Greenpeace and the Green parties. These had their origins in radical action at the grassroots level, but have sought to become agents of change at the institutional level by organising into national bodies, developing a formal bureaucratic structure, and professionalising into entities with considerable technical, legal and scientific expertise. The success of this strategy has been measured in the legitimacy they have achieved, which, in the case of the Green party, has led to gains in British local, national and European elections.

By contrast to this rational and pragmatic approach is that of the groups referred to by Dryzek (1997) as the 'Green romantics'. These idealistic groups believe that there is a need for a profound change in the way people relate to each other and to the natural world, and that constitution into formal structures or engagement with institutions and policy makers is irrelevant:

> Instead, their main concern is with the nurturing and development of different kinds of subjectivity, or ways that individuals can experience the world.
>
> (Dryzek, 1997: 155)

Green groups embrace a wide range of contrasting and sometimes competing philosophies, but tend to share a concern for harmony between mind, body, spirit and nature. In the US and parts of continental Europe there are a number of organised 'deep green' offshoots such as eco-feminism, spiritual ecology, social ecology, eco-theology, and the Gaia movement, but the UK has seen a more diffuse 'alternative' movement associated with 'hippy' communes and tipi villages, alternative health and healing movements, eastern philosophies and pagan practices, and radical bookshops, cafés and food cooperatives (see Doherty, 2002).

During the 1990s, however, elements of the alternative movement in the UK began to become more organised and involved in direct action. In part this was due to resistance to the measures adopted by an increasingly authoritarian state to repress protest and undermine individual freedoms, as expressed particularly in the action taken by the Conservatives against New Age travellers. But it was also a response to the increased sense of urgency in regard to the environmental problem, especially following the warnings of the 1992 Rio Earth Summit. Thus it was, for example, that a British branch of Earth First! was established in 1991, that more people became involved in 'anti-globalisation' protests, and that a more concerted eco-warrior and anti-roads campaign emerged – with the character Swampy as a 'symbolic referent' (Doherty, 2002: 167).

Towards ecological, holistic and responsive design

Governments and institutions have been slow to respond to the environmental imperative in regard to the design and construction of housing, despite the fact that it is housing that is one of the major contributors to environmental degradation and carbon dioxide emissions. However, as the sustainability agenda has assumed greater prominence there have been a few advances, although these reflect a somewhat fragmented and uncoordinated approach. Thus on the one hand there has been the high profile, high cost and hard to replicate demonstration project, such as GMV (see Chapter 6), and on the other the introduction of advanced technological systems and scientific ratings mechanisms against which environmental performance can be measured, such as the new EcoHomes standards (see Chapter 5).

Some private sector housebuilders, housing associations and architectural firms are also beginning to recognise that by promoting their designs as sustainable they can gain increased legitimacy. This has resulted in a rhetoric which maximises the use in publicity of words such as 'sustainable', 'ecological' and 'energy efficient', although in reality the true environmental gain is often minimal. There are, however, some notable exceptions to this general rule. These include the much acclaimed carbon neutral development BedZED, the work of the 'intelligent and green' partnership INTEGER, the Sherwood Energy Village in Nottinghamshire and the often unsung contributions of numerous housing associations (see BedZED, 2004; INTEGER, 2002; Sherwood Energy Village, 2002; Sustainable Homes, 2004).

More serious, committed and imaginative approaches to the design of environmentally aware and sustainable housing have largely been the province of individuals, be they architects, theorists, visionaries or people convinced of the need for simpler lifestyles. In this regard the work of the ecologically minded architects Robert and Brenda Vale made an early and significant contribution in the form of their design for a self-sufficient or 'autonomous' house, entirely free of mains services (Vale and Vale, 1975).

Since then many people, including the Vales themselves, have begun to appreciate that what is really needed at the present time is a more holistic approach, in which not only must the built form become more environmentally benign, but also people's expectations, attitudes and ways of relating to their home must undergo a transformation. This requires attention to a whole range of factors: respect for site; the impact of local climate; the use of natural and non-polluting materials; reduction in energy requirements; environments which are conducive to physical and mental health; and the achievement of the more ambivalent notions of balance, harmony and well-being. Ideas about how these aims might be realised have led to a proliferation of instructional and advisory texts, and the promotion of the concepts of the 'natural', 'green', 'organic', 'eco' and 'healthy' home (see, for example, Baggs and Baggs, 1996; Borer and Harris, 1998; Pearson, 1998, 2001a; Roaf, 2003; Vale and Vale, 1991). In some cases it is advocated that recourse should be had to more traditional modes of design, albeit modified to suit the contemporary situation. Thus, for example, there are those who believe in the merits of 'earth sheltered' housing, an energy saving house form adapted from the ancient underground dwellings of Asia and China, or who consider that harmony and well-being can only be achieved by following the principles of 'feng shui', the esoteric and ancient Chinese art of auspicious design based on astrology and geomancy (see Baggs and Baggs, 1996; Carpenter, 1993; Pearson, 2001a).

For some, holistic design must go still further and reflect the most deep-seated human yearnings: connection with place and other people; physical, emotional and aesthetic harmony; and spiritual sustenance. Often this involves seeking to elucidate and reproduce those aspects of design which have been experienced since time immemorial as life and spirit enhancing – that 'timeless way of building' that Alexander sought to distil through his pattern language (see Chapter 5). Others have looked elsewhere for inspiration. The architect and writer Christopher Day, for example, has been influenced by the philosophy or anthroposophy of Rudolf Steiner in the creation of his organic, flowing forms and the way he uses the play of light to instil a spiritual dimension (Day, 2004). Another 'alternative' architect and founder of the Ecological Design Association is David Pearson, who has drawn inspiration from the Gaia principle and the ideas of deep ecology. Pearson's ambition is to create a new natural and organic domestic architecture which can contribute to a total harmonious living ecosystem, and which employs the archetypal and universal forms rooted in the mysticism of ancient philosophies and cosmologies:

> The[se] ideas have led to a desire for many to find more fundamental ways of living in harmony with the land and rebalancing their relationship with nature; making self-sustaining lifestyles with an emphasis on personal and planetary self-healing and repairing.
>
> (Pearson, 1994: 72)

This recourse to established cultural traditions in the search for a new approach to contemporary house form is also reflected in the interest that began to be shown in vernacular and spontaneous forms of shelter in third world countries as early as the 1960s (see, for example, Habraken, 1972; Hamdi, 1991; Rudofsky, 1964; Turner, 1976; Ward, 1985). In particular, it was the user led and self-built aspect which became the focus of attention, and the way that this seemed to result in housing which was in harmony not only with the environment but also with people's needs and aspirations. It was a conviction that such dweller controlled housing might result in more responsive design in this country that led to the development of a self-build housing movement, inspired initially by John Turner and the appeal of his work to three other unconventional people: Colin Ward, anarchist and radical writer on housing and self-help; the émigré architect Walter Segal, long interested in indigenous housing; and Jon Broome, later founder of the cooperative architectural practice, Architype.

As a result of their pioneering efforts the London Borough of Lewisham was persuaded to support a self-build development (see Towers, 1995), and subsequently several other community self-build projects have been completed, many using the Segal method (see Borer and Harris, 1998; Walter Segal Self Build Trust, 2004). However, the actual number of these, or indeed any type of self-build or community scheme, including cooperatives, has always been small in the UK (see Broome and Richardson, 1991; Clapham and Kintrea, 1992). This contrasts to the situation in the rest of Europe, and indeed, the world, where self-build, community involvement and various forms of cooperative and collective housing are commonplace. The advantages of such housing are not only the benefits that accrue from user control of the process of design (even if the actual construction is then left to others), but also the contribution that is made to the creation of a supportive community. It is from these principles that the Scandinavian form of collective housing known as cohousing has been derived; a concept which is now attracting interest in the UK and which is elaborated in the following section of the chapter.

Another type of communal and democratic housing which has begun to emerge in the UK has been initiated by certain individuals committed to the environmental movement. Here the principal aim is to lead a way of life which is more self-sufficient and sustainable, but in which people share resources and live according to democratic principles. In some cases this has involved the adaptation of existing large properties and the establishment of radical housing cooperatives. In others the self-build method has been used to construct environmentally friendly dwellings, as for example at the Hockerton Housing Project, a self-built, earth sheltered scheme designed by the green architects, the Vales (Hockerton Housing Project, 2001; White, 2002). But some of those most committed to alternative modes of dwelling have gone further, choosing to reject nearly every aspect of conventional living and subsist on minimal resources in temporary structures made of locally available materials. It is this type of 'low impact development' which is the hallmark of those who are affiliated to the 'ecovillage' movement and which is discussed later in this chapter.

Cohousing

The concept of cohousing has been derived principally from the Danish system of collective living known as *bofællesskab*, meaning literally living communities. *Bofællesskab* first emerged in the 1970s as communities of families and individuals who felt isolated by the stresses of modern urban living, but who were not attracted to the shared household model of communes (McCamant and Durrett, 1988). Instead they wanted to combine the autonomy and privacy of individual dwellings with the benefits that could be gained from a community setting, such as neighbourliness and social support; shared playspace and child care; communal preparation of food and eating of meals; provision of laundries, workspace and guest rooms. Also important was the democratic principle, with residents themselves responsible for organisation, planning, design and management, with recourse to professional support only where necessary.

Similar forms of collective housing also have a history in the Netherlands and Sweden. In Sweden the model of the *kollectivehus* has existed since the 1930s (see Vestbro, 2000), whilst in the Netherlands *Centraal Wonen* began to emerge in the 1970s and have subsequently become popular as a solution for the housing and support needs of older people (see Brenton, 2001). Elsewhere, interest in what became known as cohousing was only stimulated following the promotion of the concept by the American architects, Kathryn McCamant and Charles Durrett. It was they who coined the term 'cohousing', and it has been as a result of their influence that cohousing has expanded rapidly in North America. Indeed there is now an American based cohousing network with its own website and journal, and in addition, many cohousing communities have become affiliated to the international web-based network Intentional Communities. This was originally set up in the US to connect groups interested in communal living, and now includes representatives of ecovillages, religious communities, communes and various types of cooperative (see Intentional Communities, 2004).

In the UK cohousing has been slower to make an appearance. Following the Dutch experience, Brenton has been keen to promote the concept as a solution for older people, and in association with the JRF and the Housing Corporation, has been working to establish an Older Women's Cohousing Project in London. But for the most part it is ordinary individuals in search of different and more supportive ways of living who have become interested in the concept. Although exact figures are hard to determine, it would appear that at the time of writing there are approximately 20 cohousing schemes completed or planned across the UK, most of which (with the exception of Stroud) consist of adaptations of existing large, often institutional, properties, sometimes with an element of new build (see Odell, 2003). Typical inhabitants are professionals desirous of escaping stressed and materialistic urban lives, and there is an emphasis on ecological practices such as energy efficiency, reduction in car use, recycling and food production.

The UK now has its own web-based cohousing network, established after the holding of a National Cohousing Convention in 1999, and with the aim of promoting cohousing as a lifestyle choice:

> Do you ever feel lonely, even when you are in a crowd? Do you distinguish between loneliness and aloneness? ... Do you ever feel you would like to live in a place where you can find some people to be with at a moment's notice – with the option that you can dive back into your private space if necessary? Would you like the choice of eating each evening with friends and acquaintances, or just by yourself at home? If so, then a CoHousing Community might be what you're looking for.
>
> (Watson, 2004)

Despite this persuasive rhetoric, it remains the case that there are numerous difficulties in establishing a cohousing community. Apart from finding a group of like-minded people there is the length and intensity of the process, which requires considerable dedication over a period of years. Additional problems occur in the finding of a suitable site and the securing of the necessary finance, often rendered difficult by the resistance of financial institutions to lend to schemes perceived as 'alternative' and organised on the principle of mutual ownership. The planning process too can be fraught with difficulty since wary planning officials and potential neighbours are almost certain to raise objections. Furthermore, as cohousing is based on a particular ideology it raises crucial problems in regard to appropriate design, since the need for both privacy and community must be respected, whilst at the same time it is important for opportunities to be provided for casual social interaction.

Solutions to some of these design problems can be drawn from the experience of other examples of cohousing schemes. McCamant and Durrett (1988) and Cooper-Marcus (2000), for example, observed in their studies of Scandinavian and Dutch cohousing that in most cases private space was located to the rear of units and cars were banished to the outer perimeter. Beyond this a number of different solutions were adopted to meet the design objectives: arranging units on both sides of a sometimes glazed pedestrian street; placing the common house at the angle at which two rows of units meet; clustering units so that they overlook a central green or garden; placing picnic tables and children's play areas at strategic points; and providing convivial spaces to sit beside front doors. Also to be considered is the need for the redefinition of the usual assignment of public, semi-public, and private space, including not only boundaries within the site, but also the ways in which connections are made to neighbouring areas.

Springhill Cohousing

Stroud is a long established market town lying on the fringe of the Cotswolds in Gloucestershire. It grew to prominence as a centre of the local woollen industry, but by the latter part of the twentieth century most of the mills had fallen idle and many had been converted into housing, offices or retail premises. Meanwhile Stroud had become a fashionable place for people in search of mystical, spiritual and artistic inspiration, drawn by the attractiveness of the town and its proximity to ancient sites and ley lines. Thus Stroud began to develop as an 'alternative' centre with specialist galleries and studios, organic food shops and cafés, a variety of arts festivals, numerous alternative health practitioners and a Steiner school. There also began to emerge a tradition of green activism and sustainable practices, including an environmental campaign against a planned supermarket, and the success of Stroud in becoming in 1990 the first town council in the UK to be run by the Green Party (see Wall, 1999). With continuing strong Green representation at both parish and district level, Stroud is committed to an agenda of sustainability and improvement of the environment. It also has a council supported car sharing system and a LETS system (local exchange trading system), trading in a notional currency referred to as 'strouds'.

In the late 1990s, a part time property developer, David Michael, began to draw together a group of people who might be interested in a cohousing scheme in Stroud. Michael had become interested in communal living from his experiences of a kibbutz in Israel, and was inspired by both McCamant and Durrett's book on cohousing and Alexander's work on the pattern language. Notwithstanding the limited success of his first cohousing scheme in Bradford-on-Avon in Wiltshire (Cunningham, 2001), Michael felt sufficiently buoyed from his initial informal contacts to believe that a scheme in Stroud would receive support. After a six month search he found a possible site in the grounds of a demolished mansion house, Uplands House, which had been designated in the local plan for housing. The location itself was ideal: only a few minutes walk from the town centre; on a south-facing slope with expansive views; bordered by a small park to the west; screened by mature trees; and with existing vehicular access off Springfield Road to the north. The only existing housing which impinged on the proposed development was a short terrace along this same road.

It took 12 months to negotiate purchase of the land, paid for upfront by Michael, and to acquire outline planning permission. By this time the project was already 30 per cent pre-sold, and with Michael as managing director and project coordinator, a Cohousing Company was formed to undertake the design and development process and to choose a construction company that would be prepared to work on the partnering principle. Aspiring members had to agree to buy £5,000 worth of shares in the company, to show they could raise sufficient finance to pay for a completed unit, to support the principles of cohousing and to agree to give the Company first refusal on resale. Word of mouth, mailings, local meetings and the setting up of a website (www.cohouses.net) brought additional interest, and by early 2003, six months after building work started, all the plots had been allocated. The 100 or so members constituted a mix of household types, and represented all ages from toddlers to old people. Most were professionals following such occupations as teaching, consultancy work, social work, alternative therapies, life-coaching and interior design, and some had had prior experiences of environmental action or alternative ways of living.

The architects appointed were Pat Borer, known to Michael as co-author of *The Whole House Book* (Borer and Harris, 1998), and, on Borer's recommendation, Jonathan Hines of the firm Architype. Borer had been a resident of the Centre for Alternative Technology (CAT), established in Machynlleth in the 1970s as an environmental demonstration and educational project, and had subsequently moved on to establish his environmental architectural practice. The firm Architype, founded by Jon Broome, was by now a large concern with a reputation for environmental design and self-build projects, including the ecological demonstration house at CAT. With Michael in control, the architects and the Cohousing Company spent many hours drawing up designs for the scheme. This was to incorporate aspects of Alexander's pattern language, and it was Architype's Jonathan Hines who was put in charge of deciding which particular patterns to use (although unfortunately it was not possible to access further details in this regard).

In December 2000 a detailed planning application was submitted for 35 dwellings, two office studios and a community house. The statement in support of the planning application describes the scheme (incorrectly) as: 'the first Cohousing Community in the UK', with an overall aim of creating: 'a sense of community, in a way which develops the site in an environmentally sensitive and sustainable way' (Cohousing Company, 2000). Cohousing, it suggests, is a 'creative' way to develop a site which presents a number of difficulties, especially those of its steep gradient and compact size (0.76 ha), which in a traditional car dependent development would produce few units. The principles to be adopted by the Cohousing Company would result in a pedestrianised scheme with parking on the perimeter of the site, whilst the minimisation of private gardens would mean that most of the remaining external space could be retained as a communal facility. The statement also asserts that the scheme will conform to the Residential Design Guide for Stroud with its emphasis on distinctive urban design and place making, and that it will be a 'sustainable settlement', with some of the most environmentally friendly and energy efficient buildings in the UK. The intention at the time was to include such innovative features as sustainably sourced timber, a turf roof for the common house, organic paints and stains, a sustainable urban drainage system (SUDS) (to minimise surface water run off into the overloaded local drainage system), a car sharing scheme and ecological management of the site.

Following the planning application there was considerable local objection, particularly in regard to the issues of parking and access, and the fact that in priding themselves on having no on-site parking, the cohousing residents were actually displacing the problem to the perimeter. A few objectors were outspoken in their opposition, referring to 'these commune people', the 'gruesome structure' proposed and the 'collective siege mentality' which was indicated by emphasis on the erection of walls and fences. The realisation that there was an orchestrated 'nimby' campaign stimulated the cohousing group to action of their own. This involved mailings to all in the vicinity, an open day and encouragement to supporters to write in to the local planning authority. The success of this strategy resulted in some 30 individual and over 100 standard letters supporting the scheme.

Although the planning officers were minded to approve the application, the committee members rejected it on the grounds that it would be contrary to the council's adopted policy in regard to layout, materials and lack of definition of private garden space. The Cohousing Company decided to appeal, but at the same time they also prepared a revised planning application. This took into account the council's verdict as well as comments received during the consultation process from bodies such as the Environment Agency and Severn Trent Water in regard to sewerage and drainage, the highways authority in regard to parking and access, and landscape architects in regard to lack of attention to hard surfacing, cycle parking and planting. But the most significant compromises were the removal of ground floor garages and first floor access balconies in the units facing the existing terrace of houses, the confinement of parking within the site and the definition of private garden space by fencing.

The revised application was approved in June 2001, but meanwhile the appeal on the original application was still pending. In his decision the inspector dismissed many of the planning committee's reservations, but concluded that the first floor access balconies would be likely to cause excessive noise and disturbance, and that this alone was serious enough to warrant dismissal of the appeal.

The Cohousing Company thus had little choice but to adopt their revised plan, for which planning permission was granted in August 2001. This was subject to a Section 106 agreement for three affordable homes on a shared equity basis, although the housing department had some reservations about the fact that the units were not for rent but for sale, and that the scheme was geared towards a particular lifestyle which might not suit its waiting list applicants. The main additional conditions related to the submission and implementation of a landscaping plan, agreement on foundations and retaining structures, measures in regard to access, traffic calming and suitable temporary car parking, and the restriction of the use of the community house and the studio offices to residents only. Later applications which were allowed as minor variations concerned the removal of the garden fences which the cohousing members had never wanted, and the replacement of the proposed turf roof of the common house with cement slate tiles, due to cost.

At the time of the research visit in December 2004, all the residential units were completed and only the common house and the car parking provision were still under construction. The boundaries of the site are clearly defined by fencing and screened by rows of trees, creating an impression of both separation and containment (Figure 10.1). Pedestrians gain entrance through three gates to the west, east and north, each with a notice affixed stating that access is for residents only (Figure 10.2). Vehicular access is at the northern edge of the site with parking on adjacent pavior hardstanding, together with a few additional covered spaces beneath the row of flats (Figure 10.3). As discussed above this was not part of the original design, and one of the consequences is that the uppermost group of houses now appear slightly cut off from the rest of the site. On the other hand it has provided an opportunity to redesign the upper entrance to the common house and to: 'define and emphasise the sense of arrival', as stated in the revised planning application.

Given the extent of car parking, the amount of remaining semi-public space is limited, and the small private gardens provide little alternative recreation space. The main pedestrian route through the site is referred to as 'Main Street' and from it

10.1 The main pedestrian approach to Springhill Cohousing across a park from the town centre. The boundaries of the development are defined by trees and palisade fencing (beyond the park railings).

10.2 The western entrance gate from the park. The warning notice emphasises access is only to Springhill Cohousing.

10.3   The pavior hardstanding for cars in the process of completion. There is also limited under cover parking below the balconied apartments on the left. Access to the upper floor of the common house is on the right of the picture. Note also the use of timber cladding and the retained vista to the landmark feature of the church.

lead a limited number of narrower pedestrian paths linking the rest of the site. Main Street itself is 3.5 to 4.5 metres wide and angled to give a variety of perspective, and the close proximity of the two rows of dwellings that front it provides a sense of enclosure and intimacy (Figure 10.4). Recessed porches or flights of steps symbolise the transition from semi-public to semi-private space, a transition further reinforced by the display of personal possessions (Figures 10.5, 10.6). Centrally located is what was intended to be the 'village green' (Figure 10.7). This small depressed green space has now become an integral part of the SUDS system, which feeds surface water through grass swales, guttered rills and stone or tile lined courses into the lower lying land, consistent with the planning authority's requirement that no more water run off should be produced than from an undeveloped greenfield site. The steepness of the site affects not only the water run off situation but also accessibility, and even though a lift is available through the common house to reach the higher level vehicular access, it is questionable whether older and disabled people would feel comfortable on the scheme. However, the steepness also has the advantage of diminishing the extent of overlooking of the rows of facing units, as well as maximising passive solar gain – not to mention the views across the valley.

The main construction materials are Scandinavian spruce (not the locally sourced timber originally planned), lime render and clay roof tiles. The latter

10.4 Main Street. This illustration also shows the drainage rills for surface water, part of the SUDS system.

10.5 The deeply recessed porches providing storage space and marking the transition towards private space

10.6 Steps and a raised platform provide an alternative transitional arrangement. Note also the large south-facing window and the upper balcony.

10.7 The 'village green'. Note the stone course for water run off from Main Street. Opposite is the common house still under construction. The stairway on the left gives access not only to the adjacent apartments but also to the upper level of the site.

form part of an integrated system with matching photovoltaic panels, hardly distinguishable to an untrained eye. These panels provide a proportion of power for hot water, and heating costs are low due to the triple glazing, the high level of insulation (provided by recycled newspaper) and the large south-facing windows. The intention to include rainwater capture for household purposes was abandoned due to costs, as was greywater recycling and the turf roof. There is also no longer to be an in house car sharing scheme, and instead residents without cars must rely on the established town wide scheme or use alternative transport.

At a central point on Main Street is the lower entrance to the three storey bay fronted common house (Figure 10.6), located here in order to ensure people regularly pass by and feel inclined to drop in. The intention is that this will be the focal point of communal activity, with evening meals eaten in the top floor dining room with its adjacent kitchen, social events and meetings taking place on the middle floor, and the ground floor providing a laundry and other facilities such as work space. However, at the time of writing these were not complete, and it remains to be seen whether such communal aspects work as intended. It is also too soon to tell whether the cohesive, democratic and supportive principles behind cohousing will actually develop, or whether the scheme, now affiliated to Intentional Communities, will continue to be controlled by the founder.

Ecovillages and low impact developments

The term ecovillage, or by extension, econeighbourhood, has begun to be loosely applied to many very diverse projects in the UK (see Barton, 2000). However, it would appear that the original intention was for the term to be restricted to ecologically sound, generally small scale, self-built, largely self-sufficient and community-sharing settlements. This can be deduced from the original use and definition of 'ecovillage', which, although not explicitly documented, appears to have originated at the Findhorn Foundation in Scotland. Findhorn was established in the 1960s as an idealistic community for spiritual fellowship, but by the early 1980s it was accepted that a more realistic approach needed to be taken to the organisation of daily life:

> It was at that time that the idea of a 'planetary' or 'eco-village' came into being: the idea of translating these early principles of cooperation and working with nature into a built environment.
>
> (Talbott, 1995: 15)

Members of Findhorn were also involved in the Gaia Trust, an international organisation set up in Denmark in 1987 following the development of Lovelock's theory of Gaia. The objective of the trust was to find a new and more holistic vision of sustainability which would include a spiritual dimension. To this end the trust held a series of seminars attended by representatives of 'alternative' communities, including Findhorn, and gradually the conviction emerged that: 'the eco-villages concept was a key component in any global strategy to manifest the eco-spiritual vision' (Jackson, 1995: 61). Subsequently the international Global Ecovillage Network (GEN) was set up to promote the ecovillage concept and exchange ideas and information, and as the internet became established GEN began to rely on this as its chosen medium of communication.

GEN's definition of an ecovillage is that it should be able to demonstrate commitment to three different dimensions: the social, involving support, responsibility, sense of belonging and participation; the ecological, involving use of local materials, protection of soil, water and air, and personal connection to the earth; and the cultural and spiritual, involving respect for the Earth and each other, shared values, the fostering of creativity, and observance of rituals and other celebrations (GEN, 2004). The UK ecovillage network, however, has placed the emphasis of an ecovillage on its ecological dimension:

> Eco-villages are citizen initiatives to model sustainable, low impact, human settlements. ... Eco-villagers utilise renewable energy technology, ecological building techniques, and human-scale design to reduce exploitation of natural resources, facilitate community self-reliance, and improve quality of life ...
>
> (Eco-Village Network UK, 2003a)

The emphasis within this definition on 'low impact' has led to the emergence of another settlement concept, that of the low impact development. This term was first adopted by Simon Fairlie, former editor of *The Ecologist*. He defines a low impact development as possessing certain key characteristics: smallness of scale; unobtrusive and temporary structures; use of local or recycled materials; protection of wildlife; enhancement of biodiversity; consumption of low levels of non-renewable resources; generation of little traffic; low impact or sustainable purposes; and a recognised positive environmental benefit (Fairlie, 1996). A harmonious relationship with the land is also a central aspect, with cultivation based on the non-intensive principles of permaculture. Derived from 'permanent agriculture', the permaculture movement was first promoted in the 1970s by the Australian Bill Mollinson and is based on the cooperative and mutually beneficial or symbiotic relationships found in the natural world. Beyond this it also has a philosophical and ethical dimension, in which care for the earth, care for ourselves and for others, and the sharing of the earth's resources are all to be regarded as part of one integrated whole.

As well as working with the land, low impact developments create dwellings from locally available or recycled materials, use renewable energy sources, derive water from local streams, and where possible avoid the use of motor vehicles or machinery. Construction may be of stone, timber, rammed earth, cob, straw bales or even old tyres, with insulation of natural or recycled materials such as newspaper, straw and sheep's wool. Turf or sedum roofs on more solid structures not only act as further insulation but also reduce the amount of water run off, help to minimise visual impact, and provide habitats for plants and small animals. Recourse is often had to the tried and tested temporary structures of nomadic peoples, such as the Asian yurt, the North American tipi and the Romany gypsy bender (see Pearson, 2001b). Examples of such low impact developments include the earliest established, Tipi Village in Carmarthenshire, and the more recent settlements of Tinkers Bubble in Somerset (also home to Fairlie), Brithdir Mawr in Pembrokeshire, Kings Hill in Somerset, and Shutway Quarry in the Cotswolds (see Eco-Village Network UK, 2003b; White, 2002).

Many of these low impact developments have in common the difficulties they have faced in regard to the planning system, and the publicity, sought or unsought, that this has brought them. The inherent rigidities of planning law, policy guidance and bureaucratic thinking, mean that there is little understanding of or tolerance towards unconventional living arrangements. Hence many such settlements are set up secretly, lost to sight in woodland, quarries or undergrowth. Here they may after a time be 'discovered' as for example at Brithdir Mawr, where a pilot surveying for the National Park observed the glint of the sun reflected from a solar panel. This can result in prolonged planning battles, and it is only as a result of persuasive and well informed campaigns that progress has been made towards greater acceptability (see Fairlie, 1996).

In this context the work of the organisation The Land is Ours, set up in the 1990s to campaign for fair access to the land, has been instrumental in seeking to change attitudes. This organisation has a dedicated planning office known as Chapter 7, named after Chapter 7 of Agenda 21, and it is suggested that the planning system should regard low impact developments as an opportunity. To this end a 15 point charter is proposed against which planning authorities can assess the merits of low impact settlements. This includes such matters as housing for people in need, integration into the local economy and community, minimisation of car use, materials of low embodied energy and with minimal environmental impact, energy conservation, autonomous provision of water and disposal of waste, and open days for members of the public (The Land is Ours, 1999). As a consequence of the work of Chapter 7 and more especially of commitments under Agenda 21, it would appear that gradually planning authorities and, perhaps more importantly, planning inspectors are indeed beginning to have a change of heart. Thus by the 1990s a number of appeals had been favourably heard, and some authorities had granted temporary or even permanent permission. There were even indications that local authorities might be prepared to change their policies, as in Gloucestershire and Somerset where draft structure and local plans have been produced which contain clauses permitting low impact dwellings under certain conditions (Fairlie, 1996).

Stewart Community Woodland

Dartmoor is a mainly upland area in Devon which was designated as a National Park in 1951. The Park is managed by the Dartmoor National Park Authority (DNPA) and this body is also responsible for local planning matters. In 2000 DNPA published a Biodiversity Action Plan as part of DNPA's commitment to sustainability and Agenda 21 (DNPA, 2000), and the local plan too reinforces the commitment to sustainability, suggesting that this is the underlying principle governing the planning and management of Dartmoor. A particular aim is to: '… encourage developments providing benefits to the global environment where these are not in conflict with the purposes of designation [as a National Park]' (DNPA, 2004: 15).

The Stewart Community Woodland project had its inception in 1997 following discussions between a group of friends who were active supporters of environmental and social justice campaigns, and members of radical groups such as Amnesty International, Greenpeace and Friends of the Earth. They felt that rather than just demonstrating, they should actually change their lives and set up a sustainable living project. Most of the group were graduates, and had previously followed careers in such fields as law, computing, graphic design and campaign management. Practical experience of sustainable living had been gained through working visits to projects such as Tinkers Bubble, Findhorn, Brithdir Mawr and the Centre for Alternative Technology.

In order to pursue their aim the friends formed a housing and workers' cooperative named 'Affinity' and investigated the reality of acquiring some land. What they were ideally searching for was a site for a low impact settlement and where permaculture could be practised. Existing farmhouses and land with planning permission for housing were prohibitively expensive, so they began to look at quarries, plantation woodlands, and degraded farm land. In 1999 one of their members was taken by a land agent to Stewart Wood on the edge of Dartmoor and about a mile from the small town of Moretonhampstead. The steep south-west facing site extended to 32 acres of mainly conifer plantation and had previously been owned and managed first by the Dartington Estate and then by the private company Fountain Forestry. There was a main road adjacent to the site, a disused railway running alongside it, a handful of inhabited properties on the perimeter, sufficient level land for a growing area, and several streams and springs. In many ways it seemed an ideal site, although it was recognised that the location within the Park boundary would mean tighter planning restrictions than would otherwise be the case.

The £50,000 purchase price was raised through the issuing of loan stock on an interest free basis, and in April 2000, 12 adults and two children moved into Stewart Wood. The day after, they delivered a letter to DNPA explaining that they had purchased the woodland and intended to set up a new community project there. No mention was made of the fact that they were already in residence. Accompanying the letter was an illustrated leaflet which had already been delivered to all of

Moretonhampstead's residents as well as to immediate neighbours. This leaflet discussed the threat to Devon's traditional woodlands and the need to comply with Agenda 21, and then went on to discuss the establishment of an 'exciting new project' based on permaculture principles, which will: 'demonstrate the value of integrating conservation woodland management techniques [...] with organic growing, traditional skills and crafts and low-impact sustainable living'. It was also pointed out that the project would benefit the environment, provide local jobs, produce sustainable products and offer a resource for recreation and education.

A few weeks later, having been informed that people were already living in Stewart Wood, officers of DNPA visited the site and photographed a number of tents as evidence of residential activity. After a month they were warned that as the statutory 28 day period had elapsed, planning permission was required. In July, on the same day that an eviction notice was served, a retrospective planning application was received. Enclosed was a letter setting out the group's ambitions and how these were consistent not only with the policies and guidelines of the local plan, but also with Agenda 21 and the European Convention of Human Rights. Details were included of the proposed management and business plans, and an offer made to enter into a Section 106 agreement to ensure that only environmentally benign low impact development would take place. A subsequent letter made further suggestions about the planning conditions they would be happy to accept, notably the restriction of planning permission to a five year period, the minimisation of the area of human habitation, and the limitation of the number of residents to a maximum of 20 and of vehicles (other than those of visitors) to three. They also emphasised that permaculture was labour intensive and required them to live on site, and proposed that their application should be determined against the 15 criteria for sustainable development established by Chapter 7 (see above).

The various consultees, such as the Environment Agency, South West Water, Moretonhampstead Parish Council, Teignbridge District Council, Highways and DNPA's own Trees and Landscape Officer, had few objections in principle to the proposals for the woodland and its management, but did object to the residential element. So too did some of the local residents. Their more negative comments referred to an 'under-experienced group of new-age, ill informed, nomadic hippies'; a 'bunch of unwashed drop-outs'; and the risk of 'spreading disease', whilst others focused on the group's lack of experience and their naivety, the potential for the attraction of 'undesirables' such as the travelling community, the increase in traffic and noise, the fact that benders, yurts and tipis were not in character with the English landscape, and the potential competition with existing crafts and trades.

In response the group themselves produced and distributed a new leaflet, established a website (www.stewardwood.org) (swiftly countered by a leaflet and website from the opposition) and contacted those whom they thought would be sympathetic. The result was some 100 letters endorsing the aims of the group. These came from some more supportive local residents, environmentalists and followers of alternative lifestyles nationwide, the EcoVillage Network and the Planning Office of The Land is Ours, and even institutional bodies such as the Dartmoor Preservation Association and the National Trust Estate Office in Pembrokeshire.

At the committee meeting of the DNPA at which the planning application was considered, the planning officer's report was supportive, stressing the sustainability contribution, the exciting nature of the proposal and its value as an example to others. However a decision was postponed to allow members to visit the site and hear at first hand from the campaigners on both sides. By the time of the subsequent committee meeting, the planning officer was recommending refusal on the grounds that the residential use was an unjustified form of development in the open countryside and hence contrary to adopted policy. Affinity were informed of this negative decision in November 2000, whereupon they decided to appeal.

At the hearing in August 2001 (at which Simon Fairlie was one of those who gave oral evidence), the inspector dismissed the appeal. His reasons for refusal were that there was insufficient evidence that a residential presence was necessary or that the project would be financially viable – both of which needed to be proved in order to comply with planning policy guidance on development in the countryside (see DoE, 1997b). In addition, he stated that the proposed dwellings were contrary to the purpose of protecting the natural beauty of the National Park. He further commented that his decision would not contravene the European Convention of Human Rights on the right to family life and a home as the group did not have to live either in a wood or in that specific location. Following this decision Affinity then made a further appeal, this time against the enforcement notice for eviction.

The inspector at the second inquiry overturned the decision on the basis that the previous inspector had not given sufficient weight either to the sustainability or subsistence aspects of the project, and that these should not be considered against a 'typical' development. Nor had account been taken of the philosophy of the group and their demonstrable commitment to sustainable living, or that these accorded with the principles of Agenda 21 and government policy on sustainability. Furthermore, he also disagreed with the assessment that there would be no contravention of the European Convention of Human Rights since these were the only homes the members of the group possessed.

In allowing the appeal the inspector granted planning permission for the structures which had already been erected and no more: six residential and one visitor's bender; a communal longhouse and kitchen; a compost toilet; and further benders for a cycle shelter, workshop and educational purposes. This permission was for a period of five years, with additional conditions that no petrol or diesel powered generator should be operated on the site, no more than three resident vehicles and ten visitor vehicles should be parked at any time, and that an annual report of activities should be submitted to DNPA. DNPA, considerably exercised that one inspector could so completely disagree with another, then appealed to the High Court. At the hearing in January 2003 the judge dismissed the appeal without even hearing the defence, since in his view the sustainability aspects of the project provided sufficient justification to allow it to 'slip through' the rigid planning policies of DNPA.

Stewart Community Woodland is approached up a fairly steep footpath from the parking point adjacent to the main road, with access to the settlement area marked by a red sign requesting visitors to telephone first (Figure 10.8). The path leads to the communal kitchen and longhouse, now combined into one structure (Figure 10.9), and from this point radiate a network of paths linking the scattered individual dwellings, referred to as 'benders' (Figures 10.0, 10.11). All the benders are self-built, with construction consisting of a platform cantilevered from the steep hillside, and a basic frame of supports and poles lashed together with rope and arched to meet at the top. Further poles are woven in horizontally, or in some cases sterling board (compressed offcuts) is used to make more solid walls, with recycled windows providing light and air. The roofs, and where necessary, the external walls, are covered with a single or double layer of army surplus tarpaulins, and additional warmth is gleaned from an interior lining of blankets. Each bender varies slightly in size and ingenuity of construction, but most have an entrance 'porch' where shoes and other effects can be stored, and contain the same facilities

10.8 The access to the settlement area of Stewart Community Woodland. The notice requests that people telephone before visiting.

10.9 The communal longhouse made from wood, recycled windows, and tarpaulin. The cantilevered construction provides extra storage space.

10.10 One of the benders, also constructed of timber and tarpaulin. The twisted chimney from the wood burning stove can be seen on the left.

10.11 A hexagonal bender, incorporating the use of sterling board. This dwelling has a panoramic view across the valley to the Devon hills.

within: a single room with a wood burning stove; a bed or beds; table and chairs; books and personal belongings; and carpeting.

The kitchen is the only structure to rest on the ground, and currently has a bare earth floor (Figure 10.12). Food (all vegan) is stored in metal cabinets to keep rodents at bay, and there is a long table with chairs, work surfaces, a wood fired Rayburn for cooking and heating water, and a sink with running water sourced from a spring and filtered through sand and gravel. This is however not fit for drinking, and more potable water is achieved by a more sophisticated system located at the lower part of the site (Figure 10.13). Although food is held in common, communal meals do not take place every day, and when they do, they are eaten either in the kitchen or round the adjacent open fire pit. From the kitchen is accessed the one other communal space, the longhouse, used for socialising, for meetings, as a children's play area, and as a library and computer room.

A limited and unreliable amount of electricity is produced by photovoltaic panels (Figure 10.14) which power the computers which most residents possess, lighting to some of the benders, the electric chain saw, and if they are lucky, the twin tub washing machine. Additional supply is generated from a simple hydro system in the stream, but this often has too small a flow to be effective. For washing purposes there is a bath house with a shower operated by gravity feed from a tank on the roof, and a 'hot tub', formed from a recycled plastic barrel and with water heated from a system rigged up from a wood fire, an old radiator and some piping. A two chambered compost toilet deals with human waste, with

10.12 The kitchen with its bare earth floor. Beyond the table is the Rayburn and on the right is the sink with running water. Above is a sleeping platform accessed by a ladder. The steps lead up to the communal longhouse, its entrance screened by tarpaulin.

10.13 The drinking water supply, with tap, filtration system, and containers

10.14 The ground mounted photovoltaic panels. One of the benders can be seen in the background, illustrating how well camouflaged they are.

each chamber used for 18 months and the contents then left to rot down (Figure 10.15). At the end of the process a perfectly pleasant friable material is produced, which like the separately composted kitchen waste, is used in the growing area. These facilities mean that the only mains services on which the group relies are telephone and broadband connections.

At the time of the research visit in April 2005 the group consisted of three single adults, a couple with a small child, and a couple with three children ranging in age from two to seven (plus three dogs). Only four of the original members remain, and the reasons why others have left have been variable, ranging from pregnancy and general tensions to a more specific conflict of interest between continuing with outside activism and devoting time to the labour intensive community activities. It is felt that the current numbers are not viable, and that ideally at least 12 adults, including some in their 50s or 60s, and some older children are needed to create a more workable and representative community. Motivations for joining are based on a desire to lead a more ecological, environmentally benign, personally fulfilling and self-sufficient way of life, and additionally all the members have 'alternative' interests and commitment to some form of spiritual awareness. The non-hierarchical principles mean that decision-making is entirely by consensus, and regular meetings are held to discuss and plan daily activities and to defuse tensions.

Stewart Community Woodland is managed according to permaculture principles, with the encouragement of natural regeneration, the control of invasive species,

10.15 The compost toilet. The small sign with its arrow directs users to the entrance up the flight of steps. The collection chamber below is protected from flies by mesh screening.

planting of new native trees, especially oak, and the creation of new wildlife habitat. A specific aim of the project is to publicise the principles and practices of sustainable living, and to that end visitors are encouraged, with opportunities to walk in the woodland, use it as an educational resource, or spend a weekend living and working with the residents. Indeed it is the educational and leisure aspects of the woodland which are more important to the community than the woodland management aspect, and it is this which may bring them into conflict with DNPA when their planning permission comes up for renewal, especially in regard to the need for on site residence. The aim of self-sufficiency has not yet been achieved, as the activities of daily living, such as wood chopping, fetching water, building and so on, are time consuming, and food growing is hampered by the ravages of rabbits and deer. Living costs are relatively low, but even so money is needed for the £10 'rent' charged to each adult to repay the original loan stock, and for food, building materials, telephone and broadband, personal items, and fuel for the one van and one car. To meet these needs several of the members have little choice but to pursue waged work. Thus there has not been time to develop as had been hoped the forest garden, the vegetable growing, and the selling of products such as logs, lengths of wood, kindling, dried herbs and flowers (with payment possible in ordinary money or the local North East Dartmoor LETS currency of 'tins'). Similarly the educational courses on topics such as forestry, plant and animal life, bender construction and personal development are still at an embryonic stage. One significant shift has been the attitude of their neighbours, who having got to know them, are no longer opposed to their activities.

Conclusion

By contrast to traditional societies the West has lost its sense of connection to the earth, to other sentient beings, and to mystical and spiritual powers. In the place of respect, humility and contentment with the satisfaction of basic needs have emerged the dominance, exploitation and quest for ever more material goods that have been the hallmarks of the social processes of the modern period. It has been the agency of individuals, pressure groups and social movements which has cautioned that this has been at the expense of the environment and our relationship to it, and that this will eventually have global impacts for the whole of humanity. As a consequence there has developed the articulation of an environmental 'problem', in which an increasingly apocalyptic and urgent message has been expressed through the use of metaphors such as 'silent spring', 'acid rain', 'the greenhouse effect', 'global warming', 'global dimming' and 'the big freeze'. The combined effect of such discourses, together with the (often disputed) scientific evidence of environmental devastation, has resulted in a belief by many that action needs to be taken. However, given the Western mantra of economic growth together with the difficulties of assessing the level of risk, the dominant responses have ranged from denial to only cautious acceptance.

Since there has been a lack of action or commitment at the institutional and organisational level, it has been the new social movements and the work and example of individuals which have assumed significance in the transformation of attitudes. Social movements, whether operating within the parameters of institutional arrangements or radically opposed to normative socio-economic conditions, have played a significant role in exposing the issues and encouraging through their example both individual and collective lifestyle changes. In regard more specifically to environmentally aware design, architects and others are using their intellectual and artistic capital to propound innovative ideas, write instructional texts and create built examples, thus providing an accumulation of practical action which can be reproduced and adapted by others. It is in this way, rather than through institutional edict, that living and responsive ecological dwellings are beginning to emerge, whether through self-building, through the adoption of organic forms and natural materials, or through the following of principles derived from ancient traditions and universal human predilections.

As well as concerns about the production of less ecologically damaging types of built form there has also been a search for forms of settlement which will overcome the sense of isolation and alienation so many people feel in contemporary urban environments. The emphasis here is on democratic involvement, responsive design and supportive communities, as evidenced in the various types of collective housing in Scandinavia and the Netherlands. This model has been introduced to the English speaking world largely through the agency of the American architects Durrett and McCamant and their coining of the name cohousing. It is they who have been directly involved in 'spreading the word', with that word also reaching the UK and being further disseminated through the medium of the internet. The result has been an increasing interest in the concept by certain middle class professionals, but apart from the interest shown by the JRF, it has yet to reach the agendas of institutional bodies.

Combining the aims of environmentally benign development with a sense of both community and spirituality has been the ecovillage concept, promoted through the agency of the Gaia Trust and again disseminated with the assistance of the internet. However over time, and in a manner not unlike that of the urban village, the term ecovillage has been appropriated by others and manipulated to apply to any development that meets even limited environmental aims. Hence the new concept 'low impact development' has been adopted to signify the mode of dwelling preferred by those who wish to live a simple life in harmony with the natural world. In an effort to persuade the institutional world to accept this concept the regulatory discourse of Agenda 21 has been appropriated and adapted, but to limited effect.

Both cohousing and low impact developments are new concepts, with salience neither to policy makers nor to the rest of the population. The two case studies illustrate the suspicion and even hostility engendered by such hints of 'different' and 'alternative' living, with the discourse of opponents demonstrating the perception of lax morals, uncleanliness, disorder and criminal tendencies: a polluting proximity of those on the fringe whose proper place should be far away – or preferably outlawed entirely. In resisting proposed plans, members of the public can give unrestrained vent to their feelings, but planning officers (whatever their personal sympathies) are under pressure to act more objectively. Their recommendations have to accord with policies at national and local level, and despite the new rhetoric of sustainability and Agenda 21, these still seem to prioritise dominant themes. Thus there is a presumption against any form of development in the countryside (especially in a National Park), and an expectation of respect for existing architectural forms (especially in a conservation area and a historic town). Once the matter goes to appeal, however, the situation is changed. With the power now in the hands of one individual (chosen because he (rarely she) supposedly possesses particular discernment) there is an opportunity for personal subjectivities to influence the decision. Thus in the case of Springhill Cohousing the planning authority was only partially supported, and in the case of Stewart Community Woodland was not supported at all – a decision which to the DNPA seemed almost subversive. However, the eventual outcome has been such as to alter policy and transform opinion: Stroud District Council will now be less disdainful both of cohousing schemes and of layouts and materials which do not conform to some preconceived norm, whilst DNPA has adopted in its most recent local plan a reference to low impact dwellings and permaculture (DNPA, 2004: 30).

In the example of Springhill Cohousing it is clear that it is the dynamism and charisma of one individual which has been the propelling force, guided by previous experience of collective living and property development, together with an interest in alternative ways of approaching design. It is due to his efforts that a committed group of people have been gathered together, and through him that two architects with interests in environmentalism, responsive design, and the merits of the pattern language were appointed. Despite the best intentions, the constraints of cost have led to a dilution of some of the ambitious ecological design features, but on the other hand the design has largely achieved its objectives of contributing to the collective ideals of the cohousing ethos. Following the example of schemes in continental Europe, private space is strictly limited, semi-private space is signalled by recessed porches and entrance steps, and semi-public space is provided in the narrow intimate pathways and the multi-functional common house with its large bay windows overlooking scenes of activity. For the residents, connections within the site and through to the surrounding area are relatively permeable and non-hierarchical, with a 'ringy' structure; however there are clear symbolic signs on the well defined boundaries which indicate that this is an exclusive development and not one for outsiders to penetrate.

Stewart Community Woodland has evolved in a far more democratic way than Springhill. From the start it has been a group initiative, in which members share the common values of green and radical action and an approach to sustainability which requires a complete transformation in their modes of dwelling and being. This has led them to direct confrontation with the establishment, and here their well educated and professional backgrounds have helped to equip them (so far) with the tools and contacts to mount and fight the campaigns to dislodge them. Their non-exploitative approach to the environment drives their ambitions to demonstrate that permaculture and living off the land can be made viable, although they still have some way to go to achieve this goal. It is their belief that others should be persuaded to emulate their example and share their enjoyment of their tranquil woodland that has led them to the idea of running educational courses and, by contrast to Springhill, of opening up some areas to visitors. The only space within the woodland from which visitors are barred without permission is that of their own settlement, a semi-private space which is symbolically demarcated by a warning notice but otherwise lacking in clear definition. Within the settlement are the well spaced private individual benders, each with their semi-private porch and connected by a permeable network of paths. At the point at which all paths converge are the shared spaces of the kitchen and longhouse, which, like the centrally located common house of Springhill, provide the focus and embodiment of communal life. In both schemes it is this commitment to shared and caring lives (whether with each other or with the environment) which transforms the act of dwelling from merely a place of shelter into meaningful connection with people and place, both now and for the future.

Part III

Conclusion

11 Making connections

The endeavour in this book has been to propose a way of accounting for and understanding how and why certain development concepts and models specific to the late twentieth and early twenty-first centuries in the UK have arisen, and then, by the use of case study examples, to elucidate the processes that impact on the shaping of particular built outcomes. This has been undertaken through the devising of a conceptual framework, as elaborated in Chapter 1, which in taking a contextual approach to the built form addresses a number of different factors: cultural, social, spatial and conceptual processes; the institutional framework; the influence of organisations and individuals; and the articulations of discourse and text. The result is a work which may in some respects be open to criticism, for example in regard to its breadth rather than its depth, or for the failure of the author to identify with one specific theoretical approach, or for the lack of critical engagement with the intricacies of theory, be they sociological or architectural. However as stated in the Introduction, these matters have not been the focus of the book, and instead the aim has been unapologetically to borrow ideas from different theoretical and conceptual approaches and from a range of disciplines and schools of thought. These ideas are the ones considered to be useful for the purpose and are arguably idiosyncratic and selective, but the justification is deemed to be in working towards a more holistic elucidation of the processes which result in the built forms in which our lives are both framed and reflected. This final chapter seeks to draw together and reflect on the different influences which have helped to shape the variety of our residential environments as we enter the twenty-first century, and ends with some speculation about what this might indicate in regard to future directions.

As denoted in Figure 1.1, at the level of the structures of society it is the cultural context, unique to a particular nation or social group, that is important in determining the nature of social, spatial and conceptual processes. All cultures, from time immemorial, have had a proclivity to classify and to categorise the world around them, to make use of ritual and symbol to mark significant events,

Conclusion

and to encode values and belief systems through myth and narrative. Classification has often been about survival and continuity: what we are allowed to eat and what we are not; the people with whom we can intermarry and those who are forbidden; the insider who is a friend and the outsider who is a threat; the time at which we become an adult and the time at which we become an elder; the domesticated world of culture and the untamed world of nature. The importance of such classifications has been emphasised through their representation not only in myth and ritual (particularly in regard to times or spaces of transition), but also in cultural artefacts, including house type and form. It is in this way that house forms have arisen that are consonant (or homologous) with ways of life and patterns of thought, and which, through necessity, have utilised those materials that are to hand. The distinctive and localised dwellings that have appeared are usually referred to as vernacular housing and include, for example, the Kabyle house (see Bourdieu, 1973), the American Indian tipi, the Mongolian yurt and Asian underground housing (see also Chapter 10). The symbolic significance of the act of construction might also be marked by rituals in relation to the choosing of auspicious times, sites and orientations, as exemplified in the ancient Chinese art of feng shui. Such rituals are indicative of the importance of the home as a locale for the reproduction of cultural and social systems; dwelling as a process as opposed to merely shelter.

As time has passed the boundaries between cultures have become more porous, and most cultures have borrowed ideas from others, especially those deemed to be superior. Hence has arisen the gradual (or in some cases sudden) adaptation of ways of life and associated artefacts, and the rejection of what has been considered outmoded and inferior. This has led to the loss of old skills and traditions, notably craftworking; to different ways of treating certain categories of people, especially the old; to migration to the cities for the presumed advantages of waged work; to the loss of connection with the spiritual and the natural world; and to the rise of the four square house built of brick, stone or concrete blocks. In many cases this has resulted in stress and the inhibition of appropriate action, since these ways of living are often not consonant with social needs and long established traditions (see Rapoport, 1977, 1982). In order to try and redress this imbalance groups and individuals have had recourse over time to various compensatory mechanisms. These include the establishment of areas referred to by Gans as 'urban villages' to help rural migrants adapt to the 'urban jungle' (see Chapter 6); the promotion by Western commentators of vernacular and spontaneous housing; the enthusiasm in the West for feng shui; and the adoption of traditional dwelling types such as the tipi and bender by those seeking to reject the trappings and values of contemporary society (see Chapter 10).

As we have seen in this book, cultural borrowing also occurs between nations or groups when one appears to have found a solution to a problem or an issue that is exercising another. Examples here include the adoption from continental

Europe of the solution of modernist mass housing blocks for workers (see Chapter 7) and foyers for homeless and jobless young people (see Chapter 8). From the US has come the influence of the loft and the gated community as new ways in which to accommodate contemporary city living (see Chapter 9), whilst a cross fertilisation of ideas from the US, Scandinavia, the Netherlands and Germany has led to the replication in the UK of the concepts of the televillage, cohousing and the continuing care retirement community (see Chapters 6, 8 and 10). That these have had varying degrees of support and success indicates perhaps that some are more consonant with British culture than others: mass housing blocks were introduced from European nations accustomed to flatted dwelling to a nation that largely was not and were eventually rejected; on the other hand cohousing with its affirmation of a small and supportive community seems to speak to people's inherent need to find identity within a caring group, and is a concept gaining in popularity.

It is cultural factors that are one of the determining influences on categories of thought, and as these are reproduced and perpetuated over time they play a key role in laying down the structural foundations of society: structures in the mind become also the organising principles of society and affect both social systems and in turn spatial arrangements. Thus there is an ongoing relationship between conceptual, social and spatial processes, in which legitimation, codification, concretisation and representation are reflected and reproduced across all three as mutually reinforcing mechanisms (see Figure 1.1). Conceptual processes use cognitive, symbolic and interpretative data, and rely to a large extent on myth, archetype, symbol, sign, metaphor and imagery. In this regard the principle of opposition, as espoused by Lévi-Strauss (1968), becomes an important element. In the context of the subject matter of this book the oppositions of country/city, sanity/madness, insider/outsider, inclusion/exclusion, independence/dependence, deserving/undeserving, work/home, centre/periphery have assumed particular relevance. The importance of oppositions such as these is that the one becomes defined by what the other is not; one is intrinsically 'good' and the other 'bad', with the 'bad' often banished to the margins. The power of this imagery of the margins is further reinforced by the fact that marginality may have a spatial or a temporal dimension, and sometimes a combination of both. Thus the country has long been considered 'backward' in relation to the civilities of the city; the space and time of work has since the onset of industrialisation been seen as separated from the space and time of leisure; and for many years the mad were separated from the sane and consigned to peripheral places. However, there is a contradiction here, for as Shields (1991) points out, marginal people and places have a capacity not only to evoke abhorrence but also fascination. There is a curiosity, an allure of the strange and the forbidden, an excitement of risk and transgression, which exerts an influence over the imagination and leads to the desire to experiment, to cross the boundaries and seek out a new reality. Through this process not only can the strange be made familiar, but also myth can be confronted with the insights of intellect and rationality and thus transformed. Hence the city can become recast as a place of alienation and crime and the country as a haven of relaxation and tranquillity; attitudes to the mad and the place of their incarceration can be reconceptualised; and a new elision can occur between the space of work and the space of home, as in the way in which domestic space has been inserted into the former workspace of mills and warehouses, and work has been reinserted into the domestic home.

The oppositions which appear to be the most powerful and enduring, perhaps because rooted in notions of cultural survival and identity, are those of insider/ outsider and inclusion/exclusion. This can be deduced from the way in which societies seem to have a continuing need to have a category of people and a category of place constructed as outcast and other. In the past in the UK these people were the indigent poor and the so-called mad, with their associated stigmatising spaces of the workhouse (the 'poorhouse') and the mental hospital (the 'mad house', 'funny farm' or 'loony bin'). Today this outcast role has been assumed by social housing as a whole: once constructed as the normative and acceptable tenure of council housing, it has fallen in esteem in step with the ascendancy of the myth of owner occupation (see Kemeny, 1981). In the popular mind (aided by media representations) social housing is epitomised by the imagery of the 'sink' estate, and inhabited by an 'underclass' of drug dealers, single mothers, scroungers, asylum seekers and teenage tearaways. The term 'affordable housing', by contrast, has yet to acquire quite these same negative connotations, despite being similarly targeted at a class of people who do not altogether fit the desirable norm. Even so, housebuilders have been quick to grasp the implications, and as illustrated in the pages of this book have been concerned to ensure that where possible these people are kept at a spatial distance equivalent to their perceived social distance.

This desire to exclude those 'not like us' or the potentially dangerous and polluting 'other' which seems to loom so large in the imagination is also borne out by the case study material. Sometimes this has involved the direct expression of suspicion and opposition, as in the examples located in Bordesley, Crickhowell, Stroud and Dartmoor, but equally it can be achieved by physical means. This may be signified symbolically, for example in the erection of territorial signs at boundary points as at Bordesley, Hartrigg Oaks and Stewart Community Woodland, or through the more concrete means of the wall, fence and gate as at Adventurers Quay, Springhill Cohousing, Exe Vale and Keeling House.

The significance of myth, collective memory, imagery and association is also of relevance in helping to account for the beliefs and ideas behind many of the development concepts discussed. Words such as 'village', 'community', 'home' and 'family' may have a logical meaning, but they are also affectively charged (see Lash, 2000) and have an appeal to the emotion and to a nostalgic vision of ourselves which far outweighs any dictionary definition. They therefore become 'good to think', and this in turn leaves them open to manipulation by those seeking to appropriate them to achieve a 'feel good' impression. However, if used (or abused) inappropriately the point is ultimately reached when the association is so far severed from its original connotations that such words are rendered almost meaningless, as has happened with the oxymoronic 'urban village' and to a lesser extent with 'Garden City'. Both of these concepts have also drawn legitimacy from their utopian idealism, thus resonating with the mythology of being able to achieve on this earth the promised land of milk and honey. Arguably it is this foundation in myth rather than reality which is a major contributory factor in the failure of such utopian ideals: a failure exhibited not only in the case of the urban village but also in the experiment of high rise living and 'streets in the sky'.

As noted in Figure 1.1 spatial processes are one of the key determinants of built form. The spatial context of social action has been captured in Giddens' (1984) concept of the locale, whilst Bourdieu's (1977) notion of space as a 'structuring structure' helps to explain how cultural and social categories become encoded in space and thereby act as a mnemonic for the rules of the social world and the place of people within it. In the modern era many of these rules became constituted around aspects of power and domination, and these have been duly reproduced in spatial arrangements. Thus as Foucault (1977), Markus (1993), Dovey (1999) and Hillier and Hanson (1984) have averred, and as discussed in Chapters 1 and 5, architecture has been made complicit in the control and classification of people through spatial devices. Such devices have been illustrated in this book in a variety of ways: the panopticon form of surveillance used in institutions such as mental hospitals and exemplified at Exe Vale (and in modified form in the atrium of Timber Wharf); the consignment of those with least power to the most intimidating and marginal spaces, such as the mass housing block and again the mental hospital; the adoption of mechanisms to exclude the stranger and potential malefactor, as in the gated community; the progression through different types of space to indicate changing categories of need and dependency, as in the foyer Occasio House and the CCRC Hartrigg Oaks; and the use of contrasting spatial syntaxes to indicate the relative positions of people to others through their degree of control over space, as indicated in the difference between the supervisory *enfilade* of progression into The Oaks care centre and the open or 'ringy' structure of Springhill Cohousing and Stewart Community Woodland. Such spatial arrangements are not, however, immutable, and can be rearranged and hence recoded. Thus what were once 'back regions' of society can be transformed into upmarket 'front regions', as has happened perhaps most markedly at Exe Vale, discussed in Chapter 7, but also in the way in which the previously marginalised areas of Bordesley (Chapter 6), and Britannia Basin and Cardiff Bay (Chapter 9) have become reconstructed as respectable locations for urban living. The spatial aspects of locale are also significant in terms of influencing built outcomes: topography and patterns of activity over time affect such matters as site conditions, adjacent uses, vistas, layout possibilities, connections, solar orientation and wind exposure (consider for example the issues that were faced in Bordesley, and the opportunities and constraints of the steep south-facing site of Springhill Cohousing); whilst the physical characteristics of neighbouring built forms (or in the case of Exe Vale and Keeling House, the building itself) influence design considerations and solutions.

Undoubtedly the parameters of space provide an important context, but it is perhaps in the trajectory of the social system and social processes that the mechanisms that have led to the burgeoning of new development concepts and models can be most clearly discerned. As Giddens has suggested, there has been a fundamental shift from the traditional principles which underpinned feudal society to the more diffuse and bureaucratic principles of modern, capitalist society. Under capitalism it was the processes of industrialisation that assumed prominence, with the focus on the taming of the natural world, the belief in science and rationality, the assumption of new powers by the state, the promotion of consumerism, the separation of home and work, the requirement to be a productive worker, and the emergence of the welfare state to compensate for some of the negative externalities that capitalism provoked. With a further shift to a post-industrial era, British society has experienced a postmodern 'turn'. This is marked by such factors as globalisation, the predominance of the market, commodification, individualisation, hazard and risk, the questioning of expert 'knowledge' and fundamental 'truths', and new approaches to the issues of lifestyle, identity and diversity (see Chapter 2). Whilst on the one hand this has created new opportunities and freedoms, by the same token it has also created new insecurities, including the loss of the sense of identity gained through family, marriage, community and the continuity of work (Bauman, 2001a). Consequently, people feel they have only themselves on whom to rely to give their life meaning, and often this involves making use of whatever props are to hand to forge an identity. In this endeavour consumer goods have become ever more important, with fashions, brands and labels chosen for their significance as signs and markers of a certain lifestyle niche rather than for their use value (Lash and Urry, 1994). As well as helping in the project of establishing identity, these give their users cultural capital and act as symbols of distinction (see Bourdieu, 1984). Appropriated first by trend setters or more privileged groups, they then become desired by those lower in the social hierarchy – as for example has occurred with the gated community, first adopted by the rich elite and now available to all who can afford to buy.

It is through such processes that housing has assumed a new significance as product, increasingly commodified as a consumer asset with numerous and diverse brands to appeal to different lifestyle sectors. These reflect the desire of people for new ways of self-expression and modes of living – as for example in the loft, the televillage, the live/work unit, the gay village, the retirement community, the 'eco' house and the reinvention of the tower block. And even for those who are not considered part of the mainstream, such as the less affluent old, the disabled and the homeless, there has been the emergence of new 'brands', such as lifetime homes, smart homes, assisted living, foyers, extra care housing, supported accommodation, core and cluster housing, and floating support. These new concepts for more vulnerable groups reflect also the postmodern appreciation of diversity and the right to self-determination and self-expression for all, as well as an awareness of the inappropriateness of the old modernist solutions of mass institutionalisation. However, the fact that many of the cited examples retain at least some aspects of institutional control suggests an ongoing tension between the desire to contain and mould to the required standard those still socially constructed as in some way problematic, and the realisation that even people needing support should be enabled to take charge of their own lives and construct their own identities.

As Giddens has argued (see Chapter 1) the social system relies on rules and resources for its reproduction over time and space. Together rules and resources constitute the institutional framework (discussed in Chapter 3), and can be discerned through the nature of the social, economic, political and juridical processes of society. In Giddens' terminology the normative, symbolic and legitimising aspects of rules underpin accepted ways of living and codes of conduct, whilst the authoritative and allocative aspects of resources are concerned with the control and distribution of material products. Thus there are longstanding norms in British society about marriage and family life, about the meaning of home and community, about the dignity of work, about acceptable standards of behaviour, and about the role of the Royal Family. These, together with other aspects of social life, are under constant threat, whether from outside under the processes of globalisation, or from within due to the pressures of social change. But failures or transgressions of established norms cause uncertainty and a sense of threat to continuity and tradition, invoking a propensity to control, punish and impose conformity. Hence the increasing emphasis on custodial sentences, the introduction of ASBOs, the marginalisation of those who do not work (whether the disabled, the sick, the old or the young), the disdain for the 'meddling' of the Prince of Wales in matters of policy, and the disquiet by the older generation about the contemporary state of marriage. In regard to resources it is the economic and political systems which assume primacy, and which are in large part responsible for the (unequal) allocation of power and wealth. This ensures the reproduction of a situation whereby there is a social and spatial polarisation between rich and poor, with the former controlling access to the 'best' in terms of spatial location, housing, food, education and health care, and the least well off consigned to peripheral estates, the poorest housing (or none), the worst nutrition and the least well performing schools and hospitals. Thus are social divisions perpetuated and power retained by the few at the expense of the many.

Again as indicated in Figure 1.1, social, economic and political processes are reproduced and mediated through the institutions and organisations established for their regulation and administration. These include institutions such as the government, the Royal Family, the professions, the housebuilding industry, the welfare system, the housing system and the planning system; and organisations such as the ODPM, housing associations, UDCs, banks and charities. As bodies with powers of action these function at the level of agency, and are necessarily peopled by individuals. But institutions and organisations also endure over time and have principles and practices which inhere in them rather than in any one individual, thus giving them an element of independent existence. The individuals who are born into or join institutions and organisations become socialised into their accepted ways of action, developing (in Bourdieu's terms) the appropriate *habitus*; a feel for the game in the field in which they are operating. For example in architecture, a *habitus* is developed in which architects consider themselves superior to clients and in which the design of each building is seen as an opportunity for the production of a uniquely individual and potentially iconic creation. By contrast the housebuilding industry instils a *habitus* of risk aversion, of not experimenting with new techniques, and of a belief that most consumers are not looking for the unique and the innovative but some variation of the traditional and the rustic.

The fact that institutions and organisations are legitimated by society for the reproduction of its structures and systems means that there is a tendency for conformist practices and an inherent resistance to change. This results in a situation in which certain issues or categories of people are constructed in a stereotyped way and solutions applied accordingly. Thus as we have seen, those with deviant behaviour are constructed as mad and placed in a lunatic asylum; older people in housing need are classed as best served by sheltered housing, regardless of their individual circumstances; and the problems of urban decline are seen as best tackled by public private partnerships. In the same way, the housing system has a routinised response to homelessness, which, by sorting people into the categories of the deserving and the non-deserving, perpetuates the approach first established in Victorian times. This has been reproduced in the concept of the foyer, discussed in Chapter 8, since it helps only those young people who can 'prove' that they can benefit, regardless of the severity of their need. This inclination for the reproduction of established practices also means that there is inflexibility in relation to matters which are not routine or which might pose a threat to the established order. For example, the planning system, first established in the post-war period to restrict uncontrolled development, is criticised for maintaining an entrenched resistance to new development proposals. This resistance becomes even more pronounced if applications are out of the ordinary and put forward by a non-traditional group, as for example in the cohousing and low impact developments discussed in Chapter 10, despite the fact that these accord with the sustainable practices promoted by more recent planning guidance. In the same way financial institutions such as banks and building societies are inherently suspicious of the unconventional, and find it impossible to 'bend the rules' to accommodate loans for non-mainstream developments.

However, the very fact that institutions and organisations are peopled by individuals, at least some of whom are capable of independent thought, means that there is always the possibility of divergence from the norm. This is particularly the case where rules are not tightly prescribed and hence there is more scope for discretion and autonomous decision-making. It is in this way that, for example, the same planning application or the same homeless young person may receive a different response from different planning or housing authorities. Thus as noted in Chapter 10, a few more open-minded planning authorities have been enlightened enough to permit low impact developments and to incorporate them in principle into local planning policy. In the same way some housing authorities have over time resisted the normalising agendas of central government and decided, for example, that tower blocks are not the residential form they wish to adopt, or that foyers are too institutionalising and supported individual tenancies are a more appropriate solution. If such divergences from normal practice are proved successful, or at least unproblematic, then they will gain legitimacy and eventually a new orthodoxy will be established. Often such a process is set in train through acts of mediation and negotiation (see Chapter 4). Indeed the importance of negotiation in determining outcomes has been a dominant theme throughout the case studies. This can be seen, for example, in the modification of the government preferred model of a UDC in Birmingham and Cardiff, discussed in Chapters 6 and 9, and in the continuous negotiations over planning applications. This is of particular significance in relation to concessions on Section 106 agreements when planning officers are confronted with the economic realities faced by development actors.

It is in organisations which are free, or relatively so, of statutory control and regulation that innovation and experimentation are perhaps most likely to be found. Such organisations include housing associations, trusts, charities, pressure groups and social movements, which not only innovate and experiment, but also support those groups or causes which are disdained by the mainstream of society. Charities, for example, have had a long history of being the main recourse for the most needy in society, and many, including for example Shelter and Age Concern, have had considerable success in changing attitudes and lobbying for new legislation. In regard to housing, the housing trusts first established in the late nineteenth century had (and continue to have) a salutary role in regard to the provision of homes for those who otherwise could not access decent housing. Amongst these early trusts were the Peabody Trust and the Joseph Rowntree Memorial Trust (now the JRF), both of which are still in the vanguard of providing innovative responses. In the case of Peabody this relates to a willingness to be at the forefront of experimentation with new construction techniques, and in the case of the JRF, active engagement with and promotion of a host of new concepts discussed in this book, such as lifetime homes, smart homes, CASPAR and the CCRC. Also of significance in regard to housing are the new types of financial institution which have stepped outside the traditional mould in their willingness to support non-mainstream developments. These include Triodos Bank, which lends to projects with social and environmental aims; the Ecology Building Society, which will support self-build schemes and those incorporating sustainable methods; and the Muslim banks which provide finance on a no interest basis according to Sharia law.

As discussed in Chapters 4 and 10, organisations first established as pressure groups have played a large part in encouraging more enlightened approaches to conservation and preservation. These include such long established organisations as the National Trust, RSPB and SPAB, as well as more recent ones such as FoE. The aim of pressure groups is to effect change by working within established structures and institutions, and this contrasts with the approach adopted by social movements. These deliberately use confrontational and aggressive tactics to expose and publicise practices which they feel are exploitative of people or the natural world. Their aim is to try to transform society, and whilst some adopt methods which are confrontational and violent, others are more interested in the rejection of materialism and capitalism and the establishment of alternative ways of living. It is this type of radicalism that is illustrated in the ecovillage movement discussed in Chapter 10. Such radical social movements should, however, be distinguished from other types of group action also often referred to as 'movements', such as self-build, gentrification, LETS systems and cohousing. In effect these are grass roots actions rather than specifically social movements, stimulated by self-belief, a lack of alternatives and a conviction of what is right for the needs of the group concerned rather than a desire to change society.

As discussed in Chapter 4, individuals acting alone also possess the capacity to exert power and effect change. This may be on the basis of status, conviction, experience, personal characteristics, or possession of the capital derived from membership of an institution or through mastery of an area of knowledge. For example the Prince of Wales as a member of the Royal Family has symbolic capital which he has used to promote his views on contemporary architecture and on urban villages (see Chapters 4 and 6); an artist has aesthetic capital, and the works of a well known one such as Damien Hirst can bestow distinction on a project (as at Timber Wharf in Chapter 9); a business man has economic capital and can use it to persuade financial institutions to support him (as with Ashley Dobbs and Triodos in Chapter 6, although as that case shows, capital can be lost and support concomitantly withdrawn); and figures who have social and political capital can be employed to lend legitimacy to ideas and projects, as for instance with Lord Rogers, who as well as chairing the Urban Task Force to promote the 'urban renaissance' has also served on boards of various regeneration bodies (including CBDC) and the panels of numerous architectural competitions (including Timber Wharf).

Other individuals have used their creativity, skills, and knowledge to introduce new ideas or find solutions to particular issues. Some are internationally famous and have assumed iconic status, as for example Le Corbusier, Ebenezer Howard and James Lovelock, whilst others have had an impact in a particular field and are known only to those within that field, as with Fowler and the design of mental hospitals (see Chapter 7), Pevsner and the appreciation of historic buildings (see Chapter 7), Christopher Day and the creation of harmonious and ecological dwellings (see Chapter 10), Sheila McKechnie and her work on homelessness (see Chapter 8) and Simon Fairlie and the concept of low impact development (see Chapter 10). Often these individuals are inspired by the challenge and excitement of finding ways to do things differently, and may have a certain visionary zeal. This is also true of those maverick developers encountered in the pages of this book who have stepped outside the safety zone of traditional modes of development, such as Tom Bloxham, David Michael, Ashley Dobbs and the Stewart Community Woodlanders. If judged successful according to institutional criteria, these individuals then have the opportunity for establishment endorsement, as has happened with Tom Bloxham and his company Urban Splash, whilst those that fail, like Ashley Dobbs, have little choice but to abandon their ambitions and look elsewhere.

Another contextual factor identified in Figure 1.1 is that of text, for in a contemporary society the powers of both structure and agency rely to a considerable extent on text and discourse. It is through these means that traditions and norms are encoded and passed from one generation to the next, that rules and regulations are fixed in policies and procedures, that ideas are transferred from country to country or person to person, and that images are created that can bring to immediate view what is otherwise out of sight. However as discussed in Chapter 2, text and discourse are not neutral, and embody the predispositions of their authors (under the influence of structural forces and institutional cultures) to interpret things in certain ways and thus ensure that it is this way, rather than any other, that is reproduced. Texts also adopt the language which will resonate with the *habitus* of the anticipated audience; for example, the discourse of architects or architectural critics in architectural publications is quite different from the discourse of sociologists in social science journals, even if on the same topic such as the merits or demerits of mental hospitals and tower blocks. By contrast to the factual and analytical language of such academic and professional publications is the rhetorical and even apocalyptic style of politicians, as illustrated in Chapter 7 with the words of Enoch Powell and John Major on those same subjects of the mental hospital and the tower block. Indeed, for politicians and policy makers it is crucial to develop a particular facility with language, since this is so formative in setting agendas and in encouraging the general public to construct certain issues in certain ways (see also Gurney, 1999b; Hastings, 1999). Thus such concepts as owner occupation, community care, economic growth and 'good' design have become legitimised and normalised, whilst on the other hand certain groups of people have become classed as problematic or threatening, notably (at the present time) older people, young people and asylum seekers. Indeed, in the project of New Labour rhetoric has become a particularly important device, as indicated in the mastery of spin and the mantra-like repetition of 'buzz' terms such as social inclusion, sustainable development, urban renaissance, joined up thinking, decent homes and, most recently, respect. However, the danger is that ultimately such terms are rendered meaningless through overuse and lack of meaningful definition, and like the words 'village', 'community' and even sustainability begin to lack credibility and legitimacy.

In any context rhetoric is a powerful and necessary device if text is to be used successfully to persuade, seduce, alarm or manipulate. This has been illustrated in this book across a range of contexts: in the professional texts of Fowler and Lasdun which seek to convince fellow architects of the rationale for their creations; in the informational and instructive texts of Pevsner; in the diatribes on the environmental question which seek to instil a sense of panic and a need for change; in the promotional texts of city boosterism and the 'selling' of cities like Manchester and Cardiff; in the journalese of the cohousing network seeking to recruit new members; or in the persuasive material sent to planning offices to try and sway planning outcomes, such as letters of support and objection, 'concept' statements, design proclamations and pertinent publications. But the use of text to seduce and manipulate is at its most pronounced in marketing. Developers are adept at manufacturing the cues of the spatial characteristics of site and built form into signs of prestige, security, convenience and discernment, often through the rhetorical devices of hyperbole and metaphor. Words are chosen which will create the appropriate image for a particular market niche and lifestyle preference, such as 'tranquil', 'vibrant' or 'sustainable', or in other cases to convey a sense of distinction, as in 'unique', 'historic' or 'discerning'. Another mechanism is to present the words of existing users to give an impression of satisfaction and success, as in the pen portraits employed by Hartrigg Oaks and Occasio House. Visual impact can be as important as words, and this includes not only the selective use of photographs and drawings but also images chosen for their symbolic or sign value (such as the yacht riding the crest of a wave for Adventurers Quay and the rare cirl bunting for Devington Park). Increasingly, videos, DVDs and promotional websites are also used. Indeed the importance of the internet as a communicative device cannot be downplayed, given its instant accessibility within the home and its capacity to reach worldwide audiences. Thus all self-respecting housebuilders, in common with almost all institutions and organisations, have a website setting out their credentials and mission statements as well as details of schemes. This predominance of the internet is further reinforced by the fact that even those who otherwise eschew the trappings of modern life, such as the denizens of low impact developments, have recourse to it as a vital cord for the maintenance of a sense of connection to the outside world.

In regard to built form, the whole emphasis of this book has been on how outcomes are mediated by prevailing cultural, societal and spatial processes and practices, as reflected also in institutional frameworks, the thoughts and actions of agents, and textual representations. All of these become sedimented in the built environment and can be elucidated from a variety of cues: the way in which space is apportioned and framed; the emergence of particular building types; the variation of built form within each type (including housing); and the layout and design style of each individual building. But built form is more than passive outcome; through its concrete presence and durability over time it also actively reinforces and reproduces the structural systems of society. Thus through its capacity to channel, classify and contain it reflects the social organisation of society; through its ability to denote distinction it lends legitimacy to the powerful (whether occupant, provider, or designer); and through its spatial hierarchies and use of symbolic embellishments it reinforces cultural identities and archetypes. These are revealed in the spatial marginalisation of outcast groups, in the construction of monumental and overpowering built forms, in the supervisory panopticon and the 'stage set' (Dovey, 1999: 114) of the atrium or entrance foyer, in the imposition of different types of spatial syntax, in the distinction between public and private sector housing, and in the erection of gates, walls and other barriers:

> The urban built form is a system of boundaries and transgression, centers and peripheries, surveillances and gestures, gazes and performances.
>
> (Short, 2000: 19)

The fact that the spatial system 'says' something about social relations means that built form too has the capacity to be read as text. This has been indicated by commentators such as Foucault (1977), Markus (1993), Dovey (1999) and Hillier and Hanson (1984) in relation to the way in which social relations and social action are facilitated or constrained through the disposition of space, and by Bourdieu (1973), Forty (2000), Biddulph (1995), and Broadbent *et al.* (1980) in relation to the way aspects of the built form serve as signs and mnemonic devices for cultural and social categories. Also encoded in built form are the changing ideas and fashions as to that which constitutes 'good' or aesthetic design, with the 'battle of the styles' inscribed for future generations in language as diverse as the plain and proportioned Georgian, the flamboyant Gothic revival, the pseudo-rustic Arts and Crafts, the functional and rational Modernism, or the eclectic and kitsch postmodernism.

By the latter half of the twentieth century the mass produced housing of the speculative housebuilder was making reference to all of these indiscriminately, and without the rigour or conviction that might have come with committed design input or more development control. Even so, a type of 'language' has developed in which each housebuilder's product can be recognised from a grammar composed of identifiable house types and elevations. These have been imposed across the country with bland disregard for the idiom of the local vernacular, and it is only with the emergence of a new type of discourse, that of urban design, that this situation is beginning to be challenged. That this is beginning to have an effect is clear from the foregoing chapters, since with the exception of Bordesley, the earliest of the case study examples in this book and conceived within the dominant paradigm of market pragmatism, all the case studies show at least some respect for urban design thinking. This does, however, vary in extent, ranging from the gesture to local context, as evinced at Hartrigg Oaks; through the preservation of distinctive form and features, as at Exe Vale and Keeling House; to a more committed consideration of such matters as mass, scale, public space, public art and themed hard landscaping, as at Adventurers Quay; and finally to more rigorous adherence to such matters as high density, domestic scale, pedestrian dominance, clear demarcation of semi-public, semi-private and private space, opportunity for social encounters, and flexible and sustainable design, as displayed at Springhill Cohousing and the Acorn Televillage.

In speculating about the future, and it can only be speculation, the same contextual approach can be adopted as has been done for the contemporary situation. At the structural level, cultural processes are likely to continue to see the perpetuation of those myths and cultural archetypes which have already proved so enduring, such as the distinction between outsider and insider. However as has happened hitherto there will be new categories of people and places constructed as outcast and in their turn relegated to the margins. Also unequivocal is a continuation of the exchange of ideas between cultures and the resultant introduction into the UK of a variety of as yet unknown new concepts and models of dwelling. It is inevitable too that there will be further transformations in social life ushered in by challenges both global and local. Possibilities here might be environmental cataclysm, a post-materialist turn, sustained global or local economic collapse, the imposition of an ideology of extremism or religious revivalism, new forms of populist political or spiritual engagement, or further significant advances in the fields of assisted reproduction, cloning, and the postponement of the natural ageing process. Any or all of these are perfectly conceivable, and their consequences will be felt in the structures of society, in new institutional frameworks, in the reallocation of resources, in the relationships between people, and in new crises of identity. If these occur they will be reflected in new lifestyles, in new modes of living, in new ways of expressing identity, in new forms of seeking community and in new types of housing.

Also with considerable impact will be the effect of further demographic and socio-economic changes, the trends of some of which can already be discerned. For example in the short term the numbers of single person households are likely to increase still further, and unless and until the size of the total population falls or housing supply is boosted this will intensify the strain that has already been placed on housing demand. Perhaps more profound will be the situation with regard to older people. As their numbers increase along with their longevity, there is likely to be an even greater diversity in regard to income, state of health and expectations. This will lead to a far wider range of accommodation options, both with and without support. Undoubtedly there will be more retirement communities on the American model as the private sector grasps the opportunity to exploit those with the greatest means, and the private sector is also likely to explore further the potential of the extra care model (see Chapter 8). Meanwhile the public and voluntary sectors will be expected, as ever, to give assistance to those from whom profit cannot be made. Increasingly this is likely to be tailor made to the needs of individuals, with a further extension of the current trend away from semi-institutionalised accommodation offering a generic level of support, to more personalised units and individualised care. This tendency is also likely to be reflected in a wider variety of options to assist people with disabilities, whether physical or mental, including the more widespread and potentially depersonalising utilisation of new technology. It seems inevitable too that developments in such 'smart home' technology will spread to the design and management of ordinary mainstream housing, whilst other technological advances will assist in another demographic trend, that of homeworking. In this latter regard housing providers will respond with more diverse and flexible arrangements for the combination of living and working space, although whether this will also include the development of more televillages, as discussed in Chapter 6, remains to be seen.

Some new development concepts and models may emerge primarily from cultural and social change, but others may be more directly influenced by changes in spatial processes. The reproduction of investment cycles whereby certain areas gradually become relegated to back regions and certain building types become obsolescent is likely to persist. As happens at the present time, such areas or building types will lie dormant until 'rediscovered', perhaps by a maverick and risk taking entrepreneur, whereupon they will be reconstructed both physically and socially as desirable front regions or residences for the discerning. It is possible to conjecture that over time the areas that might be affected could include industrial estates, out of town shopping centres, the waterfront developments of the 1980s, the 'urban villages' of the late 1990s, or even airport sites, should air travel be abandoned due to environmental costs or tourism truncated due to the effects of global over-heating. Possible structures for future obsolescence might include foyers, should they eventually be deemed too institutionalising; almshouses, should their mediaeval form and associations prove too outmoded; power stations and their cooling towers, should nuclear power and renewables replace coal and gas; or monasteries and convents, should the religious vocation continue to dwindle in appeal. Any or all of these, and many more, could provide scope for the fashioning of new types of residential space and the transformation of old built forms into new.

Conclusion

Other different types of living space might arise from changing institutional preoccupations and priorities, such as new forms of governance, the reversal of the commitment to economic growth, more (or less) government control over development and design, greater regulation over each person's and each building's carbon footprint, and new approaches to the needs of vulnerable and disadvantaged people. All of these might then be expressed in built environments, discourses and forms of words as yet undreamt of. There will also in the future be the scope for the rise of new professions, charities, trusts, pressure groups and social movements. These may lead to new ways of perceiving environmental issues, the championing of new groups of people and types of place, or attacks on different aspects of social life. Housing providers are also likely to develop a variety of new organisational concerns, whether of their own volition or through being forced to do so by pressure from institutions or consumers. This again would lead to the development of new concepts or to greater variation in house type and design – or on the other hand to more standardisation. And as throughout history, individual inspiration and commitment will also play a part in terms of critiques of contemporary design and the devising of new concepts and examples, whether by architects, visionaries, maverick developers, commentators or users.

In regard to the possible future shape of built form, there are already a few significant and interesting trends which have emerged in recent years and which may increase in popularity. One of these is the elitist, autocratic, and highly engineered new tower blocks of High Tech Modernism. Currently promoted by high profile architects, they still need to gain the full acceptance of planning authorities and the target market of the mobile elite. If this occurs then they are likely to multiply, especially in the face of greater pressures on urban space. And once perceived as markers of distinction they will become desired by those lower in the social hierarchy, and may eventually even be imposed once more as a 'solution' to the mass housing of the poor. At the other extreme is the responsive, democratically designed and ecologically benign dwelling. At present favoured by a fraction of the middle classes with environmental concerns and a desire for meaningful identity and a real sense of community, they include self-build schemes, eco-dwellings, cohousing, and low impact developments. Currently the benefits accrue only to a tiny and privileged minority and are generally achieved in the face of opposition from the entrenched attitudes of institutions and the population at large. However, as demand for more environmental awareness grows, as it assuredly will, then consumers, regulators and providers will all respond. The impact will be felt in the normalisation of what are now seen as 'alternative' dwellings, and the incorporation of more sustainable methods into the standard housing product.

This standard housing product is also likely to see other significant changes in approaches to construction. As discussed in Chapter 3, the current government is already keen to encourage both an increased use of prefabrication and more productive and democratic working practices. Here they have faced resistance from a public still reacting to the unsuccessful experiment of systems built housing in the 1960s, and a housebuilding industry resistant to change. However, the case study material indicates that the idea of a partnership approach to procurement has gained considerable favour across all sectors, although it is, as ever, the housing associations which are the most willing to experiment. New technologies will also bring further innovations in materials and assembly methods, and this may create a new generation of house types and styles which are also of lower cost. In the face of crises of supply and affordability this will be further driven by demand from young people and low paid workers in their desire to gain access to the owner occupied sector unless, of course, renting gains a new legitimacy. Already we have seen the devising in the Netherlands of a prototype in this regard; the 'space box', currently used to provide student accommodation (R. Weaver, 2005). Constructed of fibreglass and resin each primary coloured dwelling unit measures just three metres by six and a half and can be connected to others horizontally or stacked vertically. As Weaver suggests, these could offer potential for starter homes or even sheltered housing, and the likelihood is that the space box or some derivative of it will be introduced here too; a new generation of 'prefabs'.

The future is of course another country, and more will happen in terms of cultural, social and spatial change than can ever be predicted. All of this will have an impact on the design of the built environments of the future, and it may be that citizens in 50 or 100 years time will have experienced such a transformation in approach to conceptions of living space that they will look back in bemusement to the domestic environments typical of the turn of this century. On the other hand, perhaps the majority of their dwellings will still, as today, be reproducing versions of the traditional pseudo rustic across the land, and new (or revived) forms such as the skyscraper or the eco-dwelling will continue to be rejected by the majority. But let us hope that in facing the challenges and problems of their age they will manage to achieve better than ourselves that conjuncture of lived, conceived and imagined space conceptualised by Lefebvre and discussed in Chapter 1. To do so they will need to have learnt from the mistakes of the past how to avoid the reproduction of residential forms which work counter to the social prerequisites, spatial harmonies and archetypal representations of the place people experience most essentially as home.

References

Abram, S., Murdoch, J. and Marsden, T. (1996) 'The social construction of "Middle England": the politics of participation in forward planning', *Journal of Rural Studies*, 12: 353–64.

Adams, D. and Watkins, C. (2002) *Greenfields, Brownfields and Housing Development*, Oxford: Blackwell.

Aldous, T. (1992) *Urban Villages: a concept for creating mixed use urban developments on a sustainable scale*, London: Urban Villages Group.

Aldous, T. (1997) *Urban Villages: a concept for creating mixed use urban developments on a sustainable scale*, 2nd edn, London: Urban Villages Forum.

Alexander, C. (1979) *The Timeless Way of Building*, New York: Oxford University Press.

Alexander, C., Ishikawa, S. and Silverstein, M. (1977) *A Pattern Language*, New York: Oxford University Press.

Allen, C. (2003) 'On the social consequences (and social conscience) of the "foyer industry": a critical ethnography', *Journal of Youth Studies*, 4, 4: 471–94.

Allison, J. (1998) *The Birmingham Heartlands Initiative*, Birmingham: BHDC.

Allmendinger, P. and Thomas, H. (eds) (1998) *British Planning and the New Right*, London: Routledge.

Altman, I. and Low, S. (eds) (1992) *Place Attachment*, New York: Plenum Press.

Altman, I. and Werner, C. (eds) (1985) *Home Environments*, New York: Plenum Press.

Anderson, I. and Quilgars, D. (1995) *Foyers for Young People: evaluation of a pilot initiative*, York: Centre for Housing Policy.

Archer, M. (2000) *Being Human: the problem of agency*, Cambridge: Cambridge University Press.

Architects' Journal (1991) 'Asylum debate', *Architects' Journal*, 193, 3, 6 January: 10.

Architectural Review (1960) 'Housing, Bethnal Green, London', *Architectural Review*, CXXVII, 759, May: 304–12.

Architecture Today (1997) 'Richard Reid's high density housing for Cardiff Bay', *Architecture Today*, 77: 10–11.

Arias, E. (ed.) (1993) *The Meaning and Use of Housing: international perspectives, approaches and their application*, Aldershot: Avebury.

At Home in the Bay (1998) 'The adventure continues …', *At Home in the Bay*, Issue 1, October: 4–5.

Atkinson, R. (2003) 'Introduction: misunderstood saviour or vengeful wrecker? The many meanings and problems of gentrification', *Urban Studies*, 40, 12: 2343–50.

Atkinson, R., Flint, J., Blandy, S. and Lister, D. (2004) *Gated Communities in England: final report of the gated communities in England New Horizons Project*, London: ODPM.

Audit Commission (1988) *Estate Management in the National Health Service*, London: Audit Commission.

Bachelard, G. (1969) *The Poetics of Space*, Boston, MA: Beacon.

Baggs, S. and Baggs, J. (1996) *The Healthy House*, London: Thames and Hudson.

Bailey, N. (1995) *Partnership Agencies in British Urban Policy*, London: UCL Press.

Bailey, R. (1973) *The Squatters*, Harmondsworth: Penguin.

Baillieu, A. (1993) 'Brooke acts over Lasdun landmark', *Building Design*, 1152/1153, 26 November: 2.

Baillieu, A. (1995) 'The price of history', *Architects' Journal*, 202, 6, 10 August: 18–19.

Balchin, P. and Rhoden, M. (2002) *Housing Policy: an introduction*, 4th edn, London: Routledge.

Baldwin, S. (1926) *On England and Other Addresses*, London: Philip Allen.

Ball, M. (1983) *Housing Policy and Economic Power*, London: Methuen.

Ball, M. (1996) *Housing and Construction: a troubled relationship*, Bristol: The Policy Press.

Ball, M. (1999) 'Chasing a snail: innovation and housebuilding firms' strategies', *Housing Studies*, 14, 1: 9–22.

Ball, M. (2002) 'The organisation of property development professions and practices', in S. Guy and J. Hannebury (eds) *Development and Developers: perspectives on property*, Oxford: Blackwell Science.

Bannister, J. and Fyfe, N. (2001) 'Introduction: fear and the city', *Urban Studies*, 38, 5–6: 807–813.

Barker, K. (2004) *Review of Housing Supply: delivering stability: securing our housing needs*, Norwich: HMSO.

Barlow, J. (1999) 'From craft production to mass customisation: innovation requirements for the UK housebuilding industry', *Housing Studies*, 14, 1: 23–43.

Barnes, C. (1990) *Cabbage Syndrome: the social construction of dependency*, London: Falmer Press.

Bartlett, K., Potter, M., Meikle, J., Duffy, F., Ozaki, R., Hakes, J., Young, R. and Hooper, A. (2002) *Consumer Choice in House Buying: the beginnings of a house buyer revolt*, York: JRF.

Barton H., Davis, G. and Guise, R. (1995) *Sustainable Settlements: a guide for planners, designers and developers*, Bristol: University of West of England and Local Government Management Board.

Barton, H. (ed.) (2000) *Sustainable Communities: the potential for eco-neighbourhoods*, London: Earthscan.

Barton, W. (1959) *Institutional Neurosis*, Bristol: John Wright.

Bauman, Z. (1988) *Freedom*, Milton Keynes: Open University Press.

Bauman, Z. (1998) *Globalization: the human consequences*, Cambridge: Polity Press.

Bauman, Z. (2001a) *Community: seeking safety in an insecure world*, Cambridge: Polity Press.

Bauman, Z. (2001b) *Work, Consumerism and the New Poor*, Buckingham: Open University Press.

BBC (2000) *Televillage Goes Bust*. Online. Available: http://news.bbc.co.uk/1/hi/business/990033.stm (accessed 1 December 2003).

BBNP (1993) 'Report to National Park Committee, agenda item 13, 12/11/1993', Unpublished Report, Brecon: BBNP.

Beck, U. (1992) *Risk Society: towards a new modernity*, London: Sage.

Beck, U. (2000) *World Risk Society*, Cambridge: Polity Press.

Beck, U., Giddens, A. and Lash, S. (1994) *Reflexive Modernization: politics, tradition and aesthetics in the modern social order*, Cambridge: Polity Press.

BedZED (2004) *About BedZED*. Online. Available: http://www.bedzed.org.uk/about.htm (accessed 23 November 2004).

Bell, D. and Valentine, G. (eds) (1995) *Mapping Desire: geographies of sexualities*, London: Routledge.

Benjamin Thompson Associates (undated) The *Inner Harbour Area Planning Brief*, Cardiff: CBDC.

Bentley, I. (1999) *Urban Transformations: power, people and urban design*, London and New York: Routledge.

Bentley, I., Alcock, A., Murrain, P., McGlynn, S. and Smith, G. (1985) *Responsive Environments: a manual for designers*, Oxford: Architectural Press.

Berger, P. and Luckmann, T. (1966) *The Social Construction of Reality*, Harmondsworth: Penguin.

Berkeley Group (1999) *Annual Report and Accounts*, London: Berkeley Group.

References

Bernard, M. and Phillips, J. (2000) 'The challenge of ageing in tomorrow's Britain', *Ageing and Society*, 20: 33–54.

Bibby, A. (2003) *Telecottages and Telecentres*. Online. Available: http://www.andrewbibby.com/ telecot.html (accessed 1 December 2003).

Biddulph, M. (1995) 'The value of manipulated meanings in urban design', *Environment and Planning B: Planning and Design*, 22: 739–62.

Biddulph, M. (2000) 'Villages don't make a city', *Journal of Urban Design*, 5, 1: 65–82.

Biddulph, M. (2001) *Home Zones: a planning and design handbook*, Bristol: The Policy Press.

Biddulph, M., Franklin, B. and Tait, M. (2003) 'From concept to completion: a critical analysis of the urban village', *Town Planning Review*, 74, 2: 165–93.

Biddulph, M., Hooper, A. and Punter, J. (2004) *Evaluating the Impact of Design Awards for Housing*, London: ODPM/RIBA.

Biggs, S., Bernard, M., Kingston, P. and Nettleton, H. (2000) 'Lifestyles of belief: narrative and culture in a retirement community', *Ageing and Society*, 20: 649–72.

Blake, R. and Golland, A. (2004) 'Housing renewal, conversion and city living', in A. Golland and R. Blake (eds) *Housing Development: theory, process and practice*, London: Routledge.

Blakely, E. and Snyder, M. (1997) *Fortress America: gated communities in the United States*, Washington, DC: Brookings Institution Press.

Blakely, E. and Snyder, M. (1998) 'Forting up: gated communities in the United States', *Journal of Architectural and Planning Research*, 15, 1: 61–71.

Blumer, H. (1969) *Symbolic Interactionism*, Englewood Cliffs, NJ: Prentice-Hall.

Boddy, M. and Parkinson, M. (eds) (2004) *City Matters: competitiveness, cohesion and urban governance*, Bristol: The Policy Press.

Borer, P. and Harris, C. (1998) *The Whole House Book: ecological building design and materials*, Machynlleth: Centre for Alternative Technology.

Bourdieu, P. (1973) 'The Berber House', in M. Douglas (ed.) *Rules and Meanings*, Harmondsworth: Penguin.

Bourdieu, P. (1977) *Outline of a Theory of Practice*, London: Cambridge University Press.

Bourdieu, P. (1984) *Distinction*, London: Routledge and Kegan Paul.

Bourdieu, P. (1989) 'Social space and symbolic power', *Sociological Theory*, 7,1: 14–25.

Bourdieu, P. (1991) *Language and Symbolic Power*, Cambridge: Polity Press.

Bourdieu, P. (1992) *The Logic of Practice*, Cambridge: Polity Press.

Bourdieu, P. and Wacquant, L. (1992) *An Invitation to Reflexive Sociology*, Cambridge: Polity Press.

Bramley, G., Bartlett, W. and Lambert, C. (1995) *Planning, the Market and Private Housebuilding*, London: UCL Press.

BRE (2004) *EcoHomes*. Online. Available: http://products.bre.co.uk/breeam/ecohomes.html (accessed 23 November 2004).

Brenton, M. (2001) 'Older people's cohousing communities', in S. Peace and C. Holland (eds) *Inclusive Housing in an Ageing Society*, Bristol: The Policy Press.

Brewerton, J. and Darton, D. (eds) (1997) *Designing Lifetime Homes*, York: JRF.

Brindley, T. (2003) 'The social dimension of the urban village: a comparison of models for sustainable urban development', *Urban Design International*, 8, 1/2: 53–65.

Broadbent, G., Bunt, R. and Jencks, C. (eds) (1980) *Signs, Symbols and Architecture*, Chichester: John Wiley.

Broome, J. and Richardson, B. (1991) *The Self Build Book*, Hartland, Devon: Green Books.

Brunskill, R. (1981) *Traditional Buildings of Britain: an introduction to vernacular architecture*, London: Victor Gollancz.

Bryant, C. and Jary, D. (1991) (eds) *Giddens' Theory of Structuration*, London: Routledge.

Building (2001) 'Project review: Harlow Foyer', *Building*, 41, 12 October: 67–72.

Building Design (1992) 'RIBA London Region urges listing of Lasdun tower', *Building Design*, 1098, 16 October: 4.

Building Design (1999) 'Lasdun helps out on Keeling refurbishment', *Building Design*, 1406, 13 August: 4.

Burnett, J. (1986) *A Social History of Housing 1815–1985*, 2nd edn, London: Routledge.

Burr, V. (1998) 'Overview: realism, relativism, social constructionism and discourse', in I. Parker (ed.) *Social Constructionism, Discourse and Realism*, London: Sage.

Burrell, J. (1985) 'A sane environment', *Building Design*, 760: 18–19.

Bynner, J., Elias, P., McKnight, A., Pan, H. and Pierre, G. (2002) *Young People's Changing Routes to Independence*, York: York Publishing Services.

CABE/DETR (2000) *By Design: urban design in the planning system*, London: Thomas Telford Publishing.

CABE/ODPM (2003) *The Value of Housing Design and Layout*, London: Thomas Telford.

Calthorpe, P. (1993) *The Next American Metropolis: ecology, community and the American dream*, New York: Princeton Architectural Press.

Cardiff County Council (2004) *A Brief History of Cardiff*. Online. Available: http://www.cardiff.gov.uk/cardiff/history/Brief_History.htm (accessed 16 August 2004).

Carmona, M. (1998) 'Residential design – not an optional extra', *Town and Country Planning*, 67, 6: 227–9.

Carmona, M. (2001) *Housing Design Quality: through policy, guidance and review*, London: Spon.

Carmona, M., Carmona, S. and Gallent, N. (2003) *Delivering New Homes: processes, planners and providers*, London: Routledge.

Carpenter, P. (1993) '*Sod It': an introduction to earth sheltered development in England and Wales*, Coventry: Coventry University.

Carson, R. (1962) *Silent Spring*, New York: Fawcett Crest Books.

Castells, M. (1977) *The Urban Question*, London: Edward Arnold.

Castells, M. (1978) *City, Class and Power*, London: Macmillan.

CBDC (1988) *Cardiff Bay Regeneration Strategy: summary*, Cardiff: CBDC.

CBDC (2000) *Renaissance: the story of Cardiff Bay 1987–2000*, Cardiff: CBDC.

Champion, A. (ed.) (1989) *Counterurbanization: the changing pace and nature of population deconcentration*, London: Edward Arnold.

Chapman Handy (1996) *People's Needs for Housing of Special Design*, Edinburgh: Scottish Homes.

Cherry, B. (2001) 'Foreword', in S. MacDonald (ed.) *Preserving Post-War Heritage: the care and conservation of mid-twentieth century architecture*, Shaftesbury: Donhead.

Cherry, B. and Pevsner, N. (1989) *The Buildings of England: Devon*, London: Penguin Books.

Clapham, D. (1997) 'The social construction of housing management research', *Urban Studies*, 34, 5–6: 761–74.

Clapham, D. (2005) *The Meaning of Housing: a pathways approach*, Bristol: The Policy Press.

Clapham, D. and Kintrea, K. (1992) *Housing Co-operatives in Britain: achievements and prospects*, Harlow: Longman.

Clarke, D. (2003) *The Consumer Society and the Postmodern City*, London: Routledge.

Cohousing Company (2000) 'Planning application supporting statement', Unpublished Paper, Bradford-on-Avon: Cohousing Company.

Cole, I. and Furbey, R. (1994) *The Eclipse of Council Housing*, London: Routledge.

Coleman, A. (1985) *Utopia on Trial: vision and reality in planned housing*, London: Hilary Shipman.

Collins, P. and Blake, R. (2004) 'Finance, procurement and marketing of housing', in A. Golland and R. Blake (eds) *Housing Development: theory, process and practice*, London: Routledge.

Colquhoun, I. (1999) *RIBA Book of 20th Century British Housing*, Oxford: Butterworth Heinemann.

Colquhoun, I. (2004) *Design Out Crime: creating safe and sustainable communities*, Oxford: Architectural Press.

Compton, N. (2004) 'The regeneration game', *Observer Magazine*, 15 February: 16–22.

Construction Task Force (1998) *Rethinking Construction*, London: DETR.

Cooper-Marcus, C. (1995) *House as a Mirror of the Self*, Berkeley, CA: Conari.

Cooper-Marcus, C. (2000) 'Site planning, building design and a sense of community: an analysis of six cohousing schemes in Denmark, Sweden and the Netherlands', *Journal of Architectural and Planning Research*, 17, 2: 146–63.

References

Croft, C. and Harwood, E. (1999) 'Conservation of twentieth century buildings: new rules for the Modern Movement and after', in G. Chitty and D. Baker (eds) *Managing Historic Sites and Buildings*, London: Routledge.

Crossley, N. (2002) *Making Sense of Social Movements*, Buckingham: Open University Press.

Croucher, K., Pleace, N. and Bevan, M. (2003) *Living at Hartrigg Oaks: residents' views of the UK's first continuing care retirement community*, York: JRF.

Crow, G. and Allan, G. (1994) *Community Life: an introduction to social relations*, London: Harvester Wheatsheaf.

Cullen, G. (1971) *The Concise Townscape*, London: Architectural Press.

Cullingworth, J. and Nadin, V. (2001) *Town and Country Planning in the UK*, 13th edn, London: Routledge.

Cunningham, J. (2001) 'Pulling down the fences', *The Guardian*, 25 July. Online. Available: http://www.society.guardian.co.uk/societyguardian/story/0,7843,526656,00.html (accessed 23 November 2004).

Curtis, W. (1987) *Modern Architecture since 1900*, London: Phaidon.

Curtis, W. (1994) *Denys Lasdun: architecture, city, landscape*, London: Phaidon.

D'Arcy, E. and Keogh, G. (2002) 'The market context of the property development activity', in S. Guy and J. Hennebury (eds) *Development and Developers: perspectives on property*, Oxford: Blackwell.

Darton, D. (1999) *The UK's First Continuing Care Retirement Community Opens Today*. Online. Available: http://www.jrf.org.uk/pressroom/releases (accessed 14 January 2003).

Daunton, M. (1987) *A Property Owning Democracy*, London: Faber.

Davidoff, L. and Hall, C. (1987) *Family Fortunes*, London: Hutchinson.

Davis, M. (1990) *City of Quartz: excavating the future in Los Angeles*, London and New York: Verso.

Day, C. (2004) *Places of the Soul: architecture and environmental design as a healing art*, 2nd edn, Oxford: Architectural Press.

Dear, P. (2003) 'Builders' profits boom as fewer homes built', *Property People*, 398, 21 August: 1–2.

Deas, I., Peck, J., Tickell, A., Ward, K. and Bradford, M. (1999) 'Rescripting urban regeneration, the Mancunian way', in R. Imrie and H. Thomas (eds) *British Urban Policy: an evaluation of the Urban Development Corporations*, London: Sage.

Dennis, C. (1989) 'Statement of evidence by JRHT to Public Inquiry, July 1989', Unpublished Paper, York: JRHT.

Dennis, N. (1970) *People and Planning: the sociology of housing in Sunderland*, London: Faber and Faber.

Després, C. (1991) 'The meaning of home: literature review and directions for future research and theoretical development', *Journal of Architectural and Planning Research*, 8, 2: 96–115.

DETR (1998a) *Circular 6/98: planning and affordable housing*, London: DETR.

DETR (1998b) *Planning for Communities of the Future*, London: DETR.

DETR (1998c) *Places, Streets and Movement: a companion guide to design bulletin 32 residential roads and footpaths*, London: DETR.

DETR (1999) *Supporting People*, London: DETR.

DETR (2000a) *Quality and Choice: a decent home for all, the housing Green Paper*, London: DETR.

DETR (2000b) *PPG3: housing*, London: DETR.

DETR (2000c) *Our Towns and Cities: the future – delivering an urban renaissance*, London: DETR.

DETR (2000d) *Building a Better Quality of Life: a strategy for more sustainable construction*, London: DETR.

DETR (2000e) *Millennium Villages and Sustainable Communities*, London: DETR.

DETR (2000f) *Conversion and Redevelopment: processes and potential*, London, DETR.

DETR (2001) *Quality and Choice for Older People's Housing: a strategic framework*, London: DETR.

DETR/HBF/The Planning Officers Society (1998) *Housing Layouts – Lifting the Quality*, London: HBF.

Development Control and Traffic Regulation Committee (1999) 'Appendix to Agenda of Committee Meeting 30 September', Unpublished Paper, Manchester: Manchester City Council.

Devington Homes (undated) *Devington Park, Exminster*, London: Adventis Group.

DNPA (2000) *Action for Wildlife: the Dartmoor biodiversity action plan*, Bovey Tracey, Devon: DNP Publications.

DNPA (2004) *Dartmoor National Park Local Plan 1995–2011*, Bovey Tracey: DNP Publications.

Dobbs, A. (1993) 'The Concept', unpublished paper submitted in support of planning application, Brecon: BBNP.

DoE (1987) *Re-Using Redundant Buildings: good practice in urban regeneration*, London: HMSO.

DoE (1991) *NHS Estate Management and Property Maintenance*, London: HMSO.

DoE (1992) *PPG3: housing*, London: DoE.

DoE (1994a) *Quality in Town and Country: a discussion document*, London: DoE.

DoE (1994b) *PPG15: planning and the historic environment*, London: DoE.

DoE (1995) *Quality in Town and Country: urban design campaign*, London: DoE.

DoE (1996) *Quality in Town and Country: urban design exhibition*, London: DoE.

DoE (1997a) *PPG1: general policy and principles*, London: Stationery Office.

DoE (1997b) *PPG7: The Countryside – Environmental Quality and Economic and Social Development*, London: Stationery Office.

Doherty, B. (2002) *Ideas and Actions in the Green Movement*, London: Routledge.

Doling, J., Ford, J. and Stafford, B. (1988) *The Property Owing Democracy*, Aldershot: Avebury.

Donley-Reid, L. (1990) 'A structuring structure: the Swahili house', in S. Kent (ed.) *Domestic Architecture and the Use of Space*, Cambridge: Cambridge University Press.

Douglas, M. (1970) *Purity and Danger: an analysis of concepts of pollution and taboo*, Harmondsworth: Penguin.

Douglas, M. and Isherwood, B. (1996) *The World of Goods: towards an anthropology of consumption*, 2nd edn, London: Routledge.

Dovey, K. (1999) *Framing Places: mediating power in built form*, London: Routledge.

Dovey, K. (2002) 'The silent complicity of architecture', in J. Hillier and E. Rooksby (eds) *Habitus: a sense of place*, Aldershot: Ashgate.

Drake and Lasdun, D. (1956) 'Housing: cluster blocks at Bethnal Green, London', *Architectural Design*, April: 125–8.

Dreyfus, H. and Rabinow, P. (1982) *Michel Foucault: beyond structuralism and hermeneutics*, Chicago: University of Chicago Press.

Dryzek, J. (1997) *The Politics of the Earth: environmental discourses*, Oxford: Oxford University Press.

Dryzek, J., Downes, D., Hunold, C. and Schlosberg, D., with Herned, H-K. (2003) *Green States and Social Movements: environmentalism in the United States, United Kingdom, Germany and Norway*, Oxford: Oxford University Press.

DTLR (2001) *Planning: delivering a fundamental change*, London: DTLR.

DTLR/CABE (2001) *By Design – Better Places to Live: a companion guide to PPG3*, Kent: Thomas Telford Publishers.

Duany, A. and Plater-Zyberk, E. (1992) 'The second coming of the American small town', *Plan Canada*, May: 6–13.

Duffy, K. (1995) *Social Exclusion and Human Dignity in Europe*, Strasbourg: Council of Europe.

Dunleavy, P. (1981) *The Politics of Mass Housing in Britain 1945–1975: a study of corporate power and professional influence in the welfare state*, Oxford: Clarendon Press.

Durkheim, E. (1964) *The Division of Labour in Society*, New York: The Free Press.

Dutton, P. (2003) 'Leeds calling: the influence of London on the gentrification of regional cities', *Urban Studies*, 40, 12: 2557–72.

Dwelly, T. (2000) *Living at Work: a new policy framework for modern home workers*, York: JRF.

East Birmingham UDA (1989) *Bordesley Development Framework*, Birmingham: East Birmingham UDA.

References

Eco-Village Network UK (2003a) *Who are We?* Online. Available: http://europe.ecovillage.org/uk/network.whoarewe.htm (accessed 20 November 2003).

Eco-Village Network UK (2003b) *Sustainable Living Projects*. Online. Available: http://europe.ecovillage.org.uk/network/articles.htm (accessed 20 November 2003).

Edginton, B. (1997) 'Moral architecture: the influence of the York Retreat on asylum design', *Health and Place*, 3, 2: 91–9.

Edwards, A. (1981) *The Design of Suburbia: a critical study in environmental history*, London: Pembridge Press.

Ellin, N. (1997) 'Shelter from the storm or form follows fear and vice versa', in N. Ellin (ed.) *Architecture of Fear*, New York: Princeton Architectural Press.

English Partnerships (2003) *Sustainable Regeneration*. Online. Available: http://www.epolitix.com/Data/Companies (accessed 20 November 2003).

Erickson, B. and Lloyd-Jones, T. (2001) 'Design problems', in M. Roberts and C. Greed (eds) *Approaching Urban Design: the design process*, Harlow: Pearson Education Ltd.

Essex County Council (1973) *A Design Guide for Residential Areas*, Chelmsford: Essex County Council.

Essex County Council (2004) *Supporting People Newsletter*. Online. Available: http://www.supportingpeople.essexcc.gov.uk/docs (accessed 23 April 2004).

Essex Planning Officers' Association (1997) *A Design Guide for Residential and Mixed Use Areas*, Chelmsford, Essex: Essex Planning Officers' Association.

Evans, B. (2003) 'Nautical, but nice', *Architects' Journal*, 217, 5, 6 February: 24–35.

ExtraCare Charitable Trust (2003) *About Us*. Online. Available: http://www.extracare.org.uk/pages/aboutus.htm (accessed 14 January 2003).

Fairclough, N. (1992) *Discourse and Social Change*, Cambridge: Polity Press.

Fairlie, S. (1996) *Low Impact Development: planning and people in a sustainable countryside*, Charlbury, Oxon: Jon Carpenter.

Featherstone, M. (1991) *Consumer Culture and Postmodernism*, London: Sage.

Felstead, A. and Jewson, N. (2000) *In Work, At Home*, London: Routledge.

Fincher, R. and Jacobs, J. (eds) (1998) *Cities of Difference*, New York and London: The Guilford Press.

Fishman, R. (1982) *Urban Utopias in the Twentieth Century: Ebenezer Howard, Frank Lloyd Wright, and Le Corbusier*, Cambridge, MA: MIT Press.

Fitzpatrick, S. and Clapham, D. (1999) 'Homelessness and young people', in S. Hutson and D. Clapham (eds) *Homelessness: public policies and private troubles*, London: Cassell.

Folkard, K. (1998) *Housing Strategies for Youth: a good practice guide*, Coventry: CIH.

Ford, J., Burrows, R. and Nettleton, S. (2001) *Home Ownership in a Risk Society: a social analysis of mortgage arrears and possessions*, Bristol: The Policy Press.

Ford, J., Rugg, J. and Burrows, R. (2002) 'Conceptualising the contemporary role of housing in the transition to adult life in England', *Urban Studies*, 39, 13: 2455–67.

Forrest, R., Kennett, P. and Leather, P. (1999) *Home Ownership in Crisis? The British Experience of Negative Equity*, Aldershot: Ashgate.

Forrest, R. and Murie, A. (1988) *Selling the Welfare State*, London: Routledge.

Forty, A. (2000) *Words and Buildings: a vocabulary of modern architecture*, London: Thames and Hudson.

Foucault, M. (1977) *Discipline and Punish: the birth of the prison*, London: Allen Lane.

Foyer Federation (2004) *Introduction*. Online. Available: http://www.foyer.net.org/mpn (accessed 22 April 2004).

Frampton, K. (1992) *Modern Architecture: a critical history*, 3rd edn, London: Thames and Hudson.

Franklin, B. (1996a) 'A new dimension to housing: context and meaning in the built form', *Environments by Design*, 1, 2: 163–84.

Franklin, B. (1996b) 'New perspectives on housing and support for older people', in R. Bland (ed.) *Developing Services for Older People and Their Families*, Research Highlights in Social Work 29, London: Jessica Kingsley.

Franklin, B. (1996c) 'Concierges in tower blocks: a strategy in the mediation of change', *Scandinavian Housing and Planning Research*, 13: 27–39.

Franklin, B. (1998) 'Constructing a service: context and discourse in housing management', *Housing Studies*, 13, 2: 201–16.

Franklin, B. (1999) 'More than community care: supporting the transition from homelessness to home', in S. Hutson and D. Clapham (eds) *Homelessness: public policies and private troubles*, London: Cassell.

Franklin, B. (2002a) 'Hospital – heritage – home: reconstructing the nineteenth century lunatic asylum', *Housing, Theory and Society*, 19, 3–4: 170–84.

Franklin, B. (2002b) 'Monument to madness: the rehabilitation of the Victorian lunatic asylum', *Journal of Architectural Conservation*, 8, 3: 24–39.

Franklin, B. (2003) 'Success or failure? The redevelopment of Bordesley as an (urban) village', *Urban Design International*, 8, 1/2: 21–35.

Franklin, B. and Clapham, D. (1997) 'The social construction of housing management', *Housing Studies*, 12, 1: 7–26.

Franklin, B. and Tait, M. (2002) 'Constructing an image: the urban village concept in the UK', *Planning Theory*, 1, 3: 250–72.

Franklin, B., Biddulph, M. and Tait, M. (2002) *The Urban Village: a real or imagined contribution to sustainable development*, End of Award Report to ESRC, Cardiff: Department of City and Regional Planning, Cardiff University.

Frey, H. (1999*) Designing the City: towards a more sustainable urban form*, London: E&FN Spon.

Furlong, A. and Cartmel, F. (1997) *Young People and Social Change: individualization and risk in late modernity*, Buckingham: Open University Press.

Gann, D., Barlow, J. and Venables, T. (1999) *Digital Futures: making homes smarter*, York and Coventry: JRF and CIH.

Gans, H. (1962) *The Urban Villagers: group and class in the life of Italian-Americans*, New York: Free Press.

Gardner, H. (1997) *Extraordinary Minds: portraits of exceptional individuals and an examination of our extraordinariness*, London: Phoenix.

Garfinkel, H. (1967) *Studies in Ethnomethodology*, Englewood Cliffs, NJ: Prentice Hall.

Garrett, A. (2002) 'Sky-high living no longer a tall order', *Observer Cash*, 1 December: 19.

GEN (2004) *What is an Ecovillage?* Online. Available: http://gen.ecovillage.org/about/wiaev.html (accessed 30 November 2004).

Gergen, K. (1994) *Realities and Relationships: soundings in social construction*, Cambridge, MA: Harvester Wheatsheaf.

Giddens, A. (1984) *The Constitution of Society: outline of the theory of structuration*, Cambridge: Polity Press.

Giddens, A. (1990) *The Consequences of Modernity*, Stanford, CA: Stanford University Press.

Giddens, A. (1991) *Modernity and Self-Identity: self and society in the late modern age*, Cambridge: Policy Press.

Giddens, A. (1993) *New Rules of Sociological Method*, Cambridge: Polity Press.

Giddens, A. (1994) *Beyond Left and Right: the future of radical politics*, Cambridge: Polity Press.

Gilleard, C. and Higgs, P. (2002) 'The third age: class, cohort or generation?', *Ageing and Society*, 22: 369–82.

Gillen, M. and Golland, A. (2004) 'The private housebuilding industry and the housing market', in A. Golland and R. Blake (eds) *Housing Development: theory, process and practice*, London: Routledge.

Gillespie, A., Richardson, R. and Cornford, J. (1995) *Review of Telework in Britain: implications for public policy*, Newcastle-upon-Tyne: Centre for Urban and Regional Development Studies, University of Newcastle-upon-Tyne.

Glass, R. (1964) 'London: aspects of change', in Centre for Urban Studies (ed.) *Aspects of Change*, London: MacGibbon and Kee.

References

Glendinning, M. and Muthesius, S. (1994) *Tower Block: modern housing in England, Scotland, Wales and Northern Ireland*, New Haven and London: Yale University Press.

Glenn Howells Architects (2004) *Practice*. Online. Available: http://www.glennhowells.co.uk/noflashtop.php (accessed 16 August 2004).

Goffman, E. (1961) *Encounters*, New York: Bobbs-Merrill.

Goffman, E. (1968) *Asylums: essays on the social situation of mental patients and other inmates*, Harmondsworth: Penguin.

Goffman, E. (1971) *The Presentation of Self in Everyday Life*, Harmondsworth: Pelican.

Goldsmith, E., Bunyard, P., Allaby, M. and Allen R. (1972) *A Blueprint for Survival*, Harmondsworth: Penguin.

Goldthorpe, J., Lockwood, D., Bechofer, F. and Platt, J. (1968) *The Affluent Worker: industrial attitudes and behaviour*, Cambridge: Cambridge University Press.

Gooblar, A. (2002) 'Outside the walls: urban gated communities and their regulation within the British planning system', *European Planning Studies*, 10, 3: 321–34.

Gosling, D. and Maitland, M. (1984) *Concepts of Urban Design*, London: Academy Editions.

Gray, E. (1994) *The British House: a concise architectural history*, London: Barrie and Jenkins.

Greed, C. (1993) *Introducing Town Planning*, Harlow: Longman.

Gurney, C. (1990) *The Meaning of Home in the Decade of Owner Occupation: towards an experiential research agenda*, Working Paper 88, Bristol: School for Advanced Urban Studies, University of Bristol.

Gurney, C. (1999a) 'Lowering the drawbridge: a case study of analogy and metaphor in the social construction of home-ownership', *Urban Studies*, 36, 10: 1705–22.

Gurney, C. (1999b) 'Pride and prejudice: discourses of normalisation in public and private accounts of home ownership', *Housing Studies*, 14, 2: 163–83.

Gurney, C. and Means, R. (1993) 'The meaning of home in later life' in S. Arber and M. Evandrou (eds) *Ageing, Independence and the Life Course*, London and Bristol: Jessica Kingsley.

Guy, S. and Henneberry, J. (2004) 'Economic structures, urban responses: framing and negotiating urban property development', in M. Boddy and M. Parkinson (eds) *City Matters: competitiveness, cohesion and urban governance*, Bristol: The Policy Press.

Habraken, N. (1972) *Supports: an alternative to mass housing*, London: Architectural Press.

Hajer, M. (1995) *The Politics of Environmental Discourse: ecological modernization and the policy process*, Oxford: Oxford University Press.

Hall, P. (1982) 'Ebenezer Howard', *New Society*, 11 November: 252–4.

Hall, P. and Spencer-Hall, D. (1982) 'The social construction of a negotiated order', *Urban Life*, 11, 3: 328–49.

Hall, T. (2003) *Better Times Than This: youth homelessness in Britain*, London: Pluto Press.

Hamdi, N. (1991) *Housing without Houses: participation, flexibility, enablement*, New York: Van Nostrand Reinhold.

Harrison, M. with Davis, C. (2001) *Housing, Social Policy and Difference: disability, ethnicity, gender and housing*, Bristol: The Policy Press.

Harvey, D. (1985) *The Urbanization of Capital*, Oxford: Basil Blackwell.

Harvey, D. (1989) *The Condition of Postmodernity: an inquiry into the origins of cultural change*, Oxford: Basil Blackwell.

Harvey, D. (1997) 'Contested cities: social process and spatial form', in N. Jewson and S. MacGregor (eds) *Transforming Cities: contested governance and new spatial divisions*, London and New York: Routledge.

Hastings, A. (1999) 'Analysing power relations in partnerships: is there a role for discourse analysis?', *Urban Studies*, 36, 1: 91–106.

Hastings, A. (2000) 'Discourse analysis: what does it offer housing studies?', *Housing, Theory and Society*, 17: 131–39.

Healey, P., Purdue, M. and Ennis, F. (1995) *Negotiating Development: rationales and practices for development obligations and planning gain*, London: E&FN Spon.

Hearnden, D. (1983) *Continuing Care Communities: a viable option in Britain?*, London: Centre for Policy on Ageing.

Hetherington, K. (1997) *The Badlands of Modernity: heterotopias and social ordering*, London: Routledge.

Hetherington, P. (2005) 'Prescott plan to provide £60,000 homes', *The Guardian*, 4 January. Online. Available: http://www.moneyguardian.co.uk/news/story/0,1456,1382967,00.html (accessed 21 February 2005).

Hewison, R. (1987) *The Heritage Industry: Britain in a climate of decline*, London: Methuen.

Heywood, F., Oldman, C. and Means, R. (2002) *Housing and Home in Later Life*, Buckingham: Open University Press.

Higgins, J. (1989a) 'Defining community care: realities and myths', *Social Policy and Administration*, 23, 1: 3–16.

Higgins, J. (1989b) 'Homes and institutions', in G. Allan and G. Crow (eds) *Lone Parents and the Home*, London: Macmillan.

Hillery, G. (1955) 'Definitions of community: areas of agreement', *Rural Sociology*, 20: 111–23.

Hillier, B. (1988) 'Against enclosure', in N. Teymur, T. Markus and T. Woolley (eds) *Rehumanising Housing*, London: Butterworth.

Hillier, B. and Hanson, J. (1984) *The Social Logic of Space*, Cambridge: Cambridge University Press.

Hockerton Housing Project (2001) *Sustainable Community: a practical guide*, Southwell: Hockerton Housing Project Ltd.

Hockey, J. and James, A. (1993) *Growing Up and Growing Old: ageing and dependency in the life course*, London: Sage.

Hodge, R. and Kress, G. (1993) *Language as Ideology*, 2nd edn, London: Routledge.

Holmans, A. (2001) *Housing Demand and Need in England 1996–2016*, London: TCPA.

Hooper, A. and Nicol, C. (1999) 'The design and planning of residential development: standard house types in the speculative housebuilding industry', *Environment and Planning B: Planning and Design*, 26: 793–805.

Housing Corporation/DETR (1999) *Housing Quality Indicators*, London: DETR.

Howard, E. (1960) *Garden Cities of Tomorrow*, London: Faber (first published 1898).

Howard, M., Garnham, A., Fimister, G. and Veit-Wilson, J. (2001) *Poverty: the facts*, 4th edn, London: CPAG.

HRH The Prince of Wales (1989) *A Vision for Britain: a personal view of architecture*, London: Doubleday.

Hutson, S. (1999) 'The experience of "homeless" accommodation and support', in S. Hutson and D. Clapham (eds) (1999) *Homelessness: public policies and private troubles*, London: Cassell.

Hutson, S. and Liddiard, M. (1994) *Youth Homelessness: the construction of a social issue*, Basingstoke: Macmillan.

Hutton, W. (1996) *The State We're In*, London: Vintage.

Imrie, R. and Hall, P. (2001) *Inclusive Design: designing and developing accessible environments*, London: Spon.

Imrie, R. and Thomas, H. (eds) (1993) *British Urban Policy and the Urban Development Corporations*, London: Paul Chapman.

Inchmarlo House (2004) *Inchmarlo*. Online. Available: http://www.inchmarlo-retirement.co.uk/ (accessed 19 May 2004).

Inman, P. (2005) 'Towns closed to first time buyers', *Society Guardian*, 22 January. Online. Available: http://www.society.guardian.co.uk/housingdemand/story/0,10488,1396231.html (accessed 24 January 2005).

INTEGER (2002) INTEGER: *Intelligent and Green*. Online. Available: http://www.integerproject. co.uk (accessed 23 November 2004).

Intentional Communities (2004) *Intentional Communities*. Online. Available: http://www.ic.org/ (accessed 9 December 2004).

References

Internal Audit Scotland (2003) *The Egan Report and Registered Social Landlords*. Online. Available: http://www.internalauditscotland.com/internalaudit/clientalerts.cfm (accessed 15 August 2003).

Jackson, P. and Thrift, N. (1995) 'Geographies of consumption', in D. Miller (ed.) *Acknowledging Consumption: a review of new studies*, London: Routledge.

Jackson, R. (1995) 'The global eco-village network', in J. Conrad (ed.) *Eco-Villages and Sustainable Communities: models for 21st century living*, Findhorn: Findhorn Press.

Jacobs, J. (1961) *The Life and Death of Great American Cities*, New York: Random House.

Jacobs, J. (1998) 'Staging difference: aestheticization and the politics of difference in contemporary cities', in R. Fincher and J. Jacobs (eds) (1998) *Cities of Difference*, New York and London: The Guilford Press.

Jacobs, K. (1999) 'Key themes and future prospects: conclusion to the special issue', *Urban Studies*, 36, 1: 203–13.

Jacobs, K. (2002) 'Subjectivity and the transformation of urban spatial experience', *Housing, Theory and Society*, 19: 102–11.

Jacobs, K. and Manzi, T. (1996) 'Discourse and policy change: the significance for housing research', *Housing Studies*, 11, 4: 543–61.

Jacobs, K. and Manzi, T. (1998) 'Urban renewal and the culture of conservatism: changing perceptions of the tower block and implications for contemporary renewal initiatives', *Critical Social Policy*, 18, 2: 157–74.

Jacobs, K. and Manzi, T. (2000) 'Evaluating the social constructionist paradigm in housing research', *Housing, Theory and Society*, 17: 35–42.

Jacobs, K., Kemeny, J. and Manzi, T. (eds) (2004) *Social Constructionism in Housing Research*, Aldershot: Ashgate.

Jencks, C. (1977) *The Language of Post-Modern Architecture*, London: Academy Editions.

Jenkins, R. (1992) *Pierre Bourdieu*, London and New York: Routledge.

Jenks, M., Burton, E. and Williams, K. (eds) (1996) *Compact City: a sustainable urban form*, London: E&FN Spon.

Jephcott, P. (1971) *Homes in High Flats*, Edinburgh: Oliver and Boyd.

Jones, G. (1995) *Leaving Home*, Buckingham: Open University Press.

Jones, G. (2002) *The Youth Divide: diverging paths to adulthood*, York: JRF.

JRF (2004) *Joseph Rowntree Foundation 1904–2004*, York, JRF.

JRF (2005) *CASPAR Developments*. Online. Available: http://www.jrf.org/housingandcare/caspar (accessed 26/04/2005).

Jupp, B. (1999) *Living Together: community life on mixed tenure estates*, London: Demos.

Karn, V. and Sheridan, L. (1995) *New Homes in the 1990s: a study of design, space and amenity in housing association and private sector production*, Manchester and York: University of Manchester and JRF.

Kellaher, L. (2001) 'Shaping everyday life beyond design', in S. Peace, and C. Holland (eds) *Inclusive Housing in an Ageing Society*, Bristol: The Policy Press.

Kelly, M. (2001) 'Lifetime Homes', in S. Peace and C. Holland (eds) *Inclusive Housing in an Ageing Society*, Bristol: Policy Press.

Kelly, P. (2003) 'Growing up as risky business? Risks, surveillance and the institutionalized mistrust of youth', *Journal of Youth Studies*, 6, 2: 165–80.

Kemeny, J. (1981) *The Myth of Home Ownership*, London: Routledge and Kegan Paul.

Kemeny, J. (1992) *Housing and Social Theory*, London: Routledge.

Kemeny, J. (2002) 'Re-inventing the wheel? The interactional basis of constructionism', *Housing, Theory and Society*, 19: 140–1.

Kemp, P. (1997) 'Ideology, public policy and private rental housing since the war', in P. Williams (ed.) *Directions in Housing Policy: towards sustainable housing policy for the UK*, Basingstoke: Macmillan.

Kent, S. (ed.) (1990) *Domestic Architecture and the Use of Space*, Cambridge: Cambridge University Press.

King, A. (1980) *Buildings and Society: essays on the social development of the built environment*, London: Routledge and Kegan Paul.

King, P. (1996) *The Limits of Housing Policy: a philosophical investigation*, London: Middlesex University Press.

King, R. (1996) *Emancipating Space: geography, architecture and urban design*, New York: The Guilford Press.

Lash, S. (2000) 'Risk culture', in B. Adam, U. Beck and J. van Loon (eds) *The Risk Society and Beyond: critical issues for social theory*, London: Sage.

Lash, S. and Urry, J. (1994) *Economies of Signs and Space*, London: Sage.

Laslett, P. (1989) *A Fresh Map of Life: the emergence of the third age*, London: Weidenfeld and Nicolson.

Lawrence, R. (1987) *Housing, Dwellings and Homes: design theory, research and practice*, Chichester: John Wiley.

Lawrence, R. (1990) 'Public collective and private space: a study of urban housing in Switzerland', in S. Kent (ed.) *Domestic Architecture and the Use of Space*, Cambridge: Cambridge University Press.

Lawrence, R. (1993) 'Can human ecology provide an integrative framework? The contribution of structuration theory to contemporary debate', in D. Steiner and M. Nauser (eds) *Human Ecology: fragments of anti-fragmentary views of the world*, London and New York: Routledge.

Lawrence, R. (1994) 'Rented housing design considered in context', in R. Danermark and I. Elander (eds) *Social Rented Housing in Europe: policy, tenure and design*, Delft: Delft University Press.

Lawrence, R. (1996) 'The multi-dimensional nature of boundaries: an integrative historical perspective', in D. Pellow (ed.) *Setting the Boundaries: the anthropology of spatial and social organisation*, Westport, CT: Bergin and Garvey.

Lawson, B. (1997) *How Designers Think: the design process demystified*, 3rd edn, Oxford: Architectural Press.

Layder, D. (1997) *Modern Social Theory*, London: University College London Press.

Leach, N. (1999) *The Anaesthetics of Architecture*, Cambridge, MA: MIT Press.

Lee, P. and Murie, A. (1997) *Poverty, Housing Tenure and Social Exclusion*, Bristol: The Policy Press.

Lefebvre, H. (1991) *The Production of Space*, Oxford: Blackwell.

Lévi-Strauss, C. (1966) *The Savage Mind*, London: Weidenfeld and Nicholson.

Lévi-Strauss, C. (1968) *Structural Anthropology*, London: Allen Lane.

Lewis, O. (1959) *Five Families: Mexican case studies in the culture of poverty*, New York: Basic Books.

Ley, D. (1996) *The New Middle Class and the Remaking of the Central City*, Oxford: Oxford University Press.

Ley, D. (2003) 'Artists, aestheticisation and the field of gentrification', *Urban Studies*, 40, 12: 2527–2544.

Llewelyn Davies (2000) *Urban Design Compendium*, London: English Partnerships/Housing Corporation.

Lloyd-Jones, T. (2001) 'The design process', in M. Roberts and C. Greed (eds) *Approaching Urban Design: the design process*, Harlow: Pearson Education Ltd.

Lodziak, C. (2002) *The Myth of Consumerism*, London: Pluto Press.

Lovelock, J. (1979) *Gaia: a new look at life on earth*, Oxford: Oxford University Press.

Low Pay Unit (2003) *Facts About Low Pay*. Online. Available: http://www.lowpayunit.org/research/factslowpay.shtml (accessed 26 June 2003).

Low, S. (2003) *Behind the Gates: life, security and the pursuit of happiness in fortress America*, New York: Routledge.

Lowe, S., Spencer S. and Keenan, P. (eds) (1998) *Housing Abandonment in Britain*, York: Centre for Housing Policy.

Lynch, K. (1960) *The Image of the City*, Cambridge, MA: MIT Press.

References

McCamant, K. and Durrett, C. (1988) *Cohousing: a contemporary approach to housing ourselves*, Berkeley, CA: Ten Speed Press.

McCracken, G. (1990) *Culture and Consumption: new approaches to the symbolic character of consumer goods and activities*, Bloomington, IN: Indiana University Press.

McKechnie, S. (1991) 'Foyers', in Shelter (ed.) *The Foyer Project: a collection of background papers Part II*, London: Shelter.

McKenzie, S. (2003) 'A decade of making a difference', *Housing Magazine*, April: 15–17.

McRae, S. (ed.) (1999) *Changing Britain: families and households in the 1990s*, Oxford: Oxford University Press.

Madanipour, A. (1997) *Design of Urban Space: an inquiry into a socio-spatial process*, Chichester: John Wiley.

Madanipour, A. (1998) 'Social exclusion and space', in A. Madanipour, C. Goran and J. Allen (eds) *Social Exclusion in European Cities: processes, experiences and responses*, London: Jessica Kingsley.

Madanipour, A. (2003) *Public and Private Spaces of the City*, London: Routledge.

Madigan, R. and Munro, M. (1991) 'Gender, house and home: social meanings and domestic architecture in Britain', *Journal of Architectural and Planning Research*, 8, 2: 116–32.

Malpass, P. (2000) *Housing Associations and Housing Policy: a historical perspective*, Basingstoke: Macmillan.

Manchester City Council (2004) *The City of Manchester*. Online. Available: http://www.manchester. gov.uk/corporate/the city (accessed 16 August 2004).

Manchester Online (2002) *Regeneration Plan is a Real Cracker*. Online. Available: http://www. manchesteronline.co.uk/news/s/12/12406_regeneration_plan_is_a_real_cracker.html (accessed 20 April 2005).

Manning, N. (1985) 'Constructing social problems', in N. Manning (ed.) *Social Problems and Welfare Ideology*, London: Gower.

Manzi, T. and Smith-Bowers, B. (2005) 'Gated communities as club goods: segregation or social cohesion?', *Housing Studies*, 20, 2: 345–59.

Marcuse, P. (1997) 'Walls of fear and walls of support', in N. Ellin (ed.) *Architecture of Fear*, New York: Princeton Architectural Press.

Markus, T. (1993) *Buildings and Power: freedom and control in the origin of modern building types*, London and New York: Routledge.

Markus, T. and Cameron, D. (2002) *The Words Between the Spaces: buildings and language*, London and New York: Routledge.

Martin, J. (1990) 'Continuing care villages', *The Planner*, 25: 15–17.

Meadows, D.H., Meadows, D.L., Randers, J. and Behrens, W. (1972) *The Limits to Growth: a report for the Club of Rome on the predicament of mankind*, London: Earth Island Ltd.

Means, R. and Smith, R. (1998) *Community Care: policy and practice*, 2nd edn, Basingstoke: Macmillan.

Meikle, J. (1995) 'The house that John built', *The Guardian*, 27 April.

Mellor, R. (1997) 'Cool times for a changing city', in N. Jewson and S. MacGregor (eds) *Transforming Cities: contested governance and new spatial divisions*, London: Routledge.

Merchant, C. (1992) *Radical Ecology: the search for a livable world*, New York: Routledge.

Merton, R. (1967) *Social Theory and Social Structure*, New York: Free Press.

Mesler, M. (1989) 'Negotiated order and the clinical pharmacist: the ongoing process of structure', *Symbolic Interaction*, 12, 1: 139–57.

MHLG (1961) *Homes for Today and Tomorrow*, London: HMSO.

Miles, S. (1998) *Consumerism as a Way of Life*, London: Sage.

Miller, D. (1995) 'Consumption as the vanguard of history: a polemic by way of an introduction,' in D. Miller (ed.) *Acknowledging Consumption*, London: Routledge.

Mitchell, P. (1990) *Memento Mori: the flats at Quarry Hill, Leeds*, Otley: Smith Settle.

Morris, E. (1997) *British Town Planning and Urban Design: principles and policies*, Harlow: Longman.

Morris, J. (1995) *Housing and Floating Support: a review*, York: York Publishing Services.

Mulhearn, C. (2000) 'A life in architecture: Tom Bloxham', *Architects' Journal*, 212, 1, July 6: 26.

Murdoch, J. and Abram, S. (2002) *Rationalities of Planning: development versus environment in planning for housing*, Aldershot: Ashgate.

National Assembly for Wales (1999) *Pattern Book Plans*, Cardiff: National Assembly for Wales.

National Assembly for Wales (2000) *Better Homes for People in Wales*, Cardiff: National Assembly for Wales.

Network East Foyers (2003) *Annual Review 2002–2003*, London: Network East Foyers.

Newman, O. (1973) *Defensible Space: people and design in the violent city*, London: Architectural Press.

NHF (1998a) *Standards in Quality and Development: a good practice guide*, London, NHF.

NHF (1998b) *Accommodating Diversity*, 2nd edn, London: NHF.

NHS/English Heritage (1995) *Historic Buildings and the Health Service*, London: HMSO.

Norwood, G. (2003) 'W is working from home', *The Observer*, 13 April. Online. Available: http://money.guardian.co.uk/property/story/0,14422,1181419.html (accessed 1 December 2003).

Nother, P. (1995) 'Sanctuary or workhouse?' *Housing Magazine*, February: 43–4.

Nyman, J. (1999) 'Continuing care retirement communities and efficiency in the financing of long-term care', *Journal of Ageing and Social Policy*, 11, 2/3: 89–98.

O'Brien, M. and Penna, S. (1998) *Theorising Welfare: enlightenment and modern society*, London: Sage.

Odell, M. (2003) 'Dream homes', *Observer Magazine*, 23 February: 35–40.

ODPM (2002) *Sustainable Communities – Delivering through Planning*, London: ODPM.

ODPM (2003a) *The Starter Homes Initiative*. Online. Available: http://www.odpm.gov.uk/stellent/groups/odpm_housing/documents/ (accessed 19 August 2003).

ODPM (2003b) *Sustainable Communities: building for the future*, London: ODPM.

ODPM (2005a) *Key Worker Living*. Online. Available: http://www.odpm.gov.uk/stellent/groups/odpm_housing/documents/page/odpm_house_026955.hcsp (accessed 11 February 2005).

ODPM (2005b) *Planning Contributions: New Clauses*. Online. Available: http://www.odpm.gov.uk/stellent/groups/odpm_planning/document (accessed 11/02/2005).

ODPM (2005c) *PPS1: delivering sustainable development*, Norwich: Stationery Office

ODPM (2005d) *Sustainable Communities: homes for all*, Norwich: Stationery Office.

Office for National Statistics (2003a) *Census 2001*. Online. Available: http://www.statistics.gov.uk/census2001/demographic_uk.aspcci/nugget (accessed 17 February 2003).

Office for National Statistics (2003b) *Households: One Person Households up 30%*. Online. Available: http://www.statistic.gov.uk/CCI/nugget.asp (accessed 27 June 2003).

Office for National Statistics (2005) *Employment: rate remains at 74.9%*. Online. Available: http://www.statistics.gov.uk/cci/nugget.asp?id=12 (accessed 3 May 2005).

Oldman, C. (2000) *Blurring the Boundaries: a fresh look at housing and care provision for older people*, Brighton: Pavilion.

Oldman, C. and Quilgars, D. (1999) 'The last resort? Revisiting ideas about older people's living arrangements', *Ageing and Society*, 19: 363–84.

Oliver, M. (1996) *Understanding Disability: from theory to practice*, Basingstoke: Macmillan.

Oliver, P. (1987) *Dwellings: the house across the world*, Oxford: Phaidon.

Oliver, P. (2003) *Dwellings: the vernacular home worldwide*, London: Phaidon.

Oliver, P., Davis, I. and Bentley, I. (1981) *Dunroamin: the suburban semi and its enemies*, London: Pimlico.

O'Rourke, M. (2001) 'The Lansbury Estate, Keeling House and Balfron Tower: conservation issues and the architecture of social intent', in S. MacDonald (ed.) *Preserving Post-War Heritage: the care and conservation of mid-twentieth century architecture*, Shaftesbury: Donhead.

O'Sullivan, T. and Gibb, K. (eds) (2003) *Housing Economics and Public Policy*, Oxford: Blackwell Science.

Pahl, R. (1968) 'A perspective on urban sociology', in R. Pahl (ed.) *Readings in Urban Sociology*, Oxford: Pergamon Press.

References

Palmer, G., Rahman, M. and Kenway, P. (2002) *Monitoring Poverty and Social Exclusion 2002*, York: JRF.

Pantazis, C. and Gordon, D. (eds) (2000) *Tackling Inequalities: where are we now and what can be done?* Bristol: The Policy Press.

Papanek, V. (1995) *The Green Imperative: ecology and ethics in design and architecture*, London: Thames and Hudson.

Parfect, M. and Power, G. (1997) *Planning for Urban Quality: urban design in towns and cities*, London: Routledge.

Park, D. and Radford, J. (1997) 'Space, place and the asylum', *Health and Place*, 3, 2: 71–2.

Parker-Pearson, M. and Richards, C. (1994) *Architecture and Order: approaches to social space*, London: Routledge.

Parsons, T. (1937) *The Structure of Social Action*, New York: McGraw Hill.

Payne, J. (2000) 'Village people', *Property People*, 10 August: 8–9.

Pearson, D. (1994) *Earth to Spirit: in search of natural architecture*, London: Gaia Books.

Pearson, D. (1998) *The New Natural House Book: creating a healthy harmonious and ecologically sound home*, New York: Simon and Schuster.

Pearson, D. (2001a) *New Organic Architecture: the breaking wave*, Stroud: Gaia Books.

Pearson, D. (2001b) *Yurts, Tipis and Benders*, Stroud: Gaia Books.

Pickard, R. (1996) *Conservation in the Built Environment*, Harlow: Longman.

Planning Officers Society/HBF/DETR (1998) *Housing Layouts – Lifting the Quality*, London: Planning Officers Society/HBF/DETR.

Popular Housing Forum (1998) *Kerb Appeal: the external appearance and site appeal of new houses*, Winchester: Popular Housing Forum.

Powell, K. (2001) *New London Architecture*, London: Merrell.

Power, A. and Mumford, K. (1999) *The Slow Death of Great Cities: urban abandonment or urban renaissance*, York: JRF.

Pred, A. (1983) 'Structuration and place: on the becoming of sense of place and structure and feeling', *Journal for the Theory of Social Behaviour*, 13, 1: 44–68.

Pride of Manchester (2003) *Urban Splash's Tom Bloxham Speaks Exclusively to Pride of Manchester*. Online. Available: http://prideofmanchester.com/interviews/TomBloxham.htm (accessed 16 August 2004).

Prince's Foundation (2000) *Sustainable Urban Extensions: planned through design*, London: Prince's Foundation.

Punter, J. and Carmona, M. (1997) *The Design Dimension of Planning: theory, content, and best practice for design policies*, London: E&FN Spon.

Quilgars, D. and Anderson, I. (1997) 'Addressing the problem of youth homelessness and unemployment: the contribution of foyers', in R. Burrows, N. Pleace and D. Quilgars (eds) *Homelessness and Social Policy*, London: Routledge.

Quilgars, D. and Pleace, N. (1999) 'Housing and support for young people', in J. Rugg (ed.) *Housing and Social Policy*, London: Routledge.

Rabinow, P. (1984) *The Foucault Reader*, Harmondsworth: Penguin.

Raemaekers, J. (2000) 'Planning for sustainable development', in P. Allmendinger, A. Prior, and J. Raemaekers (eds) *Introduction to Planning Practice*, Chichester: John Wiley.

Rapoport, A. (1969) *House Form and Culture*, Engelwood Cliffs, NJ: Prentice Hall.

Rapoport, A. (1977) *Human Aspects of Urban Form*, Oxford: Pergamon.

Rapoport, A. (1982) *The Meaning of the Built Environment: a non-verbal communication approach*, Beverly Hills: Sage.

Rapoport, A. (1985) 'Thinking about home environments: a conceptual framework', in I. Altman and C. Werner (eds) *Home Environments*, New York: Plenum Press.

Rapoport, A. (2001) 'Theory, culture and housing', *Housing, Theory and Society*, 17: 145–65.

Ravetz, A. (1974) *Model Estate: planned housing at Quarry Hill, Leeds*, London: Croom Helm.

Ravetz, A. (1980) *Remaking Cities*, London: Croom Helm.

Ravetz, A. (2001) *Council Housing and Culture: the history of a social experiment*, London: Routledge.

Ravetz, A. with Turkington, R. (1995) *The Place of Home: English domestic environments, 1914–2000*, London: E&FN Spon.

RIBA (2003) *Policy Unit: Main Responsibilities*. Online. Available: http:/www.riba.org/go/RIBA/News/Policy-350.html (accessed 5 September 2003).

Richard Reid Associates, (2004) *Urban Design*. Online. Available: http://www.richardreid.co.uk/urbandesign/1urbandesign.html (accessed 31 August 2004).

Richardson, H. (ed.) (1998) *English Hospitals 1660–1948: a survey of their architecture and design*, Swindon: Royal Commission on the Historical Monuments of England.

Rickford, F. (1994) 'Don't fence me in', *Community Care*, 29 September/5October: 16–17.

Roaf, S. (2003) *EcoHouse2: a design guide*, Oxford: Architectural Press.

Roberts, M. (1991) *Living in a Man Made World: gender assumptions in modern housing design*, London: Routledge.

Roberts, M. and Greed, C. (eds) (2001) *Approaching Urban Design: the design process*, Harlow: Longman.

Robson, B. (1988) *Those Inner Cities*, Oxford: Clarendon Press.

Robson, B., Parkinson, M., Boddy, M. and Maclennan, D. (2000) *The State of English Cities*, London: DETR.

Robson, D., Nicholson, A. and Barker, N. (1997) *Homes for the Third Age: a design guide for extra care sheltered housing*, London: Spon.

Roger Tym and Partners (1988) *Birmingham Heartlands Development Strategy for East Birmingham*, London: Roger Tym and Partners.

Ross, M. (1996) *Planning and the Heritage: policy and proceedings*, 2nd edn, London: E&FN Spon.

Rudlin, D. and Falk, N. (1999) *Building the 21st Century Home: the sustainable urban neighbourhood*, Oxford: Architectural Press.

Rudofsky, B. (1964) *Architecture without Architects*, London: Academy Editions.

Rugg, J. (ed.) (1999) *Young People, Housing and Social Policy*, London: Routledge.

Rugg, J. (2000) *Hartrigg Oaks: the early development of a continuing care retirement community 1983–1999*, York: Centre for Housing Policy, University of York.

Sarre, P. (1986) 'Choice and constraint in ethnic minority housing: a structurationist view', *Housing Studies*, 1, 2: 71–85.

Saunders, P. (1990) *A Nation of Home Owners*, London: Unwin Hyman.

Saussure, F. de (1915) *Cours de Linguistique Générale*; trans. W. Baskin (1978) *Course in General Linguistics*, London: Fontana.

Savage, M. and Warde, A. (1993) *Urban Sociology, Capitalism and Modernity*, Basingstoke: Macmillan.

SAVE (1995) *Mind Over Matter: a study of the country's threatened mental asylums*, London: SAVE Britain's Heritage.

Sayer, A. (2000) *Realism and Social Science*, London: Sage.

Schumacher, E. (1973) *Small is Beautiful: economics as if people mattered*, New York: Harper Row.

Schutz, A. (1972) *The Phenomenology of the Social World*, London: Heinemann.

Scoffham, E. (1984) *The Shape of British Housing*, London: George Godwin.

Scott, A. (1990) *Ideology and the New Social Movements*, London: Routledge.

Scott, J. (1995) *Sociological Theory: contemporary debates*, Aldershot: Edward Elgar.

Scott, J. (1999) 'Family change: revolution or backlash in attitudes?', in S. McRae (ed.) *Changing Britain: families and households in the 1990s*, Oxford: Oxford University Press.

Scull, A. (1982) *Museums of Madness: the social organisation of insanity in nineteenth century England*, Harmondsworth: Penguin.

Shelter (1992) *The Foyer Project: a collection of background papers*, London: Shelter.

Sherwood Energy Village (2002) *Sherwood Energy Village*. Online. Available: http://www.sherwoodenergyvillage.co.uk (accessed 11 November 2002).

Shields, R. (1991) *Places on the Margins: alternative geographies of modernity*, London: Routledge.

References

Short, J. (2000) 'Three urban discourses', in G. Bridge and S. Watson (eds) *A Companion to the City*, Oxford: Blackwell.

Silicon Alley (2003) *Silicon Alley – Newcastle's Urban Televillage*. Online. Available: http://www.silicon-alley.co.uk (accessed 1 December 2003).

Silverstone, R. and Hirsch, E. (eds) (1992) *Consuming Technologies: media and information in domestic spaces*, London: Routledge.

Simmie, J. (1974) *Citizens in Conflict: a sociology of town planning*, London: Hutchinson Educational.

Skultans, V. (1979) *English Madness: ideas on insanity 1580–1890*, London: Routledge.

Smit, J. (1997) 'All that granny can buy', *Building Homes*, 8, August: 20–2.

Smith, N. and Williams, P. (eds) (1986a) *Gentrification of the City*, Boston: Unwin Hyman.

Smith, N. and Williams, P. (1986b) 'Alternatives to orthodoxy: invitation to a debate', in N. Smith and P. Williams (eds) *Gentrification of the City*, Boston: Unwin Hyman.

Social Exclusion Unit (1998) *Bringing Britain Together: a national strategy for neighbourhood renewal*, London: Stationery Office.

Somerville, P. (1992) 'Homelessness and the meaning of home: rooflessness or rootlessness?', *International Journal of Urban and Regional Research*, 163: 529–39.

Spring, M. (1987) 'Clearing mental blocks', *Building*, 1 May: 28–9.

STBI (2004) *STBI Summary Report*. Online. Available: http://www.towerblocks.org.uk/html_summary/index.htm (accessed 21 January 2004).

St David (undated) *Adventurers Quay*, Cowbridge: St David.

Stephenson, J. (2001) *The Building Regulations Explained: 2000 revision*, London: Spon.

Stewart, W. (1970) *Children in Flats: a family study*, London: NSPCC.

Strauss, A., Schatzman, L., Ehrlich, D., Bucher, R. and Sabskin, M. (1963) 'The hospital and its negotiated order', in E. Freidson (ed.) *The Hospital In Modern Society*, London: Free Press of Glencoe.

Sturge, M. (2000) *Continuing Care Retirement Communities in the UK: lessons from Hartrigg Oaks*, York: JRF.

Suchman, D. (2001) *Developing Active Adult Retirement Communities*, Washington, DC: the Urban Land Institute.

Sudjic, D. (2004) *Background, Munkenbeck and Marshall Architects*. Online. Available: http://www.mandm.uk.com/philosophy.htm (accessed 4 February 2004).

Sustainable Homes (2004) *What is Sustainable Homes?* Online. Available: http://www.sustainablehomes.co.uk/about2htm (accessed 2 December 2004).

Suttles, G. (1968) *The Social Order of the Slum*, Chicago, IL: University of Chicago Press.

Swenarton, M. (1981) *Homes Fit for Heroes: the politics and architecture of early state housing in Britain*, London: Heinemann.

Tai Cymru (1998a) *Development Quality Requirements for New Dwellings in Wales*, Cardiff: Tai Cymru.

Tai Cymru (1998b) *Site Layout Design for New Housing Schemes*, Cardiff: Tai Cymru.

Talbott, J. (1995) 'The Findhorn Community', in J. Conrad (ed.) *Eco-Villages and Sustainable Communities: models for 21st century living*, Findhorn: Findhorn Press.

Tarn, J. (1973) *Five per cent Philanthropy: an account of housing in urban areas between 1840 and 1914*, Cambridge: Cambridge University Press.

Taylor, J. (1991) *Hospital and Asylum Architecture in England 1840–1914: building for health care*, London: Mansell.

Taylor, N. (1973) *The Village in the City*, London: Temple-Smith.

TCA (2003) *Telework News*. Online. Available: http://www.tca.org.uk/news/news.php (accessed 1 December 2003).

Teignbridge District Council (1999) *Former Exe Vale Hospital, Exminster: draft planning brief*, South Devon: Teignbridge District Council.

The Builder (1846) 'Editorial', *The Builder*, CLXXXI, 25 July: 349–55.

The Land is Ours (1999) *Defining Rural Sustainability: 15 criteria for sustainable developments in the countryside*. Online. Available: http://www.thelandisours.org/chapter7/defining.html (accessed 25 November 2004).

The Times (1997) 'Acorn Televillage', *Times Weekend*, 7 June: 9.

Thomas, H. (2003) *Discovering Cities: Cardiff*, Sheffield: Geographical Association.

Thomas, H. and Imrie, R. (1999) 'Urban policy, modernisation and the regeneration of Cardiff Bay', in R. Imrie and H. Thomas (eds) *British Urban Policy*, 2nd edn, London: Sage.

Thompson-Fawcett, M. (1996) 'The urbanist revision of development', *Urban Design International*, 1, 4: 301–22.

Thompson-Fawcett, M. (1998a) 'Leon Krier and the organic revival within urban policy and practice', *Planning Perspectives*, 13: 167–94.

Thompson-Fawcett, M. (1998b) 'Envisioning urban villages: a critique of a movement and two urban transformations', unpublished thesis, University of Oxford.

Thorp, S. (2003) 'Enemy at the gates?', *Housing Magazine*, March: 24–6.

Tibbalds, F. (1992) *Making People Friendly Towns: improving the public environment in towns and cities*, London: Longman.

Tinker, A. (1996) *Older People in Modern Society*, 4th edn, Harlow: Addison Wesley Longman.

Tomlin, J and Sewell, G. (eds) (1993) *Good Practice Handbook for Foyer Managers and Developers*, London: Foyer Federation for Youth.

Towers, G. (1995) *Building Democracy: community architecture in the inner cities*, London: UCL Press.

Towers, G. (2000) *Shelter is Not Enough: transforming multi-storey housing*, Bristol: The Policy Press.

Townsend, P. (1962) *The Last Refuge*, London: Routledge and Kegan Paul.

Townsend, P. (1981) 'The structured dependency of the elderly: creation of social policies in the twentieth century', *Ageing and Society*, 1, 1: 5–28.

Townshend, T. and Madanipour, A. (2001) 'Urban design in the planning system', in M. Roberts and C. Greed (eds) *Approaching Urban Design: the design process*, Harlow: Pearson Education Ltd.

Tugnutt, A. and Robertson, M. (1987) *Making Townscape: a contextual approach to building in an urban setting*, London: Mitchell.

Turner, J. (1976) *Housing by People: towards autonomy in building environments*, London: Marion Boyars.

Unwin, S. (1997) *Analysing Architecture*, London: Routledge.

Upper House Farm (2002) *For Others*. Online. Available: http://www.upper-house-farm.com/choice.html (accessed 28 November 2002).

Urban Splash (2002) *Annual Review 2002*, Manchester: Urban Splash.

Urban Splash (2004) *Urban Splash*. Online. Available: http://www.urbansplash.co.uk (accessed 10 August 2004).

Urban Task Force (1999) *Towards an Urban Renaissance*, London: DETR.

Urban Villages Forum/English Partnerships (undated) *Making Places: a guide to good practice in undertaking mixed development schemes*, London: Urban Villages Forum/English Partnerships.

URBED (1998) *Tomorrow: a peaceful path to urban reform*, Manchester: URBED.

URBED, MORI and the School for Policy Studies, University of Bristol (1999) *But Would You Live There? Shaping attitudes to urban living*, London: Urban Task Force.

Vale, B. and Vale, R. (1975) *The Autonomous House: design and planning for self-sufficiency*, London: Thames and Hudson.

Vale, B. and Vale, R. (1991) *Green Architecture: design for a sustainable future*, London: Thames and Hudson.

Vestbro, D. (2000) 'From collective housing to cohousing – a summary of research', *Journal of Architectural and Planning Research*, 17, 2: 164–73.

WAG (2002) *Update on Rethinking Construction*. Online. Available: http://wwwhousing.wales.gov.uk/content/English (accessed 15 August 2003).

References

WAG (2005) *Rethinking Construction*. Online. Available: http://www.housing.wales.gov.uk/index. asp?task=content8a=ez (accessed 22 February 2005).

Walker, A. (1997) 'Introduction: the strategy of inequality', in A. Walker and C. Walker (eds) *Britain Divided: the growth of social exclusion in the 1980s and 1990s*, London: CPAG.

Wall, D. (1999) *Earth First! and the Anti-Roads Movement: radical environmentalism and comparative social movements*, London: Routledge.

Walter Segal Self Build Trust (2004) *Examples of Projects*. Online. Available: http://segalselfbuild. co.uk/projects/projectcontents.html (accessed 4 November 2004).

Ward, C. (1985) *When We Build Again: let's have housing that works*, London: Pluto Press.

Wates, N. (1976) *The Battle for Tolmers Square*, London: Routledge and Kegan Paul.

Wates, N. (ed.) (2000) *The Community Planning Handbook: how people can shape their cities, towns and village in any part of the world*, London: Earthscan/Princes Foundation/South Bank University.

Watson, D. (2004) *CoHousing Communities: honouring both privacy and community*. Online. Available: http://www.cohousing.co.uk/whatiscoho.htm (accessed 28 October 2004).

WCED (1987) *Our Common Future, The Brundtland Report*, Oxford: Oxford University Press.

Weaver, M. (1999) 'The height of fashion?', *Housing Today*, Issue 133, 13 May: 16–17.

Weaver, M. (2005) 'Ministers in right to buy compromise', *Society Guardian*, 24 January. Online. Available: http://www.society.guardian.co.uk/housing/story/0,7890,1397311,00.html (accessed 24 January 2005).

Weaver, R. (2005) 'Dutch box clever over housing', *The Observer*, 20 February. Online. Available: http://www.observerguardian/cash/story/0,6903,1418233,00.html (accessed 7 March 2005).

Webster, C. (2001) 'Gated cities of tomorrow', *Town Planning Review*, 72, 2: 149–70.

Westwood, S. and Williams, J. (1997) 'Imagining cities', in S. Westwood and J. Williams (eds) *Imagining Cities: scripts, signs and memories*, New York: Routledge.

Wheway, R. and Millward, A. (1997) *Child's Play: facilitating play on housing estates*, Coventry: CIH.

White, N. (ed.) (2002) *Sustainable Housing Schemes in the UK: a guide with details of access*, Southwell, Notts: Hockerton Housing Project.

Whyte, W. (1943) *Street Corner Society*, Chicago: University of Chicago Press.

Wilcox, S. (2002) *Housing Finance Review 2002/3*, York, Coventry and London: JRF/CIH/CML.

Wilcox, S. (2003) *Can Work: Can't Buy: local measures of the ability of working households to become home owners*, York: JRF.

Williams, G. (2003) *The Enterprising City Centre: Manchester's development challenge*, London: Spon.

Williams, R. (1975) *The Country and the City*, St Albans: Paladin.

Wilson, D. (1992) 'Space and social reproduction in local organisations: a social constructionist perspective', *Environment and Planning B: Society and Space*, 10: 215–30.

Wright, P. (1985) *On Living in an Old Country: the national past in contemporary Britain*, London: Verso.

Young, M. and Willmott, P. (1962) *Family and Kinship in East London*, London: Penguin (first published 1957).

Zukin, S. (1989) *Loft Living: culture and capital in urban change*, Baltimore. MD: Johns Hopkins University Press (first published 1982).

Zukin, S. (1995) *The Cultures of Cities*, Malden, MA and Oxford: Blackwell.

Zukin, S. (1996) 'Space and symbols in an age of decline', in A. King (ed.) *Re-Presenting the City: ethnicity, capital and culture in the 21st century Metropolis*, Basingstoke: Macmillan.

Zukin, S. (1998) 'Urban lifestyles: diversity and standardisation in spaces of consumption', *Urban Studies*, 35, 5–6: 825–39.

Index

Abercrombie, Patrick 80, 81

Acorn Televillage scheme 129; Acorn logo 128, 129(fig.); aims not achieved 132; central piazza 129, 130(fig.); courtyards 129(fig.); critical assessment 135, 136; design awards 132; flexible interior design 132; former farmyard 129, 131(fig.); pedestrian way 129, 130(fig.); rear access road 129, 131 (fig.); sustainability 129, 132

Acorn Televillages 125, 128, 129

Acts of Parliament; Children's Act (1989) 181; County Asylums Act (1808) 142; Disability Discrimination Act (1995) 57; Employment Act (2002) 124; Homeless Persons Act (1977) 58; Homelessness Act (2002) 59, 181; Housing Act (1956) 151; Housing Act (1964) 53; Housing Act (1974) 54; Housing Act (1988) 56; Housing Act (1996) 56; Housing and Town Planning Act (1919) 52; Housing of the Working Classes Act (1890) 51; Lunacy Act (1845) 142; National Assistance Act (1948) 57; NHS and Community Care Act (1990) 57, 58, 168; Planning and Compulsary Order Act (2004) 62, 71; Rent Act (1957) 53; Town and Country Planning Act (1947) 52, 141; Town and Country Planning Act (1944) 141

Adventurers Quay 194, 196, 212–18, 222; award winning project 217; canal bridge 215, 216(fig.); conditions imposed 214; courtyards 215, 218(figs); design 213, 214; 'drawbridge' approach 215, 216(fig.); flagship development 217; 'gated' aspect 214–15, 217,

222; landmark feature 213, 213(fig.); landscaped area 217, 219(fig); marketing brochure 214, 222; planning 213, 214; surveillance aspect 222; waterfront walkways 214, 217(fig.)

aestheticisation of urban space 44

aesthetics 23

affordable housing 60, 70, 71, 76, 84, 98, 158, 260

age, categories of 165, 166, 179, 189

Age Concern 77, 265

agency 5, 67, 264

Agenda 21 (United Nations Division for Sustainable Development) 241, 242, 243, 252

Ainscow, Carol, Artisan 201

Aldous, Tony 211

Alexander, Christopher 111; pattern language 88, 228, 232, 233

Allerton Bywater, Millennium Village 113

alternative lifestyles 195, 252; negative public perception 233, 243, 252, 260

'alternative movement' 226; communities 240; development funding 264, 265

Ancient Monuments Society 202

Anti-Social Behaviour Order (ASBO) 188, 263

Archer, M. 14, 20

architects 73–4, 75, 163, 264; asylums 142–3; influential 81–3; modernist 139

architecture; asylums 142–3; community 74, 83; cultural anthropology 12, 13; disciplinary power 23, 24; form 23; key figures 81–4; modernist 26, 28, 81, 87, 141, 151; postmodernist 44, 83, 87; styles 81–3, 86, 87; UK 29, see also design

Index

T - #0051 - 250123 - C0 - 234/156/15 [17] - CB - 9780415336185 - Gloss Lamination